Too Much Schooling, Too Little Education:
A Paradox of Black Life in White Societies

Too Much Schooling, Too Little Education:

A Paradox of Black Life in White Societies

Mwalimu J. Shujaa, Editor

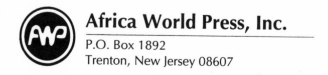

Africa World Press, Inc.

P.O. Box 1892
Trenton, New Jersey 08607

Africa World Press, Inc.
P.O. Box 1892
Trenton, NJ 08607

Copyright © 1994 Mwalimu J. Shujaa
First Printing, 1994

Book Design: Jonathan Gullery
Cover Art: Amon Ra Ptah Hotep Imhotep
Cover Design: Carles J. Juzang

Library of Congress Cataloging-in-Publication Data

Too much schooling, too little education : a paradox of black life in
    white societies / Mwalimu J. Shujaa, editor.
        p.   cm.
    Includes bibliographical references and index.
    ISBN 0-86543-385-2. -- ISBN 0-86543-386-0 (pbk.)
        1. Afro-Americans--Education--Social aspects. 2. Afro-Americans-
    -Education--History. 3. Discrimination in education--United States.
    4. Critical pedagogy--United States.
    LC717.T66   1993
    370' .8996073--dc20
                                                    93-45417
                                                        CIP

Contents

Dedication ix

Acknowledgements xi

Foreword Cultural Work:
Planting New Trees with New Seeds.................1
Haki R. Madhubuti,
*Gwendolyn Brooks Center, Chicago State
University and the Institute for Positive
Education*

Part One
Evaluating Our Assumptions About Education and Schooling:
Developing African-centered Orientations to Knowledge

Introduction to Part One..9
Mwalimu J. Shujaa
State University of New York at Buffalo

Chapter 1 Education and Schooling:
You Can Have One Without the Other...........13
Mwalimu J. Shujaa,

Chapter 2 Black Intellectuals and the
Crisis in Black Education 37
Jacob H. Carruthers,
*Center for Inner City Studies
Northeastern Illinois University and
The Kemetic Institute*

Chapter 3   African-American Cultural Knowledge and
             Liberatory Education: Dilemmas, Problems,
             and Potentials in Postmodern
             American Society..57
             Beverly M. Gordon,
             The Ohio State University

Part Two
African-American Education Initiatives:
Historical Resistance to Schooling

Introduction to Part Two 81
             Mwalimu J. Shujaa

Chapter 4   Outthinking and Outflanking the Owners of the
             World: An Historiography of the African-
             American Struggle for Education.....................85
             Ronald E. Butchart
             University of Washington at Tacoma

Chapter 5   The Search for Access and Content in the
             Education of African-Americans....................123
             Joan Davis Ratteray
             Institute for Independent Education

Chapter 6   Historic Readers for African-American Children
             (1868-1944): Uncovering and Reclaiming a
             Tradition of Opposition...............................143
             Violet J. Harris, *University of Illinois*

Part Three
African-American Experiences in Schools and
Perspectives on Schooling

Introduction to Part Three 179
             Mwalimu J. Shujaa

Chapter 7   Reproduction and Resistance:
                   An Analysis of African-American Males'
                   Responses to Schooling...............................183
                   Vernon C. Polite
                   The Catholic University of America

Chapter 8   African-American Principals:
                   Bureaucrat/Administrators and
                   Ethno-Humanists..203
                   Kofi Lomotey
                   Louisiana State University

Chapter 9   Educating for Competence in Community
                   and Culture: Exploring the Views of
                   Exemplary African-American Teachers..........221
                   Michele Foster
                   University of California-Davis

Chapter 10   Literacy, Education, and Identity Among
                   African-Americans: The Communal Nature
                   of Learning...245
                   Vivian L. Gadsden
                   University of Pennsylvania

Part Four
African-Centered Pedagogy:
An Absolute Necessity for African-Centered Education

Introduction to Part Four..265
                   Mwalimu J. Shujaa

Chapter 11   BEing the Soul-Freeing Substance:
                   A Legacy of Hope in AfroHumanity..............269
                   Joyce Elaine King
                   Santa Clara University
                   Thomasyne Lightfoote Wilson
                   San Jose State University

Chapter 12   African-Centered Pedagogy:
              Complexities and Possibilities......................295
              Carol D. Lee, *School of Education and
              Social Policy, Northwestern University*

Chapter 13   Notes on an Afrikan-Centered Pedagogy 319
              Agyei Akoto
              NationHouse Positive Action Center

Part Five
Patterns of Resistance to European-Centered Schooling:
Reclaiming Responsibility for Educating Our Own

Introduction to Part Five...341
              Mwalimu J. Shujaa

Chapter 14   The Emergence of Black Supplementary
              Schools as Forms of Resistance to Racism
              in the United Kingdom 343
              Nah (Dorothy) E. Dove
              State University of New York at Buffalo

Chapter 15   Afrocentric Transformation and
              Parental Choice in African-American
              Independent Schools..................................361
              Mwalimu J. Shujaa
              State University of New York at Buffalo

Chapter 16   The Rites of Passage: Extending Education
              Into the African-American Community..........377
              Nsenga Warfield-Coppock
              Baobab Associates

Afterword   The Afrocentric Project in Education 395
              Molefi Kete Asante
              Temple University

              Contributors...399

              Index 405

This book is dedicated to

the Afrikan People's Action School, to the Nile Valley Shule and to the committed and visionary sisters and brothers whose creativity, labor and understanding of African cultural history have maintained these institutions as part of our generation's legacy to our children.

my children, Kenya and Kwame. Every minute devoted to this project has been inspired by my hope that you will remember your mother and father as two people who did their best; that you will learn from our mistakes and build on the things that we did well; and know that we love you.

the Council of Independent Black Institutions (CIBI) for 22 years of leadership in African-centered education and pedagogy.

Acknowledgements

This book has been a three-year project. It has been my good fortune to be the recipient of tremendous support and sound advice from many people during this time period. Kassahun Checole, publisher of Africa World Press/Red Sea Press provided the initial encouragement to develop the book. His patience and understanding throughout have been monumental. Thank you, Kassahun.

I am deeply indebted to each of the contributing authors for their confidence and for their cooperation. Often I have reflected on the fact that many of the people who wrote chapters did not know me personally at the time that I approached them. Yet, they agreed to contribute to this book because they shared with me the same belief in and commitment to the statement that this book makes about education as a cultural imperative for all African people who aspire to be truly self-determining.

There are many others to acknowledge. Austin D. Swanson made resources available to me in the Department of Educational Organization, Administration and Policy in the Graduate School of Education at the State University of New York at Buffalo. Carol Norris and Sally Claydon of the departmental office staff provided word processing for several chapters. The contributions by my long-time graduate assistant, Catherine Priser, were invaluable in fine tuning the manuscripts and providing stylistic consistency. Other graduate students made important contributions as well. Sharon Johnson did word processing to incorporate final corrections after copy editing. Shawgi Tell assisted with the indexing, and other tasks that seemed to be without end as the project neared completion.

Pat Glinski and Nancy Myers of the Center for Educational Resources and Technology in the SUNY-Buffalo Graduate School of Education helped to reconstruct chapters from printed copies and back-up diskettes when a case containing recently updated diskettes mysteriously disappeared in 1992. Dianne L.H. Mark and Dia N. Sekayi (Kimberly L. Ballard) voluntarily took on the tedious task of transcribing an audiotaped lecture that eventually became Jacob H. Carruthers' chapter. Many thanks go to the students in my Spring 1992 seminar, "African American Education in Critical Sociological Perspective," for their comments and feedback on drafts of several chapters. A special thanks go to the following graduate students for their proofreading assistance: Ginni Doolittle, Mark Garrison, Illana Lewis, Pat Maloney, Laura Watts, Virginia Batchelor Robinson,

Barbara Shircliffe, and Shawn Vecellio.

I owe much to Mwalimu Hannibal Tirus Afrik and to Kofi Lomotey for their ever available and freely given encouragement, and to Aggei Akoto for his example and consistency. A special thanks also to Margaret Wilder for looking over my shoulder.

Finally, I want to thank the members of my family — my wife, Kweli, my son, Kwame, and especially my daughter, Kenya (who completed the indexing) — for their love and support. And, from those whose contributions I may have failed to acknowledge here, I humbly ask for forgiveness.

Mwalimu J. Shujaa
Buffalo, New York
August 1993

Cultural Work: Planting New Trees With New Seeds

Haki R. Madhubuti
Gwendolyn Brooks Center
Chicago State University
and Institute of Positive Education

In America people of African descent are caught between a hurricane and a volcano when it comes to the acquisition of life giving and life sustaining knowledge. Too many of our children are trapped in urban school systems that have been "programmed" for failure; and, all too often, the answer to what is to be done to correct this injustice is left in the very hands of those most responsible for the problem. If your child is sleeping and a rat starts to bite at his/her head you don't ask the rat to *please* stop biting at your child's brain. If you are sane, normal and a loving parent you go on the attack and try your damnedest to kill the rat.

When it comes to the education of African-American children, rats are biting at the doors, floors, desks and gym shoes of the nation's public schools. Jonathan Kozol in his heartfelt book *Savage Inequalities* documents the near collapse of urban public education. He writes of young people who "have no feeling of belonging to America." If public schooling is the first formal state sponsored orientation into becoming a productive citizen, we are in deep, deep trouble. If public schooling is supposed to stimulate the nation's children into becoming poets, doctors, teachers, scientists, computer experts, musicians, business people, carpenters, professors, etc., get ready to throw in the towel. This is the eleventh round and the only answer that is forthcoming from most school systems is to change the superintendent.

Rather than looking at the system, we personalize the problem as if one man or woman can effect real change. In a city like Chicago where 60 years of "boss" politics control a 2.7 billion dollar Chicago school budget, change and child-centered education are back seated to economics and patronage. To bring an "unschooled" outsider in as superintendent is like a chicken prescribing chicken soup for a cold.

Why is it that in 1993 we still lie to ourselves? Some of the most intelligent advocates of public school education continue to blame the victim as if our children have the capacity to educate themselves. They overlook the ever present political, racial and economic reality of the major consumers of public education, Black and Latino children. The rat I speak of is white supremacy (racism) manifesting itself freely in the structured and systematic destruction of millions of unsuspecting children and their parents.

It is argued in some quarters that in order to "survive" in the Black community a public school education can be a handicap. Young brothers seen too often with books (without pictures) are grouped into a category that is viewed as unmanly and negative. However, this view is unenlightened and is a small slice of the miseducation that is accepted and encouraged by a growing number of people with enslaved minds enclosed in short-circuited memories. On the other hand, white supremist ideology has a way of making another type of enslaved mind think that by acquiring pieces of paper (degrees) he/she is indeed free. Yet, the one freedom that is openly accessible to all Black folks in America is the freedom to self-destruct.

Memory is instructive here. Africans did not swim, motor boat or free fly to America. There is a horrible connection between Africans and Europeans that must not be forgotten, negated or minimized. The African holocaust is seldom explored or taught in our schools. This relationship of white slave trader to enslaved African has been the glue connecting us for over a millennium.

There are over 100 million people of African descent in the Western hemisphere and we all face similar problems. Whether one is in Canada, the United States or Brazil, the fight for self-definition and self-reliance is like digging a hole with a shovel in steel-reinforced concrete. There are over 69 million people of African descent in Brazil speaking Portuguese, there are 35 million plus people of African descent in the U.S. attempting to speak English, and we Africans don't talk to each other. I maintain that this is a learned activity and acutely cultural. Over one hundred million Africans moving and working for the same goals, in the same hemisphere, are a threat to anyone's rule. Our clothes, names, street address, employment and articulations in their languages have changed, but the basic relationship has remained the same. Black folks are still dependent upon white folks in America. To Africanize or to liberate this system from its exclusive Euro-American paradigms is indeed a progressive and often revolutionary act.

Another memory. I'll never forget a trip I made to Tanzania in the seventies for an international conference. After the day's work, I walked alone in the city. As the sun set and the street lights illuminated the city of Dar es Salaam, I noticed three children huddled close together about a block away under a lamp post. As I approached them, I noticed that my presence was not important to them. I smiled at the reason why. The three of them, two boys and a girl, under a dimly lit lamp post, were deeply engrossed in reading and discussing a book. I walked on without disturbing them in their obvious joy. It was clear to me that these were poor African children using the only light available at that time. This used to be the reality of the great majority of African-Americans.

The fight to educate African-Americans is a little told history in this age of integration. In fact if truth is to be liberated, it was the students in Black schools along with the Black church that led the modern fight for full educational and political equality. This fight was never a battle to sit next to white children in a classroom. It was and still is a struggle for an equal and level playing field in all areas of human endeavor: finance, law, politics, military, commerce, sports, entertainment, science and technology, and, of course, education.

Many believed that if we had first rate facilities/buildings, supplies, environment, teachers and support personnel, a quality education would follow. This is obviously not true. We now understand that there is a profound difference between going to school and being educated. We know that close to a half-million children frequent the Chicago Public Schools each day and less than twenty percent (20%) are truly receiving a first-class education that could stand remotely close to the best private schools.

For the last twenty-five years, I have been involved in the independent Black school movement. This movement grew out of the Black empowerment struggles and initiatives of the sixties and has developed African-centered schools around the country. It also has established a national professional organization, the Council of Independent Black Institutes (CIBI). The great majority of the first generation persons involved in this movement were products of the public school system. We knew first hand the type of school not needed. From the beginning, we were (and continue to be) cultural workers who had been tremendously influenced by Black struggle and the works of W.E.B. DuBois, Carter G. Woodson, Frantz Fanon, Paulo Freire, Marcus Garvey, Harold Cruse, Chancellor Williams, E. Franklin Frazier, Mary McLeod Bethune and others.

The critical examination of schooling and education always has been central in our analysis. The question of schooling vs. education is not a question of becoming an "educated fool"; the fear of book learning disconnecting one from community concerns has a long tradition in the Black community. In fact, in our community there has always been a distinction made between schools and education. Since we had to fight so hard to get a foot into the schoolhouse door, the struggle to go to school in itself meant to most African-Americans that a quality education would not necessarily be the results of such an endeavor.

James D. Anderson in his brilliant book, *The Education of Blacks in the South 1860-1935*, makes it clear that African-Americans viewed education as a birth right in the same light as freedom. The first two institutions that Africans built from the ground up with their own hands and resources were schools and churches. This new inquiry into the state of Black education is an insightful and important one. Therefore, our query must be one that asks the difficult questions:

1. What is more important than the enlightened education of our children? Should one's children have any obligation to their own people and culture? Who is ultimately responsible for providing an education - the family, state or others?
2. Education in the past has been used politically against the advancement of African-Americans. Is it any different today? Will African centered studies connect education to the political, economic and racial reality of today's world?
3. The European-centeredness of today's education continues to place conscious Blacks on a collision course with its basic

premise: that European culture stands at the center and is pivotal in one's understanding of the world. Is European culture universal? Will the introduction of African centered thought broaden our students or pigeonhole them into a false sense of security and narrow nationalism?

4. All education is value based. Whose values are our children learning? Will African centered studies teach a value base that will encourage and allow competition at a world level and cooperation at a local one?

All education must lead to deep understanding and mastery. Introduction to many forms of knowing is absolutely necessary. The problem is that most of our understandings about life that are being taught to our children have ceased to be life giving and life sustaining and do not lend themselves to self-reliance.

African centered cultural studies must lead, encourage and direct African-American students into the new technologies: computers, environmental sciences, finance, bio-chemistry, food technologies, bio-genetics, communications, electronics, etc. This is where the new statements about power, control and wealth are being made in the world today.

Black students must have deep understandings of the political, racial, economic, scientific and technological realities that confront the very survival of African people locally, nationally and internationally. They must be grounded in a worldview that promotes cross-cultural communication, understanding and sharing, yet be self-protective enough to realize that the world is not fair and that one's own interests often come into conflict with the interests of others, especially when race is involved. Therefore, if we want our children to achieve significantly they must:

A. Possess a deep understanding of the world in which they will have to function. However, we do know that the foundation of their knowledge must be anchored in positive self-concept and an environment that encourages growth. It is clear that if one is secure in one's self, that which others project - in all areas - will be less appealing, confusing or threatening.

B. Realize that all education is foundational. That is, the values we practice are introduced early and often in school and non-school settings such as family, media, church, entertainment, sports functions, etc., and can either work for or against development.

C. Understand that successful development is difficult with a quality education, but almost impossible without one. Further, education can be fun, but it is often hard and boring work and requires a commitment far beyond picking up a basketball or learning a new dance or handshake. It demands deep study and quiet time.

Most children are born into the world at the top of their game, genius level. The culture that receives them will either nurture and develop the genius in them or silence their minds before they reach the age of six. Most children remain in a learning mode. However, those that truly explode with ideas, creativity and unbounded talent are the ones introduced to knowledge in creative environments by talented and caring people. It is our responsibility as African-American parents, educators and citizens to develop educational settings - formal and informal - where cultural understandings (political, historical, literary, technological, financial, health, law, etc.), are not transmitted accidently, but by design. *Too Much Schooling, Too Little Education* is an overneeded addition to the ongoing search for meaningful African-centered education. Dr. Shujaa has edited a collection that is not only a first in this field, he has also assembled in one volume some of the best thinkers and practitioners working today. This book is more than impressive, it is required reading.

Copyright 1993 Haki R. Madhubuti

Part One

Evaluating Our Assumptions About Education and Schooling: Developing African-centered Orientations to Knowledge

Introduction to Part One

While working on this book I often envisioned the project as being like the planning of a very special benefit concert. This "concert", however, would be *read* by its audience rather than *listened* to. As editor/author, I saw my role as somewhat like that of the orchestra leader whose job it is to recruit a group of outstanding musicians for an all-star ensemble. I wanted people who not only played extremely well, but who also understood the importance of the cause for which the concert would be performed and shared a sense of commitment to it. It was up to me to decide what the range of instrumentation would be, the pieces that would be performed and the order of presentation. In this metaphoric role my aim was/is to deliver to the audience a concert-on-paper built on meaningful parts that meld into a dynamic whole. The 16 chapters in this book are contained in five theme-related parts. A brief introduction is provided for each part to present the reader with a sense of its particular rationale.

Part One provides the conceptual framework. These three opening chapters offer a problem statement and lay out the theoretical foundation that the remainder of the book builds upon. The opening theme, *Evaluating Our Assumptions About Education and Schooling: Developing African-centered Orientations to Knowledge*, was chosen to evoke the idea that some serious rethinking is in order. The position taken in this book is that this rethinking must call into question the way we, as African[1] people, approach education and schooling. This opening part sets a tone of African-centered analysis. These analyses put the interests of African people first. The authors are concerned with the extent to which the education afforded Africans (or what has passed for education) has benefitted others more than we. Consequently, the writing is not constrained by attempts to define what is best for African people in ways that are linked to the best interest of European-centered hegemonic nation-states. There are no "trickle-down" approaches taken here; this book is about what African people must do for ourselves.

In this introduction to Part One, I want to make clear some of my own assumptions that underlie the development of this book. I believe that for Africans in the United States (and elsewhere, for that matter) education must be recognized as a process that should reflect our own interests as a cultural nation and be grounded in our cultural history. It should be a process of identity development within the context of Pan-African kinship and heritage. Education is our means of providing for the inter-generational transmission of values, beliefs, traditions, customs, rituals and sensibilities along with the knowledge of why these things must be sustained. Through education we learn how to determine what is in our interests, distinguish our interests from those of others, and recognize when our interests are consistent and inconsistent with those of others. Education prepares us to accept the staff of cultural leadership from the generation that preceded ours, build upon our inheritance and make ready the generation that will follow us.

Whenever I hear an African person in the United States equate schooling with education, I become more concerned for our future as a cultural nation. By drawing distinctions between education and schooling I hope to shed light on the problems that must be overcome by African people in the United States in order to offer ourselves the best of what we produce. We in the United States live out our lives in a white-supremacist social order in which the economic, political and cultural interests of a European American elite dominate societal institutions—including the determination of what is taught in schools. The schooling process is designed to provide an ample supply of people who are loyal to the nation-state and who have learned the skills needed to perform the work that is necessary to maintain the dominance of the European-American elite in its social order. For African-Americans, individual success in schooling is often simply a matter of demonstrating one's ability to represent the interests of the European-American elite. Through such a process, African people as a group are able to derive little benefit from the schooling of our members and, even then, it is most likely to be in the interests of the European-American elite for us to do so.

Too many of our best and brightest have been rendered virtually inaccessible to us largely because they have experienced too much schooling and too little education. Our situation is such that we can ill afford to consider ourselves to be educated solely on the basis of the number of years we spend in school or because of the diplomas and degrees we obtain from schools. I have personally met African people who hold doctorates and who still refer to European-type hair as "good" and African-type hair as "bad"! Such ideas are not simply matters of personal preference. They are produced by a racist ideology that ascribes a hierarchy to human worth in which the physical characteristics commonly associated with Africans are thought to be inferior to those of Europeans. Here we see that perhaps 20 or more years of schooling have not countered these particular influences of white supremacy on the sensibilities of these Africans. We dare not call this preparation to reproduce the cultural hegemony of the European-American elite education! To the contrary, the education of Africans in America should counteract the hegemonic intent of schooling. This is why making critical distinctions between education and schooling is a necessary act for African people. But, the mere drawing of such distinctions is not enough. Our positioning relative to the European-American elite demands that we develop the infrastructure within our cultural nation to support the education of all of our people with or without holding state power.

In the opening chapter "Education and Schooling: You Can Have One Without the Other", I describe schooling as a societal imperative necessary for the maintenance of existing relations of power and privilege. Education is described as a process that locates the members of a culture within their cultural history, facilitates the transmission of cultural knowledge, and affirms the cultural identity. In societies where multiple cultures exist and where the power relations among them are unequal, the existence of a politically dominant cultural group ensures that schooling and education can not be assumed to be overlapping social processes. I argue that the ability of Africans in America to fulfill their cultural responsibilities is dependent upon drawing critical distinctions between education and schooling.

In Chapter Two, "Black Intellectuals and the Crisis in Black Education", Jacob H. Carruthers examines the often overlooked role of early Black nationalist thinkers and discusses the necessity of reclaiming the intellectual tradition they established. Dr. Carruthers argues that, in order to resolve the crisis in Black education, contemporary Black intellectuals must achieve intellectual freedom from European-centered constructions of knowledge and reconstruct Black education on an African-centered foundation.

In Chapter Three, "African-American Cultural Knowledge and Liberatory Education: Dilemmas, Problems, and Potentials in Postmodern American Society", Beverly M. Gordon further articulates the role of African intellectuals. She argues that African-American scholars, although marginalized in U.S. society, can still disseminate liberatory education by using cultural knowledge as a form of discourse. Dr. Gordon's view is that African-Americans must counter European-centered hegemony by continuing to employ liberatory and emancipatory pedagogy in schools and other learning institutions and situations.

In concluding, let me state that this book essentially offers a critical examination of the schooling and education of Black people in the United States of America. While the emphasis is on the United States, the analyses presented here are thought to have a great deal of relevance for Black people in other societies where, as in the United States, white-supremacist ideology has produced institutions that sustain anti-Black racism. Nah Dove's chapter on Great Britain, the only contribution whose social context is not the Unites States, attests to the likelihood that the analyses presented here are generalizable to other social contexts.

1. I use the term African in the Pan-Africanist sense put forward by Kwame Nkrumah: "All peoples of African descent, whether they live in North or South America, the Caribbean, or in any other part of the world are Africans and belong to the African nation." See "Extracts From Class Struggle in Africa" in *Revolutionary Path* (London: Panaf, 1973), 517.

Chapter One

Education and Schooling: You Can Have One Without the Other*

ᐒ◸◅ᘋᐁ◊ᐁ◊ ◸ᐓᐁ◅◅ᘋᐁ◊ᐁ◊ ◸ᐓᐁ◅◅ᘋᐁ◊◊ ᐁᐓ ◸ᐓᐁ◅◅ᘋᐁ◊◊ᐁᐓ ◸ᐓᐁ

Mwalimu J. Shujaa[1]
State University of New York at Buffalo

In African-American folk language the phrases "going to school" and "getting an education" are typically used in ways that imply that "schooling" and "education" are overlapping processes. It is not uncommon to hear people say, for example, "I am going to finish school and get a good education." The implied expectation is, of course, that "education" will be an outcome of "schooling." However, African-American folk language also contains expressions to signify that "going to school" is not always thought to be

* Earlier versions of this chapter were (a) presented at the Annual Meeting of the American Educational Research Association, San Francisco, April 1992 and (b) published in *Urban Education*, 27(4) (1993), 328-351.

consistent with "getting an education."[2] Anyone growing up in an African-American community has more than likely heard the rhyming verse:

bought you books and sent you to school,

but you still ain't nothing but—an educated fool!

This is obviously an insult intended for someone for whom "schooling" has not overlapped with "education." This type of signifying is often reserved for college-trained persons who are perceived to look condescendingly on the common folk in the community because they consider them uneducated. Folk expressions are instructive because they reflect reality as it is experienced and interpreted in African-American communities.[3] They bring to light the fact that African-Americans have long understood that schooling can both serve as well as betray their interests.

In this chapter I argue that a strategic differentiation between "education" and "schooling" is fundamental to the transmission, maintenance, and development of an African-centered cultural orientation and identity. I contend that "education" and "schooling" are different processes and that, while it is possible for them to overlap, it is also probable that most African-Americans receive more schooling than education. Using the United States as a social context, I present a conceptual model that links the process of schooling to the perpetuation of existing relations of power within the society. I use examples taken from interview data collected during my involvement in an earlier study of African-American participation in independent African-American schools to support the model.[4]

Conceptual Background

The failure to take into account differing cultural orientations and unequal power relations among groups that share membership in a society is a major problem in conceptualizations that equate schooling and education. Cultural orientations "involve cognitive, affective, and directive processes in people's strategies to solve problems.

. . . They are tenacious, persistent, superorganic principles that resist pressures for change brought about by the institutional transformation of society."[5] However, cultural orientations must be understood to exist in the context of group historical experience.[6] The African-American cultural identity has been and continues to be influenced by the U.S. social context, but it is essential to note that the African-American cultural orientation also represents an experiential context. Thus, while African-Americans exist within the U.S. social context, they also exist within an African historical-cultural continuum that predates that social context and would continue to exist even if the nation-state and its societal arrangements were to transform or demise.

Schooling is a process *intended* to perpetuate and maintain the society's existing power relations and the institutional structures that support those arrangements. All societies must provide a means for their members to learn, develop, and maintain throughout their life cycles adequate motivation for participation in socially valued and controlled patterns of action.[7] However, what is crucial to understand for this discussion is that when multiple cultural orientations exist within a nation-state, it is the leadership among the adherents to the politically dominant cultural orientation that exercise the most influence on the "concepts, values, and skills" that schools transmit. Such is the case with White Anglo Saxon Protestants in the United States. It is the leadership within this cultural group whose world view largely determines what is socially valued and controls patterns of action within the society. Education, in contrast to schooling, is the process of transmitting from one generation to the next knowledge of the values, aesthetics, spiritual beliefs, and all things that give a particular cultural orientation its uniqueness. Every cultural group must provide for this transmission process or it will cease to exist.

Education and schooling processes are not mutually exclusive, they can and do overlap. There are aspects of schooling that can serve the common interests of all members of a society, regardless of their particular cultural orientations. Carol D. Lee, Kofi Lomotey and myself list three such areas of overlap.[8] We believe that public schools in the United States can and should:

1. Foster the development of adequate skills in literacy, numeracy, the humanities, and technologies that are necessary to negotiate economic self-sufficiency in the society;
2. Instill citizenship skills based on a realistic and thorough understanding of the political system, and support such citizenship skills by promoting questioning and critical thinking skills and teaching democratic values[9];
3. Provide historical overviews of the nation, the continent, and the world which accurately represent the contributions of all ethnic groups to the storehouse of human knowledge.[10]

The attainment of goals such as these would constitute a significant step toward providing all citizens with the kinds of skills needed for full and equal participation in the society.

While the broad dissemination of these skills would, no doubt, be of benefit to the society, it would do little to enable individuals who lack adequate knowledge about their own cultural history to put such skills to use for the uplift of their cultural communities. We acknowledge this limitation of schooling and conclude, ultimately, that it is an inappropriate interpretation of public schooling's societal role to expect that it will provide for . . .

> the achievement of ethnic pride, self-sufficiency, equity, wealth, and power for Africans in America. . . . These goals will require a collective (although not monolithic) cultural and political world view.[11]

The world view we speak of can only be transmitted through a process of education strategically guided by an African-American cultural orientation and an understanding of how societal power relations are maintained. Moreover, it is the responsibility of each adult generation of African-Americans to ensure that the educational infrastructure for transmitting this knowledge to their progeny exists.

The first step in fulfilling our responsibilities to our culture is to develop collective practices for determining what cultural knowledge is to be transmitted. This could begin among groups of families, within organizations, and eventually include entire communities. The next step is to assess the extent to which our cultural knowledge is being transmitted in schools, churches, early childhood programs, and other settings where organized learning takes place. The third step is to create new resources to satisfy any aspects of the cultural knowledge base that are not addressed by existing facilities.

In this infrastructural model, independent African-centered schools represent institutions fully committed to collectively determining what aspects of cultural knowlege are to be transmitted. This process is reflected in the schools' curricula and the means by which the curricula are developed. In the current reality, however, relatively few of our children attend such institutions. The majority of our children are in European-centered public, private, and religious schools. The process of assessing the extent to which our cultural knowledge is taught must include an examination of what is happening to our children who attend these schools. The inherent shortcomings must be met with demands for culture affirming curricula. However, while these struggles are being waged, resources must be created to provide for the transmission of cultural knowledge among students who attend European-centered schools. Here, the Black supplementary school movement in the United Kingdom offers a useful model.[12] The supplementary schools operate on weekends and evenings to provide a culture affirming environment for students who would otherwise be at the mercy of Britain's state-run schools. In the United States, Saturday academics, after school programs, rites-of-passage organizations and study groups have been developed to facilitate the transmission of cultural knowledge.

Our ability to meet our cultural responsibilities is facilitated by our understanding of the linkages that exist between the process of schooling and the oppression of people of African descent. In the next section I analyze factors that influence our understanding of these linkages and suggest the conditions that are necessary for making critical distinctions between schooling and education.

The Strategic Differentiation of Education and Schooling: A Conceptual Model

Figure 1 is a conceptual model that represents decision making about schooling and education as a flow that bifurcates at four critical points. The model shows how decisions are influenced by the interplay between a society's structural conditions and members' achievement expectations and perceptions about the quality of their lives (achieved outcomes). Structural conditions are the "institutionalized arrangements of human life."[13] The influence of society's structural conditions on an individual's achievement expectations is cumulative. Schooling exerts an influence on members' achievement expectations through policies (e.g., tracking and testing), reward systems (e.g., grading and awarding credentials), and patterns of human interaction (e.g., social inclusion and exclusion) that reinforce and are reinforced by the society's structural conditions.

Bifurcation #1 represents any point in a person's life at which s/he evaluates the quality of his/her life. An individual will probably do this several times in the course of a life span. The individual will either conclude that the quality of his/her life is consistent with his/her achievement expectations or that it is not. The upper branch

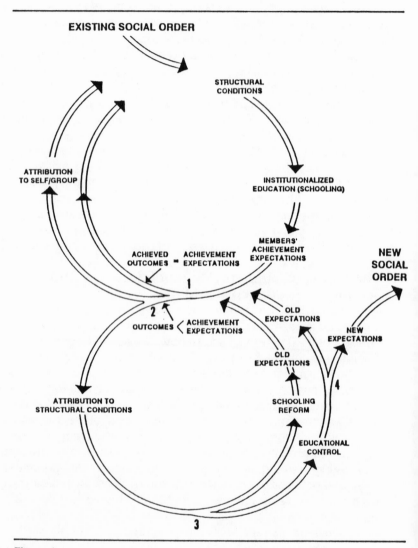

Figure 1

at Bifurcation #1 represents congruence between achievement expectations and outcomes. This situation exists when a person's perceptions about the quality of his/her life are consistent with his/her expectations. A person who expects to achieve prosperity and is prosperous is likely to be highly motivated to support the social arrangements that are believed to be conducive to his/her prosperity. Therefore, in the model, the path branches back toward the existing social order to symbolize the perpetuation of the prevailing structural conditions.

If the existing structural conditions contribute to expectations of poverty for an individual and s/he is, in fact, poor, s/he may fatalistically accept his/her condition. Believing that things cannot be changed, such individuals are unlikely to challenge the social order. Fatalistic attributions can occur among African-Americans because, as a group, we have experienced generations of oppression in the United States. When individuals believe that their subordinate condition is inherent in the order of the society, they may withdraw from what they consider to be a useless pursuit of social mobility.

Thus, in either case, prosperity or poverty, if the existing social order and its structural conditions are not challenged, the social order and its power relations are perpetuated. Consequently, the motivation to challenge the social order does not develop for two reasons. The first is because of the congruence between the individual's social expectations and the quality of life s/he is experiencing. The second is because of the individual's belief that the existing social order and its structural conditions should not or cannot be changed.

The lower branch from Bifurcation #1 represents an individual's unmet achievement expectations. These are attributed either to self or group characteristics or to the society's structural conditions. Bifurcation #2 illustrates these possibilities. The upward flowing branch symbolizes unmet achievement expectations that are attributed to self (individual) or group characteristics. The downward branch represents an attribution to the society's structural conditions. I will discuss the upper branch first.

The maintenance of the social order depends upon the development of this pattern of thinking among some of the society's members. It is one of schooling's functions to facilitate the "selection" of individuals to occupy low-status, but necessary, roles in the society. What better way to accomplish this selection process than to imbue some members with the idea that they (or their group) are unworthy or unprepared for the quality of life they see enjoyed by others? The adoption of this kind of thinking has often led African-Americans to support all kinds of programs and projects intended to "fix" the things that are "wrong" with us. Individuals pursue these courses of action when they internalize explanations for unmet achievement expectations that focus on self/group deficits rather than explanations that de-legitimize the social order. This is as much a part of the selection process as pushing some members of the society toward high-status roles by enmeshing their thinking with the idea that they (or their group) can accomplish anything.

When African-Americans attribute unmet achievement expectations to their own characteristics, we see the realization of racism's ultimate impact as a strategy for maintaining and perpetuating social domination. Its most overt manifestation is the internalization of the racial inferiority ideology. The most insidious manifestation is the adoption of the "minority" perspective. In the former instance "Whiteness" is perceived as superior. In the latter case there is the perception that White people will always be in power because they are the majority. The internalization by African-Americans of White supremacist ideologies is painful to discuss (and many of us do not discuss it); but it can and does occur. Frazier illustrates this problem through a statement from an interview with a 20-year-old African-American high school graduate.

> Our chances aren't as good by any means as the White man's and never will be unless the White man's attitude changes and [Blacks] make adjustments in their training and study. It's a situation like that [which] makes fellows like me not want to waste years studying to do what? I know there's no difference between the White man and me, *but I can't help feeling he is better than I am when he is trained to do his work and then has all the chance of doing it.*[14] [emphasis mine]

This excerpt provides an indication of the weight that racist treatment has placed upon this young man. He has to struggle with himself to avoid feeling that he, and not the structural conditions of his society, are responsible for the incongruence between his social expectations and the quality of his life. To the extent that he attributes his condition to himself, there will be no stress placed upon the society's structural conditions to change.

The overall concern here has to do with schooling's role in perpetuating this kind of attribution. Woodson opened the *Mis-educa-*

tion of the Negro with these words:

> The "educated Negroes" have the attitude of contempt toward their own people because in their own as well as in their mixed schools Negroes are taught to admire the Hebrew, the Greek, the Latin and the Teuton and to despise the African.[15]

Woodson's reasoning has been further developed by contemporary African-American writers, particularly in the field of psychology, such as Wilson,[16] Akbar,[17] and White & Parham.[18] The critical issue is that the leadership within the politically dominant culture in the U.S. utilizes schooling to inculcate its world view as universal. The effects of exclusion that Woodson describes continue to be problematic for African-Americans because the nature of our schooling in U.S. society is unchanged. Essentially, this means taking the position that the support given the schooling of African-Americans by government and "philanthropy" is and has historically been intended to serve the interests of the politically dominant members of U.S. society.[19]

The lower branch from Bifurcation #2 represents courses of action that can occur when unmet achievement expectations are attributed to the structural conditions of society. Individual attention is focused on countering the society's structural conditions to make achievement expectations obtainable. This degree of consciousness is the basic prerequisite for social activism in education and other areas of social life. There is, of course, a long history of activism that has coalesced African-American constituencies to work toward achieving some measure of change in the structural conditions of U.S. society. The civil rights movement is a prime example. However, any reasonable analysis of the civil rights movement would indicate that not every African-American who opposed Jim Crow shared the same vision of the course of action that would best serve the interests of African-Americans in a post-Jim Crow society.[20]

Marable argues that in the 1990s the belief that racial equality has been achieved is a post-Jim Crow spectre that haunts African-Americans.[21] He explains why this belief has emerged and persists:

> The number of Black elected officials exceeds 6,600; many Black entrepreneurs have achieved substantial gains within the capitalist economic system in the late 1980s; thousands of Black managers and administrators appear to be moving forward within the hierarchies of the private and public sector.[22]

Marable continues with an explanation of why he considers racial equality to be an illusion:

> The true test of any social thesis is the amount of reality it explains, or obscures. And from the vantage point of the inner-cities and homeless shelters, from the unemployment lines and closed factories, a different reality emerges. We find that racism has not declined in significance, if racism is defined correctly as the systematic exploitation of Blacks' labor power and the domination and subordination of our cultural, political, educational and social rights as human beings.[23]

The significance of Marable's argument for this discussion is that it helps to illuminate the fact that African-Americans view their relationship to the social order in different ways. A key factor influencing such views is the tension between individualistic and group orientations. Some African-Americans view themselves as being essentially individuals competing with other individuals to achieve the best the society has to offer them. Others take the view that individual achievement has no significance outside the quality of life experienced by African-Americans as a group. An individual's perceptions about the legitimacy of the schooling options available to African-Americans will reflect the extent to which s/he has adopted an individualistic or a group orientation. Accordingly, not all African-Americans who attribute their unmet achievement expectations to society's structural conditions, reflect the same view of reality in their analyses of what needs to be done about schooling.

Bifurcation #3 symbolizes how differing interpretations of one's relationship to the social order are evident in choosing between public school reform (the upper branch) and the rejection of public schooling (the lower branch). In my conceptual model schooling reform is an avenue leading to the attainment of achievement expectations that reinforce the existing social order. My reasoning is that our notions about quality of life are relative. Achievement expectations are constructed within the societal context and shaped by its institutions and hierarchies. Schooling reforms are not intended to produce fundamental changes in the role schooling plays in reproducing both the value system of the politically dominant culture and the social ordering that serves its elite. For example, in a capitalist society like the United States the accumulation of personal wealth is held up as a standard for measuring success. Thus, many symbols of success take on meaning in relationship to the perceived lifestyles of the wealthy. Many schooling reforms gain public support because they imply changes that will make these symbols of success accessible to more people.

Beyer discusses this fallacy of schooling reform in a critique of *A Nation at Risk*.[24] He describes the rationale for the schooling reforms supported in that document as . . .

> a pretext that justifies current social practices and institutions, a way of covertly supporting the *status quo*, a way of diverting attention away from basic social, political, and economic disparities and forms of oppression, and resultant forms of inequality. . . . By recasting the frustration, impatience, and anxiety that typify American social life in terms that safeguard those social institutions that support current inequalities, this report provides a "sleight of hand" that is at once ideologically ingenious and socially injurious.[25]

Beyer's description illustrates how reforms can address changes in schooling's packaging and methods of delivery while reinforcing the individualistic and materialistic value orientations that serve the interests of those in power.

Fundamental change in schooling can only be accomplished within the framework of fundamental change in the society's power relations. While there are many who would cast schooling reforms as vehicles that can facilitate the attainment of unmet achievement expectations, I believe this is possible only when such expectations are not contradictory to the existing power relations. Reforms do not challenge schooling's role in the maintenance of status quo power relations in society. Therefore, in my conceptual model, schooling reform is placed on a path that perpetually leads back to decision making about whether or not the quality of an individual's life is consistent with his/her achievement expectations in the existing social order (see Bifurcation #1).

The lower branch at Bifurcation #3 represents the decision to seek a better quality of life by controlling the schooling process. This is accomplished by utilizing options outside public schools such as home schooling and independent schools. The rate at which African-Americans are enrolling in independent schools has increased steadily since the late 1960s.[26] The Institute for Independent Education reports that more than 330,000 African-American students are enrolled in independent schools.[27] The schools these students attend represent a wide range of types. Most

(226,590) students are in Catholic schools. The next highest category is independent neighborhood schools (52,744); these schools have predominantly African-American enrollments. The remainder are spread among schools associated with the National Association of Independent Schools and various denominationally affiliated Christian schools.

Ratteray and myself reported that independent neighborhood schools deal with cultural and religious orientations in a variety of ways.[28] In particular, we found that there were very definite differences in both the quality and quantity of the attention given to maintaining and developing African-centered cultural orientations among their students. All of the parents who were interviewed at these schools indicated that they had decided against public school, however, they expressed different expectations regarding the extent to which an African-centered cultural orientation was important to them in choosing their children's schools. Some parents' choices were influenced by concerns that a particular school might be "too Black" and others had consciously chosen schools that would help their children develop African-centered cultural orientations.[29] Thus, these schools can be viewed as vehicles that are used by African-American parents to pursue very different achievement expectations.

These varied expectations are symbolized at Bifurcation #4. In discussing these expectations I will use segments from interviews conducted with parents of students who attend African-American independent schools to illustrate how schooling and education are differentiated in their thinking. The left branch from the bifurcation point symbolizes decisions based on achievement expectations that reinforce the existing social order. Here, independent schools are used as alternative pathways to achieving goals that reinforce existing power relations and value orientations of the society's politically dominant culture.

One mother we interviewed in Baltimore believes that it is important for her children to believe in themselves. She wants the school to help her children develop enough self-confidence and motivation to work as hard as necessary to overcome any feelings of personal shortcoming relative to someone else. In addition to academic needs, the parent describes the school's contribution in terms that relate to the development of a positive self-image:

> [School name] instills in the children a better self-image as far as living up to your full potential and trying harder, you know basi-

cally what you can do, and not having no one say that because you may be a little slower than the next child that if you don't work just a little bit harder, you can come up to the level of the child that you think you are a little slower than. . . . I think they instill . . . a better self-image in the children and give them a better motivation as to want to try harder. [1.002-94]

This mother is making a comparison that is based on what she feels happens to children in public schools and what she expects her children to gain from the independent African-American school they attend. She believes that success for African-American children is determined by the resolve that they have to overcome personal shortcomings. She favors the independent African-American school because she feels its teachers have the skill and dedication to develop this attribute in her children. This viewpoint implies a belief that individuals vary in their abilities and that relative shortcomings can be overcome through hard work, and an optimism about meeting achievement expectations. One does not get a sense that this mother enrolled her children in an African-American independent school because of a sense of contradiction between personal goals and mainstream notions of personal success. The African-American independent school is viewed as a way of offsetting barriers to achieving personal success. The barriers, however, are perceived in terms of personal attributes and not in the context of the structural conditions of the society. My interpretation is that this parent is not making a critical distinction between schooling and education. She is not challenging the social order, but attempting to offer her children an alternate means of access to its rewards.

Another parent we interviewed also sees the development of personal attributes as the most important contribution the independent African-American school can make. In this instance the personal attribute is described as "the ability to adapt." The adaptation is to being "a minority." What the parent wants is for her son to learn how to compete in U.S. society as a "minority." She is concerned that her child's enrollment in the independent African-American school, because its students are all African-American, may result in a "lack of exposure" to minority status.

Exposure to and the ability to cope with and adapt to being a minority, for lack of a better term, in the world is something that has to be developed. . . . In a black environment or a black school you can be under-exposed so that you develop a sense of com-

placency. . . . Or, that you don't develop your abilities to adapt.
[1.003-338]

According to her perception of "minority" status, this mother believes that her son will always be competing with Whites for social rewards. Unless he learns to compete, she feels, he will not be successful in meeting his achievement expectations. Again, the African-American independent school is viewed as a means to overcoming barriers to achieving success in the context of the society's existing structural conditions. There is no challenge to the social order implied here.

The right branch from the bifurcation point symbolizes the strategic differentiation of education from schooling. This process is motivated by achievement expectations that are based on new values and the realization that the power to educate is conditioned upon freeing the process from the controlling influences of the politically dominant culture. Education becomes part of the infrastructure needed to preserve progress made toward the emergence of a new social order.

A mother in Washington, D.C. indicated that her son had negative experiences in public school even though he was enrolled in classes for the academically gifted. His inquisitiveness was stifled and often interpreted as insolence. This mother was raised "on the picket lines" and has always involved her children in community issues. She is deeply concerned that her children develop a commitment to uplifting African-American people. Several times during our interview she stressed that "each one must teach one" is a principle that she lives by and attempts to instill in her children. She also indicated that she wants her children to learn self-assuredness because she believes they would need it in order to overcome White racism. While we were discussing her feelings about her children's enrollment in an all African-American school she made this comment about her expectations of the schooling process:

In the first place, most public schools in the District are Black. So, I mean, there's no difference really here as far as that is concerned. The other thing is that nurturing and the positive imagery that takes place here is so necessary, I think, to making people who are well adjusted, strong, and creative who then can go out into the work force and say, you know, I respect you. You *will* respect me. . . . Because that's what I tell them, they don't have to like you and don't think that they will. You get along as well as you can. You succeed as well as you can. . . . The whole thing is that while you're in the learning process, you need to learn from your own, with your own and that type of thing. [1.004-809]

She went on to describe what she perceives to be the role of the independent African-American school in providing education that will help her children to achieve what she expects them to as adults:

. . . I want the children to be taught not that you get educated and you learn as much as you can so you can work for someone else. But that we, you know, you get educated, you develop your own. They could even go so far as to have the junior achievement programs here, that type of thing. [1.004-926]

Evident in these statements is the mother's concern that her children be agents for change. She sees the independent African-American school and the home as extensions of each other in fostering the achievement of this goal. Thus, for her, involvement in the independent African-American school is a part of parenting:

These children are so awesome. You know? I mean, we have just heavy discussions at my household and I want them to be politically aware and economically sound. . . . They need to learn economics and these kids with these minds that are going out like this need to learn to manage money and that kind of thing. They could have a bank, a school store, anything in here. Those are some of the things I'd like to see develop and I'm on the curriculum committee. I'm going to try and work at that. [1.004-1048]

This mother is one who has made a strategic distinction between schooling and education. She acknowledges the importance of being prepared to earn a living amid the social conditions that exist. Beyond that, however, is the emphasis she places on helping her children appreciate the significance of contributing to the uplift of African-American people.

When African-American parents strategically differentiate education from schooling the decisions they make about where to enroll their children are based on their perceptions of the social and cultural realities that influence their lives. They involve careful consideration of other schooling options, most often public systems, that are well integrated into the societal infrastructure. They include assessments about the relationship of schooling to the social order and schooling's role in the attainment of individual achievement expectations. Most significantly, these decisions entail taking stock of both one's individual and group relationship to the existing social order and determining how to provide one's children with the best preparation for assuming their responsibilities in the maintenance and perpetuation of an African cultural orientation.

Overcoming Schooling: A Cultural Imperative

My conceptual framework emphasizes the exigencies of our African cultural orientation over those of the nation-state (U.S.). Consequently, I treat schooling and education as differentiated processes. Schooling ties me to the social order framed by the nation-state. Education informs and locates my thinking within an African historical-cultural context.

Cultural orientation makes a difference in the way one critiques society. This can be illustrated through contrasting examples taken from the writings of John Dewey and W. E. B. DuBois. These men were social contemporaries, however the writings presented here indicate that they saw U.S. society in very different ways. First, consider Dewey's discussion of the function of education in a democratic society. In the following statement, he explains the criteria needed to evaluate education's role in a society:

> Since education is a social process . . . a criterion for educational criticism and construction implies a *particular* social ideal. The two points selected by which to measure the worth of a form of social life are the extent to which the interests of a group are shared by all its members, and the fullness with which it interacts with other groups.[30]

Of course, the social ideal that concerns Dewey is democracy. He regards a democratic society as one which . . .

> makes provision for participation in its good of all members on equal terms and which secures flexible readjustment of its institutions through interaction of the different forms of associated life is in so far democratic.[31]

He then describes the role of education in democratic society:

> [It] gives individuals a personal interest in social relationships and control, and the habits of mind which secure social changes without introducing disorder.[32]

Dewey's notion that a particular kind of education can bring about change "without introducing disorder" is problematic. Although, by his own words, Dewey understood that the United States is "composed of a combination of different groups with different traditional customs,"[33] he, nonetheless, ignores the dialectics of domination and resistance associated with these cultural differences. There is no mention of how the power over institutionalized education held by the politically dominant members of the society is used to maintain the order he wants to preserve. He also avoids the issue of oppressed peoples' challenge to that power. For Dewey, social change is to be determined by the rational thinking of the politically dominant members of the society.

DuBois and Dewey shared membership in the same society, but related to different primary cultural groups. Dewey's cultural orientation was European-American; DuBois' was African-American. DuBois presents a quite different analysis of education's role in society than Dewey. To begin with, DuBois focuses on the cultural conflict in the United States and its impact on the African-American cultural identity. He saw the legislation of equal rights in voting and education as the ". . . beginning of even more difficult problems of race and culture." He also reckons with the question of what would become of the African-American cultural identity in a United States where equality was supposedly the law of the land:

> . . . what we must now ask ourselves is when we become equal American citizens what will be our aims and ideals and what will we have to do with selecting these aims and ideals. Are we to assume that we will simply adopt the ideals of Americans and become what they are or want to be and that we will have in this process no ideals of our own? . . . We would take on the culture of white Americans doing as they do and thinking as they think.[34]

DuBois considered the cultural assimilation of African-Americans into the politically dominant culture in the United States to be unacceptable. He saw a clear dilemma for African-Americans—refuse to go to school or go to school and run the risk of becoming alienated from the African-American cultural community:

> Here for instance, is the boy who says simply he is not going to school. His treatment in the white schools . . . is such that it does not attract him. Moreover, the boy who does enter the white school and gets on reasonably well does not always become a use-

ful member of our group. Negro children . . . often know nothing of Negro history. . . . Some are ashamed of themselves and
their folk.[35]

The dialectics of power do not escape DuBois' analysis, as they do
Dewey's. The exigencies of culture, not society, establish imperatives
for DuBois. He is unwilling to accept social arrangements that restrict
the ability of the African-American to understand and appreciate
his/her relationship to the African historical-cultural continuum.

Freire gives an indication of having reached conclusions similar
to DuBois' regarding the importance of culture.[36] He points out that
an attack on a people's culture is the first step in any process of domination:

Cultural identity is the first point the dominative people, or class,
or nation, or individual [attempts] to destroy in the dominated people. In other words, there is no oppression, no domination without the attempt . . . to destroy the cultural identity of the invaded.

There is much to suggest that one of the functions of schooling in the
United States has been to effect a gradual destruction of the cultural
identity of African-Americans. This process has been justified as being
consistent with the promulgation of a common American culture.

The common culture concept is inherently one-sided in favor of
the politically dominant culture. It is put forth typically by people
who already believe that their cultural orientation is "the" common
culture. Consequently, they have little to lose by demanding the
acquiescence of others. They assign little or no significance to the
different cultural orientations of the people with whom they share
societal membership nor are they concerned with the fact that other
people attach importance to their own cultural identities. An illustration of how the cultural diversity in U.S. society is downplayed is
found in Hirsch's discussion of his concept of cultural literacy.

By accident of history, American cultural literacy has a bias toward
English literate tradition. Short of revolutionary political upheaval,
there is absolutely nothing that can be done about this. . . . We
have kept and still need to keep English culture as the dominant
part of our national vocabulary for purely functional reasons.[37]

Hirsch's is the particularistic view of an individual who is privileged
and empowered by the politically dominant culture in the United

States. He is essentially arguing that the political dominance of the White Anglo Saxon Protestant is incontestable and all who live within its influence are compelled to accept it, if for no other reason than in the interests of national unity.

Hirsch's argument rests on a conception of social history that is in reality the history of the society's politically dominant culture. And therein lies the problem with "common culture." The United States is, as Asante[38] and others have argued, a hegemonic society, in which the relatively powerful members trace their ways of thinking, their philosophical foundations, and their canons of knowledge to the cultures of Western Europe. These people, over the generations, have used societal institutions and resources to glorify their Western European cultural heritage while, at the same time, devaluing through processes of omission, distortion, and misrepresentation knowledge centered in the cultures of others in the same society who do not trace their origins to Western Europe. African-Americans are among these "other" groups that are systematically oppressed through institutionalized relations of power and resource distribution based on race. "Whiteness" has served as the biological symbol of Western European cultural descendence. Hare points out that immigrants who left Europe as Poles, Italians, Germans, or Russians, became "Whites" when they reached the shores of the United States.[39] They became part of an institutionalized set of social relations that offered them inclusion into the family of "Whiteness." Schooling facilitated this process for them because it was through schooling that they learned they could aspire to a place in the U.S. social order and its "common culture." "Blackness", then, becomes the criterion on which "non-Whites" are assigned to a caste status of perpetual subordination to "Whites."[40]

Education is, indeed, a cultural imperative for African-Americans. Men and women of African descent in the United States and in the Caribbean have maintained a long tradition of cultural resistance based on the recognition that their abilities to preserve and perpetuate their own cultures have been consistently under attack. This thinking is evident among the published works of David Walker,[41] Edward Wilmot Blyden,[42] Drusilla Dunjee Houston,[43] Carter G. Woodson,[44] and W. E. B. DuBois,[45] to name just a few.

Woodson proposed that African-Americans establish a new program of education for themselves to undo the mis-education inculcated by schooling in the United States. He supports his reasoning in the following manner:

The so-called modern education, with all its defects, however, does others so much more good than it does the Negro, because it has been worked out in conformity to the needs of those who have enslaved and oppressed weaker peoples. For example, the philosophy and ethics resulting from our educational system have justified slavery, peonage, segregation, and lynching. The oppressor has the right to exploit, to handicap, and to kill the oppressed. Negroes daily educated in the tenets of such a religion of the strong have accepted the status of the weak as divinely ordained . . . [46]

To Woodson, it clearly makes no sense to expect a system of schooling controlled by the politically dominant culture for its own interests to provide education for African-Americans. Yet, for the most part, this is what we have done.

I foresee no change in this situation that does not involve African-Americans taking control of our own education. When education is strategically differentiated from schooling, there is no reason this cannot be done. It means empowering ourselves to ensure that African-centered cultural knowledge is systematically transmitted to our children. In many cities, African-centered independent schools are providing a means for acquiring educational control. Where such schools do not exist or are not accessible, families, groups of parents, community-based organizations, churches, and rites-of-passage organizations can and have become networks for passing on cultural knowledge. This is our cultural imperative.

Conclusion

In concluding I want to share a personal recollection that focuses much of what I have said in this essay. In 1957, when I was a second grader at Frederick Douglass School in Parsons, Kansas, my teacher, Miss Lacy Clark, taught a lesson that illustrates how African-Americans who understood the importance of doing so have always had to make strategic distinctions between education and schooling. One morning Miss Clark asked us to stop what we were doing and put everything on our desks away. She then distributed to each of us a copy of a drawing that looked as if it had come from a coloring book. The drawing showed an autumn scene in which a group of children were playing among piles of raked leaves. There were oak trees in the drawing with leaves tumbling from their branches. The children were dressed warmly in caps, jackets, and scarves.

Miss Clark's instructions were simple. We were to use our crayons to color in the picture. Although it was not necessary, she added an incentive—a prize would be given to the student who did the best job coloring the picture. Miss Clark collected our drawings when the bell for recess rang. When we returned after recess and took our seats, Miss Clark announced the winner of the prize. It turned out to a boy who had colored the faces of the children in the picture brown to match his own. He was the only student among this class of 25 African-American children to do so. The rest of us had colored in every detail of that picture except the faces of the children.

Because 1957 was the last year of Douglass School's existence, Miss Clark was doing what she could to prepare us for that inevitable day when our teachers and most of our classmates would be White. She knew that we would have to fight for our cultural identities in the formerly all-White schools. Miss Clark intended to prepare us to participate in and contribute to both the larger society and to our own cultural community. At times, her teaching emphasized knowledge specific to the African-American cultural identity she shared with her students; at other times its focus was on the second grade curriculum prescribed by the all-White school board.

As a teacher, Miss Clark was strategically differentiating between education and schooling. What she did for my classmates and me is done by many, but unfortunately not all, African-American teachers and administrators everyday. The actions of individuals like Miss Clark and the teachers and administrators described by Foster[47] and Lomotey[48] provide indications that human agency can and often does intervene in the reproduction of politically dominant ideology. The critical task confronting us is broadening our understanding of the role that the strategic differentiation of education and schooling can play in the success of African-American resistance to political and cultural domination and in guiding the development of our cultural nation in a new world order in which egalitarian relationships between cultures replace exploitative hierarchies.

Notes and References

1. I wish to thank Prof. Susan Noffke for her comments on my conceptual model. I also wish to thank the following graduate assistants: Catherine Priser and Damon Revelas, for their all around assistance and Vance Agee for his help with the analysis of the parent interview data.
2. V. Gadsden, "Literacy, Education, and Identity among African-Americans: The Communal Nature of Learning," *Urban Education* 27(4) (1993): 352-369.
3. J. Ogbu, *The Next Generation: An Ethnography of Education in an*

Urban Neighborhood (New York: Academic Press, 1974), 16.

4. J. D. Ratteray and M. J. Shujaa, *Dare to Choose: Parental Choice at Independent Neighborhood Schools* (Washington, DC: Institute for Independent Education, 1987).

5. N. K. Shimahara, *Adaptation and Education in Japan* (New York: Praeger, 1979), 2.

6. A. Akoto, *Nationbuilding: Theory and Practice in Afrikan-Centered Education* (Washington, DC: Pan Afrikan World Institute).

7. T. Parsons, *Societies: Evolutionary and Comparative Perspectives* (Englewood Cliffs, NJ: Prentice Hall), 5-18.

8. C. D. Lee, K. Lomotey, and M. J. Shujaa, "How Shall We Sing Our Sacred Song in a Strange Land? The Dilemma of Double Consciousness and the Complexities of an African-Centered Pedagogy," *Journal of Education* 172 (1990): 45-61.

9. A. Gutmann, *Democratic Education* (Princeton: Princeton University Press, 1987); L. McNeil, *Contradictions of Control: School Structure and School Knowledge* (New York: Routledge & Kegan Paul, 1988).

10. Lee et al., "How Shall We Sing Our Sacred Song," 49.

11. Lee, Lomotey, and Shujaa, "How Shall We Sing Our Sacred Song," 49.

12. N. Dove, "The Emergence of Black Supplementary Schools: Resistance to Racism in the United Kingdom," *Urban Education* 27(4) (1993): 430-447.

13. Shimahara, *Adaptation and Education*.

14. E. F. Frazier, *Negro Youth at the Crossways: Their Personality Development in the Middle States* (Washington, DC: American Council on Education, 1940), 136-137.

15. C. G. Woodson, Mis-Education of the Negro (1933; reprint, Washington, DC: Associated Publishers, 1969), 1.

16. A. Wilson, *The Developmental Psychology of the Black Child* (New York: Africana Research, 1978).

17. N. Akbar, *Chains and Images of Psychological Slavery* (Jersey City, NJ: New Mind Productions, 1984).

18. J. L. White and T. A. Parham, *The Psychology of Blacks: An African-American Perspective* (Englewood Cliffs, NJ: Prentice Hall, 1990).

19. J. D. Anderson, *The Education of Blacks in the South, 1860-1935* (Chapel Hill, NC: University of North Carolina, 1988); R. E. Butchart, "Outthinking and Outflanking the Owners of the World: A Historiography of the African-American Struggle for Education," *History of Education Quarterly* 28 (1988): 333-366.

20. S. Stuckey, *Slave Culture: Nationalist Theory and the Foundations of Black America* (New York/Oxford: Oxford University Press, 1987); J. H. Clarke, *African World Revolution: Africans at the Crossroads* (Trenton, NJ: Africa World Press, 1991).

21. M. Marable, "Toward Black American Empowerment: Violence and

Resistance in the African-American Community in the 1990s," *African Commentary* 2 (1990): 16-21.

22. Marable, "Toward Black American Empowerment," 16.
23. Marable, "Toward Black American Empowerment," 16.
24. L. E. Beyer, "Educational Reform: The Political Roots of National Risk," *Curriculum Inquiry* 15 (1985): 37-56.
25. Beyer, "Educational Reform," 48.
26. P. L. Benson, *Private Schools in the United States: A Statistical Profile, with Comparisons to Public Schools* (Washington, DC: Department of Education, 1991); Institute for Independent Education, *African-American Enrollment in Independent Schools (Research Notes on Education)* (Washington, DC: Author, 1990); Ratteray and Shujaa, *Dare to Choose.*
27. Institute for Independent Education, *African-American Enrollment.*
28. Ratteray and Shujaa, *Dare to Choose.*
29. M. J. Shujaa, "Parental Choice of an Afrocentric Independent School: Developing an Explanatory Theory," *Sankofa* 2 (1988): 22-25.
30. J. Dewey, *Democracy and Education* (1916; reprint, New York: The Free Press, 1944), 99.
31. Dewey, *Democracy and Education,* 99.
32. Dewey, *Democracy and Education,* 99.
33. Dewey, *Democracy and Education,* 21.
34. W. E. B. DuBois, "Whither Now and Why," in *The Education of Black People: Ten Critiques, 1906-1960 by W. E. B. DuBois,* ed. H. Aptheker (New York: Monthly Review Press, 1973), 149.
35. DuBois, "Whither Now and Why," 151.
36. P. Freire, *The People's Education and Participant Research,* Cassette recording no. RA-1-35.15 (Washington, DC: American Educational Research Association, 1991).
37. E. D. Hirsch, Jr., *Cultural Literacy: What Every American Needs to Know* (Boston: Houghton Mifflin, 1987), 106-107.
38. M. K. Asante, "Multiculturalism: An Exchange," *American Scholar* 60 (1991): 267-276.
39. B. R. Hare, *The Effectiveness of Desegregation as a Strategy for Improving the Quality of African-American Education,* Keynote address at the Beyond Desegregation: Perspectives from the 1990s Conference held at the State University of New York at Buffalo, November 1991.
40. S. Wynter, *Do Not Call Us Negroes: How "Multicultural" Textbooks Perpetuate Racism* (San Jose, CA: Aspire Books, 1992), 9-10.
41. D. Walker, *Walker's Appeal in Four Articles, together with a Preamble to the Coloured Citizens of the World, but in particular, and very expressly, to those of the United States of America,* ed. C. M. Wiltse (1829; reprint, New York: Hill and Wang, 1965).
42. E. W. Blyden, *Black Spokesman,* ed. H. R. Lynch (London: Frank

Cass and Co., 1895).

43. D. D. Houston, *Wonderful Ethiopians of the Ancient Cushite Empire* (1926; reprint, Baltimore: Black Classics Press, 1985).

44. Woodson, *Mis-Education of the Negro.*

45. DuBois, "Whither Now and Why."

46. Woodson, *Mis-Education of the Negro,* xxxii.

47. M. Foster, "Educating for Competence in Community and Culture: Exploring the Views of Exemplary African-American Teachers," *Urban Education* 27 (1992): 370-394.

48. K. Lomotey, "African-American Principals: Bureaucrat/Administrators and Ethno-Humanists," *Urban Education* 27 (1992): 395-412.

CHAPTER TWO

Black Intellectuals and the Crisis in Black Education

Jacob H. Carruthers
Center for Inner City Studies
Northeastern Illinois University
and
The Kemetic Institute

Defining the Crisis

E. Franklin Frazier died in 1962. Ironically, it was that very same year that he began to speak of embarking on a new direction in his thinking—a change in course that caused him to reflect on matters that he had avoided for most of his scholarly life. As his life flame was about to go out, Frazier turned his attention to the problem of the Negro intellectual. In a 1962 essay, "The Failure of the Negro Intellectual," he said among other things, that,

> educated Negroes or Negro intellectuals have failed to achieve any intellectual freedom. In fact . . . it appears that the Negro intellectual is unconscious of the extent to which his thinking is

This essay is based on Dr. Carruthers' presentation at the Council of Independent Black Institutions' (CIBI) Distinguished Black Educators Forum, Chicago, Illinois, 1983.

restricted to sterile repetition of the safe and conventional ideas current in American society.[1]

He then added,

We have no philosophers or thinkers . . . men who have reflected on the fundamental problems which always concerned philosophers such as the nature of human knowledge and the meaning or lack of meaning of human existence.[2]

Frazier confronted the crisis of the Black intellectual rather late in his life. However, the fact that he did confront it is important because many of us at the time had not really started thinking about the problem, including those of us who were supposed to be Black intellectuals. We did not begin to focus on this problem until people like Frazier and Harold Cruse directed our attention to it. However, despite our failure to address the issue, it must be understood that this was not actually a new concern and that Black thinkers had focused on the crisis of Black thought for quite some time. In fact, from the very beginnings of Black educational development, but specifically during the period following the U.S. Civil War and preceding the partitioning of the African continent, Black thinkers had focused much of their attention on Black intellectual development and the problem of Black education.

Frazier's criticism was aimed at Black intellectuals in the United States. Unfortunately, however, he disregarded an important element in the historical development of Black thought —the group of Black intellectuals whom we identify as nationalist thinkers. Harold Cruse later reminded us of the role played by nationalist thinkers in his book *Crisis of the Negro Intellectual*.[3] He echoed Frazier's concerns about the failure of Black intellectuals to articulate a theory of knowledge grounded in the "Afro-American ethnic group consciousness."[4] Yet, even though Cruse extracted much from Frazier's original probe, he must be credited with reminding us that there had been a line of nationalist Black thinkers in this country as far back as the early 19th century.

These thinkers represented what Cruse called the "rejected strain" of intellectuals although many of them, in fact, had dealt with quite a few of the fundamental concepts that would have made them eligible to be considered philosophers—even by Frazier's standards. Among this group of Black intellectuals were men like Hosea Easton, Martin Delany, Edward Wilmot Blyden, and Alexander

Crummell. Delany and Blyden, who had both done field studies in Africa prior to its partition by European colonialism in 1884-85, documented the existence of a distinct and universal world view among African people. In the early 1800s, Hosea Easton helped establish the tradition of comparing ancient Ethiopian-Egyptian civilization with contemporary Africa as part of African-centered scholarship.[5] Crummell, an Episcopal priest, traveled to Africa seeking land to repatriate enslaved Africans.[6]

Frazier's oversight is understandable if we consider the problems he faced in overcoming the contradictions in his own training as a sociologist. In general, however, his criticisms should be well taken. In this chapter I will discuss how we came to blur the distinction between those individuals whom we refer to as "educated" purely on the basis of the number of years of schooling they have accumulated and those we should consider to be intellectuals by virtue of the reasoning and understanding they contribute to problems affecting African people. Moreover, I will explore the origins of this situation and its significance.

The Illusion of Intellectual Attainment

Frazier defined the African-American intellectual as being equivalent to or synonymous with any African-American having received advanced schooling—whether an individual wanted to be considered such or not and whether he or she aspired to that role or not. Such a generalization is not valid. Among most other ethnic groups there is a broad group of people with advanced schooling, within which there is a smaller group that comprises the intellectual segment.

One of the best examples of Black intellectualism is Edward Wilmot Blyden who was born in St. Thomas, Virgin Islands, in 1832. Blyden lived for a short time in Venezuela and in the United States before emigrating to Liberia. He committed himself to the development of African education for Black people in West Africa. In 1872, during a two-year stay in Sierra Leone, Blyden included the following in a letter to the governor of the then British colony, John P. Hennessey:

All educated Negroes suffer from a kind of slavery in many ways far more subversive of the real welfare of the race than the ancient physical fetters. The slavery of the mind is far more destructive than that of the body. But such is the weakness and imperfection of human nature that many of those who bravely fought to remove the shackles from the body of the Negro transfer them to his *mind*.[7]

Blyden's ideas about the role of schooling in the mental enslavement of Black people could be found reverberating some 50 years later throughout the pages of Carter G. Woodson's *Mis-Education of the Negro*.[8] Woodson challenged African-American people to abandon the kind of education that made them versed in the stories of Europeans but left them with nothing positive to say about their own history and culture:

> The only question which concerns us here is whether these educated persons are actually equipped to face the ordeal before them or unconsciously contribute to their own undoing by perpetuating the regime of the oppressor.[9]
>
> The so-called modern education, with all its defects, however, does others so much more good than it does Negroes because it has been worked out in conformity to the needs to those who have enslaved and oppressed weaker people. For example, the philosophy and ethics resulting from our education system has justified slavery, peonage, segregation and lynching. . . . The Negro, thus educated is a hopeless liability to the race.[10]
>
> When a Negro has finished his education in our schools, then he has been equipped to begin the life of an Americanized or Europeanized White man, but before he steps from the threshold of his alma mater he is told by his teachers that he must go back to his own people from whom he has been estranged by a vision of ideas, which in his disillusionment he will realize that he can not attain.[11]
>
> Even if the Negroes do successfully imitate the Whites, nothing new has thereby been accomplished. You simply have a larger number of persons doing what others have been doing. The unusual gifts of the race have not thereby been developed, and an unwilling world therefore continues to wonder what the educated Negro is good for.[12]

By calling into question the value of the so-called educated Negro for the development of the race, Woodson got to the heart of the problem confronting Black intellectuals. And, as we have noted, E. Franklin Frazier had also taken up this problem when he died in 1962, nearly 30 years after Woodson's *Mis-Education of the Negro*.

It is important to understand that this problem is not unique to African-Americans. Mis-education has also been a critical issue in Africa since the late 1950s as newly independent African states struggled to decolonize their education systems. Julius K. Nyerere, former President of Tanzania, addressed the problem in his important essay, "Education for Self-Reliance."[13] Nyerere believed that Tanzania's potential to produce the intellectual leadership it needed would not be realized until his country "questioned the basic system of education we took over at the time of independence."[14] He found that there were

> basic elements in the [education] system which prevent . . . the integration of the pupils into the society they will enter, and which encourage attitudes of inequality, intellectual arrogance, and intense individualism among the young people who are to go through our schools.[15]

Thus, after several years of independence from British colonialism, Nyerere found his country's development hampered by an education system that better served the interests of the European colonialists who created it than it did those of the people of Tanzania who depended on it.

The crisis in Black education is, indeed, world wide. I submit that this crisis is and has been perpetuated and maintained in large measure by the failure of contemporary Black intellectuals to address the problems in their own thinking. These problems are directly attributable to schooling founded on European-centered constructions of knowledge. The crisis in Black education will not be resolved until Black intellectuals achieve intellectual freedom and reconstruct Black education on an African-centered foundation. These are the preconditions to the real liberation of the African race all over the world. To understand how I arrived at such a conclusion, it is necessary to take a tour through history and reflect on the underpinnings of Black education under White control.

Intellectual Control as a Weapon

There is a myth that traditional African education was totally confined to the kind of practical on the job training depicted in many anthropological accounts of African societies. One of the better explanations of that tradition is found in *Facing Mt. Kenya* by Jomo Kenyatta in which we are presented with a picture that shows African education as being extremely practical.[16] This was not formal education; it was an education process that was designed to integrate individual children into Gikuyu society. The children learned by doing and, indeed, they received the wisdom of their elders through that educational system. It was a quite useful and functional education and was well adapted to the situation for which it was designed.

Certainly, the kind of education Kenyatta described did occur and continues in Africa as well as here in the United States in some instances. Essentially, it is the same kind of education my grandfather and my great-grandfather received. They received practical education in such things as milking cows, but they were also taught how to understand the wisdom of their ancestors. While this was a creditable kind of education in its own right, we have to understand today that this was only one aspect of African education. It represents only one part of the heritage of traditional African education.

Alongside the practical education just described, there was another form of traditional education in all of the urban societies established and maintained by African people which provided what we might call formal or higher education. In ancient Egypt, for example, there was an institution called the *at seba*[17] which literally means the "house of instruction,"[18] where young people were instructed in the higher aspects of knowledge. They were taught first of all simply how to write, read, do mathematics, and other kinds of basic skills. This was a very rigorous kind of education. Youngsters entered around the age of twelve and sometimes stayed in those schools until they were 28 years old. In the process, they became highly educated people.

Ancient Egyptian society depended on the people who successfully negotiated this education to do the more meticulous, intellectual, and skilled jobs. The scribes, as they are now called, maintained control of the governing apparatus. They were the ones who entered the priesthood and various other types of professions, including medicine and architecture. The kind of education they received combined teaching of the morals and the ethics of society with the wisdom and the skills necessary for people of this culture to achieve high intellectual goals. This kind of education was so profound, so significant, and so impressive that people from all over the world went to Egypt to study. The ancient Egyptians were the teachers of the world.

Through the centuries, one of the great preoccupations of European historiography has been to try and eradicate this information from the pages of history. If one read only European-centered versions of history, it would seem that no African had ever been educated formally before Europeans "discovered" them. When Egypt was finally defeated militarily, the gate to Africa stood wide open. Conquerors came slowly at first, but inevitably they came. After about 3,000 years they were able to subdue the African continent completely. As they came, they brought in, wherever they could, an alien education system. The early Christians, who arrived begging for refuge, came in with an education agenda. They were followed by the Moslems who also came with an education agenda. We could go into what the early Christians and the Moslems did in Africa, but it is more important to this discussion that we understand fully the influence of the European Christians who arrived later. I will begin with the arrival of the Portuguese around 1480.

When European expansionists encountered Africans many centuries after the decline of Egypt as a world power, they found that formal educational institutions continued to exist. When the Portuguese reached the middle of Africa—the Congo-Angola region—they knew that they had found exactly what Europe needed to redevelop itself after centuries of warfare among feudal lords. Africa was the richest continent in the world. From the time of Caesar, Europeans had heard about it, but only when they finally gazed upon it did they fully realize its wealth—including all of its man power and woman power.

The Portuguese decided on a plan of intellectual control. They had been experimenting for about 40 or 50 years with the education of Black people in the Senegal-Gambia area; therefore, when they reached the Congo, their plan was very well mapped out. The first step was to convince the king, the Mani Congo Nzinga a Nkuwa, that he and his people would benefit by European education.[19] The Portuguese took African children to Lisbon and enrolled them in the university there. They also set up missionary schools in the Congo.

The Portuguese were also successful in converting the king to Christianity, and, under their influence, he baptized his son Afonso I. When Afonso had a son, he, too, baptized his son who carried the name Dom Henrique. Young Dom Henrique, grandson of Mani Congo Nzinga a Nkuwa, was so versed in the ways of Europe that he managed to astonish the Pope. Kwame Nkrumah paints a vivid picture of how well this education system served the Portuguese in *Challenge of the Congo.*

In 1513 a mission from the Mani Congo led by his son . . . Dom Henrique, visited the Pope, travelling overland from Portugal and carrying with them gifts of ivory, rare skins and the fine woven raffia textiles then manufactured in the Congo. Dom Henrique who was at the time 18 years old, was able to address the Pope in Latin and five years later . . . he was elevated to the rank of Bishop of the Congo.[20]

The experience of the Congo illustrates the fact that the Europeans' discovery of the advantages of providing some Blacks with a European education was evident a decade before Columbus opened up the Western hemisphere for European expansion. In fact, Nkrumah considered this strategy so effective that he referred to its continuing influence on African education five centuries later.

The Portuguese, with the support of the Mani Congo, set out on a systematic policy of Westernization in the Congo. At this point emerged the contradiction that has haunted European and African relations ever since.[21]

One example epitomizes the effectiveness of European education as a tool of intellectual control. It is to be found in the biography of Jacobus Capitien, an African who was born in the early 18th Century in what we now call Ghana, but was then known to Europe as the Gold Coast. A Dutch trader found Capitien, as a little boy, to be very bright. He decided that rather than put Capitien into slavery, he would make him his "boy." The Dutch trader took the young African boy all over Europe. During their travels the trader once got into an argument with another European which led him to boast that Capitien had as much sense as any European—a claim that the other European said was nonsense. In order to prove his claim the Dutch trader said he would put the young African into the University where he would get the equivalent of a Ph.D. and thus prove that he could think just like any White man—and so he did. To complete his European education Capitien wrote a dissertation on the defense of slavery. A detailed description of Capitien's schooling is provided by G. K. Osei:

J. E. J. Capitien was brought from Africa when about seven years old, and purchased by a slave dealer. He studied Latin, Greek, Hebrew, and Chaldic languages. He published at The Hague an elegy in Latin verse, on the death of his instructor. From The

Hague he went to the University of Leyden; on entering which, he published a Latin dissertation on the calling of the Gentiles.[22]

Capitien was so successful and popular that he was sent back to the biggest slave factory in Africa, Cape Coast Castle, where he was made chaplain. Capitien's role was to pacify the slaves and get them resigned to their eventual fate. So distinguished was he in the performance of that role that he was buried in Cape Coast Castle amongst the Europeans who lived in that slave factory. The education of Jacobus Capitien continues to be the model for Black education. That model was pushed into the Western hemisphere including here in the United States.

Mis-education and "Dis-education"
Today, we can identify two patterns of intellectual disruption used among African-Americans. First, there exists a very sophisticated system of mis-education aimed at a small Black elite. This is the same kind of mis-education that Carter G. Woodson, and Edward W. Blyden before him, wrote about. Essentially it is a schooling process through which Black people are taught to think and act in European ways.

The second pattern is actually a process of "dis-education" aimed at the Black masses. The disastrous experiences of Black students in public schools provide ample testimony to both the mis-education of the Black elite and the dis-education of the Black masses. In the midst of the tragedy, the mis-educated elite are unable to propose remedies while the dis-educated masses continue to experience pervasive, persistent, and disproportionate underachievement in comparison with their White counterparts.[23]

The Negro Mis-Education System
It is commonly known that prior to the Civil War enslaved Africans in the southern United States were forbidden to learn to read and write because White people were fearful, and rightfully so, that these skills would facilitate rebellions. However, not all Africans in the United States were deprived of schooling. It was possible for some Black people in the United States to get the kind of education that J. E. J. Capitien had received. Since colonial times, there have been educated Black people in the United States. They were supported by Whites who recognized the necessity and the advisability of educating them in the traditions of Europe. By 1774,

Anthony Benezet, a Philadelphia Quaker, had established what is generally considered to be the first school for African children in the colonial United States.[24] Thus, while there was a (rather unsuccessful) movement against the education of Blacks in the South, a liberal or enlightened interest in the education of Blacks was kept alive in the North. In fact, prior to the Civil war, two colleges for Blacks were established in this country—Lincoln in Pennsylvania and Wilberforce in Ohio.

When the chattel slave system was destroyed by the Civil War, one of the first acts of the victors was to provide for the schooling of Blacks on a wide scale. Northern industrialists, through their philanthropic alter egos, began funding and establishing Black colleges. These colleges were intended to sit atop a Negro education system. By the turn of the century, even southern Whites were making use of this Negro education system to facilitate the transition from the old chattel slavery to a new, but equally effective, system of Black exploitation. This system is generally called segregation, but I choose to describe it as the "neo-slave system" following the thinking of Thomas Carlyle in his essay "The Nigger Question." The new system depended upon the cultivation of a Black elite to serve as examples for the masses of Blacks and to demonstrate the rewards of obedience.

The educated Black elite demonstrated time and time again their ability to do what they had been trained to do. Eventually, a few of them were invited to manage the segregated colleges that were established to train Black teachers. In this manner, a small, educated Negro elite became the overseers of the educational affairs of millions of Black people.

The Lake Mohonk Conferences: Deciding What's Best for the Negro

The Negro education system was carefully planned and implemented. As a case in point consider the Lake Mohonk Conferences on the Negro Question. Some of the leading White educators of this country met at Lake Mohonk, New York (a resort area) on June 4-6, 1890, and June 3-5, 1891, to read papers and discuss what they officially called the "Negro question." By the time the second conference ended they had decided that the primary goals of education for Blacks should be morality and the dignity of labor (i.e., working for White folks).

Rutherford B. Hayes, former president of the United States, was credited with proposing the conference and was elected to chair it in 1890. In his opening address, Hayes expressed optimism that the African could be lifted to "the full stature of American manhood." Moreover, he exhorted the conference participants to take "full encouragement" from the "brighter side" of the Negroes' experience which he described in the following manner:

> A century or two ago the ancestors of the great majority of the present [Negro] population of the United States were African barbarians and pagans of the lowest type. . . . They had no skill in any kind of labor, nor industrious habits, and knew nothing of any printed or written language. This heathen people, brought from the Dark Continent, after several generations in bondage, followed by few years of freedom, have all of them learned to understand and speak the English language. All of them have been taught the first, the essential lesson in civilization: they can all learn their own living by their own labor.[25]

A "platform" intended to influence education policy related to Negroes was adopted at the close of the 1891 conference. Its first 4 planks were:

> 1. The accomplishing of the primary education of the Negro by the States themselves, and the further development of means and methods to this end, till all Negroes are creditably trained in primary schools.
> 2. The largely increased support of schools aided by private benevolence, which shall supply teachers and preachers for the Negro race.
> 3. The grounding of the vast majority of these teachers and preachers in common English studies and in the English Bible, with the further opportunity for any of them to carry on their studies as far as they may desire.
> 4. The great extension of industrial education for both men and women.[26]

The emphasis on industrial education for African-Americans in the 1890s had very little to do with the DuBois and Washington debates. The well-known philosophical argument between W. E. B. Dubois and Booker T. Washington came after the Lake Mohonk Conferences. General Samuel Armstrong, who founded Hampton Institute, was among the leading figures at the Lake Mohonk Conferences. Armstrong recommended Booker T. Washington, his best pupil at Hampton, to be the principal of a new school at Tuskegee in 1881, and developed the educational model that Washington implemented at Tuskegee. DuBois and Washington never addressed the issue of White control over African-American education and indirect White control of the Black population through an educated Negro elite. These fundamental issues had been decided upon by the powerful Whites who participated in the Mohonk Conferences and in other similar discussions of "the Negro question."

Integration and the Dispersal of Black Intellectuals

This educational process for African-Americans was replicated in virtually every state, city, town, and village in the United States. Enlightened educators like Carter G. Woodson, who recognized this exploitative system for what it was, held out little hope for Black men and women educated within it to contribute meaningful leadership for their race. Woodson assessed the leadership potential of the educated Negro elite in the following statement,

> With "mis-educated Negroes" in control . . . it is doubtful that the system would be very much different from what it is or that it would rapidly undergo change. The Negroes thus placed in charge would be the products of the same system and would show no more conception of the task at hand than do the Whites who have educated them and shaped their minds as they would have them function.[27]

The Black elite served as the gatekeepers to social status for the masses of Black people in the United States. Children who were thought to be uneducable, primarily because they posed discipline problems for the teachers, were simply put out of school. Without schooling, Blacks were literally relegated to the cotton patch for the rest of their lives. Hard labor in the fields was the lowest status level; for all intents and purposes it was simply a continuation of the old plantation system that existed during chattel slavery.

The students who satisfied their teachers' expectations and successfully climbed the education ladder received the best jobs available, such as they were for African-Americans. High school graduates could expect no more than to obtain jobs waiting tables or to become maids or chauffeurs for wealthy White families. The select few who went on to college became leaders of the Black community. This system of education remained intact until the early

1950s. By then, there were signs that it had become obsolete. Its fate was sealed in 1954 with the *Brown vs. Topeka Board of Education* decision.

A number of things happened in the United States that created misgivings among powerful White people about the capabilities of the Negro education system to meet their future needs. In fact, the dismantling process had begun by the 1930s. Some of the leading White intellectuals had become concerned about it and had funded research to find out why Black children in segregated schools were rebelling. The American Youth Commission assembled a group of Black social scientists, including E. Franklin Frazier, to study "the proscriptive influences of American society on personality development of Negro youth."[28] These researchers wrote some very remarkable reports on what happened in the segregated education system. They were so well done, in fact, that they put the White establishment on guard that the segregated education was not working. They predicted that a full scale Black rebellion was likely if that system was not changed.

The desegregation process proceeded slowly, of course, but in 1960 events occurred which drastically altered the course of history. On February 1st, four young men walked into a Woolworth's lunch counter in Greensboro, North Carolina and sat at a segregated lunch counter. When the young men announced that they were not going to leave until they were served, they were arrested and jailed. One month later students at practically every Black college in this country organized similar revolts against segregation.

These acts of defiance stirred something in this country that, I think, has been unique in this century at least. A general student rebellion began to take form. White students got involved in the anti-war in Vietnam movement and the country was shaken up for the next ten or twelve years as a result of that Black student revolt. What made the actions of these African-American students historically significant was that these students, by taking things into their own hands, deviated from the pattern of behavior established hitherto by Black intellectuals and other educated Black people. In doing so, they disconnected themselves from the control that Whites had exercised over the direction of African-American protest. A new strategy for cultivating establishment-oriented African-American leadership was needed.

The student revolts quickened the pace of desegregation at predominantly White colleges and universities. Black students were recruited to attend colleges and universities that many of them did not even know existed prior to 1960. The White establishment, while professing to be interested in its moral responsibilities, was also aware of the advantages of keeping Black students dispersed and disempowered as minorities on predominantly White campuses. This became a major social control strategy. Some of the best young Black minds are still being removed from African-American communities in their early teens, if not before, and enrolled in predominantly White schools. These young people are often never able to re-establish themselves in the African-American community, but nonetheless become role models for black excellence and black possibilities. This process amounts to a domestic "brain drain."

The Challenge to Black Intellectuals

Transcending Slave Rebellion Research

In addition to training the Black masses for their caste status, educated Blacks in the United States were also depended upon to provide the White elite with insights into the lifestyles and viewpoints of the Black masses. Whenever rebellions occurred during the period of African enslavement, Whites would establish an inquiry commission to determine what happened and how such a rebellion could be prevented from happening again. More precisely, the slavery advocates were interested in how they could repress the enslaved Africans' will to revolt. This is what I call the "slave-rebellion research" model for Black intellectual development. Such roles for African-American scholars became a tradition in sociological research.

John H. Stanfield explains this use of African-American social scientists as a function of White Anglo-Saxon Protestant male ethnocentrism and of its influence on the progressive movement in the United States:

Many progressives . . . became interested in using survey instruments to collect data on the poor; the information so gathered was then to be used for social control and for the correction of social problems . . . In their questionnaires about social habits and morals, progressives and their researchers explored the degree to which racial minorities and the poor conformed to the cultural values of Anglo-Saxon notions of morality, and used them for such tasks as describing the behavioral differences of the black middle and lower classes.[29]

A number of Blacks were sent to the University of Chicago and other prestigious institutions to learn these high skills in social research. One such person was Dr. Charles S. Johnson who eventually became the president of Fisk University and in many respects was a distinguished scholar. Dr. Johnson was appointed to conduct a study of Chicago's African-American community following the 1919 race riot. What made the 1919 Chicago riot particularly interesting to Whites was the fact that it was not a one way affair in which angry White mobs killed Blacks and burned down the Black community. This was a confrontation in which some of the Blacks fought back, and though some were killed, the fact that some White people were also killed made it imperative that some determinations be made about what was happening in the African-American community.

Educated Black people have not been the producers of their own intellectual or research agendas. In this context, we must take note of the fact that Dr. Johnson's research on the 1919 Chicago rebellion, as brilliant as it may have been, was commissioned to provide information about African-American life that would be useful in taking measures of social control. Our scholars have been trained to approach these tasks using theoretical and cognitive frameworks developed by Whites and reflective of Euro-centric viewpoints. It is important that we do not deceive ourselves in this respect. We have to understand this situation in these terms so that we know what we must confront. Schooling that was always intended to instill loyalty to and prepare us to serve a social order that oppresses us must be rejected and replaced with a liberating education.

Education for Liberation

African-centered education represents a point of departure whereupon African-American intellectuals can declare their intellectual freedom. The ideal that many Blacks, especially those with advanced schooling, have held on to since the end of the civil war is that Blacks must prove that they can take their place in this world on an equal basis with Whites. Thus, their intellectual efforts are continually intended to demonstrate to Whites that they have the ability to make significant contributions to world civilization. This is an ideal that is extremely dangerous for the advancement of our culture.

If we are to save the African race, we Black intellectuals (a term that operationally has included all educated Blacks) must, at the very least, Africanize ourselves. This process is, first, a matter of physically empowering ourselves wherever we can by pushing for

Blacks to take power. However, this simple concept of empowerment can be hazardous if it is all that we do. Therefore, we must
also transform the world.

The processes of Africanization and transformation cannot be
separated neatly into two stages—they overlap. To transform the
world according to an African-centered worldview means establishing a new African culture and a new African world civilization. We
have to restore the African value system. Rather than continually
struggling to make European-centered value systems more humane,
we have to replace those value systems with one that is African-centered. We have been dealing with the alligators, me must now face
the possibility that the solution to our problems may require that the
swamp be drained. Too few of us have prepared ourselves to deal
with this possibility.

The institutional form of our restored African value system will
not be the same as it was in antiquity, but the basic values must be
reclaimed. What we must do ultimately transcends the abolishment
of classism, racism, and sexism. Certainly, those three "isms" have
to be eliminated because they are horrible social contradictions, but
what we have to do goes far beyond this. The processes of transforming, reorganizing, and truly Africanizing the world require that
we also free our thinking from the limitations imposed by other
"isms," such as sciencism and communism, that are so much a part
of Western civilization.

These ideologies all emanate from what I call the "ancient Aryan
project." The ancient Aryan project starts from the fundamental
premise that "man" must redesign nature and transform it. It also
includes the notion that human life is by nature miserable and that
"man" has an obligation to perfect it, to rewrite the plan of creation.
This way of viewing the world has a long history. It is found throughout the folklore of the Greeks, Romans, Teutons, Iranians, and
Hindus. It has been institutionalized so successfully over the last
500 years that it almost seems to be a part of the natural intellectual order.

Some members of the Black intellectual elite seem unable to
conceive of a way of looking at human problems and the human
condition except through the eyes of European-centered science —
a perspective from which the key to solving African problems is to
be found in learning to use science and joining in the transformation of nature. This view of the world is very dangerous. We can see
some of its effects now, in terms of diseases that appear suddenly,

are of unknown origin, and cannot be cured. We live with air that cannot be breathed, water that cannot be drunk. There is something about the structure of this universe that resists the kind of transformation of nature embodied in the ancient Aryan project and, ultimately, dooms that kind of transformation to disaster. However attractive we may find the way Europeans and their descendants have tried to shape the world, it is in our interest to make a thorough study before racing to join them in perpetuating their world order.[30]

The concept of an African-centered worldview must be distinguished from any connotation of ideology. Ideology is largely associated with the rationalization of class interests, but it does not encompass the concept of worldview which includes the way a people conceive of the fundamental questions of existence and organization of the universe. While those who merely parrot European-centered theorists may not be able to see or appreciate the difference, they will, however, if and when they cease to regurgitate and begin studying and thinking independently.

In concluding, I want to point out that I am deeply aware that I may appear to be anachronistic or, perhaps, to express some form of reverse racism when I speak of Africanization, an African value system, and an African reconstruction of the world. My advocacy of these things may sound very much like the advocacy of a system similar to the one that I want to replace. However, let me share a thought that Edward Wilmot Blyden expressed more than a hundred years ago and that conveys my feelings as well:

> It is sad to think that there are some Africans, especially among those who have enjoyed the advantages of foreign training, who are blind enough to the radical facts of humanity as to say, "Let us do away with the sentiment of Race. Let us do away with our African personality and be lost, if possible, in another Race."
> This is as wise or philosophical as to say, let us do away with gravitation, with heat and cold and sunshine and rain. Of course the other Race in which these persons would be absorbed is the dominant Race, before which, in cringing self-surrender and ignoble self-suppression, they lie in prostrate admiration. Some are really in earnest, honestly thinking that by such means they will rise to the cloudless elevation of Olympus or reach the sublime heights of Parnassus, but the verdict of spectators is that they qualify themselves for Bedlam. There is, only then, one fatal influence against all this teaching, and *that is the whole course of nature.*

Preach this doctrine as much as you like, no one will do it, for no one can do it, for when you have done away with your personality, you have done away with yourselves. Your places have been assigned you in the Universe as Africans, and there is no room for you as anything else.[31]

Our intellectuals are caught between the philosophy of liberation and the methodology of oppression. Let us resolve the contradiction and put our own program in place. This is the challenge that confronts the African-centered intellectual.

Notes and References

1. E. F. Frazier, "The Failure of the Negro Intellectual," in *The Death of White Sociology*, ed. J. A. Ladner (New York: Random House, 1973), 58.
2. Frazier, "Failure of the Negro Intellectual," 60.
3. H. Cruse, *The Crisis of the Negro Intellectual: From its Origins to the Present* (New York: William Morrow, 1967).
4. Cruse, *Crisis of the Negro Intellectual*, 6.
5. J. H. Carruthers, "Reflections on the History of the Afrocentric Worldview," *Black Books Bulletin* 13 (1980): 4-7.
6. J. H. Franklin and A. A. Moss Jr., *From Slavery to Freedom*, 6th ed. (New York: Alfred A. Knopf, 1988).
7. E. W. Blyden, "Letter to Governor Hennessey, Freetown, December 11, 1872," in *Black Spokesman: Selected Published Writings of Edward Wilmot Blyden*, ed. H. R. Lynch (London: Frank Cass and Co., 1971), 228-229.
8. C. G. Woodson, *The Mis-Education of the Negro* (1933; reprint, Washington, DC: The Associated Publishers, 1969).
9. Woodson, *The Mis-Education of the Negro*, xxxi.
10. Woodson, *The Mis-Education of the Negro*, xxxii-xxxiii.
11. Woodson, *The Mis-Education of the Negro*, 6.
12. Woodson, *The Mis-Education of the Negro*, 7.
13. J. K. Nyerere, *Freedom and Socialism—Uhuru Na Ujamaa: A Selection from Writings and Speeches, 1965-1967* (London: Oxford University, 1968).
14. Nyerere, *Freedom and Socialism*, 267.
15. Nyerere, *Freedom and Socialism*, 275.
16. J. Kenyatta, *Facing Mount Kenya* (London: Secker and Warburg, 1961).
17. R. O. Faulkner, *A Concise Dictionary of Middle Egyptian* (1962; reprint, Oxford: Printed for the Griffith Institute at the University Press by V. Ridler, 1976).
18. J. H. Carruthers, *Essays in Ancient Egyptian Studies* (Los Angeles:

University of Sankore Press, 1984).

19. B. Davidson, *The African Awakening* (London: Alden Press, 1955).

20. K. Nkrumah, *Challenge of the Congo: A Case Study of Foreign Pressures on an Independent State* (New York: International Publishers, 1967), 3.

21. Nkrumah, *Challenge of the Congo*, 2.

22. G. K. Osei, *The African: His Antecedents, His Genius, and His Destiny* (New Hyde Park, NY: University Books, 1971), 140-141.

23. K. Lomotey, "Introduction," in *Going to School: The African-American Experience*, ed. K. Lomotey (Albany, NY: SUNY Press, 1990).

24. Franklin and Moss, *From Slavery to Freedom*.

25. I. G. Barrows, ed., *Mohonk Conference on the Negro Question* (New York: Negro Universities Press, 1969), 10.

26. Barrows, ed., *Mohonk Conference*, 109.

27. Woodson, *Mis-Education of the Negro*, 23.

28. Franklin and Moss, *From Slavery to Freedom*, 568.

29. J. H. Stanfield, "The Ethnocentric Basis of Social Science Knowledge Production," in *Review of Research in Education*, ed. E. W. Gordon (Washington, DC: American Educational Research Association, 1985), 406.

30. J. H. Carruthers, *Science and Oppression*, 2nd ed. (Chicago, IL: The Kemetic Institute, 1972).

31. E. W. Blyden, "Study and Race," in *Black Spokesman: Selected Published Writings of Edward Wilmot Blyden*, ed. H. R. Lynch (London: Frank Cass and Co., 1971), 200-201.

Chapter Three

African-American Cultural Knowledge and Liberatory Education: Dilemmas, Problems, and Potentials In a Post-Modern American Society*

Beverly M. Gordon
The Ohio State University

The early 1990s have been characterized as being part of the postmodern era. To get a sense of these times, it seems appropriate to try to understand the societal context within which we are currently operating. This is an age of such increasingly overwhelming exposure to media that it allows us to "graze" through an almost limitless number of cable channels and still find nothing to satisfy us. While there appears to be more visibility for and soci-

A version of this chapter was first published in Urban Education 27(4) (1993): 448-470.

etal inclusion of African-Americans, questions about whose interpretive frameworks for analyzing the status and views of African-Americans are legitimate become as problematic as the concepts of tolerance, diversity, inclusion, and heterogeneity within contemporary society.

The theoretical frameworks, paradigms, and perspectives generated by African-Americans have, for the most part, been marginalized within the literary and academic circles of the dominant culture in the United States. Consequently, efforts to disseminate such knowledge have obtained mixed results. Despite such invisibility, African-Americans, other people of color, and those committed to moving toward a democratic society must counter Anglo-hegemony by continuing to employ liberatory and emancipatory pedagogies in schools and other learning institutions and situations. One goal of such pedagogies is to provide other lenses through which to view, perceive, and understand reality and, subsequently, take action to produce social change. In this chapter I provide examples of how perceptions of social relations differ when viewed through the lens of "the other" and of the implications of these differences for educational liberatory efforts.

Much of what I have written over the last several years focuses on the cultural knowledge that African-Americans have produced and the marginalization of that knowledge within the dominant literary and scholarly communities in the United States. It has become very obvious to me that African-Americans have produced and still are producing voluminous amounts of work. From these cultural artifacts of African-American scholars, artists, and authors, emerge at least two recurrent themes: the struggle against Anglo-American hegemony in sciences and policies; and the necessity to articulate, beyond the parameters of Anglo-American hegemony, a social theory endogenous to the African-American community that is both unique to the African experience in America (i.e., USA) and interweaved within the American fiber.

I have identified what I believe to be some common currents of thought that flow through portions of this scholarship. The six foci that emerge are: self-help, self-reliance, service, economic autonomy, political power, and nationalism. The work of African-American scholars and authors within these themes reveals paradigms, values, meanings, and interpretative schemes reflective of the interests of the African-American community. Moreover, it is precisely within the diversity of this work (from scholarly writings, to popular culture as manifested in literary works, film, jazz to rap music, and to theology) that there emerges a body of cultural knowledge.

Postmodernism and the Marginalization of African-American Practices

In order to more fully understand what "postmodernism" is, I have relied on Cornel West's writings for insights into the nature of the concept and for analyses of how it does and does not relate to the African-American community.[1] While there are numerous and varied definitions of what "postmodern"[2] is, the aspects of postmodernism that have some meaning to this author are the so-called "First World" (that is the Euro-Anglo-American) reflections on the decline of European cultural dominance and the rise of the United States as the predominant military, political, and cultural power. It is no small instance, as West points out, that these "First World" reflections on postmodernism are very much European-Anglo-American—very much "parochial and provincial."[3]

The academic and popular components of postmodernism come from a revolt against the domesticated, diluted modernisms of museums, the academy, architectural forms, and literary circles. Within the academy, for example, the postmodern discourse has focused on difference, marginality, and otherness; the relationship between popular culture and resistance; and the push toward inclusion, diversity, and heterogeneity. This discourse, however, is far removed from the realities that confront people of color, the poor, and others dwelling in their daily lives on the fringes of U.S. society. While both the popular and academic postmodern discourses may sound like kinder, gentler national views, West has grave reservations about postmodernism:

> First, because the precursor term 'modern' itself has not simply been used to devalue the cultures of oppressed and exploited peoples, but also has failed to deeply illumine the internal complexities of these cultures. Under the circumstances, there is little reason to hold out hope for the new term 'postmodernism' as applied to the practices of oppressed peoples. Second, the sheer facticity of Black people in the United States historically embodies and enacts the 'postmodern' themes of degraded otherness and subaltern marginality. Black resistances have attacked notions of exclusionary identity, dominating heterogeneity, and universality—or in more blunt language, White supremacy. Yet the historical experiences of Black people in North America, as well as

Latinos, women, workers, gays, and lesbians, always require that one examine the relation of any Eurocentric (patriarchal, homophobic) discourse to Black resistance . . . the point is to engage in a structural institutional analysis to see where the debate is taking place, why at this historical moment, and how this debate enables or disenables oppressed peoples to exercise their opposition to the hierarchies of power.[4]

In sum, the dialectic in both the academy and literary circles has ignored the issue of race, specifically the voices of African-American literary artists, painters, and other Black intellectuals. This has been partly due to the wariness of African-American writers and partly because the Black voice epitomizes "otherness"—it is the voice of the fringe dwellers, not quite believable and/or adequate.

West's depiction is reminiscent of Harold Cruse's lamentation that Black intellectuals during the debates of the 1960s era were "moved by the world" but hardly moved with it.[5] For Cruse, the Black intelligentsia defaulted on their obligation to provide guidance and direction for social participation on all levels—philosophical, social, and political. This lack of participation of Black intellectuals resulted from a variety of difficulties, ranging from not controlling or owning cultural apparata or forums from which to disseminate knowledge (such as book publishers, theaters, halls), to the Black community's naive understanding of its role and task in supporting the intellectuals. These difficulties, coupled with the seeming unwillingness or inability of the Black intelligentsia to enter into the social criticism of the larger society already being waged by the emerging radical intelligentsia of the 1960s (which had its own problems),[6] pointed to the necessity of generating a mode of rationality that would bring together the fragmented pieces.

Just as West argues today, Cruse, too, saw the function of the Black intelligentsia as cultural. It was the Black intellectuals and literary writers who would have to critique the Black experience in America and present counter arguments to dispel misguided and inaccurate perceptions in research (the academy) and in society (popular culture), by placing the Black experience into its appropriate historical, racial, and capitalist contexts within American society. Cruse argued that the weakness of the Black movement was that it lacked the necessary "corps of intellectuals" to lead it. Other Black scholars during that decade echoed Cruse's discontent.[7] The Black intelligentsia were criticized for their lack of involvement in theoretical and intellectual debates. In contemporary times, however, the issue is not that there is a paucity of African-American intellectuals or literary writers or film producers, etc., or that they are not involved; it is that most of their work, policies, interpretative lenses, recommendations, etc., are antithetical to the present societal hierarchy and are either marginalized or condemned.

The Perspective of Otherness:
An Imposed World View

During these times of postmodern discussions, the dialogue and debates in the academies and in literary and artistic (and now architectural) circles are again guided by European thought. In the academy and in the popular view, the debate centers on the relationship between popular culture and resistance and how culture is conceived. This feels for me very much like the debates of the 1960s and 1970s when European critical thought was concerned with high theoretical discourse focusing on such issues as domination, hegemony, and structuralism. Yet, while issues of difference, marginality, and otherness come to the foreground, issues of race and the cultural and academic forms that challenge current structures have simultaneously been placed on the fringe of the discourse. Two examples of the marginalized view of the other or "otherness" come to mind. One is the California textbook adoption controversy. The other is the attack upon Afrocentricity. I will discuss the California case briefly and then focus on the criticisms leveled against Afrocentricity.

The controversy in California was over placing the Houghton Mifflin set of K-8 Social Studies textbooks on the accepted textbook adoption list for the state of California. Complaints by people of color, among other groups, focused on the issue of whose interpretation of "the minority perspective" of the United States and of United States history should be portrayed as the official or most representative perspective. African-Americans[8] protested their lack of inclusion and the way they were depicted, as well as the perspectives attributed to them within the textbooks. To the defense of the publisher, Houghton Mifflin, came an interesting array of advocates from the academy and popular media. Among the notables were: Diane Ravitch, at the time an adjunct Professor of history and education at Teachers College, Columbia University[9]; Arthur Schlesinger, Jr., the Albert Schweitzer Professor of the Humanities at City University of New York[10]; David Nicholson, a writer for the

Washington Post;[11] and John Leo, a writer for *U.S. News & World Report.*[12]

The issue in this controversy is fundamentally one of control—that is, who will control the perspectives and interpretations given to children in American schools? Who will make the decisions about how various groups are depicted in textbooks? For the mass culture, Diane Ravitch is being touted as providing the best analysis on this struggle between mainstream and "other" social studies/historical interpretations.[13] The framework Ravitch employs to interpret and argue against "Afrocentricity" recasts this multicultural-multiracial curriculum issue into a simplistic dichotomy: the *pluralistic* (the true democratic) vs. the *particularistic* (the true racist) perspective. The "Afrocentric" perspective is cast as one that revolves around an ideology of ethnic separatism and is situated within the Black nationalist movement. Ravitch and others argue that such ethnic studies are un-American when they go beyond a critique of the flaws of mainstream social studies and history curriculum and replace them with equally "bad" if not worse history and social studies. The so-called equally "bad" history and social studies curriculum has been generated by "Afrocentric" scholars such as Molefi K. Asante, Asa G. Hilliard III, Cheikh Anta Diop, George G.M. James, Ivan Van Sertima, Ali Mazrui and Chancellor Williams. This history is "bad" because it is built on what are called unsubstantiated claims that Africa is the true cradle of civilization giving the world math, science, philosophy, astronomy, refuting the common sense notions that the sciences and philosophy came from Greek society, etc. Moreover, the Afrocentric scholars argue that studying this ancient history, math, etc., will enhance the desire to learn in African-American students.

Ravitch perceives her pluralistic view as democratic, and dismisses the Afrocentric (particularist) perspective as suspect primarily because what are perceived as vulgar inaccuracies challenge proven historical canons. Clearly, the works of Asante, Diop, Hilliard, James, and others do fly in the face of Eurocentric Anglo-American world history. However, perhaps the more specific issue is that the Afrocentric historical perspective challenges the philosophical, historical, and cultural antecedents of Western civilization and makes problematic the Anglo universalism of human history. Such an attack unveils the extent to which there is uneasiness with knowledge that challenges the dominant canons within the academy and within popular American culture.[14]

The type of critique that Ravitch and others have presented

seems situated within the framework of postmodernist discussions that trivialize the issue of race. The African-American community is viewed in this framework as being misguided by a group of "Afrocentric scholars" into believing that "fewer Black girls will get pregnant and fewer Black boys will drop out of school if they are taught that they are descended from the builders of the pyramids."[15] Such distortions gnarl the intent of teaching African history in U.S. public schools. One of the many assets of studying African history and civilization is that Eurocentric Anglo history is put into perspective. It becomes the record of only one of many vast, rich, and powerful civilizations in the history of the world, one that rose and one that will no doubt inevitably fall to yet another even more powerful civilization in due time. But, there is also something else. In the critic's view, "Afrocentricity" must be defended by its proponents and debated within the academy. To have the academy seen as arbitrator of this debate is to place it within a dominant societal institution, wherein one can expect that attempts will be made to discredit African-American work by using the dominant discourse as the measure of truth and scientific reliability/most accurate and unbiased common canon.

The debate about the nature and role of the African in the history of the world has been of particular interest to Africans and African-Americans alike. It is of no small import that now that African, African-Caribbean, and African-American scholars are bringing to the fore knowledge and information that has been negated or ignored by the dominant Eurocentric anthropological, historical, and sociological communities, the research produced by Black scholars and authors is automatically deemed suspect and must be verified and re-documented by their Anglo-European colleagues in order to be afforded a modicum of acceptability. And, since it was within the academy that bigoted ideologies such as racism and social Darwinism were justified through the use of science and measurement, such a debate is from the outset stacked against those who view the dominant ideology as, at the very least suspect, if not bankrupt and inaccurate.

Fear of the challenge to and possible dismantling of the common canons is not limited to the discipline of education. The political classroom has given rise to other canons, specifically the African-American and feminist perspectives. Consequently, in liberal arts, there are now other challenges to "the common canon." Charles Sykes' book, *The Hollow Men*, argues that the structures for liberal arts in institutions of higher learning are producing "men" who are hollow because they do not adhere to a common canon. The structures within the academy are hollow because the interpretations are not what they used to be and, consequently, European men are emerging with new interpretations. The structure of the academy itself is viewed to be in jeopardy and Anglo males are called upon to reclaim and reinstate the common canons. The corruption of the common canons is argued to have begun with the diversification of the disciplines in the liberal arts. This is when in the 1960s and 1970s African-American and feminist scholars came into their own. Many of these scholars are now entrenched in institutions of higher education. The political base for these radicals is considered to be the classroom wherein, Sykes argues, "we" who are telling lies are protected by tenure. There is also the problem of the minimalist requirements for students. In these radical classes, the required reading lists are perceived to be minimalist because they lack the canons and their interpretations. Moreover, even when the canons are employed, they are discussed as problematic.

Culture, Knowledge, and Liberation from "Otherness"

African-American cultural knowledge—as expressed through the beliefs, values, perspectives, and worldview—can be found in the autochthonous cultural artifacts generated within the African-American existential condition. This existential condition reflects the African-American cultural, social, economic, historical, and political experience. Coupled with the wealth of literature and information on African-American cultural knowledge in the academy—for this work occurs primarily in the field of education—is popular culture which I define in terms of the literary arts, dance, media, theology, athletics, music, cinema, and so forth. Embedded within these artifacts are the six currents of thought I discussed early on: service; self-reliance; nationalism; self-help; economic autonomy; and political power. These currents of thought speak to the desires and aspirations of the community.

During the 1990s African-American intellectual and artistic materials have gained some visibility. The question now is, what is the nature of that visibility? As seen earlier, the visibility has taken the form of refuting African-American scholarship that directly challenges the traditional canons. Acts of liberation and empowerment are manifested when African-Americans *recast* their paradigms, theoretical and methodological frameworks, policies, and procedures as *normative and not otherness*. While "otherness" has been useful in identifying those whose voices are heard in discussions about "others," let us not become sedimentary in our thinking and adopt a pejorative language of otherness. While the term "other" helps to identify the problematic situation, it imposes its own form of cultural hegemony by keeping the discourse within the dominant perspective of deviancy.

Knowledge and scholarship generated by African-Americans are not learned in an effort to curtail the high attrition rates of students who do not complete secondary education and/or get pregnant. Becoming knowledgeable about one's culture is part of the manner in which cultures perpetuate themselves—knowledge about culture and history is passed on to the next generation. The information, facts, values, stories, legends, ideals, mythology, etc., that are passed on inter-generationally, provide students with the worldview/context through which they learn history and cultural and societal identity. The critical issue, however, is the nature of the cultural and historical knowledge included in this process. Such knowledge can assist African-Americans to place themselves and their history in the global history of humankind. Moreover, this knowledge demonstrates definitively that people can engage in action to change societal structures in ways that result in the improvement of their lives. These, I believe, are at least some components of an education that is liberatory.

Students do not learn to read and write; they read and write in order to learn. Liberatory education provides them with the heuristic tools and skills to critique ideas. They learn how to make problematic common sense understandings and to question what is *not* being said as well as what is stated. Liberatory education expands one's horizons and challenges the cultural hegemony of the traditional canon: Therein lies its threat to the status quo. Perhaps this is why persons like Charles J. Sykes[16] and Diane Ravitch are pushing for the recanonization of the "traditional" points of view. Liberatory education goes beyond the reductionist and reverse racist arguments that oversimplify and vulgarize its potential and purpose and, more importantly, limit or marginalize liberatory discourse.[17]

Curriculum development for liberatory education addresses such issues as the infusion of critical consciousness; incremental learning for various ages and levels; the selection of knowledge (e.g., the knowledge of "the others") and pedagogical practices (i.e, how to teach?). Questions about socially interactive classrooms, Socratic style, the employment of higher order questioning techniques (i.e., why and how questions, interpretations, analyzing various viewpoints, etc.) are issues that must be addressed by teachers who are interested in infusing such practice within their classrooms. While this would go beyond the scope of the present discussion, examples of how liberatory education could be constructed will be discussed in the next section.

The role of the African-American scholar/writer is, then, multifaceted. These scholars must provide members of the community with the heuristic skills they need to begin to take social action in their own interests, and close the gap between the academy and the community. The African-American scholar/writer is able to generate and disseminate cultural knowledge in the academy and in the popular culture through a variety of means, including the production of scholarly writings, public discussions, media (newspapers and television broadcasts), literary writings, and films. It is also the responsibility of the scholar/writer to not overlook the involvement of the African-American community in discourse. In turn, the African-American community is ultimately responsible for the infusion of liberatory education efforts within our own community institutions such as churches, organizations, and community centers. The curriculum that is disseminated must provide the students with the heuristic tools they need to critically read and evaluate what is presented to them by the dominant societal institutions, and to make informed decisions that assist in improving their lives and the lives of those within their community.

The Generation of Cultural Knowledge:
A Force for Social Transformation
in the Interests of African People

The employment of paradigms and frameworks for viewing social reality that are generated in African-American intellectual, artistic, and literary work is a political, ideological, and psychological struggle for the hearts and minds of the African-American people. The ideas of Sekou Toure, the Guinean writer, theoretician, and the country's first president, are most helpful in revealing the role of cultural knowledge in the shaping and transformation of the community.[18] Although culture has been used as a weapon of domination, for Toure it has the potential to be a weapon of liberation. While the leaders of the dominant (colonizer) society—"the imperialists," as Toure calls them—use its culture, science, art, technology, and so on to justify and perpetuate their domination, the oppressed can also use cultural values to fight more effectively against ideological domination.

Contemporary scholars have come to similar conclusions. The framework Hazel Carby employs to interpret the contexts and meanings of the works of early African-American female authors offers a valuable perspective for understanding contemporary educational scholarship of African-Americans.[19] Carby argues that language is a shared context through which different groups express their specific interests. Moreover, she adds that the terrain of language is a terrain of power relations. Carby's theorizing about and critical analysis of African-American female novelists operates "within the theoretical premises of societies structured in dominance by class, race, and gender and is a materialist account of the cultural production of Black women intellectuals within the social relations that inscribed them."[20]

When scholarship has a liberatory intent, it seeks to inform and reeducate the community for understanding itself. In doing so it makes the social configurations and assemblages of the dominant culture problematic. The dominated (the colonized) must "reconquer" themselves, and "decolonize" their minds by demystifying the manifestations of the systems that justify their domination and their inferiority complexes. Toure writes:

> One cannot extirpate from the mind of the colonized man the culture which has been imposed upon him and which has poisoned him, except by offering him a substitute culture, namely his own culture, which implies an action to restore to life, re-valorize and popularize that culture.
>
> However, this action is possible only in a larger framework of the struggle for national liberation and social promotion. . . . The cult of authenticity by activating the awareness of popular masses and their mobilization, activates the process of political and social liberation as well as forging the nation through the creation of a melting pot in which the simple citizen is formed without any consideration of tribe or race.
>
> This free man within a free people who has rediscovered his physical and mental balance thence forward assumes the entire responsibility for his own destiny.[21]

Reclaiming one's culture (cultural history and knowledge) is an essential aspect of an authentic being. Like the colonized in Africa, African-Americans have preserved many of their cultural institutions and organizations to varying degrees in spite of the yoke of domination. Collections of writings such as the present one are needed to demonstrate the interconnection between African-American literary, cultural, and intellectual work. They give a coherent *raison d'etre* to support the formation of political, scientific, aesthetic, and philosophical cultural coalitions. The intellectual and cultural communities must set the stage for the debates to follow, unearthing and studying the cultural artifacts and historic traditions that have become obscure. They must analyze this cultural knowledge and situate it in the struggle against domination and the struggle for authentic being.

Autochthonous knowledge and institution building accomplish at least two tasks: First, they help us better understand that institutions come into being as a response to a communal call or need. Second, they unveil new research paradigms, conceptual frameworks, and interpretative schemata that can be employed in curriculum theorizing and development undertaken in our own interests. There is an indication in contemporary African-American scholarship that such frameworks are becoming the foundation for praxis in the Black nationalist movement.[22] The emergence of alternative and endogenous scientific and philosophical paradigms for systematically analyzing African-American culture articulates social theorizing and philosophical reasoning that is grounded in the experiences of African-Americans. Curriculum development in schools and the reform efforts in teacher education are key points at which the infusing of this knowledge can occur. This section of the chapter will provide some examples of knowledge generated by African-Americans in the academy and in popular culture at large. Specifically, these examples are taken from history, psychology, sociology, education, philosophy, literature, and the arts. The limitation of this discussion is that it does not include specific examples of curriculum development. However, it does provide valuable references and resources to assist educators and practitioners to identify the authentic African-American perspective.

In the fields of history and psychology, African-American scholars have problematized the traditional canons. James D. Anderson has written a compelling history about the education of southern Blacks and refutes the idea that Booker T. Washington worked in the interest of Black liberation to the best of his ability in extremely difficult circumstances.[23] African-American psychologists such as James Jones now argue for revisionist approaches in research paradigms and interpretative schemes in the study of culture on the grounds that Western cultural domination (specifically United States culture) negates ethnic and cultural differences.[24] As an answer to this conceptual inadequacy, Jones offers his own analytical paradigm—a cultural quintet of time, rhythm, oral expression, improvisation, and spirituality (TROIS)—as a more precise analytic tool to bring aspects of Black culture into focus. Joseph L. White and Thomas A. Parham's *The Psychology of Blacks: An African-American Perspective* is an example of an alternative lens through which to view the community.[25] Still another example is the work of psychologist A. Wade Boykin who argues that African-American children possess greater "psychological/behavioral 'verve' than do their White counterparts in more placid [White and middle-class] suburban settings."[26]

Cheikh Anta Diop also challenges Western hegemony by arguing that Africa, and not ancient Greece is the origin of civilization.[27] Aime Cesaire[28] and William T. Fontaine[29] both generated conceptual/analytic paradigms through which to view the African experience in America, France, and the West Indies. Cesaire used aesthetics, ethics, religion, philosophy, history, psychology, and science as subjects that constitute culture. Fontaine, on the other hand, conceptualized the Black experience in terms of space, time, community, and culture.

The conceptual frameworks of Boykin, Jones, Cesaire, and Diop have universal African features that could be viewed as categories within a cultural mode of rationality that is essentially African. This "cultural capital" represents the source of the fibers that form the African-American essence. I believe that such cultural knowledge will illuminate a shared cultural context among Africans throughout the world. It has implications for African liberation pedagogy. To one who has read Ivan Van Sertima's *They Came before Columbus*[30], such a cultural unity appears quite reasonable, particularly in light of John Mbiti's[31] discussion of philosophy, ethics, religion, history (especially oral history), science, psychology, and human nature as components of African philosophy.

In the field of sociology, Joyce Ladner, in her edited volume, *The Death of White Sociology*, moved beyond the accepted sociological paradigms of social science.[32] In this anthology, she and many others reconceptualized scientific paradigms, frames of reference, and assumptions. The overall goal of the volume was for African-American sociologists to critique the dominant sociological tenets of the field, illuminate the myth of value-free research, call attention to the political and ideological interests in the field, and address "a conciliation between culture (theory) and politics (practice), or as Nathan Hare has described it, the 'uniting of the Black academy and the street.'"[33]

I, too, have grappled with how and why the notions of African-American epistemology have become marginalized while Euro-American intellectual and social theories are taken as the primary and sometimes exclusive examples of social science development. A very salient example of this is, of course, the relatively well-known history of social theory associated with the Frankfurt school. In contrast, the history of DuBois' work and the resulting series produced at Atlanta University almost two decades before the emergence of the Frankfurt school are virtually unknown or studied in the academy.[34]

Another example of alternate paradigms can be found in the contemporary work of African-American educators. A selection of papers given in a 1990 American Educational Research Association symposium on African-American teachers' wisdom and pedagogical practice, for which I served as a discussant, serve for me as exemplars to clarify my concept of African-American epistemology.[35] The reported research represented knowledge generated from the perspectives of African-American teachers to give the African-American experiences in the United States and Canada meaning and a social and political context even though situated within societies "'structured in dominance' by class, race, and gender." The works of Michelle Foster,[36] Annette Henry,[37] Etta Ruth Hollins,[38] and Gloria Ladson-Billings,[39] presented at the symposium provided me with alternative examples to the works of Ira Shor, Sylvia Ashton Warner, and Chris Searle.[40] In the truest sense, as Ladson-Billings pointed out, the talk of Black teachers is the "missing voice" in teacher education programs.[41] The work of Foster, Henry, Hollins, and Ladson-Billings as well as the work of Joyce King[42] are indicative of the current autochthonous knowledge that is being generated about and within African-American intellectual circles. While these particular works are specific to education, they represent intellectual, literary, and artistic knowledge generated across the disciplines. These works have great potential to inform future education of African-Americans, and, indeed, all of us.

In the field of philosophy, we see that African-American scholars have called for a revised critical theory of society. In response to what they see as the bankruptcy of dominant social science paradigms, they pursue models of meaning generated from the "life-world" and in the interest of their constituency. Again, the role of epistemology is crucial: they see cultural knowledge, which is generated from human activity, as forming the bases for assumptions, paradigms, models, and social theory for African-Americans that would allow for self-reflection and self-understanding, initial steps toward emancipation from domination. Furthering the notion of the emancipatory relationship between knowledge and human activity, Lucius Outlaw believes that in order to serve the emancipatory efforts of African-Americans, as well as to be a guiding influence in the struggle of all oppressed groups against cultural imperialism, domination, and ideological hegemony, it is necessary to place "praxis in the concrete needs and inspirations of African-Americans."[43] For Outlaw, the modes of rationality that hold the most promise for emancipation will be found in the life-world of African-Americans.

> . . . in the mediated folk tales; in religious practices; in political language and practices prevalent during various times and under various conditions. . . . Reclaiming [these forms of life praxes] through acts of reflection will provide understandings of the historically conditioned concerns of Black people. Such acts of reclamation are fundamental, for the orientation of present and future philosophical and practical activities in the interest of African-American people.[44]

Cultural artifacts that have implications for the education of African-American people continually emerge. Some of these that might be useful to the educational community may not focus specifically on educational issues but more broadly on understanding the culture of the African-American community beyond college course textbooks. Examples include biographical works such as those of Sara Lawrence Lightfoot[45] and James Comer.[46] We can also point to international perspectives and issues, addressed in documentaries such as the 1986 PBS documentary series, *The Africans*, written and directed by Ali Mazrui.[47] In the 1970s, 1980s, and 1990s, the works of writers such as Toni Morrison (*Beloved; Sula*); Gloria Naylor (*The Women of Brewster Place; Linden Hills*); Alice Walker (*In Search of our Mothers' Gardens; The Color Purple*); Ishmael Reed

(*Mumbo Jumbo; The Last Days of Louisiana Red; The Free-lance Pallbearers*); and of film directors such as Spike Lee (*Do the Right Thing; Malcolm X; School Daze*) or Euzhan Palcy (*Sugar Cane Alley; A Dry White Season*), take us on forays that illuminate various dimensions of and the complexities in the culture of the African communities in the United States, the Caribbean, and Africa. Moreover, these works respond to our condition of situated dominance by emotional cultural hegemony.

Conclusion: Implications for Teacher Education

As we conclude, let us return briefly to Cornel West's work on the impact of African-American culture on the American way of life and the dilemma of the African-American intellectual in the post-modern era.[48] West has identified organic intellectual traditions in African-American life, a Black Christian tradition of preaching, and a Black tradition of performance. He urges collective intellectual work and critique and the creation of institutions to provide the infrastructure for strengthening African-American scholarship and promoting discourse and "high quality critical habits." To develop these critical habits, West urges African-American scholars to embrace the Foucauldian model, which

> encourages an intense and incessant interrogation of power-laden discourses in the service of . . . revolt. And the kind of revolt enacted by intellectuals consists of *disrupting and dismantling of prevailing "regimes of truth"*—including their repressive effect—of present day societies. This model suits the critical, skeptical, and historical concerns of progressive Black intellectuals. . . . The problem is the struggle over the very status of truth and the vast institutional mechanisms which account for this status. . . . The new key terms become those of "regime of truth," "power/knowledge," and "discursive practices."[49] (emphasis mine)

He calls for a reconceptualization of the "specificity and complexity of Afro-American oppression" throughout educational and social theorizing in general and among African-American scholars in particular. What is needed, West believes, is

> the creation or reactivation of institutional networks that promote high quality critical habits primarily for the purpose of Black insurgency. . . . The central task of postmodern Black intellectuals is to stimulate, hasten, and enable alternative perceptions and prac-

tices by dislodging prevailing discourses and powers.[50]

West argues that the role of African-Americans in the academy and in literary and cultural circles is the production of culture—to be the producers of postmodern products that are relevant to African-American life. He defines African-American culture in terms of "kinetic orality, passionate physicality, and combative spirituality." Moreover, West asserts that African-American cultural products and practices can be identified in music forms and style (such as African-American popular music which has had a profound influence on American culture and music) through such contexts as sermonic discourse (particularly that of charismatic leaders such as Malcolm X, Martin Luther King, and Jesse Jackson); and athletics (including sports, dance, etc.) which, again, have had a profound effect on mass culture in American society. These African-American cultural practices are in response to and in resistance of White supremacist practices.

The knowledge generated, and products offered, by African-American scholars have far-reaching implications for teacher education; however, the current marginal usage of only a few categories of thought may prove stifling and debilitating. Black people have created a body of knowledge, cultural knowledge (cultural meaning across the disciplines in science, social theory, art, philosophy, etc.). The marginalizing of its substance—theoretical constructs, paradigms, and models of viewing and seeing the world—in the dominant body of knowledge is troublesome. Perhaps such terms as *inclusion, multiculturalism*, and *pluralism* are used and defended in the United States because such language assists the dominant power in maintaining its structures. When we speak of a multicultural, pluralistic, and/or inclusive system, part of the rationale is that everyone must fit in. However, in this instance the United States is neither pluralistic nor multicultural but a White-male-dominated system, coupled with the particularity/specificity of racism. Anglos have defined themselves as White in relation to African-Americans. While multicultural and cross-cultural categorizations have been useful as ways of identifying certain types or genres of work, it is problematic whether or not they can encompass the specific needs and purposes of Black insurgency for African-American and other African scholars around the world. Categories such as "critical, emancipatory, or liberatory pedagogy" may be better suited as descriptors because they not only expand narrow frames of reference, but also make it possible for us to move our thinking from a pejorative frame to one of self-reflection, critique, and social action.

At the present time, it is probably more helpful to focus our attention on separating content from pedagogy than to talk about a unique learning style for Black children. For example, the "verve" learning style scholarship of the early 1980s suggested that highly active children were not necessarily deviant, but that this was a display of high energy levels. Thus, it was argued that these children required a pedagogical style which matched their cognitive and learning styles. The discussion of the possible vervistic learning style of African-Americans was transformed into very interesting political issues. These issues had to be addressed so that in the discussion of learning styles it would not be misconstrued to mean that African-American children could only be effectively educated using a particular learning style or used to divert attention away from the very clear position that the African-American community wants good quality education for their children. While neither time nor space allows for elaboration here, the larger discussion of reconstructed alternative interpretative paradigms and the reaction to such perspectives within the dominant education structure merits critical examination.[51]

Our research agenda must open up fields of inquiry and identify territory to be explored and data to be collected. African-American psychologists have data on a holistic view of Black culture. So far, however, there are few ethnographic studies on African-American or Caribbean culture that are similar to Annette Henry's work that indicates how teachers (and/or parents) incorporate this view in their lives and pass it on to their children.[52] John Ogbu emphasized the homogeneous culture of the African-American community in the 1960s.[53] Where are the studies about what is happening within heterogeneous African-American communities of the 1980s and 1990s where we find such contrasts as those that exist between life in middle-class suburbs and inner-city tenements; the social status of officials and professionals compared to those of the working class and under-classes and gang and drug cultures? The charge of African-American scholars is to put such issues into the mainstream research arena.

We must also study the attitudes and techniques of teachers, African-American and Anglo, who are effective with African-American children. By introducing their practices in school situations we can study and document content, process, and school interaction. Again, the call is for applied research. If there is such a thing as culturally compatible pedagogy, we must attempt to identify and apply it to see whether it can be widely transfused into public schools and teacher preparation. Additional research focusing on, for example, what "regimes of truth" means for education (particularly school knowledge—its creation, production, and dissemination) and/or on challenges to disrupt and dismantle such regimes could prove a provocative litmus test for mainstream educational theory and practice from school classrooms to college campuses.

Dialogue that does not marginalize African-centered intellectual discourse allows for scholarly engagement. This could result in the production of school knowledge that promotes social participation for change. Such dialogue between those African-Americans in the academy and in popular culture and their Anglo counterparts—which goes beyond "otherness" to acknowledge the validity of the Black perspective and unpack the issues of White supremacy and the unwillingness/fear/mean-spiritedness of many members of the Anglo-European culture to face the inevitable reality of having to share the resources and power with the true majority of the world's population—is long overdue.

Notes and References

1. This discussion is based on Cornel West, "Black Culture and Postmodernism," in *Remaking History*, eds. Barbara Kruger and Phil Mariani (Seattle: Bay Press, 1989), 87-96; and Cornel West, "Postmodernism and Black America," *Zeta Magazine* 1 (1988): 27-29.
2. Todd Giltin, "Postmodernism Defined, at last!" *Utne Reader* (July/August 1989): 52-61.
3. West, "Black Culture," 88.
4. West, "Black Culture," 91.
5. Harold Cruse, *Crisis of the Negro Intellectual* (New York: William Morrow and Co., Inc., 1967).
6. Herbert Marcuse, "Failure of the New Left," *New German Critique* 18 (Fall 1979): 33-11.
7. James Turner and W. Eric Perkins, "Towards a Critique of Social Science," *The Black Scholarly Journal of Black Studies and Research* 7 (April 1976).
8. Robert Reinhold, "Class Struggle," *The New York Times Magazine* (September 29, 1991): 26-29, 46-47, 52. While there were other People of Color, such as Asian-Americans, as well as those who represented viewpoints such as women's issues, alternative lifestyles etc., all of whom objected to this series for a variety of reasons, this discussion will be primarily concerned with the concerns of African-Americans.
9. Diane Ravitch, "Multiculturalism E Pluribus Plures," *The American*

Scholar 59 (1990): 337-354.

10. Arthur Schlesinger, "When Ethnic Studies are Un-American," *Social Studies Review* 5 (1990): 11-13.

11. David Nicholson, "D.C.'s 'African-Centered' Curriculum. What Will the New Program Really Teach? 'Afrocentrism' and the Tribalization of America—The Misguided Logic of Ethnic Education Schemes," *The Washington Post* (Sunday, September 23, 1990): B1, B4.

12. John Leo, "A Fringe History of the World," *U.S. News & World Report* (November 12, 1990): 25-26.

13. Leo, "Fringe History."

14. The author anticipates discussing the issue of the politics of textbook adoption and the minority image therein at greater length in an upcoming manuscript.

15. Nicholson, "D.C.'s African-Centered Curriculum."

16. Charles Sykes, *The Hollow Men: Politics and Corruption in Higher Education* (Bluff, IL: Regnery Gateway, 1990).

17. David Nicholson, "'Afrocentrism' and the Tribalization of America. The Misguided Logic of Ethnic Education Schemes," *Washington Post* (September 23, 1990): B1, B4. Nicholson asserted that parents, educators, and others within the African-American community who called for the adoption of an Afrocentric curriculum were operating "on the naive assumption that fewer Black girls will get pregnant and fewer Black boys will drop out of school if they are taught that they are descended from the builders of the pyramids."

18. Sekou Toure, "A Dialectical Approach to Culture," *The Black Scholar* 1 (1969): 11-26.

19. Hazel V. Carby, *Reconstructing Womanhood—The Emergence of the Afro-American Woman Novelist* (New York and Oxford: Oxford University Press, 1987).

20. Carby, *Reconstructing Womanhood*, 17.

21. Toure, "Dialectical Approach," 19.

22. Manning Marable, "The Third Reconstruction: Black Nationalism and Race in a Revolutionary America," *Social Text - No. 4* 2 (1981): 3-27.

23. James D. Anderson, *The Education of Blacks in the South, 1860-1935* (Chapel Hill and London: University of North Carolina Press, 1988).

24. James M. Jones, "Conceptual and Strategic Issues in the Relationship of Black Psychology to American Social Science," in *Research Directions of Black Psychologists*, eds. A. Wade Boykin, A. J. Franklin, and J. F. Yates (New York: Russell Sage Foundation, 1979).

25. Joseph L. White and Thomas A. Parham, *The Psychology of Blacks—An African-American Perspective* (Englewood Cliffs: Prentice Hall, 1990).

26. A. Wade Boykin, "Psychological/Behavioral Verve: Some Theoretical Explorations and Empirical Manifestations," in *Research Directions of*

Black Psychologists, eds. A. Wade Boykin, A. J. Franklin, and J. F. Yates (New York: Russell Sage Foundation, 1979).

27. Cheikh Anta Diop, *Black Africa—The Economic and Cultural Basis for a Federated State*, trans. Harold J. Salemson (1978; expanded edition, Chicago: Lawrence Hill books, 1987). See also, C. A. Diop, *The African Origin of Civilization—Myth or Reality*, ed. and trans. Mercer Cook (Westport: Lawrence Hill & Co., 1974).

28. Aime Cesaire, *Discourse on Colonialism*, trans. Joan Pinkham (New York: Monthly Review Press, 1972).

29. William T. Fontaine, "Social Determination in the Writings of Negro Scholars," in *Philosophy Born of Struggle—Anthology of Afro-American Philosophy from 1917*, ed. L. Harris (Dubuque: Kendall Hunt, 1983). See also, W. T. Fontaine, "An Interpretation of Contemporary Negro Thought from the Standpoint of the Sociology of Knowledge," *Journal of Negro History* 25 (1940): 6-13.

30. I. Van Sertima, *They Came before Columbus—The African Presence in Ancient America* (New York: Random House, 1976).

31. John S. Mbiti, *African Religions and Philosophy* (Garden City: Anchor Doubleday, 1970).

32. Joyce Ladner, ed., *The Death of White Sociology* (New York: Vantage Books, 1973).

33. Ladner, *Death of White Sociology*, xxvii.

34. Beverly M. Gordon, "Toward Emancipation in Citizenship Education: The Case of African-American Cultural Knowledge," *Theory and Research in Social Education* 12 (1985): 90-108.

35. *Capturing the Black Teacher's Voice: A Research Symposium on African-American Wisdom and Pedagogical Practice* (AERA, Boston, 1990). Presentations/Participants: Etta Ruth Hollins, CSU, Haywood, "A Reexamination of What Works for Inner City Black Children"; Gloria Ladson-Billings, Santa Clara University, "Making a Little Magic: Teacher's Talk About Successful Teaching Strategies for Black children"; Michelle Foster, UNC, Chapel Hill, "Black Teachers and the Politics of Race"; Annette Henry, OISE, "Black Women/Black Pedagogies: An African-Canadian Context."

36. Foster, "Black Teachers."

37. Henry, "Black Women/Black Pedagogies."

38. Hollins, "Reexamination."

39. Ladson-Billings, "Making a Little Magic."

40. Beverly M. Gordon, "Critical and Emancipatory Pedagogy: An Annotated Bibliography of Sources for Teachers," *Social Education* 49 (1985): 400-402.

41. Ladson-Billings, "Making a Little Magic."

42. Joyce E. King, "Diaspora Literacy and Consciousness in the Struggle Against Miseducation in the Black Community," *Journal of Negro Education* 61 (1962) : 317-340

43. Lucius Outlaw, "Philosophy, Hermeneutics, Social-Political Theory: Critical Thought in the Interests of African-Americans," in *Philosophy Born of Struggle—Anthology of Afro-American Philosophy from 1917*, ed. L. Harris (Dubuque: Kendall Hunt, 1983).
44. Outlaw, "Philosophy," 66.
45. Sarah Lawrence Lightfoot, *Balm in Gilead—Journey of a Healer* (Reading, MA: Addison-Wesley Pub. Co., Inc., 1988).
46. James P. Comer, *Maggie's American Dream—The Life and Times of a Black Family* (New York: New American Library, Division of Penguin Books, USA Inc., 1988).
47. For a discussion on this series, please see: B. Gordon, "The Marginalized Discourse of Minority Intellectual Thought in Traditional Writings on Teaching," in *Research Directions in Multicultural Education*, ed. Carl Grant (London and Philadelphia: Farmer Press, 1991).
48. C. West, "The Dilemma of the Black Intellectual," *Cultural Critique* 1 (1985): 109-124.
49. West, "Dilemma," 121.
50. West, "Dilemma," 122.
51. Boykin, "Psychological/Behavioral Verve"; B. M. Gordon, "Towards a Theory of Knowledge Acquisition for Black Children," *Journal of Education* 164 (1982): 90-108; Janice E. Hale-Benson, *Black Children: Their Roots, Culture and Learning Styles*, rev. ed. (Baltimore and London: John Hopkins Press, 1986); Asa G, Hilliard, "Teacher and Cultural Styles in a Pluralistic Society," *Rethinking Schools*, 4 (1989): 3; Joseph L. White and Thomas A. Parham, *The Psychology of Blacks—An African-American Perspective* (Englewood Cliffs: Prentice Hall, 1990).
52. Henry, "Black Women/Black Pedagogies."
53. John Ogbu, *The Next Generation* (New York: Academic Press, 1974).

Part Two

African-American Education Initiatives: Historical Resistance to Schooling

Introduction to Part Two

In his introduction to a recently republished edition of Carter G. Woodson's *The Education of the Negro Prior to 1861*, John Henrik Clarke wrote the following about the educational experiences of African people from 1619 to 1861 in the former British North American colonies and later in the United States:

> It must be understood that during this critical period in the life of African Americans they believed that any education was better than no education at all. Of course, a lot of what they thought was education was training and miseducation.[1]

Clarke's analysis that everything that is called education is not, is consistent with the theme articulated throughout this volume. Self-determination for African people requires that education and schooling must be critically distinguished from one another. One is hard pressed to find any schooling (or training and miseducation) provided for Africans by any European American elites that has not been carried out in accordance with White self-interests.

Woodson divides ante-bellum schooling into two periods. The first period began in 1619 with the introduction of African enslavement in the colonies and ended about 1835 at the peak of the African insurrection movement. This was followed by a second period marked by industrialization in the North and servile insurrections in the South that were organized by literate, enslaved Africans with the encouragement of African and European-American abolitionists. During the first period, White self-interests were served by the prevailing notion that enslaved Africans who had a modicum of training in western civilization and understood their masters' language were more valuable than those who did not. Of course this all changed when it became apparent that literate Africans were a threat to White self-interests because they used their skills in the interests of their own liberation. Woodson noted that by the mid-1830s "most southern white people reached the conclusion that it was impossible to cultivate the minds of Negroes without arousing overmuch self-assertion." [2]

James D. Anderson provides a forthright analysis of the post-Civil War era in his classic work *The Education of Blacks in the South, 1860-1935.*[3] What Anderson makes clear is that following the Civil War the European American elites unified, despite differences over strategy, to exploit the formerly enslaved Africans.

During discussions in my graduate seminars on African American education I find that misunderstandings about the role of White self-interests in shaping the type of schooling made available to Africans are common. Anderson's work shatters typical portrayals of this period. He presents carefully documented examples of the ways in which European American elites, from both the North and the South, systematically undermined African efforts to develop their own educational institutions.[4]

The authors of the three chapters that form Part Two use historical research to examine educational initiatives by Africans in the United States. Chapter Four, "Outthinking and Outflanking the Owners of the World: An Historiography of the African-American Struggle for Education," by Ronald E. Butchart critiques historical research on African-American education. Dr. Butchart focuses squarely on the political purposes articulated for African-American schooling by European-American elites. He argues that a need exists for historians to employ analytic methods that explain not only what African-American education should have been and should be, but that also have the capability to explain why it was not and is not.

In Chapter Five, "The Search for Access and Content in the Education of African-Americans," Joan Davis Ratteray focuses on initiatives by Africans in the United States dating back to the early 1790s to establish and maintain their own schools. Dr. Ratteray discusses the history of struggles within independent African American schools to develop curriculum content to meet the needs of African Americans. Her work builds a context for better understanding contemporary African American independent educational institutions.

Finally, in Chapter Six, "Historic Readers for African-American Children (1868-1944): Uncovering and Reclaiming a Tradition of Opposition," Violet J. Harris discusses her research on African American children's books. Between 1868 and 1944 African-Americans created a variety of literacy materials especially for African-American children. These materials presented values and goals including the characterization of education as a form of liberation. Dr. Harris argues that the creators of these materials represent "an unknown historical vanguard in literacy education."

These chapters inform us about traditional sensitivities to the distinctions between schooling and education among African people in the United States. Reading them leaves little to doubt about the strategic importance the European American elite places on controlling the thinking of African people through schooling. Resistance to this encroachment by White self-interest is shown here to have taken many forms. Let us learn from the recounting of these experiences.

1. J. H. Clarke, "Introduction," in *The Education of the Negro* (Brooklyn, NY: A&B Books Publishers, 1992)
2. C. G. Woodson, *The Education of the Negro Prior to 1861: A History of the Education of the Colored People of the United States from the Beginning of Slavery to the Civil War* (Washington, DC: Associated Publishers, 1919), 2-3.
3. J. D. Anderson, *The Education of Blacks in the South, 1860-1935.* (Chapel Hill, NC: University of North Carolina, 1988), 279-282.
4. For example, John W. Davison, founder and principal of Fort Valley (Georgia) High and Industrial School, was forced to seek financial assistance from wealthy White people in the North in 1896. In 1903, Davison's resignation as head of the school he founded was demanded by a board of directors now under the control of White "philanthropists." Davison was forced out because he resisted pressure from his White "benefactors" to adopt the Hampton-Tuskegee (industrial education) model at Fort Valley.

Chapter Four

Outthinking and Outflanking the Owners of the World: An Historiography of the African-American Struggle for Education[*]

Ronald E. Butchart
University of Washington at Tacoma

Introduction

W. E. B. DuBois once argued that the proper education for oppressed groups such as African-Americans had a special, critical purpose. He knew that education was always and everywhere political. For the oppressed, the political role of education had to be aimed precisely at finding the means to end the oppression. In 1930, speaking before the graduating students at Howard University, he put the issue this way:

Let there be no misunderstanding about this, no easy going opti-

* A version of this chapter was first published in History of Education
  Quarterly 28 (1988): 333-366.

mism. We are not going to share modern civilization just by deserving recognition. We are going to force ourselves in by organized far-seeing effort—by outthinking and outflanking the owners of the world today who are too drunk with their own arrogance and power successfully to oppose us, if we think and learn and do.[1]

It is clear from his own life's work that to "think and learn and do"—the "outthinking and outflanking"—required education.

If history is to have value beyond a literary form of collecting antiques, it must provide a guide to action. For those struggling against oppression and for justice, history must assess the past to suggest political, social, and economic strategies for the present and future. Like education, history is inescapably political. Our purpose here is to assess the historiography of African-American education in terms of its assessment of the Black struggle for learning, and its ability to contribute to action for the emancipation of African-Americans. We shall do so by examining the historiography in distinct periods, assessing the topical and thematic content, and the dominant interpretive stances of each period.

Themes in the Historiography of African-American Education

For nearly a century, historians have traced the relationships between education and the struggles of the African-American community. The resulting historiography breaks rather naturally into three distinct eras, each with its own subject matter, themes, and interpretations. The first era dates from before the turn of the twentieth century into the depression. Two tendencies dominated the period: a triumphalist history arising from the Dunningite tradition and a corrective and vindicationist history written as a defense against the fabrications of the former. That era was replaced by a second period that lasted from the early 1930s into the late 1960s, with echoes that reverberated into the 1980s. Embracing neither the White supremacist pretensions of the triumphalist historians, nor the defensive posture of the vindicationists, writers in the second era spoke from liberal progressivist assumptions. Finally, emerging from the political crisis of liberal progressivism, a third era has blossomed in the last two decades. Marked by iconoclastic revisionism, this period has produced the broadest range of studies, the least unity of interpretation, but perhaps the greatest commitment to a liberatory political agenda.[2]

Exculpation and Accommodation: The 1890s-1940s

The earliest scholarly writing on African-American education's history dates from the 1890s. It ushered in a tradition that extended well into the depression decade. During that time two mutually exclusive traditions vied for attention. Black historians dominated one tradition, writing corrective histories; White Southern historians dominated the other, producing White supremacist accounts. The Black scholars' interests were eclectic. Antebellum schooling for enslaved and free Blacks received classic treatment in Carter G. Woodson's *The Education of the Negro Prior to 1861*. Others supplemented his work on religious education under slavery. Higher education and other specialized forms of post-secondary education, along with studies of more informal educational forces and institutions such as newspapers, magazines, and literary societies, also appeared as important foci of early writing on Black education's history. Not surprisingly, perhaps, the South was the almost exclusive focus for these early writers. Indeed, virtually the sole sources of historical information on Black education in the North to emerge in this period were portions of *The Negro Common School* edited by DuBois, and Woodson's *The Education of the Negro Prior to 1861*.[3]

In this early period, postbellum southern Black education received greater emphasis than the antebellum or northern efforts. Perhaps because of their drama, their heroism, and their promise, the early years of the postbellum period, the era of freedmen's education, received special attention. W. E. B. DuBois, writing some of the first and finest African-American education history, set the terms for the subsequent debates on post-emancipation education. Northern aid and "the crusade of the New England schoolma'am" was far-sighted and noble, he argued. Southern opposition was rooted in fear of the educated Negro. Free, public southern education was the legacy of freedmen's education. If apologists for southern racism choked on those assertions, they simply fell silent in the face of his most fundamental premise: "The whole nation was responsible for slavery . . . it was . . . the undoubted duty of the whole nation to reimburse the slave in some slight degree for years of stolen toil. The smallest return thinkable was free elementary education to black children." His contemporaries also wrote on the schooling of the freedmen, but none matched his power or his poetry.[4]

Studies of postbellum elementary schooling frequently used the state as their unit of analysis. They concentrated on the legislation concerning schools and on the response of the Black community to educational opportunity, often emphasizing Black initiative. Only seaboard and border states received early scrutiny from Black historians. Few writers were willing to attempt analyses of the region as a whole.[5]

That subject matter served to highlight a narrow range of historical themes. Instructively, the predominant themes of the following two historiographic periods—segregation and integration—were of little interest to this first generation of historians.[6] Remarkably, too, industrial education figured only peripherally in their analyses. Industrial education as a practice in Black schooling was over a half century old by the time this earliest historiographic tradition had played itself out. Some of the era's historians had been outspoken critics of industrial education and of Booker T. Washington, its chief promoter. Others were surely supporters. Yet if, like DuBois, they wrote about industrial education, they wrote as critics and essayists, not as historians.[7] They did not document frequently or insistently either the erosion of Black education that had been underway since at least the late 1880s, although Thomas Jesse Jones called their attention to the trend in 1917, and DuBois was speaking of the issue in 1901. That theme was deferred for the next generation of historians.[8]

The themes which did predominate were those concerned with the images of Black America—the image projected to White America and the image reflected back into the Black community. On the one hand, there was the theme of Black education as moral uplift, the "civilizing" of a people. Because of education, Richard R. Wright asserted in his *Historical Sketch of Negro Education in Georgia,*

No people in the world has made greater ADVANCEMENT IN MORAL AND CHRISTIAN character. The schools have given them eyes to see themselves as other people saw them, and year after year vice and ignorance have become more odious.

Anticipating the thrust of the Atlanta Compromise address by a full year, Wright used his history of Black education in Georgia to assure the White South that racial peace was guaranteed by the schoolhouse. Through the good offices of Black educators, Georgia's

Negroes were

> becoming more sensitive with regard to discourtesies and insults.
> . . . It must be evident to all that the solution to the so-called Negro
> or Southern problem finds its key in what has already been done
> for all parties by the state and benevolent societies in the way of
> education in the past 20 years.

For historians in this stream, White prerogatives dictated the subject matter and the theme. Documenting moral progress defined the agenda. Their interpretation was thoroughly accommodationist.[9]

On the other hand, many more early Black historians took as their theme Black autonomy and self-help. Documenting civic and community progress defined their agenda. While that agenda had its roots in Western White value structures, it did not necessarily imply White prerogatives. It could be, and often was, used to legitimate the Black community to Whites. Yet it could also, without paradox, be used as a source of race pride, as "indications of the activity of self-educative influences in Negro life," in the words of Dorothy B. Porter. These historians wrote at length of the range of efforts by southern Blacks to appropriate Western culture and to grasp intellectual and aesthetic opportunities. From the struggles of impoverished communities to build rustic schoolhouses to the triumphs of Black college graduates; from the difficulties of obtaining a Black teacher to the satisfactions of training scholarly Black ministers; from clandestine schools for slaves to state systems of free public Black education; from Black literary societies to Black magazines—"These agencies at work among the Negroes enabled them to show what they could do toward their own uplift. They did well."[10]

This group of education historians held a narrow range of interpretive positions. DuBois, already moving toward a rigorous materialist interpretation by the first decade of the century, had the most fully articulated interpretation. He took justice to Black and working people as the central imperative, studied industrial and economic relations for their impact on institutions and on class formation and race relations, and spoke out forthrightly about his conclusions. Until long after this first period of Black educational historiography, he held strongly to the faith that education was the key to race and class problems. "Racial antagonism can only be stopped by intelligence," he wrote, though the logic of his argument seemed to indicate that economic development, not ignorance, lay at the heart of the race and class problem.[12]

Other Black writers of the period followed DuBois in writing corrective history, but stopped well short of his interpretive stance. In Woodson, one finds glimmers of a DuBoisian fury for justice, but for most of the other writers the issue of justice was muted. The majority of them sought through their writing to vindicate or exculpate the race, to portray a people who, despite oppression, poverty, and exclusion, were progressing heroically. Their work answered the canard of racists, documenting the community's educability and respectability. Because Blacks were human beings with aspirations not unlike those of Whites, their logic implied, Whites should welcome Black efforts and grant the race educational opportunities equal to those of Whites. One writer assured White readers that graduates of the college about which he wrote "are concerned about the same values with which other Americans are concerned."[13]

Their vindicationist stance left them without the clear analysis of the sources of oppression that DuBois brought to his work. Racism, their work implied, was the result of mistaken impressions. Correct those impressions, show the dominant race the worthiness of the Black race, and then Whites would provide opportunities. Given that position, few were willing to be critical of White actions toward Black education. They were even reticent to point out the contemporary deterioration in Black education. They did not seek to confront White America with its criminality, but to appeal to its higher nature. Luther P. Jackson's observation that the religious training of enslaved Africans a century earlier was paradoxical, "at one and the same time an expression of Christian ideals and an instrument for social control," was about as critical an observation of White actions as that generation of historians was willing to hazard.[14]

During this same early period a second group of historians labored to document a different history of Black education. They were White historians working from within a White supremacist interpretation. Black education was frequently secondary to their larger purposes, but they created an important, if objectionable, body of literature that their Black contemporaries, and subsequent historians of both races, have felt compelled to address.

Within African-American education historiography, these writers had but one focus: postbellum southern Black education, particularly the freedmen's education phase. Three themes arose from that one topic: northern venality in meddling in southern race issues;

Black ignorance; and southern paternalistic concern for the freedmen's moral training. Edgar W. Knight, one of the most prolific writers from this group, claimed, for instance, that northern-imposed and northern-directed freedmen's education was

> to make for much insane intolerance in [the South],
> . . . actually retard public interest in public education and leave in [its] wake abortive educational efforts that passed under the name of schools . . .

Central to this tradition was the argument that southerners would have educated the freedmen if left to themselves; it was the intolerable intervention of a people with "little or no sympathetic understanding of conditions and needs in the South," i.e., northern teachers, that created the violence toward freedmen's schools in the Reconstruction period, and that in the long run poisoned race relations.[15] Henry L. Swint's *Northern Teacher in the South*, one of the last statements by this group of writers, summarized the White supremacist case against freedmen's education. He was less virulent in his racial bias, but no less firm in his condemnation of northern educators. His interpretation was not answered for fully 4 decades.[16] When White supremacist writers did go beyond freedmen's education to investigate subsequent postbellum Black education, they did not flinch from the evidence of the deteriorating condition of southern Black schooling as did contemporary Black historians, but they found convenient means to shift blame for that deterioration to Blacks. Stuart G. Noble, for example, noted the wildly unequal conditions between White and Black schools in Mississippi by 1910, including Black classrooms averaging 67 pupils per teacher, twice the White average, and salaries for Black teachers less than half those paid White teachers. The classroom size discrepancy he dismissed as regrettable. As for salaries, "Negro teachers, with a lower standard of living, with fewer social wants, and with lower qualifications, do not deserve as high salaries as were paid White teachers." He did not investigate teacher qualifications, though he had noted wide discretion given administrators in assigning grades of certificates. Thus the issue of qualifications was never established. The other issues were racist slurs and tautologies.[17]

The White supremacist historians were apologists for the emerging social order in the South. They sought historical evidence to justify racial oppression and exclusion. They found it, to their satisfaction, in a racist view of the African-American and in the errors of Reconstruction. Blacks and northern Whites were to blame for any evidence of southern backwardness.

To a large extent, it was that interpretation to which the vindicationists and accommodationists were responding, but in doing so they granted too much of their opponents' argument. What was needed were demands for justice based on rigorous historical evidence of American injustice, and an interpretive stance that did not concede the White supremacists' primary assertions, but that posed clear alternative analyses. DuBois offered that, but his was a voice crying in the wilderness.

Liberal Progressivism and Integration: The 1930s-1960s

Vindicationist, corrective histories were written into the 1940s, but, with a handful of exceptions, the first wave of writing on Black education had spent itself by the end of the Depression. Before its spokesmen had fallen silent, however, a new generation was at work. It shared some of the topical interests of the first generation, but shifted the thematic content and constructed new interpretive foundations for its work. Liberal progressivism and integrationism replaced exculpation and accommodation in a historiographic period that ran from the 1930s to near the close of the 1960s.

DuBois had been among the earliest writers in the first period. His agenda, methodology, and analysis were rigorous and penetrating. They were also ignored by his contemporaries. Yet his works have survived while the others, excepting Woodson's, are little known. The second period was also ushered in by a writer whose interpretation and insights apparently had little effect on other writers of the era. Yet today, Horace Mann Bond's *Education of the Negro in the American Social Order* and *Negro Education in Alabama* stand head and shoulders above most of the other histories of Black education written in this era.

Like no other writer until Louis Harlan in 1958, Bond grounded his studies in a firm sense of education's social embeddedness. Education was a dependent force, he held, capable neither of developing autonomously nor of reforming its economic or political contexts. The vindicationists hoped to win White concessions for Black schools in the faith that improved schools would bring improved social conditions; Bond countered, "Strictly speaking, the school has never built a new social order; it has been the product and interpreter of the existing system, sustaining and being sustained by the social complex."[18]

He thus brought an analysis that could look steadfastly at the eroding condition of southern Black schooling from the 1880s onward and provide an explanation. That explanation was not designed to please southern Whites. It did not either offer easy panaceas nor support for faith in a liberal progressive solution to the African-American struggle for freedom. In *Negro Education in Alabama*, Bond wrote of freedmen's education that, so long as both Conservatives and Radicals assumed "that the Negro was to be inducted into the new social order with the same standing as Whites and with the same social and economic stratification," full educational entitlement logically followed. As sharecropping emerged as the primary determinant of social relations, however, it was "obvious that an educated labor force, intelligent regarding rates of interest, cognizant of even the simplest methods of accounting, would be a distinct liability to the system rather than an asset."[19] Thus did Horace Mann Bond announce the beginning of a new period in Black education historiography. His bold position was not destined to guide the new era, however.

Like the earlier historians, this second generation generally failed to study systematically the differences between rural and urban schooling. Also like their forebears', their focus was almost exclusively southern. They began to view southern education more broadly, however, attempting toward the end of this second period to interpret African-American education regionally—Louis Harlan on the seaboard South after the turn of the twentieth century, William P. Vaughn on the roots of integration in the Reconstruction South, and Henry Allen Bullock with the first attempt to provide an interpretation of the entire history of southern Black education. Generally, however, the primary geographical focus remained the individual southern state.[20]

Freedmen's education during Reconstruction was of little interest to historians of the second period. Swint's 1941 interpretation held sway throughout the period. Beginning in the mid-1950s, however, historians began cautiously and tentatively to test minor points in the Swint tradition. Their work was part of the broader challenge to the Dunning interpretation of Reconstruction. They succeeded in rescuing the Freedmen's Bureau from the worst of its detractors' opprobrium and in raising the possibility that Black education was the Bureau's most enduring legacy.[21]

In contrast to earlier historians, writers in midcentury were freer to document discrimination in southern education. They exposed as myth the rationalizations put forward by southern apologists. Using language even the more forceful vindicationists would have winced at, William R. Davis argued in *Negro Education in East Texas* that Black schooling had been "a dual system in name only; the Texas system is essentially a White system with Negro education incidental to it." In *Separate and Unequal*, Harlan went further:

> It is misleading to think of the dual system as a financial burden when the two systems are grossly unequal. Discrimination against Negro schools represented a fiscal saving and was a basis for compromise between tax payer and tax layer.

State and regional studies from the period were frequently heavy with quantitative material detailing the myriad forms of discrimination.[22]

Writing on Black higher education lacked the richness of earlier studies. Largely gone, remarkably, was the expectation of DuBois and others of his generation that higher education would produce the race's leadership cadre. The implication, at least from writers on Black higher education right up to the 1960s, was that the Talented Tenth had taken their talents elsewhere. One writer suggested approvingly that higher education served to provide "acceptance and integration in the general culture of the United States," and the handful of other, largely sociological, studies of Black higher education concurred. Charles S. Johnson's outstanding 1938 study, *The Negro College Graduate,* argued somewhat contradictorily that Black graduates "provide a fairly large proportion of the Negroes who are contributing notably to the development of the Negro group itself and to American life generally," yet noted that college education broke the connection with Black folk traditions, and documented a move away from the community. The institutional biographies from the period were generally unexceptional.[23]

Black industrial education began to come under the scrutiny of these second generation Black education historians. Bond had given it brief attention in the context of his appraisal of the influence of personalities in Negro education. He essentially dismissed Booker T. Washington as the father of Black industrial education, claiming that he "borrowed" the term. Later writers went further. Willard Range questioned the importance of the industrial education movement as a whole in *Negro Colleges in Georgia*, remarking that "it is safe to say that after 1900 most schools [in Georgia] had abandoned their dreams" of industrial education. August Meier more fully debunked Washington, tracing the antecedents of racial industrial education to White educational innovations in the nineteenth century. In place of Washington, Meier argued the prior claim of Samuel Chapman Armstrong as architect and of the Slater Fund as promoter.[24]

Histories of the middle period focused on two other topics that were essentially new to the historiography: philanthropy and segregation. Through most of the writing of this period, the philanthropists received a good press. Ullin Whitney Leavell's *Philanthropy in Negro Education*, the first systematic study of Black education's benefactors, distinguished between the early philanthropy of the churches and the later philanthropy of the major capitalists, concluding that "This newer educational philanthropy is not alone nor even primarily interested in the teaching of any doctrine or creed. . . ." His assertion of the disinterest of the major educational funds held sway among most historians throughout the period. Bond, whose early class analysis might be expected to have raised doubts, saw no class advantage to be gained through giving to southern education. Others had high praise for the vital assistance flowing to Black education at a crucial time.[25]

These writers asked if the philanthropists might gain from their activities economically or ideologically. Cast deterministically, the question seemed to yield a negative response. Only Bullock found a positive answer. He argued that philanthropic acts salved the consciences of men whose wealth was gained in ways not fully sanctioned by American culture, and legitimated that wealth to American society. Harlan and others, however, anticipating the revisionists, posed different questions. For them, the issue was not primarily one of motives, but one of social and racial philosophy and purpose. The philanthropists' accommodation and racism, not their putative class advantages, were central. Measured thus, the Southern Education Board, for instance, "failed in its program of Negro education and also failed to challenge or deflect the anti-Negro movement which it paralleled." Others began to suspect that the funds not only failed to stem racism, but indeed contributed to drawing the color line.[26]

Segregation, an issue seldom mentioned by early writers on the history of African-American education, loomed large in this second period. The key to this new interest does not lie solely with the 1954

Supreme Court decision. Several writers had begun researching the origins of segregation and advocating integration more than a decade before the Brown decision, but the decision, and the momentous events unleashed by it, opened the gates for a veritable flood of studies, not only of the desegregation battle, but of the roots of southern educational discrimination generally.[27]

The second historiographic generation distanced itself further thematically than topically from the first generation. Self-help, autonomy in educational endeavors, and uplift had primacy of place in earlier studies. The self-help theme all but dropped from sight after the Depression. Interracialism —efforts by liberal Whites on behalf of or in concert with Blacks—took its place as one of the major themes explored in the histories of the era. Much of the literature of the period documented the efforts "through which the better elements of both races have been able to find expression in co-operative effort for the common good." The era's keen interest in the philanthropists grew out of this dedication to interracialism.[28]

Interracialism rested, to a degree, on a second theme, an appeal to American ideals. This call to righteousness depended on moral suasion and the faith that when people saw the contradiction between racist behavior and democratic virtues, they would be emboldened to take the ethical high ground; they would seek "to make educational practices consistent with democratic ideals." Writers limning that theme preceded Gunnar Myrdal and contributed to the stream of liberalism from which *An American Dilemma* drew its ideological sustenance.[29]

The appeal to moral prophesy and to interracial cooperation woven into the histories of the period were logical responses to the era. This was, after all, the heyday of the NAACP, the interracial commissions in dozens of cities and states, and other efforts to mute the racist legacy in America. European fascism had held a mirror close to the American face. Socialism was making headway in the former European colonies, in part by noting to the world's people of color how Blacks were treated in the leading capitalist democracy. White liberals began moving toward moderate reformism. That movement seemed to historians to offer greater promise of delivering a measure of justice than Black self-help. It was, at the same time, more congenial than issues of class, capital, and conflict, the themes Bond and DuBois had called upon their contemporaries to consider.

As noted, segregation was a central topic for investigation by the second generation of historians. It also served as a major theme in the period. Indeed, it was Jim Crow discrimination that brought interracialism to the fore. Black progress in education, Black assimilation into the society, interracial cooperation in racial uplift and the "advancement of colored people" through education, it was hoped, would undermine separation. As one historian intoned the faith in 1950, "educational advance among Negroes creates a public opinion . . . before which all artificial barriers must eventually fall."[30]

Those three themes—interracial cooperation, democratic ideals, and segregation—arose in turn out of the interpretive stance of the majority of writers in the period. Their work was founded upon two mutually supportive traditions, integrationism and liberal progressivism.

Integrationists presumed that segregation would, or should, wither away. They were frequently assimilationist as well. They sought evidence of greater White tolerance and of greater Black immersion in White culture. Indeed, the Washingtonian roots of their faith meant that the former was largely dependent upon the latter. The integrationists argued that discrimination resulted from caste, caste resulted from attitudes, and attitudes resulted from experiences. Thus to alter discrimination, alter experiences. The experiences that culminated in racial discrimination were White experiences with Blacks. The social condition of the majority of African-Americans resulted in negative White attitudes which led to racial discrimination. Given those premises, education was an obvious key for it could change the social condition of Blacks and also give Whites positive experiences with Blacks. Buell Gallagher concluded *American Caste and the Negro College* with words that defined the integrationist position from his day forward: "Education is the best answer to the challenge of caste."[31] That faith also guided social policy in the United States for the next 40 years.

The liberal position assumed that if the marketplaces of status and reward could be freed of artificial encumbrances— legal proscriptions, unequal access to public services, atavistic traditions of exclusion, separation, and discrimination—racism would fade and discrimination would end. Racism was a result, not a cause, of racial oppression. Guarantee truly free social, political, and economic marketplaces, and the self-balancing mechanisms of liberal society would take over. Social position would accrue to merit, not race, class, or privilege. The fundamental, though unstated, premise upon which the liberal position was founded was that consensus, not conflict, lay at the heart of the historical process. Undermine that premise and the whole structure would crumble.

The labors of the second generation of historians of Black education, then, were guided by a concern to document progress toward assimilation, or progress toward integration, or progress toward fuller realization of the promise of democracy. They also sought to document Black assent to the liberal consensus, and if one looked in the right places by midcentury, there appeared to be progress and consensus. Black education was not as abysmal by 1950 as it had been in 1920; it was certainly better in 1870 than it had been in 1850, at least in the South; the notable Black struggle for knowledge suggested consensus on American values.

Sustaining a progressive analysis required that historians choose their topics with care, however. It was best not to look too closely at the North, for, as the revisionists of the next period were to document, Black educational opportunities and conditions slumped badly rather than improved in the northern Black communities, at least from the Great Migration onward. The postreconstruction era in the South was also problematic for a liberal or integrationist interpretation, except as it created a gloomy background against which to contrast a brightening present. Antebellum education was of little service. As Woodson had long before documented, Black education in the North improved little from colonial times to the Civil War, while an increasingly market-oriented, yet paranoid, slave society reversed whatever minuscule gains in literacy the enslaved of the post-Revolutionary period might have earned. It was not a good idea either to enquire too closely about the sorts of cultural institutions that provided informal education to the Black community for, while there were many of them, as the earlier historians had begun to document, they were too frequently short-lived. Whether crushed by the systematic opposition of White society or by the inertial weight of a community without the leisure or the social resources to support them, they failed to indicate sustained progress. Meanwhile, conflict between the races, between classes, and among competing purposes for education, threatened to overwhelm consensus.

More fundamentally, liberal and integrationist interpretations lacked explanatory power. They described, often with a measure of grace. They were less successful as modes of analysis. Why was America racist? Why did its schools, presumably the mainstays of democracy, deny equality to millions of its children? The liberal tradition could imagine little beyond the possibility that racism was a mistake, a misunderstanding, simply a case of bad faith that could be rectified through institutional adjustments. For the assimilationists, the answer lay in the character of the Black community itself: its tangle of pathologies, its failure to adopt the speech, dress, interests, ideologies, and neuroses of the majority culture.

Neither the liberal nor the assimilationist tradition took power and conflict seriously as categories of analysis. In liberal ideology, power is a formal aspect of the liberal state which is spread relatively evenly among all parties in the state. Birth, wealth, caste, and other ascriptive traits that may once have determined political and social power have been, by this analysis, removed from their traditional seats and distributed among all the sovereign people. Conflict, then, is reduced to resolvable issues between relative equals. Thus one need not even ask seriously about the uses, allocation, or consequences of power or conflict.

There were dissenting voices during this period. A handful of writers spoke from outside the progressive and integrationist consensus. After the work of Horace Mann Bond in the 1930s, however, it was 1958 before a major study appeared that suggested new questions and interpretations. Like DuBois and Bond before him, Louis R. Harlan, in *Separate and Unequal*, spoke from a sense of outraged justice. His basic premises departed from those of his consensus contemporaries. His premises included principled antiracism, an insistence that economic and institutional factors were of primary importance in the development of southern educational practices, and an historically grounded conviction that education alone "would never solve the major race problems." The residual integrationist strain detectable in the book resulted from Harlan's demand for justice rather than from a belief that integration or assimilation were solutions to racial conflict. Dissenters such as Harlan did not change the thrust of historical writing in their period, but they did suggest strategies and agendas for the next period.[32]

In 1967 Henry Allen Bullock published *A History of Negro Education in the South*, about the most ambitious survey of the field yet attempted. It marks the high tide of liberal progressivism and integrationism. It also marks roughly the end of the second historiographic period. The book encapsulated well the thrust of the entire period. Its dominant subjects were the dominant subjects of the period—a southern, largely rural focus, superficial treatment of antebellum education, extended analysis of freedmen's education and of the philanthropists, moderate attention to higher education. Interracial cooperation, segregation, and the contradictions between

Black education practices and the ideals of democracy were consistent themes, though the volume also reflected earlier historians' interest in self-help. It also illustrated clearly the poverty of liberal progressivism by the 1960s.

Bullock's central problem in this prize-winning volume was to find some unifying theme, some mode of explanation that would tie the study together. Disinclined ideologically to search for explanations in social and economic systems, convinced of the righteousness of participants in the liberal consensus, blind to conflict, Bullock was reduced to inventing an elaborate system of explanation that invested history with progressive purposes of its own. He secularized nineteenth century Protestant historians' faith that the divine hand could be discerned in history. He argued from an uncritical Hegelian idealism that the dialectical reaction of intended and unintended effects created historical change. Thus the task of the historian was simply to identify the intended and the unintended.[33]

The methodology was marvelously tautological. Every putatively progressive element in historical evolution could be linked, without logical possibility of rebuttal, as the unintended consequence of some earlier intended act. Thus, for instance, Bullock argued that the very existence of Blacks in the slave South—the very fact of racial slavery, we might say —"enhanced an unintentional development of their educational opportunities and an increase in their social position among Southern White people," an argument virtually indistinguishable from the argument of slavery's apologists that the presence of Blacks in America was a positive good, for it put them in contact with a superior, Christian culture. The crushing near-reenslavement of African-Americans after Reconstruction was, for Bullock, merely a "Great Detour." White racists may have intended to create a dual society, but the unintended consequence was eventual desegregation and movement toward a multicultural society.[34]

Thus one of the central events affecting southern Black education, the industrializing of the South, Bullock dismissed in a single paragraph. What we learn there is that industrial education failed to prepare Blacks for industry, a fact Bullock could describe but was incapable of analyzing on the level of ideology. Meanwhile, he ignored at his own peril Bond's haunting prophesy, made 30 years earlier, that whereas the Black was indispensable under the domination of southern agriculture, under the domination of industrialism "the Negro producer as a Negro is by no means indispensable."[35] Similarly, nowhere in the study did he mention racism, much less treat it as an analytical category. Astonishing as that seems in a book about African-American history, it is a characteristic the book shares with most others written from within the same interpretive framework.

Revisionism: The 1960s-Present

The remarkable topical, thematic, and interpretive unity of the first two historiographic periods was shattered in the third period. Beginning in the 1960s, this period featured great diversity in approaches, methodologies, foci, and premises. The result was an unparalleled richness in the field of African-American education history. In analytical rigor, many of the recent offerings rivaled the best of DuBois, Bond, and Harlan. The period was marked by a thorough-going revisionism.

The revisionists introduced several new topics to the history of African-American education. We know much more, for instance, about slavery as an educative institution, both from general studies of slavery and from studies that focus specifically on purposeful training within slavery. The debate that rages around these studies concerns the difficult issue of the degree of autonomy of slave culture.[36]

The education of northern Blacks was virtually ignored in the first two periods. After the mid-1960s, however, northern Black schooling received more attention than southern Black schooling, and most of that attention focused on urban schooling.[37] Further, historians began to investigate the people who made up schools, the students and teachers without whom there would be little to write in the first place. Much remains to be done in this area, but we now have strong studies of students in the 1920s and in the civil rights era, and of teachers, particularly in the 1860s and 1870s.[38]

There was also more empirical study of the response of the Black community to educational opportunity, and of Black educational achievement. Earlier studies often noted Black enthusiasm for education and faith in its ameliorative power, but their evidence was impressionistic for the most part. The recent empirical studies provided striking corroborating evidence, finding that historically Blacks have attended school at higher proportional rates, and for longer periods, than contemporary immigrant groups.[39]

In a related arena, scholars began to probe the history of scientific racism and its insinuation into the school in the form of intelligence tests and other standardized tests. Their documentation of the ways in which racist ideology consistently overwhelmed empirical science is chilling; the implications for the ways in which that ideological science has killed children's spirits in America's schools are devastating.[40]

Revisionist historians built on the topics developed in earlier periods as well, offering greater depth of insight or challenging earlier interpretations. The prevailing view of freedmen's education, and hence to a degree the view of postbellum southern Black schooling more generally, remained tied to Henry Lee Swint's White supremacist interpretation well into the 1970s. Though a less malevolent view of the Freedmen's Bureau was emerging in that decade, it was not until 1980 that the Swintian tradition was frontally assaulted.[41]

Likewise, industrial education continued to generate interest, but in this period investigators were less concerned with dating its years of influence or assessing its success as a strategy of modernization. The more interesting work sought instead to probe its ideological functions. In one of the more provocative essays, James D. Anderson argued that the fact that graduates of industrial schools did not go into trades or craft positions—which overwhelmingly they did not—does not indicate the failure of industrial education. To the contrary, Anderson held that the intention was not to train Black craftsmen, but rather to create a cadre of Black school teachers steeped in a conservative social and economic ideology. Industrial education, training thousands of teachers for the South's Black schools, provided a means to diffuse an ameliorist, gradualist ideology throughout the Black South.[42]

Philanthropy in Black education also attracted critical scrutiny. The resulting revisionism was as thoroughgoing concerning philanthropy as it was concerning freedmen's education. The philanthropists were humanitarians, wrote the historians of the middle period, men of vision and courage perhaps, or at least beneficent individuals whose failings trace simply to a pragmatic accommodationism. Their efforts could not reasonably be interpreted as motivated by economic or ideological considerations, according to those writers. Nonsense, retorted the revisionists. Philanthropists were men of vision, indeed, but it was a vision arising precisely out of economic and ideological considerations. In clumsy hands, this threatened to degenerate into reductionist determinism. However, the best studies remained sensitive to contradiction and conflict among competing visions, and also retained a firm grip on the analysis of ideology and economic development.[43]

Historians revitalised the history of Black higher education since its doldrums in the fifties. Most notable was a spate of outstanding institutional biographies, including Rayford W. Logan's *Howard University* and Clarence A. Bacote's *The Story of Atlanta University*, one of whose themes concerned the role of higher education in the creation of Black leaders. These studies dealt not only with their respective colleges' intentions in regard to training for leadership, but also with the accomplishments of their graduates, particularly in the field of civil rights and service to the community. Additionally, the related histories of Black professional training and of Black professional and scholarly organizations flowered, providing insight into professional education and affiliation, and important glimpses into the upper strata of the Black community.[44]

Segregation remained the major topic, however. Many recent historians appeared to assume that school desegregation was the end, rather than a means, in Black education. Hence several studies focused exclusively on the degree to which segregation did, or did not, decline. Others continued to probe the origins of educational discrimination.[45] In two areas, however, the current generation of historians moved segregation studies in new directions. First, some studies began to document the civil rights struggles as they impinged on schooling. Second, a few voices began to be heard asking critical questions about the historical context of desegregation, about the racism within desegregation's fundamental premises, and about the relationship between desegregation strategy and power.[46]

In only one topical area did the third wave of historians show decreased interest. The last two decades produced only a handful of statewide studies, though at one time the state study was a staple in the historical literature. Histories of urban education have taken the place of state histories. While an important corrective—too little was done on urban education previously, despite the urbanization of African-Americans—state studies such as Carleton Mabee's splendid *Black Education in New York State* remind us that even in the North, many Blacks have always lived in villages and towns, and were educated there in one way or another.[47]

The flowering of African-American educational history since the 1960s has nurtured a diversified thematic content. Two of the three dominant themes from the post-Depression era reemerged. The perspective on each changed, however. Thus, while interracialism continued to be woven into the fabric of many recent histories, several of them were critical of the ways in which Whites have manipulated interracial efforts for conservative ends. Similarly, segregation and integration continued to fascinate historians three decades after Brown. Yet writers played out that theme less frequently than in the middle period of historical writing. Further, in the last decade, the failure of desegregation, both as an institutional goal and as a social ameliorist strategy, added a critical and skeptical edge to this theme. Meanwhile, the appeal to democratic conscience was increasingly banished to the margins.[48]

On the other hand, themes previously unexploited by historians of African-American education emerged as central concerns in the revisionist era. For instance, historians gazed unswervingly at racism as a category of analysis and a primary problematic in the history of African-American education.[49] Likewise, several recent writers used the material base of the society as a theme. Concluding with Doxie Wilkerson that "the effectiveness of the Negro's struggle for education is conditioned by his relations to the dominant economic and political forces in any given period," they sought to clarify those forces as the terrain on which the struggle for knowledge and power goes on.[50]

Others began to use the history of African-American education as a means to explore the effects of Black cultural values on education. The degree of autonomy of slave culture is the focus of a current debate on the "schooling" of enslaved Africans. In a very different vein, Judy Jolley Mohraz, in *The Separate Problem*, argued that the diverging cultural allegiances in the Black communities of three northern urban centers yielded significantly different educational strategies, although the more egregious patterns of northern educational discrimination wracked all three communities about equally.[51] Cultural nationalism revived a major theme of the vindicationists, the self-help motif. Once again, writers noted the autonomous educational activities of the African-American community. Importantly, this revived concern with self-help has shed the early attachment to theories of racial "uplift" and is little interested in vindicating the race to the White community.[52]

Interpretation shifted dramatically in this period. The liberal progressivism of the middle years did not fade away, as had vindicationism before it, but it was no longer the primary lens through which historians viewed the educational world. Liberalism was eclipsed by revisionist tendencies due to its collapse and retreat as an interpretive mode.

In the early post-Brown years the liberal history of Black education waxed celebrational. God was clearly in his heaven, and all would be right with the world, but somewhere on that tortured road from Little Rock to Boston and beyond, liberalism lost its confidence. It could no longer easily document progress nor the ameliorative effects of the marketplace. Despite institutional tinkering and good intentions, despite laws and court decisions, America was not moving toward a desegregated society. American liberal theory lacked the ability any longer to explain that.

Liberal history retreated. It took with it its individualist bias and its disinclination to investigate ideology, power, or conflict. The result so far has not been the collapse of liberal faith, but an abandonment of its progressivist and integrationist strains. Robbed thus of its ethical and prophetic core, reduced to little more than methodology and focus informed by ideology, its historiographic products in the last 20 years have tended toward antiquarianism. Liberal historians provide richly detailed pictures, but they have abandoned the historical task of deepening political and social consciousness; they did not explain historical processes.

An aggressive revisionism upstaged the liberal posture, and was largely responsible for the vibrancy and diversity of the scholarship of this most recent period. The revisionists were held together by a skepticism toward the liberal notions of race and American institutions, a mistrust of consensus history, and a conviction that justice will not be achieved through gradualism or reliance on the marketplace, but it is a loose coalition, not all of whose contradictions are yet clear.

The disparate tendencies of revisionists betray a lack of ideological unity among them. Beyond a shared antiracism, to which many liberal historians subscribe as well, the group splinters along a number of lines. Marxists, antimarxists, Black nationalists, anarchists, democratic socialists, and those disabused liberals who have not moved to neoconservatism, fill the ranks. Consequently, revisionism cannot be said to have a clear voice. We may find eventually that its main tendencies are in fact unique lines of interpretation, each leading to exclusive conclusions.

Historiography at the Crossroads: Liberation or Resignation

Where is the field, then, after 90 years of scholarship? Our knowledge of schooling in the history of African-American life has grown enormously. Our understanding of the means by which "the owners of the world" have sought to use Black schooling to serve their own purposes has increased perhaps even more. That growth has been important if the point is to contribute to "outthinking and outflanking" those owners. Yet in the service of that end, much more remains to be done.

It is not yet clear what educational effects flowed out of various Black social movements. Black abolitionism, postreconstruction westward migrations, the Harlem Renaissance, Garveyism, Pan-Africanism, and various forms of separatism, among others, would appear to have implications for the ways in which the community educated itself, and perhaps for the ways White society sought to structure that education. To date, historians have not gone far toward probing those implications.

Similarly, the history of Black female education is neglected. Beyond occasional mention of domestic training in industrial education, the current literature says little about specific schooling for Black women, or about the content of the curriculum in Black schools as it attempted to mold perceptions of race and sex. Black fiction is filled with images of strong, independent Black women, yet nowhere in the historical literature do we learn where that characterology might have been learned outside the home; what agencies contributed to the education of Black womanhood? And what have been the sources and content of the schooling of the female children of the Black elite?

Thus far historians have focused overwhelmingly on the purposes for schooling—the intentions of educators, civic leaders, reformers, philanthropists, and perhaps even parents and students. They have paid much less attention to the effects of African-American schooling. Moreover, to the extent that scholars have addressed effects, they have interpreted effects in narrow, marketplace terms: What was the degree of mobility or assimilation resulting from schooling?

But surely the effects of education embrace more than "getting ahead." Among other things, historians need to ask the question that is assiduously avoided when speaking of "getting ahead": getting ahead of whom? What was the effect on family, community, and relationships as a result of the advanced schooling of individuals? Who got ahead of whom, and why, and with what consequences for the community? Those questions must eventually lead us to confront the sticky issues of the relationship of education to the creation of the Black leadership elite, the relationship of that class to the Black masses and to the White elite, and the role of its education in inculcating an ideology amenable to the continued social domination of White economic interests.

Ultimately, investigations of the effects of African-American education must grapple with a more basic conceptual problem. Is there an irresolvable contradiction between the core value of African-centered culture and that of education as defined by bourgeois society in the United States? The point of education in liberal culture is individualistic and privatised. The aim is to allow the atomised individual the opportunity for self-fulfillment in a social setting conceived as a marketplace; she can do so only (or most effectively) through a systematic process of severing communal obligations, and by privatising as commodities the knowledge gained in the educational setting. African-centered culture, on the other hand, values a communal ethos. Community and mutuality, not atomisation and privatisation, define the good. To the extent that that is true, scholars need to explore the implications of the contradiction and the ways in which African-Americans have sought to resolve it.

Related to that problem are two others having to do with the Black community and an educational ideology. First, we have been assured repeatedly of African-Americans' universal faith in schooling as a key to the future of the race. Yet we have no systematic attempts to test that assurance, and impressionistic evidence raises important questions. For instance, the exodusters and founders of the all-Black communities in the South, Midwest, and West built a number of other social institutions before turning their attention to schooling. The freedmen supported schooling heartily but showed by their actions that their hope for liberty lay in land, protection, and political power. We need a better understanding of where schooling stood in relationship to other social institutions for various groups and at various times, and a better sense of the content of the educational ideologies.

Second, historians have themselves accepted uncritically the adequacy of schooling as the panacea for the liberation of Black America and the resolution of America's racism. They have asserted as true what must be proven: that schooling is the key to Black progress in isolation from other social changes. The issue can be posed as an empirical question, and the answer available from African-American history is not comforting to the believers. After a century and more of expression of the faith, it is time to pose Doxie Wilkerson's counter-claim: "It is not the education of Black men that will achieve their liberation; it is the liberation of Black men that will assure their effective education." Let the two positions contend in rigorous historical debate rather than either holding place by virtue of frequent repetition.[53]

Two observations concerning future interpretation in the history of African-American education will close this study. The first observation has to do with interpretive scope. Historians of African-American education have not always spoken clearly heretofore of the broader intellectual currents in American society and how, filtered through the lens of race, they came to influence Black education.

They have been uneven in their attempt to place schooling within its larger educational context. In the large majority of studies, readers gain no sense of contemporaneous practices in mainstream schooling, and hence little sense of the degree to which African-American schooling was unique. Yet in general it can be argued that since at least the last third of the nineteenth century, African-American schooling differed primarily in degree rather than in type from the schooling offered White children.

However, what is most needed in the history of African-American education is an end to the segregation of its interpretive insights by placing it in the broader social context in which African-American schooling was practiced, for African-American schooling is part of the struggle of and against working people in America as a whole. The modes of worker control developed in African-American schooling, whether aimed at ideological hegemony or skill training, were being developed simultaneously, if under different names, for use against immigrant and working class White people. Those modes demeaned African-American working men and women more than White working men and women, doubtlessly, and wrought greater economic devastation on African-American workers than on White ones; the inequality and social conflict endemic to capitalism, linked to racist presumptions, assured that. The broader purposes were the same, however. Both groups were denied the sort of rigorous, critical education they needed.

The second observation involves the interpretive stance of African-American education's historians in the coming era. Revisionism has clearly taken the high ground, but the very disparateness of revisionism calls for a reconceptualization, a rethinking of fundamental premises, to move toward a post-revisionist stance.

The outlines of post-revisionism are not yet clear, but there are at least two contradictory possibilities. The shape of post-revisionism will directly affect the ways the Black community and others think about the community, and conceptualize appropriate social, political and economic action. One possibility may move toward "outthinking and outflanking the owners of the world"; the second possibility would move in much less liberatory directions.

The first possibility for post-revisionism would be to accept the revisionist agenda and vision, but from within a more consolidated position than that held by the current revisionists. Revisionists are not ideologically unified as were the vindicationists, White supremacists, or liberal progressivists, and hence are not in a position to fill the political void created by the retreat of liberal progressivism. There appear to be three tendencies within revisionist historiography: one that considers White culture and institutions and their intersection with African-American life; another that considers African-American culture in and for itself; and a third that takes both seriously but brings a materialist analysis to bear in its interpretation of either.

The first of these tendencies illuminates the levers of power, but frequently omits any sense of African-American perspectives, and often lacks an analysis of the sources and nature of power. The second tendency takes seriously the lives, thoughts, and actions of Black folk living, thinking, and acting for themselves. However, that culturalist approach often fails to address the material base which forms the context in which Black people lived, thought, and acted, even for themselves. It tends, then, to be as politically vacuous as history written by liberal progressives, for it does not offer an understanding of the sources of the oppression within which Blacks experienced life. Thus, the third tendency drawing on the heritage of DuBois and Bond, provides the best hope for a sensitive, informed post-revisionism. It would be a post-revisionism built upon the priority of African-American liberty, but bringing with it an ability to explain rather than simply lament the denial of liberty. It would have a vision of what African-American education should have been and should be, but would be able to explain why it was not and is not. Its explanation, like DuBois' and Bond's, would be capable of leading to political and economic strategies to guide the African-American community in its struggles toward "outthinking and outflanking."

The second possibility is that post-revisionism will turn its back decisively on the heritage of DuBois and Bond. Revisionism flowered in what has come to be known as the Second Reconstruction—

that era in which African-Americans and their supporters forced America back to the unfinished business of Reconstruction, but a Second Redemption, though not yet decisively in the saddle, looms larger in American social and political life, and has been seeking intellectual legitimacy. To judge from the early efforts of scholars moving in that direction, a post-revisionism nurtured by redemptionist sensibilities promises to return the history of African-American education to the historiographic fashions of 90 years ago.[54] It would find little reason to exploit the scholarly opportunities in the field as outlined earlier. Such a post-revisionism would be replete with triumphalist treatises that indict the African-American community and its White allies for the community's problems and many of the country's woes, and revisionist historians fighting rearguard battles to vindicate the race. And such a post-revisionism could only fortify "the owners of the world," for it will suggest few actions beyond resignation.

Notes and References

1. W. E. B. DuBois, *The Education of Black People: Ten Critiques, 1906-1960*, ed. Herbert Aptheker (New York, 1973), 77. The history of education is intimately related to all other areas of history, and cannot be understood in isolation from political, social, economic, and institutional history. Nowhere is that clearer than in African-American history, in which the social embeddedness of education is sharply illustrated. However, in order to keep this discussion within reasonable bounds I have limited the discussion and the notes to the scholarship specifically related to the history of black education, with a handful of exceptions.

2. For alternative periodization, see Vincent P. Franklin, "Changing Historical Perspectives on Afro-American Life and Education," in *New Perspectives on Black Educational History*, eds. Vincent P. Franklin and James D. Anderson (Boston, 1978), 1-18; and August Meier and Elliott Rudwick, *Black History and the Historical Profession, 1915-1980* (Urbana, 1986). Franklin relies on a traditional historiographic periodization; Meier and Rudwick are less concerned with changing interpretation than with the growth of Black history. Both add important dimensions to the dialogue, much of which I have not sought to repeat in this essay.

3. Carter G. Woodson, *The Education of the Negro Prior to 1861* (1919; rpt., New York, 1968); W. E. B. DuBois, ed., *The Negro Common School* (Atlanta, 1901); C. W. Birnie, "Education of the Negro in Charleston, South Carolina, Prior to the Civil War," *Journal of Negro History* 12 (1927): 13-21; Luther P. Jackson, "Religious

Instruction of Negroes, 1830-1860, with Special Reference to South Carolina," *Journal of Negro History* 15 (1930): 72-114; Faith Vibert, "The Society for the Propagation of the Gospel in Foreign Parts: Its Work for the Negroes in North America before 1783," *Journal of Negro History* 18 (1933): 171-212; on post-elementary education, see e.g., W. A. Daniel, *The Education of Negro Ministers* (1925; rpt., New York, 1969); Rufus E. Clement, "The Church School as a Social Factor in Negro Life," *Journal of Negro History* 12 (1927): 5-12; Reid E. Jackson, "Rise of Teacher-Training for Negroes," *Journal of Negro Education* 7 (1938): 540-547; and W. E. B. DuBois and August Granville Dill, eds., *The College-Bred Negro American* (Atlanta, GA, 1910); for informal agencies, see e.g., Charles S. Johnson, "The Rise of the Negro Magazine," *Journal of Negro History* 13 (1928): 7-21; Dorothy B. Porter, "The Organized Educational Activities of Negro Literary Societies, 1828-1846," *Journal of Negro Education* 5 (1936): 555-76; Birnie, "Education of the Negro in Charleston"; Jesse E. Moorland, "The Young Men's Christian Association Among Negroes," *Journal of Negro History* 9 (1924): 127-38; Campbell C. Johnson, "Negro Youth and the Educational Program of the Y.M.C.A.," *Journal of Negro Education* 9 (1940): 354-62; Marion Cuthbert, "Negro Youth and the Educational Program of the Y.W.C.A.," *Journal of Negro Education* 9 (1940): 363-71; few institutional biographies were written in this period, but see Francis Greenwood Peabody, *Education for Life: The Story of Hampton Institute* (Garden City, NY, 1918); and Luther P. Jackson, "The Origins of Hampton Institute," *Journal of Negro History* 10 (1925): 131-149; on education in the North, see also J. C. Carroll, "The Beginnings of Public Education for Negroes in Indiana," *Journal of Negro Education* 8 (1939): 649-58.

4. W. E. B. DuBois, *The Souls of Black Folk* (1903; rpt., New York, 1969), 64, 67, 71; DuBois, *Negro Common School*, 21-42, quotation from 40; DuBois, *Black Reconstruction in America, 1860-1880* (1935; rpt., Cleveland, 1964), 637-669. See also Luther P. Jackson, "The Educational Efforts of the Freedmen's Bureau and Freedmen's Aid Societies in South Carolina, 1862-1872," *Journal of Negro History* 8 (1923): 1-40; Charles Kassel, "Educating the Slave—A Forgotten Chapter of Civil War History," *Open Court* 41 (1927): 239-256; G. K. Eggleston, "The Work of Relief Societies during the Civil War," *Journal of Negro History* 14 (1929): 272-299.

5. Henry S. Williams, "The Development of the Negro Public School System in Missouri," *Journal of Negro History* 5 (1920): 137-165; Carter G. Woodson, *Early Negro Education in West Virginia* (Institute, WV, 1921); Alrutheus Ambush Taylor, *The Negro in South Carolina during the Reconstruction* (1924; rpt., New York, 1969), 82-105; Taylor, "The Negro in the Reconstruction of Virginia,"

Journal of Negro History 11 (1926): 379-415; W. Sherman Savage, "Legal Provisions for Negro Schools in Missouri, 1865-1890," *Journal of Negro History* 16 (1931): 309-321; Savage, "Legal Provisions for Negro Schools in Missouri from 1891-1935," *Journal of Negro History* 22 (1937): 335-44; DuBois, *Negro Common School*; Lance G. E. Jones, *Negro Schools in the Southern States* (Oxford, 1928).

6. DuBois, Woodson, Taylor, and others, documented segregation and exclusion, of course, but separation remained a minor issue in these studies, not a theme of significance. Savage, "Legal Provisions for Negro Schools in Missouri, 1865-1890," *Journal of Negro History* 16 (1931): 309-321; Savage, "Legal Provisions for Negro Schools in Missouri from 1891-1935," *Journal of Negro History* 22 (1937): 335-44; and Savage, "Early Negro Education in the Pacific Coast States," *Journal of Negro Education* 15 (1946): 134-39, focused more fully on legal and legislative issues than most contemporary African-American education historians, and hence his studies are among the few that make racial segregation a theme.

7. Even the few studies whose theme appears to be industrial education frequently do not provide rigorous histories of the idea or its effects. Peabody's *Education for Life*, for instance, is an extended panegyric.

8. Thomas Jesse Jones, ed., *Negro Education: A Study of the Private and Higher Schools for Colored People in the U.S.* (Washington, 1917); DuBois, *Negro Common School*, 42; see also Booker T . Washington and W. E. B. DuBois, *The Negro in the South . . .* ([1907?]; rpt., New York, 1970), 102-03, 114. Jones, however, wrote largely in support of continued segregation.

9. Richard R. Wright, *A Brief Historical Sketch of Negro Education in Georgia* (Savannah, 1894), 50, 52 [caps. in orig.]; see also, Peabody, *Education for Life*; Loretta Funke, "The Negro in Education," *Journal of Negro Education* 5 (1920): 1-21; Margaret A. Diggs, *Catholic Negro Education in the United States* (Washington, 1936).

10. Porter, "Organized Educational Activities of Negro Literary Societies," 576; see also Taylor, "Negro in the Reconstruction of Virginia, " 414; Birnie, "Education of the Negro in Charleston"; Woodson, *Early Negro Education in West Virginia*; DuBois, *Negro Common School*, 21-42, 91; Charles S. Johnson, "Rise of the Negro Magazine"; Reid E. Jackson, "Rise of Teacher Training for Negroes"; Clement, "Church School as a Social Factor"; Kurt F . Leidecker, "The Education of Negroes in St. Louis, Missouri, during William Torrey Harris' Administration," *Journal of Negro Education* 10 (1941): 643-49.

11. DuBois, *Souls of Black Folk*, 127; Daniel, *The Education of Negro Ministers*, 28 and passim; Clement, "Church School as a Social Factor."

12. DuBois, *Negro Common School*, 118 .

13. E. Horace Fitchett, "The Influence of Claflin College on Negro Family

Life," *Journal of Negro History* 29 (1944): 459; see also Emmett D. Preston, Jr., "Development of Negro Education in the District of Columbia," *Journal of Negro Education* 9 (1940): 595-603; Preston, "The Development of Negro Education in the District of Columbia, 1800-1860," *Journal of Negro Education* 12 (1943): 189-98; among others.

14. Luther P. Jackson, "Religious Instruction of Negroes," 72.

15. Edgar W. Knight, "The "Messianic" Invasion of the South after 1865," *School and Society* 57 (1943): 649, 645. See also Knight, "Reconstruction and Education in South Carolina," *South Atlantic Q.* 18 (1919): 350-364; 19 (1920): 55-66; Knight, *Public School Education in North Carolina* (1916; rpt., New York, 1969), esp. 265; J. G. deRoulhac Hamilton, "The Freedmen's Bureau in North Carolina," *South Atlantic Q.* 8 (1909): 53-67, 154-163. Henry Lee Swint, *The Northern Teacher in the South, 1862-1870* (1941; rpt., New York, 1967).

16. Henry Lee Swint, *The Northern Teacherr in the South, 1862–1870* (1941; reprint, New York, 1967)

17. Stuart Grayson Noble, *Forty Years of the Public Schools in Mississippi, with Special Reference to the Education of the Negro* (New York, 1918), 75-89, quotation on 82. See also Charles Dabney, *Universal Education in the South*, 2 vols. (Chapel Hill, 1936).

18. Horace Mann Bond, *The Education of the Negro in the American Social Order* (1934; rpt., with new preface and additional chapter, New York, 1966), 13; hereafter cited: *Educ. of the Negro.*

19. Bond, *Negro Education in Alabama: A Study in Cotton and Steel* (1939; rpt., New York, 1969), 141.

20. Louis R. Harlan, *Separate and Unequal: Public School Campaigns and Racism in the Southern Seaboard States, 1901-1915* (1958; rpt., New York, 1968); William Preston Vaughn, *Schools for All: The Blacks and Public Education in the South, 1865-1877* (Lexington, 1974); Henry Allen Bullock, *A History of Negro Education in the South: From 1619 to the Present* (1967; rpt., New York, 1970). On the history of northern Black education written during this period, see e.g., L. D. Reddick, "The Education of Negroes in States where Separate Schools are not Legal," *Journal of Negro Education* 16 (1947): 290-300; Frederick A. McGinnis, *The Education of Negroes in Ohio* (Wilberforce, OH, 1962); Marion Manola Wright, *The Education of Negroes in New Jersey* (New York, 1941). Southern state studies include William R. Davis, *The Development and Present Status of Negro Education in East Texas* (New York, 1934); Daniel J. Whitener, "The Republican Party and Public Education in North Carolina, 1867-1900," *No. Car. Hist. R.* 37 (1960): 362-96; Bond, *Negro Education in Alabama*; Hugh Victor Brown, *History of the Education of Negroes in North Carolina* (Raleigh, NC, 1961). Cf.

Hollis Moody Long, *Public Secondary Education for Negroes in North Carolina* (New York, 1932), a sociological approach.

21. See, among others, William T. Alderson, Jr., "The Freedmen's Bureau and Negro Education in Virginia," *So. Car. Hist. R.* 29 (1952): 64-90; W. A. Lowe, "The Freedmen's Bureau and Education in Maryland," *Md. Hist. Mag.* 47 (1952): 29-39; Martin Abbott, "The Freedmen's Bureau and Negro Schooling in South Carolina," *So. Car. Hist. Mag.* 57 (1956): 65-81; Joe M. Richardson, "The Freedmen's Bureau and Negro Education in Florida," *J. of Negro Ed.* 31 (1962): 460-67.

22. William Davis, *Negro Education in East Texas*, 137; Harlan, *Separate and Unequal*, 269; see also Ellis O. Knox, "The Origins and Development of the Negro Separate School," *J. of Negro Ed.* 16 (1947): 269-279; Marion Wright, *Education of Negroes in New Jersey*.

23. Jeanne L. Noble, *The Negro Woman's College Education* (New York, 1956), 18; Charles S. Johnson, *The Negro College Graduate* (1938; rpt. College Park, MD, 1969), 339; see also Willard Range, *The Rise and Progress of Negro Colleges in Georgia, 1865-1949* (Athens, GA, 1951); Buell G. Gallagher, *American Caste and the Negro College* (1938; rpt., New York, 1966); Marian Vera Cuthbert, *Education and Marginality: A Study of the Negro Woman College Graduate* (New York, 1942); Dwight Oliver Wendell Holmes, *The Evolution of the Negro College* (1934; rpt., New York, 1970); Horace Mann Bond, "The Evolution and Present Status of Negro Higher and Professional Education in the United States," *J. of Negro Ed.* 17 (1948): 224-235; Bond, "The Origin and Development of Negro Church Colleges," *J. of Negro Ed.* 29 (1960): 217-26. Among institutional biographies from the period, see Frederick A. McGinnis, *A History and Interpretation of Wilberforce University* (Wilberforce, OH, 1941); and Leedell W. Neyland and John W. Riley, *The History of Florida Agricultural and Mechanical University* (Gainesville, FLA, 1963). Elisabeth S. Peck, *Berea's First Century, 1855-1955* (Lexington, 1955): deals briefly with Berea while it was an integrated college.

24. Bond, *Negro Education in Alabama*, 215. Range, *Negro Colleges in Georgia,* 78; August Meier, "The Beginning of Industrial Education in Negro Schools," *Midwest J.* 7 (1955): 21-44; Meier, "The Vogue of Industrial Education," *Midwest J.* 7 (1955): 241-266. Bullock, *Negro Education in the South* addresses industrial education desultorily, but is less willing to dismiss industrial education altogether; see esp. 100-02, 159-60. xxx

25. Ullin Whitney Leavell, *Philanthropy in Negro Education* (1930; rpt., Westport, CT, 1970), 57-58; Bond, *Educ. of the Negro*, 148-50; see also Bond, *Negro Education in Alabama*, 262-86; Lance G. E. Jones, *The Jeanes Teacher in the United States, 1908-1933: An Account of Twenty-Five Years' Experience in the Supervision of Negro Rural*

Schools (Chapel Hill, 1937); Holmes, *Evolution of the Negro College,*
esp. 14, 69-71; Raymond B. Fosdick, *Adventure in Giving: The Story
of the General Education Board, a Foundation Established by John
D. Rockefeller* (New York, 1962).

26. Harlan, *Separate and Unequal,* 254; see also Bullock, *Negro
Education in the South,* 117-20; Meier, "Vogue of Industrial
Education," 241-66; William P. Vaughn, "Partners in Segregation:
Barnas Sears and the Peabody fund," *Civil War Hist.* 10 (1964): 260-
274; cf. Earle H. West, "The Peabody Education Fund and Negro
Education, 1867-1880," *Hist. of Ed. Q.* 6 (1966): 3-21.

27. Knox, "Origins and Development of the Negro Separate School";
Lillian G. Dabney, *The History of Schools for Negroes in the District
of Columbia, 1807-1947* (Washington, 1949), esp. 252-253; Leonard
Levy and Harlan B. Phillips, "The Roberts Case: Source of the
'Separate but Equal' Doctrine," *Am. Hist. R.* 56 (1951): 510-18; Harry
E. Groves, "A Re-examination of the 'Separate but Equal' Doctrine in
Public Education," *J. of Negro Ed.* 20 (1951): 520-34; "How
Imminent is the Outlawing of Segregation?" *J. of Negro Ed.* 20 (1951):
495-98; Howard J. Graham, "The Fourteenth Amendment and School
Segregation," *Buffalo Law Review* 3 (1953): 1-24. Post-Brown studies
of the origins of segregation and the antecedents to desegregation
include Franklin, "Jim Crow Goes to School"; Alfred H. Kelly, "The
Congressional Controversy over School Desegregation, 1867-1875,"
Am. Hist. R. 64 (1959): 537-63; Harlan, *Separate and Unequal;*
Harlan, "Desegregation in New Orleans Public Schools during
Reconstruction," *Am. Hist. R.* 67 (1962): 663-75; William P. Vaughn,
"Separate and Unequal: The Civil Rights Act of 1875 and Defeat of the
School Integration Clause," *Southwest Soc. Sci. Q.* 48 (1967): 146-
54; Vaughn, *Schools for All;* Carleton Mabee, "A Negro Boycott to
Integrate Boston Schools," *New England Q.* 41 (1968): 341-61;
August Meier and Elliott M. Rudwick, "Early Boycotts of Segregated
Schools: The East Orange, New Jersey, Experience, 1899-1906,"
Hist. of Ed. Q. 7 (1967): 22-35; Meier and Rudwick, "Early Boycotts
of Segregated Schools: The Alton, Illinois Case, 1897-1908," *J. of
Negro Ed.* 36 (1967): 394-402; Meier and Rudwick, "Early Boycotts of
Segregated Schools: The Case of Springfield, Ohio, 1922-1923,"
Am. Q. 20 (1968): 744-58; Donald M. Jacobs, "The Nineteenth
Century Struggle over Segregated Education," *J. of Negro Ed.* 39
(1970): 76-85. For histories of desegregation written in this period, see
e.g., Benjamin Muse, *Ten Years of Prelude: The Story of Integration
Since the Supreme Court's Decision* (New York, 1964); Albert P.
Blaustein and Clarence C. Ferguson, Jr., *Desegregation and the Law:
The Meaning and Effect of the School Segregation Cases* (New
Brunswick, NJ, 1957); Daniel M. Berman, *It is So Ordered: The
Supreme Court Rules on School Segregation* (New York, 1966); Gary

Orfield, *Reconstruction of Southern Education: The Schools and the 1964 Civil Rights Act* (New York, 1969); Numan V. Bartley, *The Rise of Massive Resistance: Race and Politics in the South in the 1950s* (Baton Rouge, 1969).

28. Among many reflecting the interracial theme, see Brown, *History of Education of Negroes in North Carolina*; Edward Jones, *Candle in the Dark*; James P. Brawley, *Two Centuries of Methodist Concern: Bondage Freedom and Education of Black People* (New York, 1974); and the sources cited in note 25 on philanthropy in Black education. Not all who developed interracialism as a theme were integrationists. Early in this period, some writers lauded interracial cooperation as a means to ease the harsher aspects of educational discrimination and make separate truly equal. See e.g., William Davis, *Negro Education in East Texas;* Jones, *Jeanes Teacher;* Wilson, *Education for Negroes in Mississippi.*

29. Marion Wright, *Education of Negroes in New Jersey,* 194; Reddick, "Education of Negroes where Separate Schools are not Equal," esp. 300; John W. Davis, "Negro Land-Grant College," *J. of Negro Ed. 2* (1933): 315; McGinnis, *Education of Negroes in Ohio,* xii; Robert G. Newby and David B. Tyack, "Victims without Crimes: Some Historical Perspectives on Black Education," *J. of Negro Ed.* 40 (1971): 192-206; Myrdal, *An American Dilemma: The Negro Problem and Modern Democracy* (New York, 1944).

30. Ambrose Caliver, "Certain Significant Developments in the Education of Negroes during the Last Generation," *J. of Negro Hist.* 35 (1950): 34.

31. Gallagher, *American Caste and the Negro College,* xiii-xiv.

32. Harlan, *Separate and Unequal,* xvii; others in this dissenting tradition include Knox, "Origins and Development of the Negro Separate School"; and Herbert Aptheker, "Literacy, the Negro and World War II," *J. of Negro Ed.* 15 (1946): 595-602; Bond, *Negro Education in Alabama;* Bond, *Educ.of the Negro.* Bond moved closer to liberal integrationism by the 1960s, however. In 1934 he wrote that it was "highly possible that [the] day will never come" when Blacks would become "full participants in the American social order." (*Educ. of the Negro,* 4). However, in the new preface and conclusion to this book, written in 1966, he expressed a cautious optimism toward assimilation, and embraced the "tangle of pathologies" explanation of Black culture. Thus he appears to have abandoned his focus on systemic bases for oppression, and rooted his analysis in the family and culture of Black America instead.

33. Bullock, *Negro Education in the South,* xiv-xi, and passim.

34. Bullock, *Negro Education in the South,* 34, 60-88.

35. Bullock, *Negro Education in the South,* 188; Bond, *Negro Education in Alabama,* 289.

36. Thomas L. Webber, *Deep like the Rivers: Education in the Slave*

Quarter Community, 1831–1865 (New York, 1978); Janet Cornelius, "We Slipped and Learned to Read: Slave Accounts of the Literacy Process, 1830–1865," *Phylon* 44 (Sept. 1983): 171–86; John W. Blassingame, *The Slave Community: Plantation Life in the Antebellum South* (New York, 1972); Blassingame, *Black New Orleans, 1860–1880* (Chicago, 1973); Eugene D. Genovese, *Roll, Jordan, Roll: The World the Slaves Made* (New York, 1974). Cf. Peter Kolchin, "Reevaluating the Antebellum Slave Community: A Comparative Perspective," *Journal of American History* 70 (Dec. 1983): 759–601

37. Doxie Wilkerson, "Ghetto School Struggles in Historical Perspective," *Sci. and Soc.* 33 (1969): 130-49; Marsha Hurst, "Integration, Freedom of Choice and Community Control in Nineteenth Century Brooklyn," *J. of Ethnic Studies* 3 (Fall 1975): 3-55; Carleton Mabee, *Black Education in New York State: From Colonial to Modern Times* (Syracuse, 1979); Linda Marie Perkins, "Quaker Beneficence and Black Control: The Institute for Colored Youth, 1852-1903," in *New Perspectives*, eds. Franklin and Anderson, 19-43; Judy Jolley Mohraz, *The Separate Problem: Case Studies of Black Education in the North, 1900-1930* (Westport, CT, 1979); Vincent P. Franklin, *The Education of Black Philadelphia: The Social and Educational History of a Minority Community, 1900-1950* (Philadelphia, 1979); Phillip T. K. Daniel, "A History of Discrimination Against Black Students in Chicago Secondary Schools," *Hist. of Ed. Q.* 20 (1980): 147-162; Michael W. Homel, *Down from Equality: Black Chicagoans and the Public Schools, 1920-1941* (Urbana, 1984); Doris Pieroth, "With All Deliberate Caution: School Integration in Seattle, 1954-1968," *Pac. Northwest Q.* 73 (1982): 50-61; John L. Rury, "The New York African Free School, 1827-1836: Conflict Over Community Control of Black Education," *Phylon* 44 (1983): 187-97; among others cited below.

38. Studies of Black students include Herbert Aptheker, "Negro College Students in the 1920s," *Sci. and Soc.* 33 (1969): 150-67; W. E. Bigglestone, "Oberlin College and Negro Students," *J. of Negro Hist.* 56 (1971): 198-215; Raymond Wolters, *The New Negro on Campus: Black College Rebellions of the 1920s* (Princeton, 1975); Cynthia Griggs Flemming, "The Effect of Higher Education on Black Tennesseans after the Civil War," *Phylon* 44 (1983): 209-16; Donald Spivey, "The Black Athlete in Big Time Intercollegiate Sports, 1941-1968," *Phylon* 44 (1983): 116-25; Linda M. Perkins, "The Impact of the 'Cult of True Womanhood' on the Education of Black Women," *J. of Social Issues* 39 (1983): 17-28; and Bertram Wyatt-Brown, "Black Schooling during Reconstruction," in *The Web of Southern Social Relations: Women, Family, and Education,* ed. W. J. Fraser, Jr., et al (Athens, GA, 1985), 46-65. On White teachers in Black education, see

Jacqueline Jones, *Soldiers of Light and Love: Northern Teachers and Georgia Blacks, 1865-1873* (Chapel Hill, 1980); Sandra Small, "The Yankee Schoolmarm in Freedmen's Schools: An Analysis of Attitudes," *Journal of Southern History* 45 (1979): 381-402; Philip S. Foner and Josephine F. Pacheco, *Three Who Dared: Prudence Crandall, Margaret Douglass, Myrtilla Miner: Champions of Antebellum Black Education* (Westport, CT, 1984). On Black teachers, see Howard N. Rabinowitz, "Half a Loaf: The Shift from White to Black Teachers in the Negro Schools of the Urban South, 1865-1890," *J. of Southern Hist.* 40 (1974): 565-94; Cynthia Griggs Fleming, "The Plight of Black Educators in Postwar Tennessee," *J. of Negro Hist.* 64 (1979): 355-364; Art Evans and Annette M. Evans, "Black Educators before and after 1960," *Phylon* 43 (1982): 254-63; Robert C. Morris, *Reading, 'Riting, and Reconstruction: The Education of Freedmen in the South, 1861-1870* (Chicago, 1981), 85-130; Ronald E. Butchart, "'We Best Can Instruct Our Own People': New York African-Americans in the Freedmen's Schools, 1861-1875," in *Afro-Americans in New York Life and History* (1988), 12, in press; and biographies of Black educators such as Louis R. Harlan, *Booker T. Washington,* 2 vols., (1972; reprint, New York, 1983); Kenneth R. Manning, *Black Apollo of Science: The Life of Ernest Everett Just* (New York, 1983); Linda O. McMurray, *George Washington Carver: Scientist and Symbol* (New York, 1981); Joe M. Richardson, "Francis L. Cardozo: Black Educator during Reconstruction," *J. of Negro Ed.* 48 (1979): 73- 83; and Linda M. Perkins, "Heed Life's Demands: The Educational Philosophy of Fanny Jackson Coppin," *J. of Negro Educ.* 51 (1982): 181-90.

39. Timothy L. Smith, "Native Blacks and Foreign Whites: Varying Responses to Educational Opportunity in America, 1880-1950," *Perspectives in Am. Hist.* 6 (1972): 309-35; Selwyn K. Troen, *The Public and the Schools: Shaping the St. Louis System, 1838-1920* (Columbia, 1975), 91-98; Alejandro Portes and Kenneth Wilson, "Black-White Differences in Educational Attainment," *Am. Soc. R.* 41 (1976): 414-31.

40. Stephen Jay Gould, *The Mismeasure of Man* (New York, 1981); Allan Chase, *Legacy of Malthus: The Social Costs of the New Scientific Racism* (Urbana, 1980).

41. Ronald E. Butchart, *Northern Schools, Southern Blacks, and Reconstruction: Freedmen's Education, 1862-1875* (Westport, CT, 1980); Joe M. Richardson, *Christian Reconstruction: The American Missionary Association and Southern Blacks, 1861-1890* (Athens, GA, 1986); Jones, *Soldiers of Light and Love;* Morris, *Reading, 'Riting, and Reconstruction;* Roberta Sue Alexander, "Hostility and Hope: Black Education in North Carolina during Presidential Reconstruction, 1865-1867," *No. Car. Hist. R.* 53 (1976): 113-32;

Keith Wilson, "Education as a Vehicle of Racial Control: Major General N. P. Banks in Louisiana, 1863-1864," *J. of Negro Ed.* 50 (1981): 156-70. Curiously, James M. McPherson, *The Struggle for Equality: Abolitionists and the Negro in the Civil War and Reconstruction* (Princeton, 1964), esp. 154-77, which anticipated many of the later revisionist arguments, was generally ignored by historians of Black education.

42. James D. Anderson, "The Hampton Model of Normal School Industrial Education, 1868-1900," in *New Perspectives,* eds. Franklin and Anderson, 61-96; see also Harlan, *Booker T. Washington.* Robert G. Sherer, *Subordination or Liberation? The Development and Conflicting Theories of Black Education in Nineteenth Century Alabama* (University, 1977); and James M. McPherson, *The Abolitionist Legacy: From Reconstruction to the NAACP* (Princeton, 1975), 203-33, contribute to Willard Range's assertion that the liberal arts remained as the core of most secondary and higher education curricula. Also on industrial education, see Allen W. Jones, "The Role of Tuskegee in the Education of Black Farmers," *J. of Negro Hist.* 40 (1975): 252-67.

43. James D. Anderson, "Northern Foundations and the Shaping of Southern Black Rural Education, 1902-1935," *Hist. of Ed. Q.* 18 (1978): 371-96; Anderson, "The Southern Improvement Company: Northern Reformers' Investment in Negro Cotton Tenancy, 1900-1920," *Ag. Hist.* 52 (1978): 31; Anderson, "Northern Philanthropy and the Training of the Black Leadership: Fisk University, a Case Study, 1915-1930," in *New Perspectives,* eds. Franklin and Anderson, 97-112; Anderson, "Education as a Vehicle for the Manipulation of Black Workers," in *Work, Technology, and Education: Dissenting Essays in the Intellectual Foundations of American Education,* eds. W. Feinberg and H. Rosemont, Jr. (Urbana, 1975), 15-40; Don Quinn Kelley, "Ideology and Education: Uplifting the Masses in Nineteenth Century Alabama," *Phylon* 40 (1979): 147-58; J. M. Stephen Peeps, "Northern Philanthropy and the Emergence of Black Higher Education—DoGooders, Compromisers, or Co-conspirators?" *J. of Negro Ed.* 50 (1981): 251-69; Donald Spivey, *Schooling for the New Slavery: Black Industrial Education, 1868-1915* (Westport, CT, 1978).

44. Institutional biographies include Edward A. Jones, *Candle in the Dark: A History of Morehouse College* (Valley Forge, PA, 1967); Rayford W. Logan, *Howard University: The First Hundred Years, 1867-1967* (New York, 1969); Clarence A. Bacote, *The Story of Atlanta University: A Century of Service, 1865-1965* (Atlanta, GA, 1969); Horace Mann Bond, *Education for Freedom: A History of Lincoln University, Pennsylvania* (Lincoln University, PA, 1976); Leland Stanford Cozart, *A Venture of Faith: Barber Scotia College, 1867-*

1967 (Concord, NC, 1976); Clarice T. Campbell and Oscar Allan Rogers, Jr., *Mississippi: The View from Tougaloo* (Jackson, Miss., 1979); Zella J. Black Patterson, *Langston University: A History* (Norman, OK, 1979); and Joe M. Richardson, *A History of Fisk University, 1865-1946* (University, AL, 1980). On other issues in higher education, see e.g., John E. Fleming, *The Lengthening Shadow of Slavery: A Historical Justification for Affirmative Action for Blacks in Higher Education* (Washington, 1976); Samuel H. Shannon, "Land-Grant College Legislation and Black Tennesseans: A Case Study in the Politics of Education," Hist. of Ed. Q. 22 (1982): 139-57; Ralph L. Pearson, "Reflections on Black Colleges: The Historical Perspective of Charles S. Johnson," Hist. of Ed. Q. 23 (1983): 55-68. On Black professional training and organizations, see Alfred A. Moss, Jr., *The American Negro Academy: Voice of the Talented Tenth* (Baton Rouge, 1981), 304; see also James Summerville, Educating Black Doctors: A History of Meharry Medical College (University, AL, 1983); Darlene Clark Hine, "The Pursuit of Professional Equality: Meharry Medical College, 1921-1938, A Case Study," in *New Perspectives,* eds. Franklin and Anderson, 173-92; Kellis E. Parker and Betty J. Stebman, "Legal Education for Blacks," *Annals of the Am. Acad. of Pol. and Soc. Sci.* 407 (1973): 144-55; Genna Rae McNeil, "To Meet the Group Needs: The Transformation of Howard University School of Law, 1920-1935," in *New Perspectives,* eds. Franklin and Anderson, 149-71; Thelma D. Perry, *The History of the American Teachers Association* (Washington, 1975); Ernest J. Middleton, "The Louisiana Education Association, 1901-1970," *J. of Negro Ed.* 47 (1978): 363-78.

45. Homel, *Down from Equality;* Bernard Schwartz, *Swann's Way: The Second Busing Case and the Supreme Court* (New York, 1986); Richard A. Pride and J. David Woodard, *The Burden of Busing: The Politics of Desegregation in Nashville* (Knoxville, 1985); George R. Metcalf, *From Little Rock to Boston: The History of School Desegregation* (Westport, CT, 1983); Meyer Weinberg, *A Chance to Learn: A History of Race and Education in the United States* (Cambridge, 1977); Richard Kluger, *Simple Justice: The History of Brown v. Board of Education and Black America's Struggle for Equality* (New York, 1976); David A. Gerber, "Education, Expediency, and Ideology: Race and Politics in the Desegregation of Ohio Public Schools in the Late 19th Century," *J. of Ethnic Studies* 1 (Fall 1973): 1-31; Pieroth, *With All Deliberate Caution: School Integration in Seattle, 1954-1968,* 50-61; J. Morgan Kousser, "Making Separate Equal: Integration of Black and White Schools Funds in Kentucky," *J. of Interdisciplinary Hist.* 10 (1980): 399-428; John Caughey, *To Kill a Child's Spirit: The Tragedy of School Segregation in Los Angeles* (Itasca, ILL, 1973); Alton Hornsby, Jr., "The Freedmen's Bureau

Schools in Texas, 1865-1870," *Southwestern Hist. Q.* 76 (1973): 397-417. Raymond Wolters, *The Burden of Brown: Thirty Years of School Desegregation* (Knoxville, TN, 1984), deals with segregation, but fits better within one of the possible post-revisionist camps described later rather than in a discussion of revisionism.

46. Mary Aickin Rothschild, "The Volunteers and the Freedom Schools: Education for Social Change in Mississippi," *Hist. of Ed. 0.* 22 (1982): 401-20; Everett E. Abney, "A Comparison of the Status of Florida's Black Public School Principals, 1965-66/1975-76," *J. of Negro Ed.* 49 (1980): 398-406; Donald L. W. Howie, "The Image of Black People in Brown v. Board of Education," *J. of Black Studies* 3 (1973): 371-84; Vincent Franklin, "Persistence of School Segregation in the Urban North," *J. of Ethnic Studies* 1 (1974): 51-68.

47. State studies include Mabee, *Black Education in New York State*; Lester F. Russell, *Black Baptist Secondary Schools in Virginia, 1887-1957* (Metuchen, NJ, 1981); John I. Scott, *The Education of Black People in Florida* (Philadelphia, 1974); James C. Carper, "The Popular Ideology of Segregated Schooling: Attitudes toward the Education of Blacks in Kansas, 1854-1900," *Kansas Hist.* 1 (1978): 254-65. Among urban studies, see Homel, *Down from Equality*; Franklin, *Education of Black Philadelphia*; Mohraz, *Separate Problem*; June 0. Patton, "The Black Community of Augusta and the Struggle for Ware High School, 1880-1899," in *New Perspectives*, eds. Franklin and Anderson, 45-59.

48. Interracialism is central to Jones, *Soldiers of Light and Love*; Richardson, *Christian Reconstruction*; McPherson, *Abolitionist Legacy*; Rothschild, "The Volunteers and the Freedom Schools"; Florence Howe, "Mississippi's Freedom Schools," *Harvard Ed. R.* 35 (1965): 141-60. More critical studies include Butchart, *Northern Schools, Southern Blacks, and Reconstruction*; Harlan, *Booker T. Washington*; Wolters, *The New Negro on Campus*; Perkins, "Quaker Beneficence and Black Control." See note 45 for studies of segregation and desegregation.

49. Homel, *Down from Equality*; Weinberg, *A Chance to Learn*; Spivey, *Schooling for the New Slavery*; Troen, *The Public and the Schools*, 91-98; Edmund Fuller, *Prudence Crandall: An Incident of Racism in Nineteenth-Century Connecticut* (Middletown, CT, 1971): among others.

50. Wilkerson, "Ghetto School Struggles in Historical Perspective," 145; see also Butchart, *Northern Schools, Southern Blacks, and Reconstruction*; Wilson, "Education as a Vehicle of Racial Control"; Fleming, *The Lengthening Shadow of Slavery*; and citations to Anderson in notes 42 and 43.

51. Mohraz, *Separate Problem*; and studies cited in note 36.

52. Moss, *The American Negro Academy*; Franklin, *Education of Black*

Philadelphia; Webber, *Deep like the Rivers*; Mabee, *Black Education in New York State*; Sherer, *Liberation or Subordination?*; Cozart, *A Venture of Faith*.

53. Wilkerson, "Ghetto School Struggles," 146.
54. This tendency is still embryonic, but can be detected in such general work as Nicholas Lemann, "The Origins of the Underclass," *Atlantic Monthly* 257 (June 1986): 31-55, and 258 (July 1986): 54-68; and more specific studies such as Wolters, *Burden of Brown*; and Thomas Sowell, *Education: Assumptions versus History: Collected Papers* (Stanford, CA, 1986).

Chapter Five

The Search For Access And Content In The Education Of African-Americans

Joan Davis Ratteray
Institute for Independent Education

The education of African-Americans has been profoundly shaped throughout history by two major problems. One is access to educational opportunities and the other is the quality of accessible schooling. Unfortunately, the struggle for access diverted the energies of African-Americans from the task of designing and providing quality schooling. In addition, the content of the schooling that African-Americans did receive was designed to meet the needs of politically empowered European-Americans and not the particular needs of African-Americans.

Against this backdrop, African-Americans have a rich tradition of developing independent educational institutions that have often been vital to the survival of their communities. This quest for independence began long before the abolition of slavery. It has at its core the ideas of liberty that have existed since the first African was brought involuntarily to North American shores. This movement toward independent institutions was a partial solution to the problem of access, and it has consistently focused on the problem of redefining content in order to provide quality education for African-Americans.

These conflicts did not exist merely as unique events on an historical continuum. There are, in fact, strong parallels with many of the problems confronting educators in the education of African-American youth today.

The Struggle for Access

Throughout the early history of the United States, African-Americans were accorded varying degrees of personal freedom. The pathways leading them to educational institutions were strewn with uncertainties. Access to schooling was possible in some instances but only under very prescribed conditions; at other times, the door was closed completely. In the struggle for access, however, African-Americans have explored several educational options, including the so-called "élite" private schools, common or public schools, religiously affiliated schools, and schools developed by and for African-Americans themselves.

Access to Elite Private Schools

Elite private schools are schools that have had the historical role of educating what are often referred to as the "upper class" or "upper income" levels of American society. This group consists primarily of relatively affluent European-Americans and their descendants, and access to these schools for African-Americans has always been considered highly experimental.

The purpose of these schools has been to inculcate students with cultural values, languages, religions, history, political theories, and economic systems in the European tradition.[1] They have tended to be financially and socially inaccessible to the masses of American students regardless of their cultural background. They have also operated, explicitly or implicitly, on the theory that only a few Africans and African-Americans could be saved from their "inferior" lot in life and be elevated to higher levels in the dominant society.

African-Americans gained access to these schools if they were considered to have exceptional ability and talent. They were usually placed there for particular purposes, which have changed only superficially over time. Reports show that in the late 19th century, African-American students "won top scholastic honors, merit scholarships, student elections and top leadership positions and moved on to leading colleges."[2] However, these youngsters were the excep-

124

tion rather than the rule and were very often the only African-Americans in an entire school. There were few of the social, cultural, or economic supports needed to sustain greater numbers of African-Americans. Essentially, educating African-Americans was a "sport" designed to intellectually uplift European-American youth rather than African-American youth.[3]

By the 1950s, there was a movement in the United States to desegregate public and private educational facilities. Elite schools responded by providing greater access to African-American youngsters.[4] This was motivated largely by moral, legal, and demographic imperatives, although in some instances, school authorities felt an obligation to make charitable gestures toward the poor and the oppressed. Legal mandates and federal guidelines, such as the *Brown* decision in 1954, the federal civil rights legislation of the 1960s, and enforcement of the Internal Revenue Service regulations on nondiscriminatory policies at tax-exempt institutions helped stem the exclusion of African-Americans. There was also a growing awareness of changing demographics as the number of school-age children among African-Americans and other cultural groups increased.

Finally, private colleges also began looking for well-prepared African-American youngsters. Pilot programs such as "Project ABC: A Better Chance" and "Independent Schools Talent Search" were designed to recruit African-American students and match them carefully with selected college preparatory schools. Early in 1982, ABC examined the effects of its program.[5] They considered the ABC program to be "a primary intervention, whereby children are moved from their local schools to others that might provide a stronger program."[6]

The ABC survey revealed that 76% of the ABC alumni respondents were African-Americans. These youngsters came from relatively large working-class and lower middle-class families. The alumni were said to exhibit positive self-concepts, were more oriented toward persons than things, were sociable, and showed strong task orientation and perseverance.

Access to the "Public School" or "Common School"

The second educational option was the "common" or public school, which traditionally has been regarded as the vehicle for schooling the masses. African-Americans originally were not included in this concept but subsequently began a concerted effort to make themselves included.

Legal mandates in various states prohibited African-American children from enjoying common schools. As early as 1740, laws were passed in South Carolina prohibiting the teaching of African-Americans. Nevertheless, in 1774, free African-Americans in Charleston, South Carolina, were educating their children in defiance of the law. Some children of enslaved Africans were able to attend school. Independent schools in the South were educational centers where free African-Americans were learning and where European-Americans could volunteer to work as missionaries. After Nat Turner's revolt in 1831, a general blanket of legal prohibitions against African-American education descended until 1861. The threat of getting caught breaking the law isolated the masses of African-Americans.[7] African-Americans began pushing for civil rights as early as the 1830s. For example, over 100 years before the 1954 *Brown* decision, in *Roberts v. City of Boston* (1849), African-American parents in Boston fought for integrated education because they believed that separate tax-supported schools were inferior in quality and lacked the necessary equipment. Even though this case became the precedent for cases involving legal segregation, Franklin notes, African-Americans realized that "public schools would not be the means through which they would attain full social, economic and political equality."[8]

The Reconstruction Act of 1867 extended the powers of the Freedmen's Bureau and led to military rule over a network of schools for African-Americans. African-American leaders in this era continued the process by assisting in passing legislation in several states designed to increase government control over education.[9] As a result, many private schools were merged with state schools.

The overwhelming majority of African-Americans were not in integrated common schools or separate tax-supported schools but attended private schools. By 1916, there were 653 schools for African-Americans. Of this number, 507 were religiously affiliated schools. There were 118 independent schools not affiliated with religious philanthropy, and only 28 were under public control.[10] However, the struggle to gain access to separate tax-supported schools that began in the 1840s eventually overshadowed the growth of independent schools for African-Americans. In fact, independent schools were seen as threatening the pursuit of racial harmony, contributing to unequal rights in the established social order, and taking away from public resources that should be directed to African-American communities in general.

Gradually, with the exception of a select group of schools, sources of private philanthropy for African-American schools dried up. Independent schools were politically isolated from the African-American community and almost completely lost their client base. The schooling of African-Americans was taken over by a federal and state government monopoly and with the blessings of civil rights advocates who stressed integration into the U.S. mainstream.

Tax-supported separate schools for African-American youngsters became schools for the masses, and they were generally considered to be in poor condition. African-American youth were left with substandard "public" facilities and little hope of an opportunity to attend any independent alternative. It was reported in the 1930s that African-Americans received less than two-fifths of the fair share of funds for public schools.[11] Today, over 90% of all African-American school-age children attend public or government-supported schools. The quality of education in many of these schools once more is considered well below the standards needed to meet national needs.

Access to Religious Educational Institutions

The third option for African-American education was aid from religious or missionary groups to educational institutions that were designed specifically for African-American youngsters. These religious groups were often at the forefront in demonstrating institutional tolerance. It was their response to the pluralistic nature of a demographically changing U.S. society. The first of these groups were the Quakers, who protested in word and deed against African enslavement and opened schools as early as the 1770s.

The first Roman Catholic school for African-American youth was opened in 1828 through the guidance of the Oblate Sisters of Providence, an African-American order of nuns. This school still operates today in Baltimore, Maryland, as an independent institution under the name of St. Frances-Charles Hall High School. The Sisters of the Holy Family, a different order of African-American nuns, founded St. Mary's Academy in New Orleans, Louisiana, in 1867. The opening of Catholic schools for African-Americans became official policy of the church by the end of the 19th century. Separate parish schools remained diocesan policy throughout the United States until the end of World War II.[12] The voluntary desegregation of these parochial schools began in the 1940s.

Catholic schools today have the largest population of African-

Americans in private schools.[13] Most studies note that African-Americans achieve at much higher levels in these schools than they do in public schools.[14] A National Catholic Educational Association study[15] found that 22% of the students in Catholic high schools were African-American youths. These African-American students reported lower grades than others when asked to appraise their academic ability. However, they reported higher self-assessments on college ability, higher educational expectations, and higher parental expectations.[16]

Access to African-American Private Schools

The fourth option in education involved schools owned and operated by African-Americans. They can be called classical in the sense that they are the earliest embodiment of principles and strategies for self-determination in education. They have offered much more than intellectual uplift because they have been part of a search for liberty and identity. This tradition in African-American independent education has a 200-year-old history. In the 1790s African-Americans who attended racially mixed public schools in 18th century Boston were harassed to the point that learning was difficult. Prince Hall, a free African-American and veteran of the Revolutionary War, petitioned the City of Boston to establish a separate tax-supported school for Africans. When the Boston School Committee declined to make any facilities available, he started an independent school in his son's house in 1798.[17]

By the late 1980s, over 200 such schools had been identified,[18] serving over 52,000 youngsters.[19] There was a marked increase in the rate at which these schools were founded in the aftermath of the great debate about community control in urban school systems like New York, in the late 1960s and the early 1970s.[20]

Ratteray and Shujaa documented the characteristics of these schools and, through in-depth interviews, examined why parents chose them for their children. They found that most of these schools serve African-American youngsters in urban areas. Many of them were founded in the 1970s, while others began early in the 20th century, and a few are over 100 years old. Approximately one-half of the schools are religious and one-half secular. Most of them enroll more than 80% African-American youth, and their curricula stress either a cultural perspective, a religious perspective, or both. They specifically affirm ethnic or religious values and the cultural backgrounds of their students. The schools often serve a broad cross-section of economic groups, although 87% of the families have incomes of less than $49,000 annually, 57% earn less than $30,000, and 24% earn less than $15,000.

The reason cited most frequently for choosing independent schools was the nature of the learning environment. The second reason was the quality of the academic program. Less frequently mentioned, although still important, was the way these schools affirm the child's cultural background, the religious teachings and affiliations of religious schools, and the low cost of tuition.

In 1984, Craig Brookins studied 10 independent school models in the midwest and eastern sections of the U.S.[21] His findings revealed, among other things, that African-American learners who attend independent Black institutions for a portion of their schooling enter public school systems better prepared than the average student because of high academic competence and exposure to a wider variety of educational content. This education, he reports, provides a context for emphasizing the African experience and how world events affect African people.

The Struggle over Content

There has been no uniform vision, among either European-Americans or African-Americans, regarding whether African-Americans should be educated for independence or whether they should be encouraged to participate in improving the existing social order. This tension is evident in four historical trends characterized by different emphases in curriculum content.

The first of these trends was typified by the use of principles and values in religious content to instruct, motivate behavior, and give meaning to the academic subjects being taught. The second trend was to select exceptionally talented African-American learners and expose them to a classical European-centered or New England-type of formal curriculum. The third trend was to emphasize industrial training as the ideal form of schooling for African-Americans as opposed to European-Americans. The fourth trend was to expand the inclusion of African and African-American history in the public-school curriculum.

Religion-Based Content Knowledge and African-American Schooling

European and European-American religious leaders established and controlled schools to teach religious content in the curricula and to use the principles articulated in this content to spread the established social and economic order. On the other hand, many African-Americans generally resisted the specific religious content as it was delivered by Europeans and European-Americans, preferring to fashion their own institutions to meet their unique social and economic needs.

Schools for African-Americans
Controlled by European-Americans

European-Americans effectively maintained a monopoly over the content of instruction in religious schools for African-Americans. They sustained this practice by determining the reasons for creating schools and by controlling the materials with which the content was delivered.

The initial rationale Europeans and European-Americans used for becoming involved in the education of African-Americans was the saving of souls. Therefore, the Bible became the primary tool for teaching rudimentary skills in reading and writing. Beginning in the 18th century, these schools introduced many African-Americans to the world of words and expanded their consciousness of world events.

In some schools, teaching consisted mainly of giving verbal instructions and having students memorize long passages from religious texts. On the other hand, groups like the Quakers and the Catholics generally adhered to strategies for teaching "with letters" to enhance the meaning of Christian doctrines, rather than teaching merely by rote memorization. Denominations such as the Presbyterians, Methodists, and Baptists attempted to reach the masses of African-American youths through Sabbath and evening schools, teaching reading, writing, and Christian principles of deliverance. Since the masses of African-Americans were more interested in learning reading and writing than in being proselytized, these early efforts at education proved to be unsuccessful and were discontinued, but they resurfaced, however, after the Civil War. In fact, the phenomenon of African-Americans taking advantage of educational opportunities in church communities but not becoming very involved in congregational activities is similar to what is happening today in many urban Catholic dioceses. Significant numbers of African-Americans enrolled in Catholic schools are not Catholic. Many bishops have expressed their concerns in the media about this state of affairs and have offered it as a reason for closing some Catholic urban schools.

European-American religious leaders also focused on the materials that were used for the schooling of African-Americans. A major issue was whether African-Americans should be provided special materials or whether they should use the same materials as European-Americans. During the 1860s, some curriculum materials were designed specifically for African-American students. The American Tract Society was a major publisher.[22] These materials included the *Freedmen's Primer*, the *Lincoln Primer*, the *Freedmen's Spelling Book*, and other readers. They were full of Bible stories, and many of the readings provided themes on the Protestant work ethic, domesticity, temperance, and piety.[23]

Criticisms of these special materials in schools for African-Americans came from two perspectives. Some argued that these materials were condescending toward African-Americans, portraying values that helped them accept their subjugated roles in life. Others denounced the need for special materials at all, as this singled out African-Americans. A group known as the American Freedmen's Union Commission believed that "the emancipated are men; that they are entitled to the best literature which American authorship can produce and to nothing inferior or different from that used by the rest of us."[24] They recommended the use of texts such as *McGuffey's Reader, Webster's Speller*, and *Greenleaf's Arithmetic* that were standard in institutions controlled by European-Americans.

This type of debate is occurring again in the 1990s. It is prompted in part by the movement to create materials for an African-centered curriculum as well as multicultural materials for a European-centered curriculum. Although most of the contemporary debate occurs in a secular, rather than a religious setting, some African-American Christian schools are beginning to discuss the need for Biblical stories that affirm African-American cultural history in the curriculum.

Schools for African-Americans
Controlled by African-Americans

African-Americans often broke away from European-Americans and formed their own religious educational institutions to meet what they perceived were their own social and economic needs. The focus on religious content appears to have been secondary, but it has had an effect on the context in which the more secular social and economic needs have been met. These needs have included an awareness of their own cultural background, an emphasis on the theoretical basis for learning, and the professional development of women in the work force.

Bishop Payne of the African Methodist Episcopal Church stressed the need for a theoretical basis in teaching and learning. In addition to courses in the Bible and discipline, Payne included texts by established authors on English grammar, geography, ancient history, church history, natural theology, popular theory, analogy, history of Christianity, and Christian theory.[25] He brought intellectual rigor to the process of curriculum development at a time when the teaching of ministers was grounded more in inspiration than in academic soundness. Unfortunately, he retained the content of the European-centered theology promoted by the established church. This is partly due to the fact that when Richard Allen and Absalom John separated from the Methodist Episcopal Church, their break was not based on a disagreement with the established theology or instruction.

Also among those who broke away were the African-American Baptists in the 1880s. By the close of the 19th century, they had developed programs emphasizing African-American culture and achievement. An example is the Virginia Theological Seminary, which was formed when a group of African-Americans separated from the Richmond Institute in 1883.[26]

Nannie Helen Burroughs, who had the only school completely controlled and supported by the Women's Auxiliary of the National Baptist Convention, stressed the professional development of women. In her words, "This school was conceived, developed, managed, owned and controlled by Negro Christian women." Her curriculum included Christian social services, cooperatives, a program for economic security, homemaking, and public speaking.

Other African-American Christian women also founded and/or operated schools. Fannie Jackson Coppin had the first practicum in teacher training, Lucy Laney was concerned with principles of child care for teachers and parents, Mary McLeod Bethune emphasized nursing, and Charlotte Hawkins Brown focused on college preparatory courses.

A more recent phenomenon is the development of Muslim schools in 1932. These institutions were created by the Honorable Elijah Muhammad who believed that . . .

[African-American] youth were not being educated in public schools to inquire into their past, be proud of their heritage prior to slavery, think for themselves, or have a desire to become economically or otherwise independent.[27]

He specifically wanted to include the teachings of Islam in his curriculum, not only as a content area in and of itself but also as a means of shaping the context within which all other subjects were taught.[28]

The Classical European-centered or New England Curriculum

This type of schooling was considered the pinnacle of American education. It meant exposing African-Americans to a classical European-centered or New England type of curriculum. It centered learning and teaching on the intellectual traditions for knowledge, culture, and history in Europe. It included instruction in writing, grammar, diction, history, Latin, Greek, and higher mathematics. Studying these subjects was the prescribed way to understand the "civilized" world.

This type of curriculum perpetuated the notion that the reason for acquiring information is the development of the individual. Its cornerstone was the European-directed philosophy of natural rights—that all men are considered to have natural and inalienable rights to life and liberty. Most importantly, it dictated a process for efficiently transmitting information that included discipline.

One of the earliest opportunities for African-American learners to be formally exposed to a classical curriculum was in 1787 through the African Free School in New York. Along with its academic content, this school was one of the first to introduce the Lancasterian method of teaching and learning. It featured military-style regimentation and provided strict punishment, rewards, and rivalry among students. In these types of schools, however, some teaching was done by the more advanced pupils.

The African Free School was created by the New York Manumission Society. Several notable individuals, including John Jay and Alexander Hamilton, helped establish an educational curriculum that was considered solid and excellent at that time.[29] In 1835, the Society relinquished its control over the operations of the school to the Public School Society. Many African-American parents became very upset with the new curriculum, the selection of textbooks, and discipline in the schools. Several years after the new management took over, teachers in the schools petitioned to change the name of the school, replacing the word "African" with "Colored." Changing the name helped change the context for learning: It de-emphasized African, which denoted both a land base and a specific culture. It also encouraged Africans to melt without a foundation into the public school mainstream, a position which is very similar to that taken by the contemporary opposition to African-centered multicultural education.[30]

Another leading institution providing classical studies to African-American youth was The Institute for Colored Youth in Philadelphia. Its curriculum included history, geography, English grammar, critical reading, Latin, composition and rhetoric, algebra, plane and spherical geometry, trigonometry, natural philosophy, and chemistry. This Quaker-controlled school often was led by African-American graduates from schools such as Oberlin, Wilberforce, Yale, and Harvard. By 1913, it became known as Cheyney Training School for Teachers. The curriculum changed from literary studies to industrial and normal training. Its focus became the preparation of teachers to serve in public schools for the masses of African-Americans.

At the turn of the century, between 1890 and 1904, the teaching of African-American youths was affected by another important change: the development of high schools. High schools were considered to be the best foundation for preparing teachers. However, they were a missing link in the schooling of African-American youth. The high school model recommended four parallel courses of study—classical Latin, science, modern languages, and English—and the number of African-American schools that met these conditions were few.[31] Funds were allocated nationally to develop high schools for European-Americans as a transition from elementary school to college. African-Americans, on the other hand, were given rudimentary content in elementary schools and in what were called "Negro colleges," but they were not given the necessary intervening stage that secondary schools provided. The clamor to establish colleges eclipsed the orderly intellectual training for African-American youth and the strengthening of an appropriate pedagogy through high school curricula. Consequently, the "Negro college," which was supported primarily by private sources, was forced to bridge the gap and offered all three levels of schooling.[32] Often, these schools were required to reduce their emphasis on classical studies in order to accommodate the need for teachers in the expanding public schools for African-American youth.

Industrial Education

The third type of schooling prescribed for African-Americans was intended to provide an industrial education that would enable African-American children and adults to read and write in order to do arithmetic, plain accounts, and needlepoint or to use their hands to cultivate the soil. Unfortunately, industrial education did not train young African-Americans to utilize the new technologies of the day. Positions such as electrical and mechanical engineering, assembly line workers, and other manufacturing positions, for the most part, were closed to African-Americans.

Some African-American leaders felt that education must have an economic underpinning, but this view was not adopted whole-heartedly by the masses of African-Americans. Frederick Douglass took the position that manual training would accentuate the "mechanical genius" of African-Americans, enabling them to get a job and become self-sustaining. His support gave new impetus to industrial education. Others believed that manual labor pedagogy might lead to economic equality and strong participation by African-Americans in the American economic order.

Many African-American young men, challenged by the notion that the African-American mind was intellectually inferior, recoiled from the idea that they should cultivate the use of their hands. They often became preoccupied with pursuing classical studies, ridiculing and shunning work with the hands. However, the seeds for conflict and disillusionment were being sown because employment for classically educated African-American men was scarce outside of the ministry and teaching.

Most of the population of African-American youth at the turn of the 20th century was in the South, and most African-American learners were considered to be candidates for industrial education. Booker T. Washington subscribed to the view that industrial education was for the masses of the people who had to toil and that young people needed it to support themselves.[33]

On the other hand, W. E. B. DuBois favored the New England style of literary training described earlier. He took the opposite view toward industrial education, writing:

It has helped bridge the transition period between Negro slavery and freedom. It has taught thousands of white people in the South to accept Negro education, not simply as a necessary evil, but as a possible social good. It has brought state support to a dozen higher institutions of learning, and to some extent, to a system of public schools. On the other hand, it has tempered and rationalized the inner emancipation of American Negroes. It made the Negro patient when impatience would have killed him.[34]

The Focus on Africa and African-American History
The fourth trend in African-American education has been to focus on Africa as a way to reinvigorate academic content for African-American youth and provide them with the self-knowledge that can lead to greater productivity in society.

The masses of African-American youth have never been exposed to a formal school curriculum that stresses an African frame of reference. The history of Africa and Africans in the Americas has not been placed in the formal order of knowledge as it is presented in the American educational system as a whole. In fact, the curricula in most schools, including many African-American independent schools, seem to be patterned on European curriculum models. Some African-American history materials and celebrations have been added in an ad hoc manner, but there is no coherent plan for the selection, introduction, usage, and evaluation of these materials.[35]

The movement to focus on Africa seeks to address directly and openly two major questions for independant schools. First, if the education of African-Americans relies heavily on European constructs and content, how can it be independent? Second, if independent schools are characterized as errant institutional responses, growing out of disillusionment with life in a European-American society, how can an independent African-American perspective sustain any intellectual integrity of its own?

Putting African and African-American History in the Classroom
This process began formally with the work of Arthur Schomburg who pointed out that there was enough known about the contributions of African-Americans to justify having "a chair of Negro history."[36]

W. E. B. DuBois, whose extensive writings stretched from 1896 to 1961, wrote that the guiding force in developing African-Americans and their leaders is a knowledge of African history and social development, as well as the history of Africans in the Americas.[37]

Carter G. Woodson, a scholar and voluminous author, contended that some African-Americans who presented themselves as educated were in fact "mis-educated" because they had been taught to admire the achievements of their oppressors and feel contempt for their own people.[38] He associated the study of history with freedom when he declared that we must use history "to build a future in which [African-Americans] can become true Americans in our nation dedicated to the concepts of freedom and unity without reference to race, creed or color."[39]

The National Association of Teachers in Colored Schools, later renamed the American Teachers Association, was one of the earliest national bodies that helped to raise the consciousness of teachers about teaching the history of African-Americans in their own classrooms. Carter G. Woodson had a major role in the ATA, systematically documenting historical materials and publishing material that reached African-American children.

Marcus Garvey actually developed what he called a "Course of African Philosophy" which he used in at least two schools he started, the Booker T. Washington University in Harlem, New York, and Liberty University in Claremont, Virginia.[40] However, Garvey's philosophy does not appear to be taken directly from Africa; rather, he developed a philosophy for Africans on the continent and in the diaspora.[41]

Twenty years ago Lerone Bennett, the historian, placed on the shoulders of African-American educators themselves the responsibility for developing "a new grammar which transcends the inherent limitations of white categories."[42]

These earlier efforts are today being incorporated in the curricula at independent schools, especially those that are attempting to examine their curricula from an African frame of reference. Ratteray and Shujaa describe how the Council of Independent African-American Institutions (CIBI), a national support group for these schools, was formed out of a movement for community control of public education in the 1960s.[43] Although this movement was aborted by public school officials, CIBI has continued to emphasize quality academic preparation in an African-centered cultural and historical context through independent schools.

Developing Guiding Principles for Teaching and Learning

A significant milestone of the 1960s was the emergence of the Nguzo Saba, a value system that emphasizes *Umoja* (unity), *Kujichagulia* (self-determination), *Ujima* (collective work and responsibility), *Ujamaa* (cooperative economics), *Nia* (purpose), *Kuumba* (creativity), and *Imani* (faith).[44] The Nguzo Saba and its derivative, the celebration of Kwanzaa, were created by Maulana Karenga from his study of the traditional African experience.[45]

A number of independent schools use these principles to organize their school curricula and teaching. CIBI has designed, in the context of these principles, a curriculum guide that includes both academic objectives for various grades from pre-primary through middle-school levels and criteria for evaluation.[46]

Scholarly attempts to study the teaching and learning of African-centered content have had little support from the American educational mainstream. For example, in 1936, only 5 institutions serving African-Americans offered instruction at the graduate level.[47] Those institutions were Fisk, Hampton, Atlanta, and Xavier and Howard. With the exception of Howard University, which is largely supported by the federal government, the other four were independent schools. Today, only one institution, Temple University, has a program that grants a Ph.D. in African-American Studies.

In other words, African-Americans have few options in the study of independent education and the structural determinants that make up the elements of an African frame of reference. Potential scholars must rely on the work of mainstream educators who have defined, almost entirely from a European perspective, the content of a "good" academic education and the controls that must be exercised over the process for setting standards of excellence. These scholars must follow both a stringent code of behavior for admission to the ranks of those considered qualified to make a scholarly pursuit of the subject and a prescribed path for research.

Prospects for the Future

Now is the time to identify in a scholarly fashion the strengths of African-American teachers and learners and to use those strengths in building a new curriculum. This curriculum should have valid, theoretically based assumptions about African-Americans and the purpose of education, as well as a clear vision of the specific elements needed in that curriculum. In this process of developing a theory of African-American teaching and learning, it is not enough to simply declare that Activity X or Activity Y is African-centered. We must be prepared to document the sources of our assumptions and ground them firmly in history, languages, cultural traditions, and other aspects of the African and African-American heritage. In addition, it will be equally important to develop effective evaluation instruments and techniques for both teachers and learners in the African-American community.

Notes and References

1. Joan Davis Ratteray, *Center Shift* (Washington, DC: Institute for Independent Education, 1990), 17.

2. D. Mallery, *Negro Students in Independent Schools* (Boston: National Association of Independent Schools, 1963), 50.

3. C. Johnson, *Negro College Graduate* (New York: Negro Universities Press, 1938), 304.

4. W. Speed-Franklin, "Ethnic Diversity: Patterns and Implications of Minorities in Independent Schools," in *Visible Now*, ed. D. Slaughter and D. Johnson, 21-31 (Westport: Greenwood Press, 1988), 22-23.

5. S. T. Johnson and S. E. Prom, *Science and Mathematics Career Choice Among Talented Minority Graduates of A Better Chance, Final Report to the Ford Foundation* (Boston: A Better Chance, 1984).

6. J. B. Griffin and S. Johnson, "Making a Difference for a New Generation: The ABC Story," in *Visible Now*, ed. D. Slaughter and D. Johnson (Westport: Greenwood Press, 1988), 35.

7. *Acts of the General Assembly of the State of North Carolina of 1830-1831* (Raleigh, North Carolina), 11; L. Fishel and B. Quarles, *The Black American: A Documentary History* (New York: Scott Foresman, 1970), 102.

8. V. Franklin, "American Values, Social Goals, and the Desegregated School: A Historical Perspective," in *New Perspectives in Black Educational History*, ed. V. Franklin and J. Andersen (Boston: G. K. Hall, 1978), 195.

9. Bureau of Education, *Report of the U.S. Bureau of Education* (Washington, DC: U.S. Government Printing Office, 1875), 283.

10. T. Jones, *Negro Education: A Study of Private and Higher Schools for Colored People in the United States* (1916; reprint, New York: Arno Press and the New York Times, 1969), 303.

11. T. Perry, "Colored Public High Schools. Remarks Delivered in 1907 by W. T. B. Williams at the Annual Hampton Negro Conference," in *History of the American Teachers Association* (Washington, DC: National Education Association, 1975).

12. V. Franklin and E. McDonald, "Blacks in Urban Catholic Schools in the United States: A Historical Perspective," in *Visible Now*, ed. D. Slaughter and D. Johnson, 93-108 (Westport: Greenwood Press, 1988), 97.

13. *African-American Enrollment in Independent Schools, 1988-89*, Research Notes, no. 6 (Washington, DC: Institute for Independent Education, 1990).

14. A. Greeley, *Catholic High Schools and Minority Students* (New Brunswick, New Jersey: Transaction Books, 1982); T. Keith and E. Page, "Do Catholic High Schools Improve Minority Student Achievement?," *American Educational Research Journal* 22 (1985): 337-349; V. Blum, "Private Elementary Education in the Inner City," *Phi Delta Kappan* 66 (1985): 644.

15. P. L. Benson et al., *Catholic High Schools: Their Impact on Low Income Students* (Washington, DC: National Catholic Educational Association, 1986).

16. M. Barnds, "Black Students in Low-Income Serving Catholic High Schools: An Overview of Findings from the 1986 National Catholic Educational Association Study," in *Visible Now*, ed. D. Slaughter and D. Johnson (Westport, Connecticut: Greenwood Press, 1988), 111-115.

17. C. H. Wesley, *Prince Hall: Life and Legacy*, 2d ed. (Chicago: Drew Sales Lodge Regalia, 1983), 77.

18. Joan Davis Ratteray and Mwalimu Shujaa, *Dare to Choose: Parental Choice at Independent Neighborhood Schools* (Washington, DC: Institute for Independent Education, 1987).

19. *African-American Enrollment*, Institute for Independent Education.

20. Joan Davis Ratteray, *Freedom of the Mind*, Essays and Policy Studies Series (Washington, DC: Institute for Independent Education, 1988).

21. Kofi Lomotey and C. Brookins, "Independent Black Institutions: A Cultural Perspective," in *Visible Now*, ed. D. Slaughter and D. Johnson (Westport: Greenwood Press, 1988), 167.

22. C. Griffin, "Religious Benevolence as Social Control, 1815-1863," *Mississippi Valley Historical Review* 44 (1957): 423-444.

23. R. Butchart, *Northern Schools and Southern Blacks and Reconstruction* (Westport: Greenwood Press, 1980), 137.

24. American Freedmen's Union Commission, *American Freedman* (May 1866), 32.

25. H. Gregg, *History of the A. M. E. Church* (Nashville: The African Methodist Episcopal Church, 1980), 74.

26. Writers Program Work Project Administration, *The Negro in Virginia*, no. 24, (Virginia: School Chapter Hastings House, 1940); L. Fitts, *A History of Black Baptists* (Nashville: Broadman Press, 1985), 208.

27. E. U. Essein-Udom, *Black Nationalism, a Search for an Identity in America* (Chicago: University of Chicago Press, 1962), chap. 9.

28. Ratteray and Shujaa, *Dare to Choose*, 45.

29. W. Bourne, *History of the Public School Society* (1870; reprint, New York: Arno Press and the New York Times, 1971), 164.

30. D. Viadero, "Battle over Multicultural Education Rises in Intensity: Issue is What Kind, Not Whether," *Education Week* 10 (1990): 13, 1ff.

31. Perry, "Colored Public High Schools," 115.

32. W. E. B. DuBois, *The College-Bred Negro* (Atlanta: Atlanta University,

1900), 16-17.

33. H. Whitney, "The Educational Philosophy of Booker T. Washington," *The Bulletin*, no. 2 (1935): 5.

34. W. E. B. DuBois, *Education and Work: The Education of Black People* (1930; reprint, Amherst: University of Massachusetts Press, 1973), 68.

35. Ratteray, *Center Shift*.

36. A. A. Schomburg, *Racial Integrity* Occasional paper no. 3 (Yonkers, NY: Negro Society for Historical Research, 1913).

37. DuBois, "Education and Work."

38. C. G. Woodson, *The Mis-Education of the Negro* (Washington, DC: Associated Publishers, 1933).

39. C. Woodson and C. Wesley, *The Negro in Our History* (Washington, DC: Associated Publishers, 1972).

40. T. Martin, ed., *Marcus Garvey: Message to the People* (Dover, Massachusetts: The Majority Press, 1985), xix-xx.

41. Ratteray, *Center Shift*, 26.

42. L. Bennett, *The Challenge of Blackness* (Chicago: Johnson Publishing Co., 1972), 224-230.

43. Ratteray and Shujaa, *Dare to Choose*.

44. M. Karenga, *Kawaida Theory: An Introductory Outline* (Englewood, CA: Kawaida Publications, 1980).

45. Ratteray, *Center Shift*, 23.

46. Council of Independent Black Institutions, *Positive Afrikan Images for Children: Social Studies Curriculum* (Trenton: The Red Sea Press, 1990).

47. Fred McCuiston, *Graduate Instruction for Negroes in the United States*, contributions to ed. no. 255 (Peabody col. bk. store, 1939).

Chapter Six

Historic Readers for African-American Children (1868-1944): Uncovering and Reclaiming a Tradition of Opposition[1]

Violet J. Harris
University of Illinois

The 1896 United States' Supreme Court decision in the case *Plessy vs. Ferguson* upheld the doctrine of "separate but equal." One result of this decision was the entrenchment of segregation and the institutionalization of inequality and racism in all cultural institutions including schools. Administrators of school systems in the South embraced the legalization of inequality with zeal. As a result of the *Plessy vs. Ferguson* decision and other laws and customs, the schooling accorded African-American children was funded and directed to insure the development of a politically powerless, disenfranchised, and economically underdeveloped group. Anderson characterized the system which spawned this type of schooling in the following manner:

From the end of Reconstruction until the late 1960s, Black Southerners existed in a social system that virtually denied them citizenship, the right to vote, and the voluntary control of their labor power. They remained an oppressed people. Black education developed within this context of political and economic oppression. Hence, although Black Southerners were formally free during the time when American popular education was transformed into a highly formal and critical social institution, their schooling took a different path.[2]

Consider the nature of that path:
1. Twenty-three Southern cities, circa 1915, with populations of 20,000 or more did not have high schools for African-Americans. Cities in this category included Montgomery, Atlanta, New Orleans, Charlotte, and Jackson. In addition, no African-Americans were enrolled in the public high schools which did exist in these cities.[3]
2. Twenty-two Southern cities with populations of 20,000 or more supported only one high school for African-Americans in 1915. These included cities such as Birmingham, Louisville, Baltimore, Memphis, Dallas, and Richmond. These schools had a total enrollment of 5,664.[4]
3. During 1929-30, 65 institutions (including state teachers colleges, state normal schools, private teacher-preparation institutions, public universities, city teachers colleges, and private colleges and universities) enrolled 25,280 students in regular sessions and 12,787 students in summer, extension, or correspondence courses during 1929–1930.[5]
4. Total high-school enrollment of African-Americans in 1940 in all Southern states, including Delaware, amounted to 240,049.[6]

The vast majority of African-Americans resided in the South until the 1950s. These data help to illustrate the extent to which significant numbers of African-Americans have had limited access to education and they further suggest that only one or two generations of African-Americans have had consistent access to schooling. Despite these bleak conditions, African-Americans viewed and continue to view education as a means of achieving equality, participating in dominant (nee mainstream) cultural institutions, and becoming middle class.[7] An examination of African-American educational historiography reveals the extent to which African-Americans cherished education. They established schools such as

Utica and Snowhill; they funded the schools with their hard-earned cash and donations of labor, livestock, and land; they boarded teachers, and, occasionally, defied White supervisors in order to provide their children with the education they deemed best.[8]

In addition to supporting schools, African-Americans also created literacy materials to instill in children fundamental knowledge and inculcate them with a particular world view. An examination of the literacy materials created especially for African-American children reveals a variety of values and goals including the characterization of education as a form of liberation. Among the explicit and implicit beliefs apparent in these materials are ones such as race pride, racial solidarity, knowledge of African-American history and culture, and commitment to achieving social equality. These sentiments are pervasive in the readers (texts used to provide literacy) created for African-American children in the period 1905-1944. These materials existed, but they were decidedly not a part of the "mainstream." That "mainstream" portrayed African-Americans as pretentious, ignorant, and overdressed buffoons.

Consider, for example, a book entitled *The Coon Alphabet*.[9] The author depicted the letter "A" in this manner:

A is fo Amos
what rides an ole mule
so he can be early
each monin ter school.

The individuals in the accompanying illustrations are gross caricatures that defame African-American physical features and interest in schooling. Further, the use of dialect and inaccurate spelling reinforce the powerful, negative title. Quite obviously, *The Coon Alphabet* was not written for African-Americans. Its racial hatred and vicious caricatures were intended to amuse non-African-Americans and help legitimate racist ideology. In contrast, Mrs. Alice Howard's *ABC for Negro Boys and Girls* portrayed African-Americans as responsible, intelligent, and assertive individuals with a sense of racial pride and solidarity:

A Stands for Afro American,
The Race that proved its worth;
One more true, more noble
Cannot be found on earth.[10]

From A Coon Alphabet

Accompanying this letter are photographs of well-dressed, healthy, and happy African-American children representing the range in physical variation found among the group. Without a doubt, this ABC book was intended for African-American children and can be characterized as liberatory or emancipatory in intent. One could argue, with a great deal of certainty, that few African-American children encountered Mrs. Alice H. Howard's *ABC for Negro Boys and Girls*. They were more than likely to interact with texts such as the *McGuffey Readers* or the *Elson Readers*. Rather than present insipid and uninspiring texts, Mrs. Howard decided to imbue her *ABC* with race pride and racial uplift themes. She justified her actions with these comments:

> I feel safe in saying that every child in the United States between the ages of three and ten receives among its toys and especially at the holiday season, an ABC Book, many of which are a reflection on the child of color. In almost every instance N stands for Nig, a black dog or cat, Ned, a Negro boy, a waiter, and so on. Firsthand observation of these facts shows the urgent need and place in the home for a book of this class which our boys and girls need not be ashamed of. Race pride is legitimate and praiseworthy. It is developed through a knowledge and understanding of the history, traditions, achievements, and characteristics of the race.

> Things that have been looked upon as a detriment and drawback
> can, through the right teaching to our children, be turned into an
> asset and thus lay the foundation for the love of and the loyalty
> to our Race.[11]

Mrs. Howard's commentary reflects an intuitive understanding of
some of the possible functions of literacy, in this case, the emancipatory and oppressive functions. Mrs. Howard perceived that others used their status, power, and control of cultural knowledge,
artifacts, and institutions to limit the access of African-Americans to
literacy and to imbue them with feelings of racial inferiority.

Many other individuals battled along with Alice Howard on the
curricular front. Individuals such as Garland Penn,[12] Silas X. Floyd,[13]
and Carter G. Woodson, along with the usually cited W. E. B.
DuBois, created curricular materials to educate, socialize, and politi-
cize youth. Readers, which were curricular materials designed to provide literacy, were created by these authors with titles such as
Floyd's Flowers or Duty and Beauty for Colored Children.[14]
These books form, quite literally, a radical "underground curriculum." Radical, not in the sense that the authors advocated socialism, but radical in terms of the depiction of African-American people
and culture, the advocacy of racial uplift, race pride refinement,
and race solidarity. These readers are "underground" materials
because most of us are unaware of their existence; one is made
aware of them through serendipity, visits to bookshops, or archival
research. Researchers will not discover any analysis of them in Nila
Banton Smith's *American Reading Instruction,*[15] a historical
analysis of reading instruction and reading materials, or in Ruth
Elson's *Guardians of Tradition,*[16] a study of school texts, or in
recent articles on the history of literacy in the United States written
by Kaestle or others. Kaestle, however, recognized this lack and
wrote that one limitation of his research and others' in the area was
the lack of analyses of issues of race and gender.

In another sense, these readers are part of an underground curriculum because 1) their creation symbolized African-American dis-
satisfaction with traditional literacy materials; 2) the readers
contradicted traditional images of African-Americans in children's
literature, hence, they are oppositional or alternative texts which
challenge what Williams labeled a "selective tradition"[17]; 3) the creators unabashedly attempted to use them to inculcate children with
specific ideologies; and 4) the readers represent some of the efforts

to gain control of the education of African-American children beyond rhetorical dichotomies of industrial or classical education. Explicit in the forewords and introductions of these readers are sentiments that literacy can either help maintain the subordinate status of African-Americans or, along with economic and political power, improve the status of African-Americans.

The purposes of this chapter are fivefold: 1) to identify the theoretical and philosophical ideas that underlie the creation of the readers; 2) to identify and analyze the contents of literacy materials created specifically for African-American children between 1868 1944; 3) to determine the conceptions of literacy held by the authors; 4) to ferret out ideological conceptions held by the authors; and 5) to assess the materials for the guidance they might provide for critical literacy education today.

Pioneering Critiques

Kliebard in his assessment of American curricula concluded that "what we call the American curriculum is actually an assemblage of competing doctrines and practices."[18] Kliebard's conception of curriculum is an apt metaphor for African-American literacy. Literacy among African-Americans encompasses numerous pedagogical, political, economic, and ideological concerns. Historically, African-American literacy has been circumscribed by law and custom; literacy has always been a contested battleground of competing theories, practices, doctrines, and ideologies. The complexity of the issues is not conducive to description; additional analyses which can account for the interrelatedness of race, class, and gender are crucial. Critical theory, as exemplified in the pioneering work of Anna Julia Cooper[19]; DuBois[20]; and Carter G. Woodson[21] and the modern work of Bowles and Gintis[22]; Williams[23]; Apple[24]; Anderson[25]; Taxel[26]; Luke[27]; and Shannon[28] provides a theoretical foundation for the needed assessment.

Most studies of African-American schooling highlight the work of Booker T. Washington and DuBois. Few studies include a discussion of Carter G. Woodson or Anna Julia Cooper. Inclusion of these scholars would lessen the influence of the belief that African American education was simply a dichotomy between the views of Washington and those of DuBois. A range of views existed between the two, and the views of Washington and DuBois varied on the basis of socio-cultural conditions. Rather than keeping the notion of a dichotomy, we should opt instead for the idea of a continuum with fluid boundaries.

Critic Henry L. Gates, Jr. characterized Anna Julia Cooper as the prototypic African-American feminist.[29] He asserted that she was, in part, responsible for the inclusion of gender in discussions of African-American literacy. The rediscovery of Cooper is crucial because she recognized that while racial oppression was pervasive, the oppression of African-American women had the additional feature of gender oppression. Cooper did not, however, argue in *A Voice From the South* that African-American men and women had any irreconcilable differences, but that oppression affected each in differing ways. She did suggest that African-American women would lead the movement for equality:

> Only the Black Woman can say "when and where I enter, in the quiet, undisputed dignity of my womanhood, without violence and without suing or special patronage, then and there the whole Negro race enters with me."[30]

Cooper urged African-American men to recognize their omission of African-American women in their arguments for higher education. She criticized those men who argued against higher education. Her basic argument was that the race would not progress unless women made up its foundation and their full intellectual potential was realized:

> It seems hardly a gracious thing to say but it strikes me as true, that while our men seem thoroughly abreast of the times in almost every other subject, when they strike the woman question they drop back into sixteenth century logic. . . . I fear the majority of colored men do not yet think it worth while that women aspire to higher education. . . . The three R's, a little music and a good deal of dancing, a first-rate dress-maker and a bottle of magnolia balm, are quite enough generally to render charming any woman possessed of tact and the capacity for worshipping masculinity.[31]

Despite Cooper's feminist proclivities and her racial consciousness, Mary E. Washington criticized her adherence to the ideal of the middle-class woman and her lack of consciousness or, at least, perceived lack of class consciousness. She wrote in the introduction of the reissued *A Voice From the South*:

> Although her sympathies were with the poor and uneducated, Cooper's images in *A Voice* are almost entirely of privileged

women: the struggling, ambitious intellectual, those fatally beautiful Southern mulatto women, a "cream-colored" aspirant to a White culture club, and an artist whose application to the Corcoran Museum school was rejected because of her race.[32]

Washington's criticism of Cooper captures the complexities and contradictions inherent in African-American education when the triad of race, class, and gender are considered. Similar complexities and contradictions manifested themselves in the contents of the readers created for African-American children.

DuBois received praise for his seminal studies on African-American education and his essays outlining plans for the restructuring of education; he was also criticized for his intellectual elitism. However, his views on literacy encompassed more than the education of the "Talented Tenth." He exhorted all African-Americans to attain the highest level of education possible:

> Colored Americans must then with deep determination educate their children in the broadest, highest way. They must fill the colleges with the talented and fill the fields and ships with the intelligent. Wisdom is the principle thing. Therefore, get wisdom.[33]

Early on, DuBois decided on a course of action which involved research, political protest, and the creation of cultural artifacts and institutions which would improve African-American literacy. DuBois enveloped his educational ideals in his philosophy of child socialization and politicization. He consistently argued that parents should apprise their children of the problems of the "color line" before children became aware of its existence in an actual racial incident. According to DuBois, knowledge would promote "strength, poise, self-dependence" and ignorance would encourage "bewilderment, cringing deception, and self-distrust."[34] Clearly, he argued for knowledge as a way of mediating institutionalized racism.

Specifically, DuBois delineated a curriculum for African-American children which would begin in infancy. He exhorted African-Americans to insure that all African-American children mastered reading, writing, and counting during the first four years of life.[35] DuBois, with this suggestion, preceded the call among some academicians for early academic programs for so-called "at-risk" students. The role of primary schooling was to refine and enhance these skills to enable children to "read for information as well as exercise, to write for self-expression as well as for mere communication, and to reason more clearly with mathematical correctness."[36] Additionally DuBois proposed that students study geography, languages, and history. Foreign language study was essential if African-Americans were to communicate with others in similar positions.

DuBois also argued that the decision to choose industrial education should be made by children themselves and not by others who wished to educate children into low status positions. He contended that vocational education should prepare students to adapt to current and future technological advances. He argued that industrial education, in practice, meant domestic service, training in menial and low-paying positions, and training in obsolete industries such as blacksmithing. Overall, DuBois labeled the education available for African-Americans "educational slavery" and an "educational caste system" that stemmed from the attempt to force industrial education as "the" model of African-American education.

DuBois asserted that industrial education developed into a system of caste education that maintained existing conditions of social inequality. He wrote "we aim not at the full development of the child but that the world regards and always has regarded education first as a means of buttressing the established order of things rather than improving it."[37] Further, he argued that caste education was exported throughout the world:

> The problem, then, of the formal training of our colored children has been strangely complicated by the strong feeling of certain persons as to their future in America and the world. And the reaction toward this caste education has strengthened the idea of caste education throughout the world.[38]

Rhetoric aside, DuBois engaged actively in the creation of institutions and cultural artifacts that would advance his educational philosophy. These creations reflected the notion of literacy for liberation. Two examples were *The Brownies' Book* and the DuBois and Dill Publishing Company (which published *Unsung Heroes*, a collective biography of African-American heroes), both noteworthy and short-lived.[39] The institutionalization of his philosophy represented an important step in disseminating it among a wider segment of the African-American population, albeit an educated, relatively prosperous segment.

Although DuBois is regarded as one of the more prominent and eminent scholars associated with African-American literacy, other scholars deserve reclamation and examination. Among these newly recovered scholars is Carter G. Woodson. Woodson in *Mis-Education of the Negro* argued for critical assessments of the structure, curriculum, and objectives of literacy for African-Americans. Woodson's philosophy arguably precedes and parallels that of Paulo Freire. Woodson asserted that "Negro" education benefited those who had enslaved and oppressed weaker peoples. He wrote:

> The Negro's mind has been brought under the control of the oppressor. . . . The same educational processes which inspire and stimulate the oppressor with the thought that he is everything and has accomplished everything worth-while, depresses and crushes at the same time the spark of genius in the Negro by making him feel that his race does not amount to much and never will measure up to the standards of other peoples. The negro thus educated is a hopeless liability of the race.[40]

Woodson, like DuBois, was not content with philosophical musings. He created cultural institutions and artifacts which still exist today.[41] In particular, Woodson published children's books that highlighted the culture and contributions of African- Americans and books that were used to develop positive racial identities. For example, he published two books written by Jane Dabney Shackleford. He advocated a type of education that would provide the impetus for emancipatory schooling linked to the realities of race and caste. Because of these endeavors, Woodson is a part of the historical vanguard in critical literacy theory. His early recognition of the perpetuation of inequality in schooling through oppressive ideologies in curriculum, philosophy, and funding still applies in contemporary education.

Several contemporary researchers offer analyses of schooling that center on the effects of class and gender. While they acknowledge the importance of race or ethnicity, they do not accord race a focal point in their critiques. These modern views coupled with the pioneering efforts of some African-Americans offer a forceful framework for the analysis of readers.

Contemporary Views

Researchers whose work is in the broad area of the sociology of school knowledge are credited with delineating the interrelatedness of family, the educational system, the economy, and the body politic.[42] In this research, family, schools, and other cultural institutions as well as artifacts are viewed as the major vehicles for the transmission of culture to individuals. These researchers have documented the inequality based on race, gender, class, and ideology apparent in most aspects of schooling.[43]

Raymond Williams has offered viable explanations of how culture functions.[44] Williams' theoretical framework explains, in part, the existence of ethnic readers and the emphasis on racial solidarity and adherence to middle-class mores apparent within their pages. Three tenets form the basis of Williams' theory of culture: 1) culture represents processes that insure the socialization of a society's members; 2) culture entails the body of intellectual and imaginative work of a society; and 3) the factor that acts as a mediator for these two conceptualizations is tradition, specifically selective tradition. Williams defined tradition as "in practice the most evident expression of the dominant and hegemonic pressures and limits. It is more than an inert historicized segment."[45] Tradition represents the power of individuals or groups of individuals to determine not only the structure and institutions of a culture, but also the knowledge and meanings of a culture. Moreover, tradition becomes selective as individuals or groups attempt to maintain their control and power.

Williams defined selective tradition as "an intentionally selective version of a shaping past and a pre-shaped present, which is then powerfully operative in the process of social and cultural definition and identification."[46] Because of the power it symbolizes, a selective tradition becomes "the tradition" and "the significant past."[47] According to Williams, selective traditions are essential components of a "hegemonic culture" which pervades the "whole process of living" and represents "the lived dominance and subordination of particular classes."[48] Hegemonic culture, comprised of artifacts, values, meanings, practices, interactions, and ideologies, becomes part of our consciousness and influences the way we perceive the world and ourselves. Hegemonic ideas and beliefs provide a sense of reality for the members of a society.

Williams delineated several functions of selective traditions. Selective traditions reinforce and recreate cultural dominance and indicate the interrelatedness of cultural institutions in these processes. Selective traditions shape behavior. The active shaping of selective traditions supports and reinforces the power of dominant groups. Perhaps, most essentially, selective traditions are used as instruments of power and are used to legitimate the established order. Selective traditions are not neutral entities or processes. The groups that exert power, especially economic power, are those groups that determine traditions and culture. Selective traditions help socialize individuals to assume a status and role which is influenced by race, gender, and class.

Selective traditions are not invariant, nor does the concept suggest conspiracy theories.[49] Oppositions to selective traditions are components of cultural processes that appear periodically, but the oppositions are not generally reinforced by power. Oppositional processes, values, artifacts, and ideologies which challenge selective traditions are either appropriated and reinterpreted, absorbed in such a fashion as to weaken their potential, or eliminated. A few works, for example, *To Be A Slave*[50] and *Roll of Thunder, Hear My Cry*[51] enter into sanctioned literary canons in their original forms despite the existence of factors designed to weaken their potential power.

The notions of selective traditions and oppositional tendencies offer one explanation for the creation of readers for African-American children. These readers embody the ideologies of their creators. However, it is necessary to document the selective tradition challenged by these readers in order to perceive their importance and the Herculean efforts required to supplant the dominant, pejorative images of African-Americans and their culture.

African-Americans and the Selective Tradition in Children's Literature

Eleazer presented the results of a study examining the inclusion or omission of African-Americans in school texts.[52] He concluded that most history and literature texts contained no suggestion that the Negro had ever made the least contribution to the literature of America or the history of America. Similarly, critic Benjamin Brawley concluded that the Negro child was depicted in the same way as the Negro adult in children's literature: stereotyped and of little consequence.[53] According to Elson, the depictions of African-Americans in textbooks advanced the view that nature conferred specific characteristics on each member of a racial group throughout historical time" and that "races could be classified according to the desirability of their traits."[54] In textbooks, especially in geographies, the superiority of the White race was assumed and African-Americans ranked at the bottom of all classification schemes. African-Americans were portrayed as "gay, thoughtless, unintelligent, and subject to violent passions."[55]

A typical depiction of African-American culture and people in children's literature resembled that given in such books as the Nicodemus stories, *Little Brown Koko*[56] and *Epaminondas and His Auntie*.[57] For example, in *Nicodemus and the Gang,* the title character and his friends are depicted as well-dressed, comic Negroes, a variation of the pickaninny stereotype.[58] An excerpt from the book supports this contention:

> "Heyo, Nicodemus!" The whole gang was outside calling.
> "Come on out!" Nicodemus looked out the window. He saw Petunia and Clara Belle and Rastus and Obadiah and Little Sim.
> "I'se a comin'," shouted Nicodemus.
> But Nicodemus only got as far as the front door, when he heard his Mammy calling . . . "Nicodemus!"
> "Yas'm, Mammy." "I wants you to min' yo' li'l sister."
> "Yes'm, Mammy." (unnumbered pages)

Nicodemus, his sister, and friends engage in typical antics of children. In this case, the children decide to build a clubhouse. The gang swims, fights, and goofs off throughout the project. On the last work day, each child brings something special for the clubhouse; one child brings a watermelon. The last actions and pictorial images are of the children eating huge slices of watermelon with enormous grins on their faces. Hogan penned six other books in the series. She missed, however, a golden opportunity to portray African-American children engaged in typical childhood antics without resorting to stereotypic dialect, mammies, and watermelon icons. This is not to suggest that African-Americans do not speak in dialect, do not engage in maternal behavior, or eschew watermelon; rather the suggestion is made that in opposition to these views, authentic depictions of folk culture existed in works by Arna Bontemps and others.

The Nicodemus stories, along with the *Story of Little Black Sambo* and others of that ilk, helped institutionalize a penetrating image of little African-American boys as stupid, incompetent, and comical that came to pervade children's literature and popular culture.[59] One cannot dismiss these books as aberrations. They were typical and they remain in circulation, often passed from one generation to the next in families as enjoyable literature. Further, one cannot dismiss these books as atypical and innocent because they were and are instruments of power and represent the images Whites received about African-Americans. Moreover, the status of African-Americans parallels public reception and acceptance of these images. If African-Americans have low status, then depictions of them are stereotyped, caricatured, and unauthentic. If the images are culturally authentic, then African-Americans have amassed some modicum of power and influence. Some of the alternative images are allowed to become a part of cultural institutions and processes as a way of diffusing their radical potential. For example, some would characterize the use of rap music in television commercials as evidence of how cultural institutions dilute radical potential.

Nonetheless, all images of African-Americans were not unauthentic. Some oppositional images were created by Whites and African-Americans. Moreover, they were not appropriated as a way of diluting their power; they represent the contradictions inherent in selective traditions. A few Whites were unusual and in fact, were progressive in their advocacy of racial equality. For example, Mary White Ovington, who wrote the oppositional novel *Hazel*, was one of the founders of the NAACP. Unfortunately, few oppositional images possess the power to eradicate stereotypes; it is a continuous process which ebbs and flows according to the relative status of the group and its power. Most African-American children received literacy instruction from texts similar to the *McGuffey Readers*. Subsequently, the images they encountered were not the more culturally authentic ones found in some of the oppositional texts.

By most measures, the *McGuffey Readers* were the most popular series for literacy instruction during the nineteenth century and continuing into the twentieth century, through the period between the world wars. Mosier examined the *McGuffey Readers* and determined that the purpose of the texts was the development of literate students with a strong moral foundation.[60] First published in 1837, the *McGuffey Readers* grew out of a conservative political tradition with antecedents in the political philosophies of Locke, Blackstone, Hamilton, and Webster.[61]

The philosophy apparent in the *McGuffey Readers* advocated the acceptance of the established political order and fostered the virtues of meekness, obedience, and subordination to the will of the clergy and the employer.[62] Recurrent themes included the advocacy of honesty, integrity, industry, and thrift as virtues more desirable than the acquisition of wealth. Additionally, Mosier found that the readers used merchants and wealthy men to exhibit kindness, tenderness, and love. The readers also taught that kindness was rewarded materially. Mosier concluded that "the great achievement of the *McGuffey Readers* is the complete integration of Christian and middle-class virtues."[63]

The *McGuffey Readers* were not geared specifically to African American children. One group, the American Tract Society, produced readers specifically for Africans newly liberated from enslavement which closely parallel the *McGuffey Readers* in terms of content and theme. These readers with titles such as *The Freedmen's Speller*, *The Freedmen's Second Reader*, and the *Freedmen's Third Reader* are steeped in overt religious dogma. Selections with titles such as "The Saviour Promised," "The Sinful Heart," and "The Christian Child's Resolve" highlight the overt religious ideology. That ideology, in the words of Trousdale, is a submission theology.[64] The publisher's note details the religious emphasis: "It is the aim of this volume to furnish easy reading lessons to those who have gone through the Primer and at the same time to impart simple instruction in the first principles of morals and religion." There is little indication that the creators wanted to prepare newly liberated Africans for a more temporal existence which would change their material status.

Although the readers were created for newly liberated Africans, the texts do not emphasize African-American history, culture, or experience. In fact, in the *Freedmen's Second Reader,* only two selections, "The Freedman's Home" and "The Free Children," relate directly to African-American experiences or historical conditions. Seemingly, the literacy the American Tract Society desired freedpersons to acquire highlighted religious piety, submission, conservativism, and restraint. The emphasis was not on the development of an educated, politicized freedperson, but on the creation of a group of submissive, morally grounded individuals.

The alternative readers created by African-Americans and progressive Whites in some ways resemble their mainstream counterparts. They include a variety of genre such as poetry, fiction, drama, stories, biographical sketches, and information pieces. They highlight certain values such as frugality, familial duty, piety, honor, obedience, and kindness. Yet, they also differ from the selective tradition in significant ways. Analyses of three of these readers from a sample of eighteen illustrates these similarities and differences and suggests how they fit within the framework of selective traditions and oppositional tendencies and texts. The three are *Floyd's Flowers*, *A Booker T. Washington School*, and *My Happy Days*.

Floyd's Flowers or Duty and Beauty for Colored Children

Hertel, Jenkins & Co. published *Floyd's Flowers* in 1905 and revised it, including title changes, in 1920 and 1922. The publisher's note contains statements indicating that they considered it an honor to have been able to acquire the services of Rev. Floyd and artist John Henry Adams. According to newspaper accounts of the time, Rev. Floyd seems to have been an educator, minister, and writer of note and prominence in Georgia and other parts of the United States. An article in the *Atlanta Independent*, an African American newspaper, announced Floyd's upcoming lecture at the local Y.M.C.A.:

> The Young Men of the Y.M.C.A. have been making strenuous efforts to secure the services of Rev. Silas Floyd at one of their meetings for a long time. . . . He is a writer of power and clearness both in prose and poetry.[65]

Reverend Floyd dedicated his life to insuring that children and adults became educated as well as practicing Christians. He wrote the materials in the text. In the introduction to *Floyd's Flowers*, he wrote of his reasons for compiling the book:

> I have endeavored to put into this book of stories for children only such things as might be freely admitted into the best homes of the land, and I have written with the hope that many young minds may be elevated by means of these stories and many hearts filled with high and holy aspirations. Our nation has a right to expect that our boys and girls shall turn out to be good men and good women, and this book is meant to help in this process.[66]

This introductory statement suggests that Floyd's purposes were the inculcation of specific religious beliefs and the creation of African American children who could easily assimilate into the dominant culture and be patriotic citizens.

Floyd attempted to accomplish these goals by using a number of genres. The content highlights appropriate social and religious behavior, and emphasizes a type of Horatio Alger motif. They are primarily stories, a few of which are in dialect. These dialect stories originally appeared in periodicals such as *Lippincott's Magazine*. Other genres include biographical sketches and information pieces on manners, dress, hygiene, diet, schooling, leisure activities, work habits, and poetry. These were not grouped on a thematic basis. Floyd's religious beliefs pervade the text. The 100 stories contain many episodes of appropriate, pious Christian behavior. In a vignette titled "The Truth About Luck," Floyd imparted the following wisdom:

> What is true in the natural world is also true in the moral and business worlds. A boy reaps that which he sows and gains the prizes for which he is willing to pay the price in labor and self-denial. A divine law controls success and defeat in this life and no stratagem or trick can take the place of hard work.[67]

Clearly, Floyd equated individual success with individual ability and hard work. He did not acknowledge the influence of racial strictures on the achievement of African-Americans, or perhaps he did not think they mattered. In this and other selections, Floyd advocated piety and hard work as the "formula" for success.

Other stories provide guidance in manners and etiquette, all designed to produce a moderate, decorous, pious person who epitomizes refined behavior. For example, "The Loud Girl," "The Rowdy Boy," "The School of the Street," "Drinking and Smoking," and "Directions for Little Ladies," model the moderate stance children should assume. For example, "Directions for Little Ladies" lists suitable public behavior:

> A little lady always says, "I thank you" whenever anybody assists her in any way, and always says, If you please . . . ; a little lady is never loud and boisterous on the streets, in public places, or at home; a true little lady will always see that her linen is clean and spotless--collars and cuffs, aprons and dress, handkerchiefs, and all articles of clothing; a little lady will not be guilty of idle gossip; a little lady will love the Sunday-school and the church; a true little lady loves her mother and she will show that she loves her mother in various ways; and every true little lady will be a Christian.[68]

Again, as this passage shows, Floyd linked appropriate behavior with Christian virtue. However, he did select a few individuals from the temporal realm as models for emulation. These models embodied the highest ideals and values Floyd desired children to acquire. They included refinement, moderation, and religious piety. The individuals who displayed these characteristics and ideals were people such as Booker T. Washington and his mentor, Samuel C. Armstrong, the founder of Hampton Institute. He also selected Frederick Douglass; Thomas Greene Bethune; Benjamin Banneker; Edmund Asa Ware, and other "Negro heroes."

Floyd seems to have subscribed to some tenets of the Gospel of Wealth. He wrote of the virtues of hard work, frugality, and investment. *Floyd's Flowers* contains a number of stories in which the hero or heroine rejects notions of getting rich quick, and in Horatio Alger fashion, opts instead for achieving solid middle-class status through hard work and perseverance. All is not Christian rhetoric, etiquette, and advice from the famous. The text contains a number of stories written for entertainment, most written in dialect. Interestingly, however, Floyd eschewed the use of dialect in the majority of the text.

Stylistically, Floyd's texts compare favorably with others published for the general market. As a commodity, *Floyd's Flowers* and the revised editions were somewhat successful. A biographical sketch of Floyd which appeared in the *History of the American Negro, Georgia Edition* indicated that 20,000 copies of the text had been sold by 1920.[69] Subsequent revisions of the text, which bore different titles, included new material, photographs, and a section for primary students written by Mrs. Alice H. Howard. Mrs. Howard's most notable contributions to the text were the the *ABC for Negro Boys and Girls*, stories, and vignettes.

Mrs. Howard's contributions are notable because she emphasized race, duty, and refinement. For example, "My Duty" is a pledge for students designed to inculcate race consciousness, duty, and refinement:

> I owe a duty to my Race,
> A debt I must repay.
> So I'm resolved to start right here
> And keep it up each day.
> First I will always truthful be
> No matter what the case.
> For falsehood always crumbles
> And leaves one in disgrace.
> Next I will be industrious,
> With eager hands and mind.
> No man who put these powers in play
> Was ever left behind.
> And then, alas, I also wish

A soldier brave to be,
But not upon the battlefield
With sword and gun you see.
I'll only battle for the Right,
When crushed beneath the Wrong.
I'll always fight to raise the Weak
When trampled by the Strong.
Then last and best of all I'll be
A martyr to my Race,
If that will give and hold for them
Their rightful, honored place.[70]

Floyd's Flowers which begins with Christian virtue, moderate behavior, and piety, ends in race pride and race duty. Perhaps, Floyd became more race conscious as the years progressed. In some ways, Floyd's organizational, religious, and institutional affiliations suggest the gradual change. Floyd was an active member of the Y.M.C.A., a minister, a teacher, and an editor. The ideologies associated with some of these entities filtered into the readers he created. Objectively, they are not ignoble, but they omit any explicit discussion of how literacy might be used to change the status of African-Americans as a group rather than the status of individuals.

Floyd's failure to acknowledge and discuss the influence of racial strictures represents a critical silence in his texts. A number of factors may account for this silence and overt conservativism, at least in the earliest edition. Floyd was a prominent clergyman in the South at a time when African-American men and women were lynched and denied equal access to and protection of laws. He could not, given this context, jeopardize his life and those of other individuals. His theology, as evident in the readers was moderate. Religion was not perceived as being instrumental in obtaining political and social equality; religion was for spiritual comfort and moral guidance. That stance, however, did not prevent clergy from using Scriptures to justify their involvement in political affairs. One need only scrutinize the actions of Richard Allen (he founded the African Methodist Episcopal Church in the 1700s) to ascertain that essentially conservative or moderate individuals could engage in actions which prompted radical change. Floyd's theology in the readers certainly could not be characterized as "liberation theology." However, in his adult sermons, he revealed a more critical consciousness. Referring to the promise inherent in the Emancipation Proclamation, Floyd wrote: "All the races of America must finally march or else hear their doom and see their proud government perish from the face of the earth." He continued with references to the Constitution: "The Constitution and the laws of the United States are just and liberal. I am far from admitting that the practice of the American people is in accord with the righteous laws of the Republic or the Republic's Constitution. . . . A government that habitually practices injustice and refuses any man the freedom to enjoy his rights cannot-and ought not to-stand."[71]

Second, Floyd taught in the public schools of Georgia and at Morris Brown College, both of which were dependent, to some extent, on the largesse and goodwill of Whites. Floyd could not adopt too assertive or radical a posture in these circumstances. Doing so would have jeopardized the availability of education for significant numbers of African-American students. Anderson documented the decreased funding, lowered salaries, and attempts to close schools which were under the direction of individuals deemed "uppity."[72]

Third, the reader appeared in 1905, a period characterized by historian Rayford Logan as the nadir. It represented the nadir because of the caste-like status accorded African-Americans, the violence used to subjugate them, and seemingly, the hopeless mood which pervaded some communities. Most importantly, this was the era of Booker T. Washington, a time in which Washington wielded considerable control and dictated the tenor of African-American opposition to White dominance and racist ideology. Individuals could suffer permanent professional censure if their views challenged Washington's.[73] Indeed, it was not until the appearance of DuBois' *Souls of Black Folk*[74] and the emergence of the Niagara movement that individuals were emboldened enough to challenge the power of Washington. Besides, Floyd adhered to some of Washington's beliefs as evidenced in his readers and sermons. Thus, the critical silence in *Floyd's Flowers*, in regard to the acknowledgment of racial strictures is understandable if assessed with this socio-historical context.

In contrast to Floyd, Mrs. Emma Akin, a White, Texan educator, incorporated more of the emancipatory functions of literacy in her readers. Three reasons that might account for the relative progressive function of her texts are the period during which they were published, her Christian Science background, and her membership in the NAACP. It is not known whether she was a member at the time her books were published. An analysis of one of her texts follows.

A Booker T. Washington School

The 4 texts comprising the Negro American Series written by Emma Akin contain many elements similar to those in *Floyd's Flowers*. They also differ. Akin's texts more closely parallel traditional basal readers. Mrs. Akin was supervisor of elementary grades for the Drumright (Oklahoma) Public Schools. She prepared the series for children who attended Drumright's school for Negroes in the late 1930s. The books were distributed throughout the South according to contemporary news accounts. In the introduction to each book, Mrs. Akin explains why they were written. For the most part, they were written to "help you learn about your own people," to provide enjoyment from "seeing real pictures of Negro children and Negro leaders," to encourage pride in the Negro race and what they were doing, to help actualize the philosophy of Booker T. Washington, to inform students of what it meant to be a good American citizen, to present stories of friendship between Black and White people, and to learn that even a small child could do much for his home and race.[75]

A BTW School features 23 stories, both narrative and expository texts, and 3 poems. Each story ends with a set of comprehension questions and each book contains a graded word list. The words were extracted from Gates' and Thorndike's graded word lists. The vocabulary sections include a note to the teacher that each word is repeated on average 18.7 times, the total number of words is 35.6, and the average number of new words per page is 2.7. The inclusion of this material suggests that Akin had training in the latest reading theory and methodology and that she modeled her texts along the lines of general texts with the exception of the emphasis on race.

A BTW School contains stories which resemble those in *Floyd's Flowers*, but the tone is less overtly religious, though no less didactic. The book opens with John Henry Jackson, the major "character" displeased with the family move to town which was done in order that his father could secure employment. As the book progresses, John Henry meets new friends, becomes an active member of his school, and experiences academic success.

Throughout the text, John Henry is polite, clean, honest, trustworthy, loyal, motivated, intelligent, and interested in learning. The text is remarkable in this regard, in that John Henry is not a dimwitted pickaninny who provides comic relief. Similarly, his parents are not stereotyped. His mother is not a mammy and his father is not a shiftless rogue. In short, John Henry is middle class, happy, and loved. For example, John Henry returns home for lunch and wants to share a game with his family, but he waits until his father returns in the evening. In the meantime, he prepares for lunch with his mother:

> I must wash my hands now. I think I shall always wash my hands before I eat. John Henry took some warm water. He found some soap. He washed and dried his hands carefully. He cleaned his nails, too. When he had brushed his hair and straightened his tie, he said "Now I am ready for lunch." He stood behind his mother's chair. He held the chair back from the table so that she could sit in it. Then he went to his place. He laid his napkin on his lap. He used his fork in eating the warm meat and vegetables. He took small bites and ate the food slowly. He drank his milk quietly. When he finished eating, he said, "That was a good lunch, Mother." "Thank you John Henry," replied his mother. "I am glad you liked it. You are a polite boy today."[76]

Clearly, John Henry and his family possess an economic status which differentiates them from the vast majority of African-Americans then. The depiction is even the more remarkable because the Jacksons are identifiably brown in skin color and not mulatto or fairskinned.

Once again, we have a text dedicated to imbuing children with refined behavior. How does the text inculcate children with a political perspective? As with personal behavior, the model of political behavior is moderation evidenced by the author's statement that she wishes to engender within children the philosophy of Booker T. Washington. In this excerpt, John Henry and his father discuss battles to be fought—a topic which gives Mr. Jackson the opportunity to present his views of political moderation:

> Now we are fighting a different kind of battle. In this battle we do not use guns. We do not kill. . . . This is a battle for friends. We do not need guns because we do not want to hurt our friends. It is a battle for the chance to do the kind of work we like to do. It is a battle for clean homes and streets. It is a battle for happiness, Mr. Jackson said. Oh! replied John Henry. It is like Booker T. Washington's chance to go to Hampton. He just stayed there until the head teacher let him show what he could do. He did not go away when he saw she did not want him. He did not become

angry. He just waited and thought what he could do when his time came. That was a friendly battle for a chance to go to school. . . . The best battles are those in which no one is hurt. The best color bearer is the one who leads them to a place where they can live and be happy instead of into a place where they will be hurt or killed. Our race is in need of such color bearers. As a race color bearer you can serve your own people and your country also.[77]

The explicit message here is that Washington's philosophy is the best way and that the struggle for social and economic independence is accommodationist, gradual, and nonviolent. In addition, struggle is placed within ahistorical contexts; there is no indication that past historical conditions influence current conditions. Essentially, "the race" is told to exhibit personal traits of cleanliness, frugality, and moderation. Further, the ideology of accommodation is implicit.

In one aspect, Mrs. Akin abandoned restraint and moderate ideologies. She wrote a story, "Black Sambo and Li'l' Hannibal," in which the two stereotyped characters come to life and ridicule the ways they have been depicted in popular culture. Betty, the major "character," falls asleep while reading *Little Black Sambo*. Black Sambo and Hannibal escape from the story crying. Sambo relates to Betty his hurt feelings which result from his stereotyped depiction in literature:

I won't have it! shouted Sambo, tearing his hair. Look at me! Just look at me! They have dressed me in those silly blue trousers. That was not enough, so they put on this awful red coat. Take a look at these shoes! Who ever heard of a real boy that wore red shoes? But that is not the worst of it. I might have stood for the blue trousers and the red coat and shoes. It is this green umbrella that is the last straw. I won't have it! I tell you, I won't have it![78]

Sambo continues venting his anger and explains to the startled Betty that the image presents him as unalterably stupid and comical.

Clown! Clown! shouted Sambo. I know I look like a clown. But this is not a play. They are sending me on a long journey. I shall meet many boys and girls. They will think I am really like this all the time. They will look at me and laugh at me day after day. They will draw pictures of me in these clothes! They will talk about the funny black boy in the bright clothes! Think of meeting fine boys and girls who might become friends if they could see me as I really am. Alas! They will think I am just a funny clown!

Black Sambo was correct. Mrs Akin quite accurately depicted the creation and perpetuation of stereotypes. She demonstrated, implicitly, that the only interaction that children would have with African-Americans would be through artifacts of popular culture. What is on the surface a humorous story, is quite damaging when coupled with pejorative pictures and reinforced by cultural institutions. Notably, one of the chapter comprehension questions encourages discussions about the reasons why Betty may have dreamed about Sambo. This type of question opens up the possibility of extended dialogue and critical thinking on a complex subject.

Mrs. Akin's offerings are traditional in structure and moderate in ideology. Yet, they contain a few progressive elements: the debunking of stereotypes in text and illustrations. The consistent images of stable, middle-class, and working-class families engaged in normal activities, speaking Standard English, and hopeful, is unique among the images in contemporaneous texts. Yet, the texts do not provide examples of the "storied tradition of resistance" (a term coined by Susan Cox) apparent in contemporary African-American children's literature. The stories contained in the books present images which are not threatening nor assertive. They are moderate and restrained, hence more suitable for segregated schooling. The third reader, *My Happy Days*, shares similarities with Mrs. Akin's text.

My Happy Days

Carter G. Woodson, in *Mis-education of the Negro*, condemned the content and purpose of African-American schooling. He argued that the schooling most Negroes received prepared them only for inferiority. Woodson, through Associated Publishers, published several readers and textbooks for children that were designed to ameliorate the impact of White supremacist ideology. One of those readers, *My Happy Days*, by Jane D. Schackelford, continues the format and content of the readers in the series developed by Emma Akin.[79] Schackelford, an African-American, spent most of her life in Indiana. She received a B.A. from the teachers college at Terre Haute and an M.A. from Teachers College of Columbia University. She taught in Terre Haute's local schools. She was active in local African-American educational and social activities. For example, she founded the Indiana branch of the Association for the Study of Negro Life and History. Most importantly, she seems to have had an educational philosophy which attempted to instill some of the ideals inherent in the Association for the Study of Negro Life and History. Towards this end, she wrote two texts for children, *My Happy Days* and *The Child's Story of the Negro*.[80] Her philosophy is evident in the preface she wrote in *My Happy Days* entitled a Message to Parents:

> In this book I have tried to present a home in which children live sanely and happily, where the parents are companions to their children, daily enriching their lives by giving them a background of fine appreciations of art, music, literature, and outstanding achievements. . . . I hope it will establish a pattern that will be followed in many homes, because we all realize that strengthening family life is a bulwark of democracy.

Here, as in *Floyd's Flowers* and *A Booker T. Washington School*, is an emphasis on moderation in behavior, refinement, and a subtle, though conservative appeal to politicization.

The editor of the Monthly Digest column of the *Negro History Bulletin* praised Schackelford's work along with that of another educator with these statements:

> At the same time one cannot but think the examples of these two distinguished workers among the lowly should be emulated by thousands of Negro teachers who never give a thought to the all but forsaken children whom they profess to be teaching. We should have such books coming from scores or hundreds of Negro teachers. They daily pass blindly over interesting materials which may be successfully dramatized for books which will interest not only the children of their race but of all races in this country and abroad.[81]

The major "characters" in *My Happy Days*, Rex and Mary Nelson, are a part of a nuclear, middle-class family. The father, Mr. Nelson, is a police officer and the mother, Mrs. Nelson, is a homemaker. From story topic, theme, and pictures, the family appears loving, kind, ambitious, and respectful of each other. In addition, the author promoted stories in which the family adhered to the tenets and values of being "Americans." Again, the implicit ideology of the text seems to suggest that assimilation is the best method for achieving success.

The reader contains three sections: "Fun at Home," with 27 selections, "Fun at School" which features 14 selections, and "Fun in the Community," which consists of 11 selections. A typical selection would be "Keeping My Body Clean." This selection emphasizes personal virtues such as cleanliness and the benefits derived from good, personal hygiene:

> Every evening I take a warm all-over bath. Boys need a bath everyday when they romp and play as much as I do. I like to rub my fingers through the soft billowy suds when I wash my hair. I like to look at the pictures Dad drew on our bathroom wall. I like to smell the fragrant odor of my favorite toilet soap. When I wash my ears, I think of all the pleasant experiences they help me to enjoy.[82]

In a similar manner, other selections present these and related virtues, almost in a "pollyanish" fashion. Yet, these are activities to which any child can relate. There is nothing peculiarly African-American about these stories. This supports the contention that Schackelford emphasized assimilation. Or viewed alternately, the lack of overt race consciousness could be construed as an attempt to highlight universal experiences. There is some race pride, but the sentiment is not as intense as it is in *Floyd's Flowers or A Booker T. Washington School*. One irony is that the family is so fair-skinned that it is somewhat difficult to detect in the beginning of the text that they are African-American. Some race pride is evident. A total absence would have been surprising given the educational ideology of Woodson, the publisher. The most overt display of race consciousness is in the selection "Growing in Self-respect." However, the emphasis is on personal appearance:

> "You are not really growing up unless you grow in self-respect." Mother always tells me. I try to improve my appearance by parting my hair straight. I keep my shoes shined and the laces tied neatly. Improving my appearance helps me to grow in self-respect. Sometimes I try to learn new skills that the other boys know. It took me several days to learn to climb the Chinese Walker but I did it. Learning new ways to develop my body helps me to grow in self-respect.[83]

My Happy Days does not offend, nor does it inspire any strong race consciousness. It simply presents daily activities of children who happen to be African-American. In terms of literary quality, the text is average, not an unusual feature of readers during this period. The language is simple and unadorned; there are few poetic phrases as in *Floyd's Flowers*. Yet, the fact that the publisher and author attempted to present authentic African-American culture signifies a type of progressive ideology when compared with contemporaneous portrayals of African-Americans.

Nonetheless, *My Happy Days* and *The Child's Story of the Negro* received considerable praise and seem to have sold well. For instance one teacher wrote to the *Negro History Bulletin* to inform other teachers of the motivating aspect of *My Happy Days*. The teacher stated that she had a slow reader who became interested in reading when given this book and who subsequently wrote a book patterned after Shackelford's.[84] Other reactions included the following:

It is appropriate to add here that *My Happy Days* is one of the most widely approved juvenile books ever published. It may not have such a large sale as many others with high-powered advertising behind them, but on it own merits the book has won its way to front rank among those who think seriously of the needs of children and have shown some judgment as to how such books should be written. The book has appealed especially to those fighting intolerance and discrimination on account of race, religion, and national origin.[85]

Finally, M. Crosby Rogers had these comments on the book's universality:

My Happy Days portrays the life of an average Negro child among self-respecting, hardworking, intelligent, and progressive members of the race. . . . It is evident that the wide distribution of *My Happy Days* in the public schools would do just this: It would show White children-some of whom need to be shown–that colored children are not "pickaninnies" and that American homes which happen to house darker-skinned folk, by and large, are the same kind of homes as those which contain those of lighter skin. . . . There is nothing particularly race consciousness about it.[86]

Evidently, a number of librarians and teachers agreed, and purchased the book. The publisher issued a second edition in 1945; a third edition appeared in 1946. *My Happy Days* remains in publication today, although in limited supply.

What then, is the legacy of these texts?

Discussion

Access to and acquisition of literacy are complex issues for any population. They become crucial issues when a group faces *de jure* and *de facto* limitations on its literacy. In this chapter, I have not intended to suggest that a conspiracy existed which sought to deprive African-Americans of education or that an evil cabal manipulated educators, representatives of philanthropic organizations, or publishers in their efforts to subjugate African-Americans. Rather, I have suggested that the attempts to deny African-Americans education were systematic, deliberate, and continuous. Anderson's groundbreaking study provided documentation to support this contention.[87] He provided evidence that demonstrated unequivocally that schools for African-American children were understaffed, underfunded, overcrowded, and constrained by political conditions. Until recently, African-Americans displayed a seemingly unending faith in the power of education to empower and liberate when combined with other institutional changes. Testament of this faith is apparent in the schools created by African-Americans, the donation of labor, materials, and funds to continue the existence of these schools, the willingness to suffer double taxation in order to gain funding for schools, and the willingness to protest attempts to foist industrial education on all African-American children.[88] Moreover, the existence of these readers suggests resistance to hegemonic schooling. As indicated in these readers, resistance assumed several forms ranging from melting pot stories (a category developed by Sims[89]) that suggested that African-Americans were no different from others, to stories that overtly advocated race consciousness and race pride.

The reclamation of these readers is important for these and other reasons. The creators of these materials represent an unknown historical vanguard in literacy education. Further, the creators—DuBois and Woodson, for example—were pioneers in the movement known today as critical theory. These theorists identified the special significance of race in schooling and the use of schooling to institutionalize the subordinate status of African-Americans. Anderson proved quite convincingly that the observations of these individuals were quite correct.[90]

There are still other aspects of these readers which are difficult, if not impossible, to assess. Unless the author was a public person of some note, involved in some organization which maintained records, or has family members who are still alive or is alive him/herself, it is almost impossible to determine the ideologies or factors that caused them to create the readers. Equally important and difficult to determine are the responses of children and teachers to these materials. Because most were published by small presses and had limited distribution, there were few occasions for revised editions which might suggest their distribution and status as commodities. The performance of these readers as commodities is of concern as well. The majority of African-American children were enrolled in schools in the South; consequently, few African-American educators and administrators were responsible for the selection of materials in school systems. More than likely, the publishers had to secure the approval of Whites which meant that the books, to a great extent, could neither challenge existing socio-cultural mores, nor encourage massive resistance to the status quo. It is probable, then, that most of these books were not available to the majority of African-American children and that they were moderate commercial successes. Yet, they were successful in another way; they represent a new, oppositional tradition evident in literacy materials.

Notes and References

1. I am indebted to the following individuals and their institutions for the guidance I received in the completion of research discussed in this chapter: Atlanta University Center Library; Herman Mason, archivist, Williams Collection of the Atlanta Public Library; Charles Blockson, curator of the Blockson Collection of Temple University; Kit Breckenridge of the Free Library of Philadelphia; Tuskegee University; The Associated Publishers; Jacqueline Rouse, Georgia State University; and Barbara Woods, Hampton University. In addition, research support received from the University of Illinois at Urbana and the National Academy of Education (Fellowship) provided the necessary time to visit libraries, museums, and historical societies.
2. J. Anderson, *The Education of Blacks in the South, 1860-1935* (Chapel Hill: University of North Carolina Press, 1988), 2.
3. Anderson, *Education of Blacks*, 194-195.
4. Anderson, *Education of Blacks*, 200.
5. Anderson, *Education of Blacks*, 147.
6. Anderson, *Education of Blacks*, 237.
7. C. G. Woodson, *Mis-Education of the Negro* (Washington, DC: The Associated Publishers, 1933).
8. Anderson, *Education of Blacks*.
9. E. Kemble, *A Coon Alphabet* (New York: R. H. Russell, 1898).
10. S. Floyd, *Charming Stories for Old and Young* (Atlanta: Hertel & Jenkins, 1922), 293.
11. Floyd, *Charming Stories*, 291.
12. G. Penn, *The Afro-American Press and Its Editors* (Springfield, MA:

Willey and Co. Publishers, 1891).

13. S. Floyd, *Floyd's Flowers* (Atlanta: Hertel & Jenkins, 1905).

14. Floyd, *Floyd's Flowers.*

15. N. Smith, *American Reading Instruction* (Newark, DE: International Reading Association, 1964).

16. R. Elson, *Guardians of Tradition, American Schoolbooks of the Nineteenth Century* (Lincoln: University of Nebraska Press, 1964).

17. R. Williams, *The Long Revolution* (New York: Oxford University Press, 1961); R. Williams, *Marxism and Literature* (New York: Oxford University Press, 1977).

18. H. Kliebard, "The Effort to Reconstruct the Modern American Curriculum," in *The Curriculum: Problems, Politics, and Possibilities,* eds. L. Beyer and M. Apple (Albany: State University of New York Press, 1988), 19-31.

19. A. Cooper, *A Voice from the South* (1892; reprint, New York: Oxford University Press, 1988).

20. W. E. B. DuBois, "The True Brownies," *The Crisis* 11 (1919): 285-286; W. E. B. DuBois, *Dusk of Dawn* (New York: Schocken Books, 1971); W. E. B. DuBois, *Writings* (New York: The Library of America, 1986).

21. Woodson, *Mis-Education.*

22. S. Bowles and H. Gintis, *Schooling in Capitalist America* (New York: Basic Books, 1976).

23. R. Williams, *Communications,* rev. ed. (London: Chatto and Windus, 1966); Williams, *Marxism and Literature.*

24. M. Apple, *Ideology and Curriculum* (London: Routledge and Kegan Paul, 1977); M. Apple, *Cultural and Economic Reproduction in Education* (London: Routledge and Kegan Paul, 1982).

25. Anderson, *Education of Blacks.*

26. J. Taxel, "The Outsiders of American Fiction: The Selective Tradition in Children's Fiction," *Interchange* 12 (1981): 201-227; J. Taxel, "The Black Experience in Children's Fiction: Controversies Surrounding Award-Winning Books," *Curriculum Theorizing* 16 (1986): 217-281.

27. A. Luke, *Literacy, Textbooks and Ideology* (London: The Falmer Press, 1988).

28. P. Shannon, *Broken Promises* (Granby, MA: Bergin and Garvey Publishers, Inc., 1989).

29. Cooper, *Voice from the South.*

30. Cooper, *Voice from the South,* 31.

31. Cooper, *Voice from the South,* 75.

32. Cooper, *Voice from the South,* xix.

33. W. E. B. DuBois, *Darkwater: Voices from within the Veil* (1920; reprint, New York: AMS Press, 1969), 210.

34. DuBois, *Darkwater,* 203-204.

35. H. Moon, *The Emerging Thought of W. E. B. DuBois* (New York:

Simon and Schuster, 1972).

36. Moon, *Emerging Thought*, 126.

37. DuBois, *Darkwater*, 204-205.

38. DuBois, *Darkwater*, 209.

39. DuBois served as founder, publisher, and/or editor of four journals: *The Moon, Horizon, The Brownies' Book, The Crisis Magazine.* Of these four, *The Crisis Magazine* remained in publication for an extended period of time. He also was the founder, along with Augustus G. Dill of the DuBois and Dill Publishing Company which published a collective biography of African-American heroes written by Elizabeth Ross Haynes. In addition, DuBois conducted numerous sociological, historical, and educational studies such as the Atlanta University studies which provided extensive documentation of the African-American experience.

40. Woodson, *Mis-Education,* xxxii-xxxiii.

41. Carter G. Woodson founded the Association for the Study of Negro Life and History. In addition, he served as founder and editor of two journals published by the Association: The Negro History Bulletin (directed to the non-historian and children) and the Journal of Negro History (aimed at scholars). Most importantly for this discussion, he founded The Associated Publishers. This enterprise was responsible for the publication of at least ten books for children, some of which remain in publication.

42. J. Demaine, *Contemporary Theories in the Sociology of Education* (London: The MacMillan Press, 1981).

43. Apple, *Reproduction.*

44. Williams, *Long Revolution*; Williams, *Marxism and Literature.*

45. Williams, *Marxism and Literature*, 115.

46. Williams, *Marxism and Literature*, 115.

47. Williams, *Marxism and Literature*, 115-116.

48. Williams, *Marxism and Literature*, 116-119.

49. Taxel, "Outsiders of American Fiction."

50. J. Lester, *To Be A Slave* (New York: Dial Press, 1968).

51. M. Taylor, *Roll of Thunder, Hear my Cry* (New York: Dial Books, 1976).

52. R. Eleazer, *School Books and Racial Antagonism*, 3rd ed. (Atlanta: Executive Committee Conference on Education and Race Relations, 1937).

53. B. Brawley, *The Negro in Literature and Art* (New York: Duffield & Company, 1921).

54. Elson, *Guardians of Tradition*, 66.

55. Elson, *Guardians of Tradition*, 67.

56. B. Hunt, *Little Brown Koko* (Chicago: American Colortype, 1951).

57. S. Bryant, *Epaminondas and his Auntie* (1907; reprint, Boston: Houghton Mifflin, 1938).

58. I. Hogan, *Nicodemus and the Gang* (New York: E. P. Dutton, 1939).

59. H. Bannerman, *The Story of Little Black Sambo* (1899; reprint, New York: Harper and Row, 1923).

60. R. D. Mosier, *Making the American Mind; Social and Moral Ideas in the McGuffey Readers* (New York: Russell and Russell, 1965).

61. Mosier, *Making the American Mind*.

62. Mosier, *Making the American Mind*.

63. Mosier, *Making the American Mind*, 123.

64. A. Trousdale, "A Submission Theology for Black Americans: Religion and Social Action in Prize-Winning Children's Books about the Black Experience in America," *Research in the Teaching of English* 24 (1990): 117-141.

65. "Announcement about an Appearance by Silas X. Floyd," *Atlanta Independent* 14 (Sept. 1916).

66. Floyd, *Floyd's Flowers*, 10.

67. Floyd, *Floyd's Flowers,*, 24.

68. Floyd, *Floyd's Flowers,*, 230.

69. A. Caldwell, *History of the American Negro, Georgia Edition*, vol. 2 (Atlanta: A. B. Caldwell Publishing Co., 1920).

70. Floyd, *Floyd's Flowers,*, 307.

71. S. Floyd, *National Perils* (Augusta: The Georgia Baptist Print, 1899), 3.

72 Anderson, *Education of Blacks*.

73. L. Harlan, *Booker T. Washington: The Wizard of Tuskegee, 1901-1915* (New York: Oxford University Press, 1983).

74. W. E. B. DuBois, *The Souls of Black Folk* (1903; reprint, Greenwich, CN: Fawcett Pub. Inc., 1961).

75. E. Akin, *A Booker T. Washington School* (Oklahoma City: Harlow Publishing Corporation, 1938), Introduction.

76. Akin, *BTW School*, 10-12.

77. Akin, *BTW School*, 99-101.

78 Akin, *BTW School*, 153-154.

79. J. Shackelford, *My Happy Days* (Washington, DC: The Associated Publishers, 1944).

80. J. D. Shackelford, *The Child's Story of the Negro* (Washington, DC: The Associated Publishers, 1938).

81. "Jane D. Shackelford and Her Book," *Negro History Bulletin* 2 (November 1938): 16.

82. Shackelford, *Happy Days*, 58.

83. Shackelford, *Happy Days*, 114.

84. "A Tribute to Jane D. Shackelford and Her Book *My Happy Days*," *Negro History Bulletin* 9 (April 1946): 166.

85. "A Tribute to Jane D. Shackelford," 166.

86. M. C. Rogers, "Jane Dabney Shackelford Receives Nation-Wide Praise," *Negro History Bulletin* 8 (February 1945): 107, 118.

87. Anderson, *Education of Blacks*.
88. Anderson, *Education of Blacks*.
89. R. Sims, *Shadow and Substance* (Urbana, IL: National Council of Teachers of English, 1982).
90. Anderson, *Education of Blacks*.

Part Three

African-American
Experiences in Schools
and Perspectives on
Schooling

Introduction to Part Three

I argued in Chapter One that where multiple cultural orientations exist in a given social context and unequal power relations sustain a politically dominant cultural group, the institutional arrangements of the society reflect the intent of the politically dominant group to reproduce those same relationships. In the United States political power has resided with White Anglo Saxon Protestant males since its formation as a nation state. I think that few would argue this point. Where we sometimes get murky in our thinking is that we do not always understand that maintaining this political dominance involves certain contradictions. It means conveying messages to the citizenry that disguise the assertion of hegemony so that it is perceived as a process of natural social ordering whereby unearned privileges derived from racialized power relations somehow become the rewards of individual merit. The role that schooling plays in these workings of society has been described extensively.[1]

No matter how systematic, how insidious or how pervasive, no form of oppression is perfect in its mission. The will to resist can never be completely subverted. It can be suppressed because some people can be confused, intimidated and coerced, but some people will always see oppression for what it is and fight against it. In the case of African experiences with schooling in the United States, there is a history of such resistance that is as old as the nation state itself as section two of this book has shown.[2] Schooling's oppressive role can be overcome and transformed into a force for change by people who are clear about the differences between schooling and education. Earlier, in Chapter One, I shared a story about my second grade teacher. This woman was able to counter the intended effects of segregated schooling and educate her students by passing on cultural knowledge that was critical to our understanding of ourselves as Africans in a society dominated by European-American racism. Another example was shown in Chapter Two where Jacob Carruthers described how segregated college campuses produced bold African students who used those very settings that were intended to ensure their inferior status as sites to plan and carry out strategies that would eventually put an end to Jim Crowism. These things are possible whenever African people see themselves as agents for change and understand that their first priority must be to do whatever they can to change conditions for the benefit of African people.

In Part Three I have included four chapters that take us inside the schooling experience to learn from the perspectives of African students, principals, teachers and adult community members. Chapter Seven by Vernon Carey Polite is titled "Reproduction and Resistance: An Analysis of African-American Males' Response to Schooling." Dr. Polite discusses his interviews with 10 African-American males in a midwestern high school. These interviews were conducted as part of a critical ethnography involving 115 African-American males in the graduating class at the same high school. He focuses on the students' perceptions of their schooling experiences and the extent of their participation in the schooling process. While one gains insights into how difficult it sometimes can be to avoid falling prey to the sorting process that takes place in schools, from this chapter, it is possible, as well, to gain a better understanding of what it takes to defeat it.

In Chapter Eight, "African-American Principals: Bureaucrat/ Administrators and Ethno-Humanists", Kofi Lomotey illustrates the differences in the role identities that two African-American public school principals assume as they go about their work. These differences represent focuses on the goals of schooling and the goals of education. He discusses the principals' movement back and forth between the two identities as well as overlapping tendencies. The descriptions Dr. Lomotey provides of these two women bring into focus their understanding of the responsibilities they bear as African adults to protect and develop the potentials of the African children in their care despite some demands associated with school administration that often tend to make doing so difficult.

In Chapter Nine, "Education for Competence in Community and Culture: Exploring the Views of Exemplary African-American Teachers", Michele Foster reports the results of two ethnographic studies she conducted with 18 African-American teachers who, through a process of community nomination, were known to be exemplary. She emphasizes the role that the teachers' backgrounds play in how they form their conceptions of the purposes and functions of schooling and its relationship to education. Dr. Foster also argues that these teachers' knowledge of their community's norms and of the position of that community within the larger society explains their success with students.

Chapter Ten by Vivian L. Gadsden concludes this section. It is titled "Literacy, Education, and Identity Among African-Americans: The Communal Nature of Learning." Dr. Gadsden's contribution is based on her study of 25 African-American adults living in a small community in rural South Carolina. She focuses on the dualism of literacy and education as an individual possession and communally embedded commodity. It is asserted that access to literacy is achieved through schools, but access to education may be accomplished only through mutual understanding, respect for the community, and a sense of cultural identity.

These authors make a powerful statement for change. Together, their contributions show that African people in the United States do, in fact, make distinctions between education and schooling. This awareness must be built upon and transformed into an infrastructure (local and national) that will ultimately ensure our ability to educate ourselves despite structural conditions in U.S. society intended to obstruct our realization of this fundamental human right and cultural responsibility.

Notes

1. See for example: Bowles, S. and Gintis, H. *Schooling in Capitalist America* (New York: Basic Books, 1975) and Giroux, H. A. and McLaren, P. (Eds.), *Critical Pedagogy, the State, and Cultural Struggle* (Albany: SUNY, 1989).

2. See Ratteray, J. D. *Center Shift: An African-centered Approach for the Multicultural Curriculum* (Washington, DC: Institute for Independent Education, 1990).

Chapter Seven

Reproduction and Resistance: An Analysis of African-American Males' Responses to Schooling

Vernon C. Polite
The Catholic University of America

In this chapter, I consider students' responses to their experiences in school as a means of understanding their schooling outcomes. The data on which the chapter is based were obtained during a three-year study of African-American male experiences in a midwestern high school. Metropolitan High School, as I will call it, was built with all the amenities of an upper socio-economic community of the late 1950s to serve a "known" population. The administrators who designed the school actually intended it for their own children, complete with a radio station, planetarium, television station, theater, and deep diving and olympic-sized swimming pools.

The school is situated in a city only approximately three square miles in area. It flanks a large, predominantly African-American, industrial city. Metropolitan City was perfectly situated to support the flight out of the inner city by upwardly mobile families seeking improved housing, lower crime rates, and better schools: first the

Jews, followed by the African-Americans and, ultimately, the Iraqis. African-Americans in this midwestern state generally have followed the migration patterns of Jews for at least eight decades.[1]

I began my examination of the quality of education for African-American males by reviewing the changes that occurred at Metropolitan High School between 1970 and 1990 and by assessing how these changes altered the school environment. There were slightly more than 100 African-American students attending Metropolitan High School in the early 1970s. This was slightly less than 9% of the total student body. These 100 African-Americans did not actually reside within the city limits, but rather lived approximately two miles away in a lower socio-economic township which was included in the school's attendance area.

African-Americans began moving directly into Metropolitan City during the mid-1970s. The district lost an average of 90 Caucasian high school students each year between 1970 and 1990, while it gained approximately the same number of African-American students annually. Conversations with adults, both African-American and Caucasian, confirmed that the Caucasian residents moved out of the district as a result of their improved socio-economic status, concern for the declining quality of education, and fear of student racial unrest at school. The most obvious change, the racial make-up of the school, was clear to teachers, parents, and students alike.

Although small in number in 1970, the African-American students expressed their anger over conditions of discrimination and alienation at Metropolitan High School. The students staged a walk-out and demanded social and curricular changes which would acknowledge African-American history and culture. Specifically, they demanded representation on all elected student organizations, a series of courses in African-American studies, Black History Month activities, and the hiring of African-American teachers.

The students were granted their demands by the school's administration. In return for these concessions, however, they were required to sign an agreement with the principal "to conduct themselves in an exemplary manner and to abide by all the rules, regulations, and policies of the school." The principal, in his remarks to the student body at an assembly conducted to discuss the walk-out and the agreements reached, concluded with the following statement:

> But I would also say that we have a great school that turns out great scholars and students who achieve and succeed in the col-

leges and universities and in the vocations of their choices to a greater degree than other schools. This is a tribute to a fine student body and to one of the finest staff of teachers I have ever worked with.

Riots, which included racial violence, occurred in both 1970 and 1974. Several Caucasian students were assaulted. The riots resulted in local school board discipline hearings which were emotional and well publicized. The State Board of Education sent representatives from the state capital to monitor the discipline hearings to assure that the decisions reached were unbiased. Several African-American males were expelled, and many others were placed on long-term suspension as a result of these hearings.

The history of African-American males at Metropolitan High School has been marred by social issues of alienation, political impotence, and resistance. This historical racial tension had a negative impact on the delivery of educational services. The unrest of the 1970s was never forgotten.

Method

In this chapter I discuss my interviews in 1989 with 10 African-American males who volunteered that they were related to some of the students who participated in the walk-out and race riots in the 1970s. Others were keenly aware of and affected by the history of racial unrest at Metropolitan High. This knowledge evolved and shaped African-American males' attitudes about the school, staff, and community. I examined changes in relations between teachers and students, parents and the school, and peer relations among the African-American males.

The overall study centered on a group of 115 African-American males who were members of the graduating class of 1989 at Metropolitan High School in the winter of 1987.[2] I followed these students over a three-year period beginning in January, 1987, the middle of their sophomore year of high school through the December following their expected June graduation date in 1989. My research made use of the traditional qualitative research strategies. Included among these strategies were participant observation;[3] in-depth and semi-structured interviews with students, teachers, staff, and community residents; analytical memoranda;[4] an analysis of official and unofficial documents;[5] and a computer aided analysis of field notes.

I was a true participant-observer in that I was employed by the district as an assistant principal at Metropolitan High School and involved professionally and personally with the students and the faculty. As a concerned African-American man, I frequently attended African-American-sponsored activities in the community, and I was a frequent guest at Jewish religious, cultural, and social activities. The fact that numerous individuals from the community, both African-American and Jewish, read and confirmed the outcomes I noted as valid was specially significant for me as the researcher.[6]

I consider my rapport with the African-American males and various teachers and members of the community to have contributed positively to my understanding of the social setting. Seven males served as key informants, providing clarification and descriptions of specific events.[7] At one point, several of these students even assisted in the development of a working vocabulary list of terms commonly associated with the drug culture in the school, e.g. "dime," "gettin' paid," "rollin'," "eight ball," "flippin'," etc. Much would have been lost had I not had the assistance of these students.

All names and other explicit details which, if used, could disclose the identity of the school, the school district, the students, and other persons associated with this story were altered or deleted in an effort to maintain anonymity.[8]

Conceptual Framework

Previous works emerging from the critical perspective on schooling tend to emphasize the capacity of both teachers and students to resist social reproduction through overt, oppositional behaviors.[9] This same work also suggests that this oppositional behavior tends to reinforce social reproduction rather than liberate students from it.[10] My examination of 115 African-American males' course selections, academic and discipline records, and the interview data showed that these 115 African-American males could be grouped into four categories that typified their responses to their schooling circumstances. These four general categories were not intended to be exhaustive. In fact, I knew that there were numerous other modes of categorizing these students based on their behaviors, for example, the athletic and socially active versus the non-engaged students; or students with strong parental and other outside support systems versus those students who had little or no support. My categorization of the 115 African-American males is represented by the following continuum, based on their responses in the areas of academic interests and achievement as well as their social interactions:

active   passive   overt
--conformist----conformist--nonconformist----resistor----

Using this continuum, the antithesis of the active conformist was the overt resistor.

Student Responses
Active Conformism:

The active conformists were fully aware of the goals, rules, and objectives of the high school. These African-American males conceptualized their future place in society and acquiesced to the school's rules and procedures with the hope of reaching their goals in life. At Metropolitan High School these students were generally functioning at or above average and were never in conflict with the school's policies and guidelines. They were determined to make their lives successful by working within the traditional academic and athletic spheres. Several of the active conformists were exceptional athletes as well as above average students. The active conformists were few in number. These students were not necessarily "perfect;" and many deliberately cut classes or engaged in minor deviant behaviors, but always with a clear understanding of their behavior and the potential impact of their behavior on their grades.

The active conformists, with very few exceptions, had strong parental support though often with little involvement in the schools. Generally, they lived with both parents and at least one of their parents was college-educated. Their parents oversaw their high school course selection, provided sufficient career counseling, assured that college entrance examinations were taken in a timely manner, and that college applications were submitted to the appropriate institutions.

Several of the active conformists were athletes who received additional incentive and support from the school's coaching staff. Their participation in the school's sports program was contingent upon their compliance with the school rules, policies, and their academic success. Grades and academic honors were the driving forces behind the active conformists. One teacher's comments pertaining to these students who occasionally cut classes were helpful in understanding the active conformist:

Polite: We have a lot of students who are regular attenders. They go to class. They don't miss their classes. How do they manage with all the loopholes? Why do some students go to class and do well and others don't?

Teacher: Well, I think that these students are highly motivated.

Polite: What is their motivation? What is their direction?

Teacher: Their grades. . . . They know that they need decent grades in order to get into the college of their choice . . . and they are very smart as far as knowing the number of days they can miss without it becoming a problem.

Polite: What are the differences between the students?

Teacher: The highly motivated, self-directed students are very selective in how they do it [cut classes]. They know what they can get away with and what their limits are.

It was apparent from my interview with Akil that he fit the description of an active conformist. He clearly understood the value of his education as compared with other students who were passive or resistant to schooling at Metropolitan High. Akil had the highest grade-point average of all the African-American males in this research population.

Polite: Are drugs consuming the school? Is that why so many Black males are uninterested in education and resist school?

Akil: A lot are interested in education, but they don't have pride and high goals for what they are going to do . . . or realistic goals I should say. They think that they can go to Western — University or Eastern — University and get C's or D's or whatever in their classes and when they get out they will be hired with a degree and all this money. . . . They don't look at getting better grades and you need to attend a better school [college or university] in order to get things that they want out of life.

Polite: How many of the Black males who graduated with you last week will be able to get into a decent college?

Akil: Maybe 10 or 15 will go on to a decent school. Some of them will go on to nowhere. Others will join the Army or one of the military forces.

Polite: Do you think that this is unusual that out of 115 Black males, only 15 will go to college?

Akil: Maybe they'll go to a junior college or something like that. I'm not knocking Eastern but that's not a school that's on the map as far as the country is concerned. In the 9th and 10th grade a lot of the students played around . . . it was high school, it was a new experience, you could skip class easily, after they got matured more, they realized that there will be some days when you don't want to go to class, but you got to pick those days that you're not going and do what you have to do in the class, but in the 9th and 10th they felt that they didn't have to go. . . . If I didn't feel like really going to a class, I just skipped. I was normal! I wasn't one of those students who just sat around and did school work all day . . . then again, I knew when I had to do work even if I didn't feel like it. I knew that I had information that I had to get or when the teacher was going to give a lecture, I had to take notes.

Generally, the active conformists viewed their conformism as the only realistic choice. They viewed the resistance and drug dealing as a sure means to a short life. Naeem, an active conformist, felt that those students who were involved in the drug world were destined for prison or murder, and he made a choice to work hard at his academics in order to be accepted into the college of his choice.

Naeem: Well, in a way it's my parents, they made sure that I didn't go in the wrong direction, but it was me also. . . . I didn't want to go that way. Too quick, it's so out of balance, you can make a lot of money, but you can also die; that's not what I'm here [in school] for.

Polite: Could you have gotten into drugs or violence if you wanted to?

Naeem: Yeah . . .

Polite: Did you know how?

Naeem: Yeah . . .

Polite: How would you have gotten into drugs for example?

Naeem: I knew a couple of people who were already dealing in drugs and sometimes they asked me if I wanted to start rollin' with them, or whatever.

Polite: Did anybody ever ask you that specifically?

Naeem: Yeah . . . first they wanted me, since I did have access to a car, to drive them to drop off drugs and they would pay me. I didn't want to do that and then they asked me if I just wanted to come in and sell with them.

Polite: What happened?

Naeem: Nothing, they just said, "You're a loss" and asked somebody else.

Polite: Do students have an opportunity to decide to follow the rules or get involved in drugs and negative behaviors?

Naeem: Probably, but they see so many others who are dealing drugs and gettin' clothes and the lifestyle that they lead and they think, "I can do that too!"

I understood from this study that the active conformists comprehended the work ethic of Western capitalist societies. They accepted their place in the capitalist system and sincerely believed that with hard work and academic success there would be opportunities for them to enjoy a productive life. They had very specific career goals; that is, they had planned to study accounting, business, pre-medicine, or pre-law. They knew the best college or university for their academic field of interest and the particulars of the college program. They understood the time commitment needed to complete a college program, but the most important factor about this group was that they were willing to comply with the rules of society in general and the school's policies specifically in an effort to reach their goals.

The active conformists, like Willis' ear'oles,[11] were often ridiculed by a few of those students who displayed various degrees of resistance to the school's policies. However, unlike the ear'oles, the active conformists at Metropolitan High School were generally very stable and popular among the majority of students, including the resistors. The active conformists "knew" what was expected of them as students at Metropolitan High School. They acquiesced to those expectations and consequently received good grades and were understood by teachers and administrators to be the "college-bound group."

Passive Conformism:

The passive conformists had little knowledge of the impact of the policies and guidelines but merely acquiesced without questioning. These students had little or no connectiveness to the purposes of schooling but viewed themselves as part of the system, even if their knowledge of the system and its operations was limited.

The passive conformists were "typical" African-American male students at Metropolitan High School. They had thoughts of college but generally avoided rigorous academic effort and those advanced courses which would have prepared them for college. They commonly lived in single-parent households with their working, divorced or separated mother.

My assertion is that if the passive conformists knew what to do about their high school careers and the social problems which haunted them, their high-school experiences would have been significantly different. They were generally consumed by personal problems and peer pressure, always on the edge of compliance and resistance.

Augustine was a typical passive conformist. He was emotionally distressed throughout much of his high school career. The following is an excerpt from my interview with August which demonstrates his passive attitude towards school:

Polite: You were doing well at Metropolitan High?

August: No.

Polite: Why?

August: Because at that point that's when the divorce and everything was going on.

Polite: With your parents?

August: Yes . . . and we [he and his mother] were living with some people I didn't like so . . .

Polite: So high school was a difficult time for you?

August: (very sadly) Yeah.

Polite: Do you think a lot of students at the high school have similar home problems?

August: Yes.

Polite: Do you know that, or do you just think?

August: You see certain kids acting up and you figure most likely it comes from their home situation.

Polite: And that can impact the way they learn and their interest in school?

August: Yes.

Polite: Did it impact you?

August: (very sad) Yeah . . . it kind of closed me off towards school. I daydreamed all the time.

Polite: What were you daydreaming about?

August: Money!

Polite: Money, why money?

August: When they got a divorce, everything went down, money went down, clothes, everything went down.

Polite: Was that a big problem?

August: Yeah, for me it was a big problem.

Polite: But I always remembered you as having everything. You were always well dressed.

August: I got it all on my own eventually.

Polite: What did you do?

August: I got a job.

Polite: What type of job did you get?

August: Worked at Farmer Jack and the A & P [two well-known grocery stores]. I moved around a lot but I always had one [job], which also interfered with my school work though.

Polite: Why was it so important for you to have all this stuff?

August: I felt more secure when I had money.

Polite: Do you see your father now?

August: Yeah . . .

Polite: What do you think that you will be doing ten years from now?

August: Hmmmm . . . probably in college still.

Polite: Ten years? What are you going to study?

August: Dentistry.

Polite: You're going to dental school? What do you have to do to get into dental school?

August: I will be a dental tech. in the Army. I have a lot of schooling to do . . . make-up for some credits from high school.

Polite: What do you mean?

August: Bring my average up.

Polite: You mentioned teachers that you liked, a number of English teachers, but now you're telling me that you want to do something that's in the hard sciences. Do you think that you will be able to make the switch to math and science? You've never taken advanced math or science.

August: Huh . . . I think that I can handle it.

Polite: Why do you want to be a dentist?

August: Huh . . . the money . . . I enjoy science. I have always done good in that . . . math is the hardest.

Polite: So you are going to four years of college after the Army and then dental school. What does your mother do?

August: She is a waitress. She's going to school to be a nurse at night.

Polite: What does your father do?

August: Huh . . . he's an insurance manager.

Augustine, like other passive conformists, had some rough short-term and long-term career goals, but lacked sufficient information to make the appropriate choices while a student at Metropolitan High School. He was intelligent, and like other passive conformists, was consumed by his personal problems. Most of the passive conformists were not emotionally free to learn. Metropolitan High's passive conformists were identified by the fact that they seemed to lack direction. They simply did not have sufficient information to make appropriate decisions about college or the work world.

Nonconformism:

The nonconformists failed to see the worth of the schooling process. These students were often regular attenders but rarely engaged in the schooling process. The "system" was covertly rejected by this relatively silent group. They saw no need to plan for the future through academic preparation for a position as a wage earner. The nonconformists made up the largest number of African-American males at Metropolitan High School. There were innumerable types of evidence to support the fact that the largest portion of the 115 African-American males saw little use for the schooling process and covertly resisted it.

Many of the nonconformists were habitual in-school truants, and when they did attend classes, they were ill-prepared and rarely contributed to class discussions nor did they produce homework on a regular basis. Many of them were influenced by the drug subculture in the school and were overly concerned with clothing and materialism. The typical nonconformist held the opinion that what was offered at the school was not meeting their interests. Many of them were extremely talented but often were eventually dropped from the school's active enrollment due to lack of regular attendance. Sekani demonstrated these characteristics:

> Polite: Sekani, as you can see what this interview is all about . . . (interrupted)
> Sekani: I know what it is. I know exactly what it is.
> Polite: What is it about?
> Sekani: It's about us Black males who messed up. I read about your project over at Bill's house.
> Polite: You wrote me a letter one time and you said . . . I still have the letter . . . you said that the reason that you didn't go to class was because . . . (interrupted)
> Sekani: I was immature when I said that, I shouldn't have wrote it . . . about the clothes and stuff? That was back when all those dope dealers were running the school. I can't say their names, right? They were dominating the school. It was hard to be a student then . . . school is not just learning, it's social too, a big part of it [is social]. All of them were dealing dope. I wanted to be in that group.
> Polite: Did you want to be in the group with the dope dealers?
> Sekani: Yeah, I wanted to be a dope dealer, but I didn't do it.
> Polite: What made you think that you would want to be a dope dealer?

Sekani: 'Cause I did (laugh). . . . I just never did anything about . . . I just thought it was cool.

Polite: Well, why didn't you get to do it?

Sekani: I just said forget it . . . played ball, I started thinking that these people who I'm trying to impress, in like 5 or 6 years I won't even remember their names, so I said it's useless . . . After school, a whole lot of things happen . . . you'll want to go to this party and do this and hang-out with these people, they won't even look at you if you are not wearing a certain type of clothing. Like this guy with all the gold and diamonds will look at you as if you ain't nothin. . . . Girls are better at handling it than boys.

Polite: Why do you think so?

Sekani: Girls don't get into all that stuff. The girls that I like, the nice girls, don't even like the dope dealers.

Polite: How many dope dealers were there?

Sekani: When I was in the tenth grade there were 1, 2, 3, 4, 5, 6, 7, 8. . . . They had to be at least a good 30 . . . at least. . . . I mean there were people rollin' that other people didn't even know, they just would wear plain clothes as long as they got a pocket full of money they would come to school and get into the lunch line and pull out $1,000 in 20-dollar bills and everybody would go like "wow," ah, and all the girls would try to talk to them . . . then they would end up going to jail.

Polite: When did you get to play basketball?

Sekani: This year.

Polite: After 3 years you were finally able to play because of eligibility rulings, right?

Sekani: I played when I was at Sprauve High. That's because I had my coach on me. If I had stayed there, I would have played all 4 years . . . 'cause he stayed on everybody about their grades. Another reason I played is because I got this girl-friend and she told me that if I didn't play, I couldn't be with her no more . . . so I played. She made me get myself together.

Polite: That's what it took?

Sekani: Yeah . . . when we were first together I was messing up. She finally told me that if I didn't get myself together, it's over . . . so I got myself together. I'm going to college in about a month, month and a half.

Polite: How did you get a GED? Did you get it already?

Sekani: Yeah . . . I just got the result the day before yesterday . . . 'cause I was talking to my coach at practice. He was having all these coaches from colleges and junior colleges come in to talk with me and they said you got the potential, you could go "pro," you could do this, you could do that . . . all you have to do is get out of high school. I talked to my counselor and she said that I had enough credits to be a junior and I would have to go to summer school and all next year to graduate. . . . I couldn't play ball until next year and my game would deteriorate. I talked to my coach and went back to talk with my counselor to ask if I could get the GED test. . . . I asked the coach could I go to college with the test and he said, "Yes." So I went to the adult education program.

Polite: When did you go, at night?

Sekani: No . . . see it was a series of classes, I didn't take them. I went to the bookstore and there is a book about the GED test . . . it's about as big as the yellow pages . . . they go over all different studies that you got to know to pass . . . I was reading every morning for a couple of hours . . . especially the parts that I didn't know. I just went through the math and the social studies . . . my writing and readin' . . . I had real high scores in that . . . and I went and took it one day . . . and I passed it. . . . I knew I passed it because it was real easy . . . and then I was thinking how stupid I was not to go on and do it in high school instead of rushin' at the last minute.

Polite: All of your teachers thought you were smart. I thought you were smart, but you would never go to class . . . why?

Sekani: Lazy, shit, that's all it was . . . lazy.

Sekani attended a small junior college in the southwestern part of the country. He came to visit me after the first year and provided me with an opportunity for a follow-up interview. He indicated that his college life was very structured. He had a strong basketball coach who required all of the players to live with a host family. Sekani's host family was White and, according to him, very wealthy. He enjoyed the relationship which he had developed with this host family. His grades were above average, and he planned to attend a major university in New Jersey for his last two years of college.

Sekani was the typical nonconformist at Metropolitan High School. He, like the other nonconformists, saw no value to the educational program and did not subscribe to it. He was sufficiently intelligent, as evidenced by his ability to pass the GED examination, which was commonly understood to be rather difficult for most high-school drop-outs. The coaches at Metropolitan High School told me that he demonstrated more natural ball-handling potential than any student who ever attended the school. He clearly had the potential to become a professional basketball player. His problem, like so many other nonconformists', was that he rejected schooling at Metropolitan High.

Overt Resistance:

The final group, the overt resistors, openly rejected schooling, rarely attended classes, disrupted the schooling of others, and engaged in a number of oppositional behaviors which were geared towards changing their status in the system. Willis saw similar aggressive behaviors among the "lads" in England as an example of this emancipatory behavior.[12]

I used three essential factors to determine whether oppositional students were actually involved in deliberate resistance. First, the resistors generally attempted to reject their structuralist environment. This rejection was seen in repeated violations of the school policies and rules and in repeated attempts to change the policies to better meet the interests of the resisting students. These efforts to change policy occurred generally by forcing acceptance or tolerance of oppositional behaviors. For example, I have listed below the disciplinary history of Jermaine. His resistance to authority and the structure of the school is quite explicit.

November 5, 1984 - Refused to return to class - suspended three days.

November 24, 1984 - Left class without permission - suspended three days.

April 23, 1985 - Fighting - suspended three days.

June 4, 1985 - Fighting - suspended three days.

March 26, 1986 - Gross Disrespect (teacher) - suspended three days.

April 30, 1986 - Gross Disrespect (teacher) - suspended three days.

May 9, 1986 - Squirted a water gun at a teacher - suspended three days.

September 12, 1986 - Refused reasonable request/profanity - suspended three days.

September 24, 1986 - Class disruption - suspended three days.

November 5, 1986 - Physically restraining a teacher from using a computer in class. He threatened the teacher with a weapon (knife) and stood on the teacher's desk. Suspended pending school board hearing for expulsion from the school system. Jermaine was subsequently expelled from school by the local Board of Education. I learned in the fall of 1991 that Jermaine had been sentenced to 10 years in the State prison for trafficking drugs throughout the community.

Second, the students associated with overt resistance generally felt subject to some form of social injustice. They were most concerned with issues of inequality, discrimination, and prejudice. They expressed feelings of inferiority or social inadequacy. I asked Glennie, a member of the class and an overt resistor, to share his thoughts on "caring teachers." His response revealed his thoughts and feelings regarding justice and caring in the school.

Polite: How can you tell if they (teachers) care?

Glennie: If they (teachers) tell me to be in class, do my work . . . or tell me that I can make it . . . that I can pass their class . . . that I can be somebody . . . words of encouragement . . . tellin' me things like that - that's carin', but somebody (teacher) that don't care only says you do this or you do that, saying that I've done well when they know that I got the majority [of the answers] wrong. There are some teachers who just can't cope with the class. A good teacher can get their class in order and the students respect them too. Mr. Adelstein is a good teacher. I had him last year. He always told us to do our work and his class was under control.

Polite: What was the work like in his class?

Glennie: He gave us homework and classwork and we had to do it too! He gave us chances, but we couldn't push him. He wasn't one of them sorry teachers that says, "oh you pass," without doing some work. With Mr. Adelstein, you had to do your work.

The third factor associated with the resisting students was their need to use symbolic interaction to build group support. These interactions were identified in their manner of dress, walking gait, vernacular, and need to identify places to "hang out." McRobbie observed similar behaviors among the working-class girls in England who used sexually explicit dress to resist the dominance and status quo dress of their society.[13]

Glennie's comments on the peer pressure and dress were typical among this group.

Glennie: Some people (students) feel that they are outcast because of their clothes and stuff. Some just can't cope with the materialistic pressure. If they don't have the money they are out [out group]. Clothes are very important to me and my boys.

Polite: How much do you spend on an outfit like the one you are wearing today.

Glennie: (long pause) . . . About 650 to 700 dollars.

Polite: But you wear a different outfit everyday.

Glennie: Yep, just like magic (big smile).

The overt resistors were generally expelled or dropped from the active enrollment at Metropolitan High School due to their repeated violations of school rules and policies, violent and aggressive behavior, or nonattendance. I established that nearly 10% of the African-American male students met the aforementioned criteria and considered them to be overt resistors.

Conclusion

It is consequential to reiterate the fact that African-American male student responses to their conditions of schooling at Metropolitan High School were clearly varied; not all African-American male students resisted schooling. Issues of human agency are closely identified with the various categories and the distinctions between the groups. The conformists seemed committed to a school work ethic which mirrored that of our capitalist society. They believed that hard mental work would be rewarded by opportunities for college and university training. Conversely, the resistors maintained an open rejection of mental labor, aligned themselves closely with street and peer cultures, and were often in deliberate violation of school policies and procedures in favor of their own personal interests. Their aggressive, sometimes violent behaviors at school often resulted in long-term suspensions and expulsions from school.

The responses displayed by the four groups of African-American males to the schooling received at Metropolitan High were most significant in determining their high school outcomes and probably their future status in the division of labor in our society. The conformists had higher grade-point averages and were more often better prepared academically and emotionally for higher education. The nonconformists had poor academic outcomes and most often failed to graduate with their class, a factor which will inevitably result in rejection from four-year colleges and high probability of underemployment and unemployed status following high school.

In the context of my overall study, one of the most consequential findings relates to the changes which occurred in Metropolitan High during the 20-year period between 1970 and 1990. The student racial and socio-economic composition steadily changed from predominantly Caucasian middle- and upper-income to African-American, lower-middle, and low income. As indicated previously, there were several racial disturbances during this same period which served as evidence that racial unrest had been part of the history of the school. Concomitantly, there were critical changes in interpersonal relationships between teachers and students over the years. At one point, the students and their parents were an intricate part of the school and community; they had knowledge and acted upon their knowledge. During the time of this research, the African-American male students and their parents maintained a very impersonal relationship with the school's teachers and administration.

African-American male students had comparative knowledge about their schooling derived from numerous outside sources and experiences with other middle- and upper-middle-income school districts. They knew that their academic experiences were not as productive as other students' in other school districts. Moreover, career planning was almost nil at Metropolitan High School. There was no evidence that detailed career planning was available to African-American male students at Metropolitan High School.

College testing, the key to entry into major colleges and universities, presented a major problem for African-American male students, along with peer pressure and the feeling that many teachers lacked caring attitudes toward them. Additionally, the fact that few African-American parents were involved in the schooling of their sons was another factor with a possible impact on the poor academic outcomes of many African-American male students. It was clear that most African-American parents knew little about the schooling of their sons at Metropolitan High School.

As a result of all these issues, I argue that many African-American males were poorly educated, received extremely low grade-point averages, and were generally not prepared for post-secondary schooling. In fact, few even attempted to gain acceptance in a college or university as compared to the 80% who went on to college from Metropolitan High School in the early 1970s.

For those students who did not graduate, in-school truancy, the drug subculture, and expulsion following aggressive behaviors were common trends. These students seemed destined for unemployment or underemployment. In short, the research presented in this chapter supports the existence of social class reproduction in that the working-class African-American males studied left school under-prepared academically. Schooling, long considered to be the traditional means to improved economic and social conditions, eluded most of the students who were the subject of this study. Many African-American males contributed significantly to their social class status by resisting mental work and favoring peer culture.

Additionally, there were examples in every academic department at Metropolitan High School of teachers who simply failed to demonstrate caring attitudes for African-American male students. In the students' own voices, the issue of teachers' lack of caring for them was most obvious. Although there were examples of positive, caring teachers, the feeling on the part of most African-American males, achievers and nonachievers alike, was that too many teachers did not demonstrate caring.

The African-American males in this study did demonstrate that they respected and positively responded to those teachers who, in their opinions, were caring, fair, and firm in their approach to students and education regardless of their race or ethnic background. This minority of strong, caring teachers included both African-American and White teachers. Interviewed Black males readily provided examples of both Black and White teachers whom they viewed as "good teachers."

The conditions of schooling experienced and responses exhibited by the Metropolitan High School's 115 African-American males in this study are not very different than the conditions of schooling and responses of African-American males in other urban areas of the United States. There are numerous similarities between the social and academic outcomes for African-American males at Metropolitan High and African-American males who are the subject of critical concern in African-American communities throughout this country.

Notes and References

1. M. F. Stevenson Jr., "Points of Departure, Acts of Resolve: Black-Jewish Relations in Detroit 1937-1962," Ph.D. diss. (University of Wisconsin, Ann Arbor, 1988).
2. Vernon Polite, "All Dressed Up with No Place to Go: A Critical Ethnography of African-American Male Students in an Urban School," Ph.D. diss. (Michigan State University, East Lansing, 1991).
3. F. Erikson, "What Makes School Ethnography 'Ethnographic'?"

Council on Anthropology and Education Newsletter 4 (1973). F. Erikson, "Qualitative Methods in Research on Teaching," in *Handbook of Research on Teaching*, ed. M. C. Wittrock (New York: Macmillan, 1985), 119-161.

4. B. Glasser and A. Strauss, *The Discovery of Grounded Theory: Strategies for Qualitative Research* (New York: Aldine De Gruyter, 1967).

5. R. Bogdan and S. Biklen, *Qualitative Research*, 2nd. ed. (Boston: Allyn and Bacon, Inc., 1992).

6. Five African-American males in the class of 1989, the subjects of this work; the Superintendent of Schools in Metropolitan City, an orthodox Jew; the Associate Superintendent, a non-Jewish Caucasian; the principal of Metropolitan High School, a non-Jewish Caucasian; two members of the Board of Education, one, an orthodox Jew and the other, a non-Jewish Caucasian; the Area Council President of the Parent Teacher Association, an African-American woman; and five tenured teachers, all Jewish.

7. N. Denzin, "Participant Observation: Varieties and Strategies of the Field Method," in *The Research Act: A Theoretical Introduction to Sociological Methods*, 2nd. ed. (New York: McGraw-Hill Book Company, 1978), 182-213.

8. The student participants were each assigned African names from: O. Chuks-orji, *Names from Africa: Their Origin, Meaning, and Pronunciation* (Chicago: Johnson Publishing Company, Inc., 1972) and other names typically given African-American males in the United States.

9. See, for example, B. Kanpol, "Teacher Work Tasks as Forms of Resistance and Accommodation to Structural Factors of Schooling," *Urban Education* 23 (1988): 173-187.

10. Paul Willis, *Learning to Labor: How Working Class Kids Get Working Class Jobs* (New York: Columbia University Press, 1977).

11. Willis, *Learning to Labor*.

12. Willis, *Learning to Labor*.

13. Angela McRobbie, "Working Class Girls and the Culture of Femininity," in *Women Take Issue*, ed. Women's Studies Group (London: Hutchinson, 1978), 96-108.

Chapter Eight

African-American Principals: Bureaucrat/ Administrators and Ethno-Humanists[1]

Kofi Lomotey
*Louisiana State University**

I have been concerned for some time with the academic under-achievement of African-American students on all schooling levels.[2] Regardless of the measures employed (e.g., standardized achievement tests, high school completion rates, suspension rates, special education placement etc.), on average, African-American students fare poorly when compared to their European-American peers.

Moreover, I am interested in improving the life chances of African-American people, in general.[3] While it is not true that schooling is the "great equalizer" or the answer to all oppression in American society, it is true that improved schooling will increase the likelihood for individuals and groups to improve their status and make greater contributions to their communities and to the society at large.

* A version of this chapter was first published in *Urban Education* 27(4) (1993): 395-412.

There is evidence to suggest that principal leadership is signifi-cant in bringing about greater success in school for African-American students. In an earlier study, I identified four qualities exhibited by principals in effective schools.[4] These include:

1) developing goals
2) harnessing energy
3) facilitating communication
4) managing instruction—which incorporates teacher supervi-sion, curriculum development, and achievement evaluation.

In this chapter, I will refer to these qualities to describe what I call the principal's "bureaucrat/administrator" role identity. While they are linked to academic success for students, these qualities also help to facilitate the socialization function of schooling in the United States. In addition to influencing the probability of academic success among students, these qualities are also effective in enabling prin-cipals to help these students move through the educational hierar-chy. Clearly, principals play a major role in enabling schools to serve their sorting, stratification and credentialling function within the American social system.[5]

I have also identified three qualities shared by some African-American principals in predominantly African-American schools. These are: commitment to the education of all students; confidence in the ability of all students to do well; and compassion for, and understanding of all students and the communities in which they live.[6] Herein, I refer to these attributes to describe what I have termed the principal's "ethno-humanist" role identity. These prin-cipals are not only concerned with the students progressing from grade to grade; they are also concerned with the individual life chances of their students and with the overall improvement of the status of African-American people. This commitment evolves from the cultural affinity that these individuals feel toward African-American students.

I have borrowed the concept of role identity from the symbolic interactionist literature. Roles are determined by the nature of the shared structured relationships that exist between human beings. Individuals may have as many different role identities as there are different kinds of structured social interactions in which they are involved.[7] In this particular discussion my intent is to describe two distinct role identities that can be detected in the perceptions of African-American principals as they describe their relationships with

African-American students. It is my contention that African-American principals often perform their bureaucrat-administrator roles. However, in addition, when they view their African-American culture as a significant bond with their students, they assume ethno-humanist roles. The affinity associated with this second role identity is facilitated, in part, by what political scientists refer to as "homophily"—the notion that people with homogeneous beliefs, values, and cultural attributes tend to interact and communicate more effectively with each other.[8]

The bureaucrat/administrator role identity facilitates what Shujaa refers to as "schooling."[9] Its objective is meeting societal goals. The principals are merely committed to facilitating the movement of their students from grade to grade. In so doing, they perpetuate the stratification and credentialling functions of schools.

The ethno-humanist role identity is more appropriately associated with Shujaa's notion of "education." Its objective is meeting a set of cultural goals. In this role, principals identify with African-American students as a member of their culture. They argue that academic success is not enough. What is needed, these principals contend, is an education about one's culture, about life, and about where these African-American students fit in the society and in the world. In essence, these leaders encourage African-American students to look at the world through an African-centered set of lenses that provides them with vision that is more focused, has a wider periphery and more depth.

This notion of education, I would argue, has been missing, for the most part, from the experiences afforded the large majority of African-American students in public schools. The result has been generations of African-American students with little sense of identity, purpose or direction and with little knowledge of the relationship between their schooling and what will occur in their later life.[10] In this chapter I look at a subset of the data from a study that focused on teachers' responses to a curriculum innovation[11] and conduct an analysis of it that illustrates the differences that distinguish the bureaucrat/administrator role from the ethno-humanist role as two African-American principals describe how they go about their work. These differences represent a focus on the goals of schooling on the one hand, and on the goals of education, on the other.

The Original Study
Shujaa's study was conducted in the Buffalo (NY) Public Schools,

where an African and African-American curriculum content infusion project was being implemented referred to as the Curriculum Infusion Project (CIP).[12] His data were collected at two schools selected by district administrators as pilot sites. The study was guided by three questions:

1) To what extent did teachers' perceptions of their role in the implementation of African and African-American curriculum content innovations match district policy goals?

2) What differences existed among teachers in the way they interpreted the task of infusing African and African-American curriculum content?

3) What differences existed among teachers' perceptions of the value to students of infusing African and African-American curriculum content?

The study was qualitative and the methods employed included in-depth interviews, document analysis, and observation. Twenty-three interviews were conducted with teachers, principals, and other staff in both schools. Both sites were elementary schools in predominantly African-American communities with overwhelmingly African-American student populations. While Shujaa was primarily interested in teachers' responses to CIP, my concern is with principal leadership as it relates to CIP. I, therefore, focus solely on the two principal interviews for this analysis. I refer to the two principals—both of whom were African-American females—as Ms. Grey and Ms. Scarlet.

Data Analysis

The analysis is presented in two major parts. I share examples of comments from the principals that characterize both the bureaucrat/administrator role and ethno-humanist role identities. I found that the principals often moved back and forth between these two identities. They were rarely focusing only on the bureaucrat/administrator role or only on the ethno-humanist role. This overlap of roles, and the tensions between them are reflected throughout the interview transcripts.

The Bureaucrat/Administrator Role Identity: Pursuing the Goals of Schooling

Goal Development

Leaders in successful organizations facilitate the development of easily understood and readily applied organizational goals. Moreover, these leaders accept and personify these goals. In schools, such an emphasis by principals helps to facilitate the principal-teacher interaction necessary for greater student success.[13] Clear goals minimize the likelihood of conflicts and misunderstandings among the staff. If principals facilitate and embody clear goals, the likelihood is greater that other members of the organization will internalize these goals,[14] thereby increasing the probability of greater organizational harmony.

The principals in this study understood, articulated, and internalized a set of goals related to the infusion project. In doing so, they demonstrated qualities that characterize effective school leaders. Ms. Grey, in explaining her understanding of the project said:

> I understand the goals of the project as to present a more real life history for young people as it portrays the role of their culture in the making of our country and the world. It gives them a sense of identity.

She went on to say that she envisioned the goals being achieved "by sensitizing the staff to include in their daily activities, where appropriate, positive aspects of Black culture and how it relates to the rest of the world."

Ms. Scarlet articulated what she perceived the goals of the infusion project to be when she said:

> I understand the goals to be [to] make the understanding or the knowledge and the awareness of the contributions of Africans and African-Americans [known] to everybody—all children. . . . The other goal is to sort of fill in the gaps [in the] textbooks and the curriculum that we have been taught.

These comments indicate that the principals held distinct views about the goals of the infusion project. And, as illustrated by Ms. Grey's remarks, there is some evidence that they also understood the significance of articulating these goals clearly to their staff—a process particularly important to energy harnessing which is discussed in the next section.

The principals also demonstrated an internalization of the project goals. For instance, Ms. Grey commented: "I bought into the project. . . . [I feel] very strong [about principals giving leadership to this project.] The principal is the leader of the building; [the principal] sets the tone."

Energy Harnessing

Co-operation is the key to the effective operation of any organization. Such cooperation among staff members in schools can only come about when principals are able to capture the energies of their teachers and encourage them to work toward collectively agreed upon goals.[15] Increased staff harmony translates into higher levels of student success.

The principals in this study understood the importance of harnessing the energies of their teachers. Ms. Scarlet expressed the following perception:

> I'm more concerned about my teachers at this point than I am for my kids, because I think if I can win the teachers over, they can set the examples the kids will follow. . . . If the teachers buy into the program, [if] they become enthusiastic about teaching about these different things that they should be teaching, then the kids will learn too.

Ms. Grey added: "When I see my teachers get interested in something and [I observe] the spirit in which they do it and the reaction of the kids, we've met a goal." In each instance the principals described their perceptions of focusing the energies of their teachers.

Perhaps, most importantly, these principals reflected an understanding that they were working with teachers who possessed varied perspectives and levels of consciousness regarding the infusion project. While some teachers may have been thoroughly committed to the project, others failed to acknowledge its significance. And, of course, there were others who fit somewhere in between. In describing her perceptions of these differences that teachers brought to the situation, Ms. Grey said:

> . . . It is one thing to do the lesson activities for young people. How teachers present and what prejudices they bring to that presentation can [make it] backfire. Something that can be very positive can be very negative. What we do is bring to it our own feelings and most people are not really objective enough . . . in our teaching because we personalize things as we see them.

Ms. Scarlet also discussed her perceptions of the varying levels of consciousness that teachers possess:

> There are some teachers [whose] children treat each other with

the utmost respect. You take these same children somewhere else, and if the environment is not the same, these same children who know how to treat one another so nicely in this environment will follow the path of another. Then you say, well, my goals haven't been met. That is not the children so much as it is the person that is doing the instructing.

At another point, Ms. Scarlet provided additional insight into the staff development implications of teacher differences:

> . . . Teachers are not born—they are made. Many teachers, as much as we hate to admit it sometimes, are not very creative. They are [a] regular, average, run-of-the-mill group. Many of them need direction, guidance, aid, and some suggestions. Once they get that, and once they feel that this is going to be a goal, then they begin to buy into it.

Here, Ms. Scarlet is not only revealing her perceptions of the differences among teachers; she is also talking about how she attempts to "bring teachers around" in an effort to have everyone working toward the same set of goals.

Beyond understanding the importance of harnessing the energies of their teachers, Ms. Grey and Ms. Scarlet were both actively engaged in focusing the energies of their faculties toward pursuing the goals of the infusion project. They were also aware of what it takes to harness the energies of teachers. Ms. Scarlet described further how she works with teachers who display a low level of commitment to the project:

> I have negative people on our staff. I won't say I don't. We know who these people are and what the rest of us do is try and say something—to be as positive as we can to counteract that. I think that has a lot to do with the success of the program. You don't let certain things stop you. You don't waste your time trying to fight it. You simply work around [it] and you shore up those edges and give those kids a little more exposure and a little more experience in a round about way rather than trying to make an enemy out of someone and then spend all your time fighting.

At another point she expressed the following optimism:

> Because I am positive, I am finding that my teachers now are

becoming a little bit more positive. I do a lot of stroking and a lot of telling people that they are doing a good job and encouraging them. I am very careful of when I say things to people, not only what I say.

Ms. Grey discussed another perception of an advantage of the project in harnessing the energy of some teachers:

I think what [the project] says to that person who doesn't see a need to teach African history or anything about Black people [is that] if they start to look at their own culture, [which] a lot of them don't know about, and see the importance, they will also begin to see the importance of someone else's culture.

Communication Facilitation

Developing goals and harnessing the energy of staff, while critically important, will only be minimally effective if the principals cannot develop and implement effective two-way communication with their staff. Two-way communication is critical. Many principals communicate with their staffs, but equally important is the degree to which teachers feel comfortable communicating with the principals on matters related to the school's goals. Research has demonstrated a link between effective two-way communication within schools and higher levels of student success.[16]

The principals in this study have developed effective two-way communication vehicles. Ms. Scarlet spoke about the importance of two-way communication in the school:

With the African infusion project, I think once we get back into the in-services, once the teachers start working on a day-to-day basis, once the coordinators have materials that they can share with the teachers, they can sit down and discuss. Okay, this is great. I can try this; we are doing a unit next week; let's see if we can give some direction. . . . I think they'll fall into line. [Whereas] if you give it to them and say: I got this at the in-service the other day and maybe you can use it, yeah, they may not look at it again for the next two weeks.

At another point, Ms. Scarlet voiced the following perception of changes she had made that were brought about by the implementation of the project:

I've learned about people. I believed before, but I know now that some of these people have to be handled a little bit differently. For example, my coordinator becomes fierce about a lot of things and what she's beginning to see is that . . . you are emotional about a lot of things and there is nothing wrong with that. But you have to get beyond that because these people over here need to see and understand that this is something they need. They may not want it, but they need it. Rather than get ornery about it, you have to understand that they are frightened; their whole life is shaken up; and that's good; and they retaliate and you have to be secure enough yourself to know this.

In the above statement, Ms. Scarlet is emphasizing the importance of effective two-way communication; but here again, implications for one's ability to harness the energy of teachers are evident. Principals must not only be aware of the varying levels of consciousness that teachers possess; they must also respond appropriately.

Ms. Scarlet expressed her perceptions of the effects of communication on staff morale: "Once we start this in-service and not just lecture but actually . . . talk about different kinds of things and break up into groups and have discussions and share ideas . . . then you'll get more enthusiasm."

In describing her perceptions of what teachers are doing differently and how their attitudes have begun to change as a result of the project, Ms. Grey said: "They communicate that to me." She went on at another point to discuss her perceptions of an increased level of communication among the teachers, brought about by the implementation of the project:

[Since the implementation of the infusion project] there's been a lot of debate . . . what you see is teachers who debate whether we should be doing this. At least they're talking. It's not under the ground or under the cover that nobody talks about it . . . I think there are some other people who use this to say to people, "What are you doing about it?"

Ms. Scarlet described how she communicated with teachers about the decision to introduce CIP at their school: "We were told in June of last year that we were going to be a pilot and I had a faculty meeting and we talked about it. I told them how I felt." Here she reflected an understanding of the importance of free and open communication with her staff.

Instructional Management

Principals in successful schools demonstrate instructional management which includes curriculum planning, teacher supervision, and achievement evaluation. These leaders often participate actively in staff meetings and other aspects of the curriculum planning process.[17] They are also involved on a regular basis in the supervision of teachers, often through regular observations.[18] Finally, principals who are instructional leaders play a meaningful role in the evaluation of student achievement. This is done through the monitoring of school-wide test results and through regular evaluative and prescriptive dialogue with teachers.[19]

I will briefly discuss the two principals' perceptions about curriculum planning and teacher supervision. Because CIP was a relatively new program at the time data were collected, there was no assessment mechanism in place to evaluate student achievement. Accordingly, little, if anything, was said in the interviews by the principals about their roles in the evaluation of student achievement in the CIP program.

Curriculum Planning

With regard to her involvement in curriculum planning, Ms. Grey provided the following comment: "I am searching out new materials and I'm being careful how monies are spent. . . . I have become more aware of what's out there and what's good and what's positive and ways to use it." At another point, she described another aspect of her input into the curriculum planning process:

> I did something different last year. I said to them let's do an international thing. Let's have lots of countries, lots of people . . . choose your country. They liked that . . . and the kids had to go and do the research.

Ms. Scarlet also stressed the importance of her involvement in curriculum matters: "[My teachers] . . . went to a couple of in-services in June and I went too. I think it is important as far as my role goes to participate along with the staff . . . I intend to continue to do that." Each of these principals understood the importance of their "hands-on" involvement in curriculum planning.

Teacher Supervision

Ms. Scarlet's perception of the importance of teacher supervision is emphasized in the following comments:

> People lose their enthusiasm because they don't have that enthusiasm in a big way. What gets measured gets done. When you stop measuring it, they slide back. Not because maybe they don't buy into the program, but because there are other things that become priority and they don't know how to make this infusion project a part of those priorities.

Ms. Scarlet also spoke about another aspect of her teacher supervision responsibilities—monitoring and feedback. She stated, "I do check lesson plans and notice when teachers have put some things in writing. I write a little note and tell them, 'I see you are using African culture.'"

To summarize, the above analyses illustrate how these principals perceive their bureaucrat/administrator role identities. The assumption of role identities by African-American leaders serves a critical function in maintaining the status quo in our schools and in our society. Schools impart information, instill values, and control people[20] and school leaders help to facilitate these functions by serving in the roles of bureaucrats/administrators.

The Ethno-Humanist Role Identity:
Pursuing the Goals of Education

Achieving a significant improvement in the level of African-American student success in public schools and in the life chances of African-American people will require a greater focus on these students by school leaders. This increased focus must be geared toward enabling these students to feel good about themselves and about their people. Moreover, these students must be encouraged to expand their world views and to learn to see the world through the eyes of Africans.

The perpetuation of African-American culture requires this redirection in the education of African-American students. African-American school leaders play a key role in bringing about these changes. Commitment to the education of all students, compassion and understanding of students and their communities, and confidence in their skill, are necessary components of this critical change effort. I will discuss how each of these attributes were evidenced in the attitudes of these two African-American principals.

213

Commitment

Both of these principals expressed their commitment to the education of African-American children. As they discussed the need for the infusion project, they recalled the lack of African-American content in their own schooling and that of their students' parents. They noted the difference between education in the northern and southern United States, and they stressed the significance of African-American churches and colleges in disseminating African and African-American history and culture.

Ms. Grey believed that the infusion project would not work for African-American students, or for any students, unless all educators—and not just African-American educators—were involved in the project: "I think . . . that there needs to be some kind of pressure or monitoring of principals and their attitude and it should not be up to Black teachers or Black principals to carry out such a project." Her concerns about the success of the project emanated from her perception of systemic problems in the American educational system and its treatment of African and African-American history and culture: "I think we have to go back to the teacher training institutions. It's got to be included . . . they've got to be sensitized. It doesn't matter where you teach, you need to do it in a sensitive kind of way." Regarding the significance of the project, she added:

> [This project] is a beginning. There should never be an end. While there are people and racism it should always be a part. It should not be related to money. We don't teach reading because of money. We don't teach math because of money. We teach it because we feel it is important that we know how to read and how to do math. It is also important that we know about people and it should be considered like that.

These statements reveal Ms. Grey's deep-felt commitment to her people—a feeling that goes much deeper than that required by her bureaucrat/administrator role identity.

Compassion

Ms. Scarlet's compassionate understanding of African-American children is articulated in the following statements:

> I am interested in children learning and knowing information, but I think we need to have our children understand where we come from. Our people are able to deal with conflict, have an inner dig-

214

nity and know how to cope with situations. Many of our kids have lost that. I grew up learning that; my grandmother taught me. I think a lot of us grew up that way. What I am seeing now, somewhere in these past 20 years or so, we have lost that with our kids; we don't know how to deal with adversity; we don't know how to deal with problems; we don't know how to be adults and get along in the world; and I think that if teachers are able to learn from reading in the African cultures that will give them another vehicle. Maybe having an additional wealth of information that you can tell children to help them understand how to deal with problems, how to relate to themselves and growing up [will help].

This statement, perhaps better than any from the data, captures the essence of the notion of the ethno-humanist role identity. Ms. Scarlet's compassion comes through as she personalizes the education of African-American students. Her recounting of what learning from her grandmother about African-American people was like and the need for such experiences to begin with today's African-American youth reflect this compassion. Implicit in this understanding is the acknowledgement of the importance of the transmission of a culture—in this case, African-American culture—from one generation to another. More evidence of Ms. Scarlet's compassion and of her immersion in African-American culture comes through in her constant inclusionary use of the term "we." She says ". . . we have lost that with our kids. . ."; ". . . we don't know how to deal with adversity . . ."; and "we don't know how to be adults."

In stressing the importance of the infusion project, Ms. Grey displayed her compassion and understanding: "[I believe this project is needed] because I came up through a system in Buffalo where we were not a part of the history of the majority of things that were taught in the school settings." Further evidence of Ms. Grey's compassion and understanding was apparent when she talked about African-American teenagers growing up unaware of their history or the current reality of racism. She noted that they are not prepared for the problems they will face once they grow up. She said: "They don't understand racism; that's why they have the problems they are having. That's why a lot of them don't hang in there. . . . nowhere were they told about it; so they run into problems they can't handle."

Involvement with implementing the infusion project itself was credited with fostering the development of at least one of the principals' sense of compassion and understanding. In this regard, Ms. Grey commented: "[Since the project] I think I am more aware [of kids], and I make sure I'm positive to a child."

Confidence

Ms. Scarlet's confidence was reflected in her understanding of the potential impact of the project on her students:

> My goal for this building is to have these children learn and grow and develop and be everything that they can possibly be. I think that if the African infusion program is done right, it is a vehicle by which the children will learn about themselves and want to be able to achieve.

This statement, while reflecting Ms. Scarlet's confidence and her deep ethno-humanism, also shows, at times, how much these school leaders' bureaucrat/administrator and ethno-humanist role identities overlap. While discussing the impact of the project on African-American youth, Ms. Scarlet is at the same time articulating school goals.

In summary, both of the principals in this study played their bureaucrat/administrator roles well. However, they were also concerned about equally important "education" issues related to the holistic development of their students. They wanted to ensure that their students had every opportunity to learn about African and African-American history and culture and they wanted their students to develop positive self-concepts and generally to feel good about themselves and their people. Moreover, they wanted the students to develop a love for and a commitment to African-American people. They were committed to the education of their students; they were confident that these children could do well; and they displayed compassion for, and understanding of the children and the communities in which they lived. In sum, these African-American school leaders were committed to doing their part to insure the perpetuation of African-American culture.

Conclusion

Principals are indeed administrators and their behavior reflects this truism. But a principal is also a member of a primary cultural group (e.g., African-American culture, Puerto Rican culture, Italian-American culture). Moreover, if principals view their cultures as significant, they consciously or unconsciously make distinctions between their bureaucrat/administrator and ethno-humanist roles. This was the case with the two African-American principals observed in the present study. While they demonstrated goal development, energy harnessing, communication facilitation, and instruction management, they also demonstrated commitment to their students, compassion for their students, and confidence in their students. Consequently, but not at all unexpectedly, the personal (ethno-humanist) and professional (bureaucrat/administrator) role identities were often intertwined.

Ms. Scarlet, in discussing the infusion project, said, "[It is intended to] make all children . . . all teachers . . . more aware of our contribution to the American culture. That's one of the goals." While Ms. Scarlet is describing one of the goals of the program (schooling) in this statement, she is, at the same time, personalizing the goal when she says "our contribution." She is making a connection between what African-American children do in school and how it affects their lives outside of school.

At another point, Ms. Scarlet further articulated her perceptions of the goals of the project:

> One of the goals is to help African-American children develop a sense of self-esteem so that they realize that they have a place in this world culture in addition to the United States culture. I think those are the broad goals of the program—not only for us but also for the majority population. So things have been rather one-sided and I think one of the goals is to show that all of us have worked together and contributed to make this world what it is.

Here again, her comments offer a clear discussion of the goals, but she also adds a more personal and cultural "editorial." She is assessing the shortcomings of the status quo and arguing that a new agenda is necessary in schools in order to insure the success of African-American students.

The ability to strike a balance between schooling and education is essential in order for public school educators to educate African-American students effectively. While it is critically important that we improve the academic achievement of African-American students, it is equally important that we enable these students to fit into and serve a meaningful role in the African-American community and in the American society. Moreover, African-American students need to be made to feel good about themselves as individuals and as African-Americans. Presently, many of these students see little connection between their educational experiences and their later lives.

Moreover, they are not developing a commitment to the development of their own communities. Only with a greater emphasis from school leaders (teachers and administrators) on "education" for African-American students will we begin to see a qualitative change in the life-chances of African-American people. African-American school leaders must take the lead in this by accentuating their ethno-humanist role identities.

Notes and References

1. I would like to thank Lucille Teichert, a graduate student in the Graduate School of Education (GSE) at the State University of New York at Buffalo (SUNYAB), for her assistance with the reanalysis of the data employed in this chapter. I would also like to thank Dianne Mark, another graduate student in the GSE at SUNYAB, for her comments on an earlier draft of this chapter.
2. K. Lomotey, "Introduction," in *Going to School: The African-American Experience*, ed. K. Lomotey (Albany, NY: State University of New York Press, 1990), 1-9.
3. K. Lomotey and J. Staley, "The Education of African-Americans in Buffalo Public Schools," in *African-Americans and the Rise of Buffalo's Post-Industrial City, 1940 to Present*, vol. 2, ed. H. L. Taylor, Jr. (Buffalo, NY: Buffalo Urban League, 1990), 157-186.
4. K. Lomotey, *African-American Principals: School Leadership and Success* (Westport, CT: Greenwood Press, 1989).
5. M. Fine, *Framing Dropouts: Notes on the Politics of an Urban Public High School* (Albany, NY: State University of New York Press, 1991); K. G. Hill, "Grade Retention and Dropping Out of School," paper presented at the Annual Meeting of the American Educational Research Association, San Francisco, CA, 1989; S. Bowles and H. Gintis, *Schooling in Capitalist America* (New York: Basic Books, 1976).
6. Lomotey, *African-American Principals*.
7. S. Stryker, *Symbolic Interactionism: A Social Structural Version* (Menlo Park, CA: Benjamin/Cummings Pub. Co., 1980), 51-65.
8. E. M. Rogers and F. F. Shoemaker, *Communication of Innovation: A Cross-Cultural Approach* (New York: The Free Press, 1971).
9. M. J. Shujaa, ed., *Too Much Schooling, Too Little Education: A Paradox of Black Life in White Societies* (Trenton, NJ: Africa World Press, 1993).
10. M. Karenga, *Introduction to Black Studies* (Englewood, CA: Kawaida Publications, 1982); K. Lomotey, "Cultural Diversity in the School: Implications for Principals," *NASSP Bulletin* 73 (1989): 81-88; Fine, *School Dropouts*.
11. M. J. Shujaa, *Teachers' Responses to the Implementation of an*

African-American Curriculum Content Infusion Policy. Final Report, unpublished manuscript, State University of New York at Buffalo, Graduate School of Education, Buffalo, 1991.

12. Shujaa, *Teachers' Responses.*
13. W. B. Castetter, *The Personnel Function in Educational Administration* (New York: MacMillan, 1976).
14. Lomotey, *African-American Principals.*
15. Castetter, *Personnel Function*; D. McGregor et al., *Leadership and Motivation: Essays* (Cambridge, MA: MIT Press, 1966); K. S. Louis and M. B. Miles, *Improving the Urban High School: What Works and Why* (New York: Teachers College Press, 1990).
16. J. B. Wellisch, A. H. MacQueen, R. A. Carriere, and G. A. Duck, "School Management and Organization in Successful Schools," *Sociology of Education* 51 (1978): 211-226.
17. California State Department of Education, *1977 California School Effectiveness Study. The First Year: 1974-75* (Sacramento, CA: California State Department of Education, Office of Program Evaluation and Research, 1979).
18. Wellisch et al., "School Management."
19. W. B. Brookover and L. W. Lezotte, *Changes in School Characteristics Coincident with Changes in Student Achievement* (East Lansing, MI: Michigan State University, College of Urban Development, 1979).
20. K. Lomotey and C. Brookins, "The Independent Black Institutions: A Cultural Perspective," in *Visible Now: Blacks in Private Schools*, eds. D. T. Slaughter and D. J. Johnson (Westport, CT: Greenwood Press, 1988), 163-183.

Chapter Nine

Educating for Competence in Community and Culture: Exploring the Views of Exemplary African-American Teachers[1*]

2ᵇᵛ⁴ᵧᵥ⁴ ᵛᵧ ᵥᵇᵥ⁴ᵧᵥᵧ ᵛᵧ ᵥᵇᵥ⁴ᵧᵥᵧ ᵛᵧ ᵥᵇᵥ⁴ᵧᵥᵧ ᵛᵧ ᵥᵇᵥ

University of California-Davis[2]

Introduction

Compared to portrayals of White teachers, positive character-izations of Black teachers are uncommon. In much the same way that scholars have planted the idea of the "culturally deprived" African-American child, so have they also sown the idea that African-American teachers are uncaring and unsympathetic indi-viduals who, rather than acting as agents of change, uphold the sta-tus quo. African-American teachers are too often described in ways which suggest that they are ill-suited to educating African-American pupils effectively.

* A version of this chapter was first published in *Urban Education* 27
(1992): 370-394.

There are, however, other images of African-American teachers embedded in essays, sociological studies, and autobiographies written by and about African-Americans that contrast sharply with such negative depictions. These accounts reveal that Black teachers have not only forged productive relationships with their pupils, but that they have been accomplished teachers who, despite overwhelming odds, have challenged the status quo by encouraging Black students to achieve beyond what society expected of them.[3]

In this chapter I examine the educational philosophies of 18 African-American teachers, most of whom have been teaching African-American students for at least two decades. I argue that because notions of education are embedded within a particular sociocultural context, individuals from various backgrounds, including teachers, are likely to have different conceptions about schooling's purpose and function and its relationship to education.

Background

Until the 1960s, African-American teachers were those most likely to be teaching African-American students. Despite this fact, the literature on teacher thinking and beliefs has failed to include the voices of this group of teachers. This literature has not considered the effect of teachers' cultural backgrounds or racial identities on their beliefs and practices. Moreover, it has not examined how teachers' awareness of their students' ethnic or cultural backgrounds positively influences and shapes their practice. Similar kinds of omission are apparent in the first-person anthropological and sociological literatures on teachers.

Most of the first-person teacher accounts were written by White teacher activists during the sixties and early seventies.[4] In fact, of over 65 first-person accounts written in English in this century and reviewed by this author, fewer than five were written by African-American teachers.

Within the sociological and anthropological literatures, African-American teachers do not fare much better. Though these literatures are somewhat more inclusive, the portrayals of African-American teachers are generally negative, with only a few exceptions.[5] In this genre, the prototypical African-American teacher is a woman who, regardless of class origins, neither identifies with nor relates well to her working-class African-American students. Consider two portrayals. The first is taken from *The Water is Wide*, a popular first-person teacher account written in the early seventies by Pat

Conroy.[6] The latter by Ray Rist is a more scholarly treatment of teachers and classrooms, and is also one of the most widely cited ethnographic studies of a classroom.[7] Rist's study examined the effect of social class on the differential educational opportunities available to African-American children in an urban classroom. In both cases, African-American teachers are portrayed as outsiders: solidly anchored middle-class women clinging tenaciously to middle-class norms. So steadfastly do these teachers adhere to middle-class characteristics, behaviors, and values, that they seem unable to identify nor to relate well to their African-American students.

A thorough analysis is beyond the scope of this chapter, though elsewhere I have offered an explanation for these decidedly negative portrayals.[8] However, as first noted in 1923 by W. E. B. DuBois and subsequently echoed by other scholars, it has been hard to fight against segregated schools and simultaneously to honor Black teachers.[9] This is a fact mirrored in much of the work of the 1960s and early 1970s. It was during this period that segregated Black schools, urban and rural, with all of their liabilities, including Black teachers, came under the sharpest attack from the White community. Thus, given the era during which these texts were written, the portrayals are understandable, perhaps.

The 1980s produced numerous policy statements that decried the decline in the number of African-American teachers. The causes were analyzed and new programs to recruit more African-American teachers were proposed. Given the attention this problem has received, one might expect to find more positive portrayals of Black teachers in the literature. Unfortunately, researchers continue to depict African-American educators negatively—despite recent scholarship by a group of Black scholars that points out the distinctive educational philosophy and pedagogy of some African-American educators.[10] An unfortunate result of these negative portrayals is that, lacking others, these descriptions are extended to all African-American teachers.

A scholarly treatment of teachers by Dee Ann Spencer exemplifies the continuation of the trend toward negative portrayals of African-American teachers.[11] Spencer's book, *Contemporary Women Teachers: Balancing School and Home*, is based on interviews with 50 women teachers and profiles the home and school lives of eight of them. The book paints a negative and harsh portrait of the only African-American teacher it depicts. Unlike the teachers portrayed by Rist and Conroy, who had middle-class family origins, this teacher was born into a poor family. Despite her upbringing, however, she demonstrates little sympathy or understanding for her students. Commenting on the teacher, Spencer observes:

> Despite Valerie's own poor background, she always blamed parents for children's problems and had little sympathy for the poor. She was concerned that people on welfare did not really use the money for needed items and said that a friend of hers who owned a grocery said the only time you see Cadillacs was on the day the welfare checks came. Valerie's animosity toward the poor reflected her own frustration at having to teach in a school not far from where she grew up—in the same cultural milieu.

Little reason exists to question the accuracy of these characterizations. However, it simply does not follow that all African-American teachers can be likened to those depicted by Conroy, Rist, and Spencer. In the characterizations presented by these authors, African-American teachers have been assigned roles in labeling children, consigning them to failure, perpetuating inequality and poverty, and maintaining the status quo. Far more than portraying the prejudices of three scholars, these images have become, for many, symbolic of the attitudes of all African-American teachers.

Eighteen Exemplary African-American Teachers: Who Are They?

The 18 individuals whose lives as teachers form the basis of this chapter participated in two separate studies of exemplary African-American teachers conducted since 1985. I located the teachers through a process of "community nomination", a sampling method and term coined specifically for this study, in which informants were secured through direct contact with the local African-American communities. This selection process was designed to capture the African-American community's conception of what it means to be a good teacher. In this instance, students were asked to identify their best teacher. African-American periodicals, organizations, and individuals provided the names of the informants. Initially, I did a case study of an African-American teacher in a predominantly African-American urban community college. At the time the study was undertaken, in 1985-86, the teacher, a woman in her forties, had been teaching for four years. Miss Morris,[12] the teacher, had been raised in a predominantly White section of a large Northeastern city, where she attended White-majority schools. Nonetheless, she had strong affiliations to the African-American community. These had been transmitted to her through stories passed down from her parents and grandmother about their lives in the pre-Brown era in New Orleans. Except for brief periods away to serve in the army and to attend graduate school, she had resided in the same city throughout her life. The study sought to discover what aspects of the teacher's behavior students considered effective. Though the study was conceived and undertaken as an ethnography of speaking, several of the themes that undergirded the teacher's pedagogy revealed a uniquely African-American perspective toward education.[13]

The 17 teachers in the second study are part of a larger on-going study of experienced, exemplary African-American teachers. In this study I extended the concept of the "emic" view, an anthropological concept meaning the insider's perspective, by building on the idea of "native anthropology" developed by Jones[14] and Gwaltney[15] and expanding the selection process utilized in the first study.

I used life and career history interviews. These interviews inquired about the teachers' family, community, cultural and economic backgrounds; their family circumstances during childhood and adolescence; their schooling (elementary, high school, and college) and teacher training experiences; their pedagogies and philosophies of education; previous teaching positions as well as the community and school contexts in which they currently teach. I conducted and recorded these interviews in teachers' homes and schools. Each interview lasted from two to four hours with follow-up interviews conducted as needed to deepen and extend previous ones.

These teachers form a diverse group. Thirteen are women, four are men. They range in age from 45-85; their teaching experience from 17-66 years. Eight are secondary teachers, eight are elementary teachers, and one teaches junior high school. Eighty percent of them teach in urban contexts. In fact, seven of the cities in which they teach are members of the Council of Great City Schools.[16] They work in 11 states and seven regions, and also hail from the same number of states and regions.[17] Six currently teach in the same region where they resided as children. Of that six, three are actually teaching in the same city including two who returned immediately after college graduation to teach in schools where they had once been pupils. The others are more transient—all currently living and working in a different region from that of their childhood.

Twelve of the teachers spent their childhoods in communities where schools were legally segregated. Four of them grew up in communities where no laws required segregated schools, and of these, three lived in cities where de facto segregation resulted in racially isolated schools nonetheless. The remaining teacher spent half of her childhood in a segregated community before moving north with her family. Four-fifths of the interviewees attended historically Black colleges, including three raised in the north who attended majority White elementary and secondary schools. All except two of those who attended predominantly White colleges spent their pre-college years in segregated schools. Whether hailing from North or South, however, all of these informants grew up, and most began their professional lives, during the time when separate but equal was the law of the United States.

Kinship, Connectedness, and Solidarity

The teachers who grew up in segregated communities spoke of the interconnections within those communities among family, school, and church. Several factors account for these interconnections. Foremost among them were the strengthened institutional ties produced by teachers' patterns of intergenerational employment and long-term residency. In small southern communities, consolidated schools that housed both elementary and secondary grades were common. The absence of a resident teaching force or school district rules requiring that all teachers live in the town where they worked resulted, in some instances, in non-resident teachers being domiciled in a teachers' residence. Moreover, when teachers were not residents of the communities in which they taught, they often boarded with local families. This practice bound the teachers to their host families and incorporated them in the communities where they were employed. Affiliations between community and school were reinforced when, after graduation, teachers returned to work as colleagues alongside those who had once been their teachers. In fact, this occurred for one quarter of the southern teachers interviewed. A final ingredient that sustained community/school connections was the required presence of all teachers at every school function. Taken collectively, these factors nourished teachers' affiliations to the communities in which they taught.

It is not my intention to romanticize segregation and the teachers did not idealize it. In fact, all of the teachers were aware of the harmful effects of segregation on African-American communities

226

and on the individuals residing in them. Many of them poignantly recalled the deprivations of the pre-Brown era—having to walk several miles to school while busses full of White students rode by; studying from torn and dirty books that were throw-aways from White schools; and cheerlessly observing White children entering the public libraries that were off-limits to Blacks.[18] These teachers also acknowledged the class and color distinctions within their own communities that gave certain members of the community, including teachers, undue privileges.[19]

The point being emphasized is that though the teachers hated the oppression of segregation, they were able to separate these conditions from the familiar experiences within their communities of origin. They neither disparaged the daily transactions within their communities nor criticized their parents and teachers. Rather, they characterized their teachers as individuals who were committed to their pupils' growth into wholesome adults and who also perceived themselves as partially responsible for this outcome. This is not to suggest that they represented their teachers as overly affectionate. On the contrary, the modal description of teachers was one of concerned individuals who commanded respect, were respectful of pupils, and who, though caring, were strict in requiring all students to meet high academic and behavioral standards.

Without exception, interviewees raised in these contexts recalled that their teachers were concerned not only with students' cognitive development, but with their affective, social, and emotional development as well. While recollecting that guiding students was one of the many functions that teachers routinely performed, a teacher who grew up in Miami explained how her teacher sought to accomplish this:

I remember the end of school, almost June, our sixth grade teacher, Miss Pascall. I won't ever forget her name. She called . . . she told us the day before she was gonna call each person up and she was gonna sit you down, we were just sixth graders, and she was gonna actually tell you what she thought about you. And what she thought your good points were and your weak points because we were getting ready to go into seventh grade and she just thought that was something important. She called me up and then she said, "OK, Pam, I'm gonna tell you what I think about you, and then ask if you have any questions." She said, "You're very bright," well, they didn't say bright in those days, they said smart, "you're smart, but personally," because I was only nine then now, "that you're too

227

young to go to seventh grade." She said, "But, don't ever let that be . . . don't ever let that hold you back, but I just want you to know that you are very young." And now for some reason that's all I remember.

A junior high school teacher raised in West Virginia during the 1930s and 1940s echoed this sentiment. Describing his teachers and characterizing the teacher/student relationships he remembered from his years as a student, he explained how the teachers from his past had influenced his own behavior as a teacher:

> Teacher: I consider my education that I received in segregated schools—I mean—a good one in the sense of the term, because of the interested people, it depends on the teachers who are willing to go above and beyond, I think this has made me do the same thing myself now.
> Interviewer: When you said they went above and beyond, what specifically did they do?
> Teacher: I think they were more interested in you as a human being, and your future, and they would go out of their way with you as a person, to give you advice and to help you, or talk about your family problems or personal problems, they were not afraid to help you. And they wanted you to move ahead, and they believed in you, and you were able to believe in them. That's why it's such a good relationship.

The conclusion to be drawn from these interviews is that the African-American teachers whom these interviewees remembered from their childhoods were vital members of their communities, and often acted as surrogate parents to the children they taught.[20] For these teachers, such stories represent key events in the formation of their ideas about the teacher's role. Predictably perhaps, these teachers have willingly embraced the characteristics they admired in their own teachers.

All of these teachers, regardless of their region of origin, expressed feelings of connection, affiliation, and solidarity with the pupils they teach. This solidarity was evident in the use of kinship terms as well as in the metaphors the teachers employed to characterize their relationships with students. Half of the elementary and non-elementary teachers interviewed used parental terms or family metaphors to characterize their relationships with their pupils. Though women elementary teachers were most likely to characterize their relationships to students using kinship terms, the use of these terms was not restricted to elementary or female teachers.

It is difficult to determine the extent to which students reciprocate in feeling kinship toward these teachers, however, several teachers alluded to mutual relationships. There is evidence, though scant, that some pupils do indeed share these feelings. An elementary teacher's recounting of what she tells her third grade pupils on the first day made it apparent that some of her pupils do reciprocate:

> In the beginning of school, I stand up there and make a speech. At the beginning of school. I say, "Now boys and girls I'm happy to have you this year," or something to that effect, "but this is my room and you are my students." And I say, "John, I'm going to be your new mother for nine months. After nine months, you can go back and be your mama's boy, but for nine months you're going to be my boy and we're going to have rules and regulations." And I say "Okay, I'm going to be your new mother for nine months." And you know what he calls me? "Mother."

Even when teachers did not use kinship terms to describe their relationships with their pupils, their use of metaphors connoted a similar conception of connectedness, solidarity, and common affiliation with the children they teach:

> I couldn't begin to tell you some of the problems I've encountered. I'm the kind of teacher who kids come and tell me their problems. I have brought kids, well one child I eventually brought home for two weeks until I could find a foster home for her because her mother put her out. I have had to take a child who tried to do an abortion on her own to take her back to the doctor and get her straightened out. Other little situations where the father was beating the child. I mean this is what my teaching job consists of, not just the physical education program, but an *extended family* program because I feel as though this is a part of what I'm about. (emphasis mine)
>
> Black people have to convince Blacks of how important it (education) is. And how they are all part of that Black *umbilical cord* because a lot of (Black) teachers, they don't do it consciously, but we are forgetting about our roots, about how we're *connected to this cord*, and about everyone we've left behind. We have it now, and we don't have time for the so-called underclass. But we have to educate ourselves as a group because otherwise what's going to happen to us all? You see what I mean. If I can't see that

kid out there in the biggest project, if I can't see how he and I or she and I are of the same *umbilical cord* and do not strive to make us more *connected to that cord with a common destiny,* then we're lost. (emphasis mine)

Educating for Competence in Community and Culture

Given these expressions of solidarity, connectedness, and kinship, what are these teachers' views about educating Black children? And, finally, how do they conceive of their roles in meeting these objectives for Black students?

These teachers are aware of how changes in society militate against easy success for African-American pupils. They understand how the rhetoric of equal opportunity—coupled with a preoccupation with materialism and assimilation into the larger societal values and norms without parallel changes in the structural conditions of society—has limited the motivation and consequent achievement of African-American students. Moreover, they are also aware that cosmetic changes in society often camouflage ongoing structural inequalities.

These teachers cited numerous instances of racism, both subtle and not so subtle, within school settings as well as in the larger society. As evidence of the latter, one woman teaching in a coastal South Carolina town since 1938, pointed to the various land-taking schemes by which community residents victimized by the recreation explosion[21] have been robbed of their ancestral lands. This same methodical displacement was repeated in the narrative of a teacher from a large city in the Northeast where urban gentrification has already dislocated long-term residents of a historically Black community and now threatens to displace hundreds of low-income residents in order to build luxury housing.

Among the teachers I interviewed, there was considerable agreement that the adoption of mainstream values coupled with an intensifying materialism have spawned subtle changes in the cultural attitudes of many Black youth who, although they are still hampered by racism, now embrace the values of the larger community. The effects of these changed conditions are best observed in the diminishing ability of the Black community to determine the meanings to be attached to particular events. This is a new racism which, though less explicit, is as virulent as the old one. An example recalled by one teacher was that, in her generation, adults frequently pointed out the achievements of famous Blacks like Jackie Robinson, the first

Black to play major league baseball. She noted, however, that their emphasis was not that Robinson was a baseball player—sports was merely the vehicle for the accomplishment—but that he had broken the color line and overcome the barriers imposed on him by the larger society. In the teacher's words, "We knew he played baseball, but he was bigger than that."

Today, however, because the accomplishments of African-Americans are filtered through the lens of the larger society, the meanings have changed. The emphasis now is on individual athletic ability and not on the overcoming of society's racism. The result is that young Blacks are being immersed in a set of values that is neither in their own best interests nor in those of the Black community.

Though the African-American community was in the forefront of the fight for desegregated schools, some polls now indicate that many are disappointed with the outcomes of school desegregation. Asked about the effects of school desegregation, almost 60% of those polled believed that the education of Black children was worse than or the same as it had been prior to the Brown decision.[22] Having observed the changes in schools for over two decades, all of these teachers were aware of the paradox of desegregated schools, a paradox expressed as early as 1934 in an essay by W. E. B. Dubois who argued:

> The Negro needs neither segregated schools nor mixed schools. What he needs is Education. What he must remember is that there is no magic, either in mixed schools or in segregated schools. A mixed school with poor and unsympathetic teachers, with hostile opinion, and no teaching of the truth concerning black folk, is bad. A segregated school with ignorant placeholders, inadequate equipment, poor salaries, and wretched housing is equally bad.

While the teachers conceded that desegregation had resulted in improved material conditions in formerly segregated schools, these same teachers spoke unhesitatingly of the systematic means—tracking, lowered expectations, and unprincipled support of athletically inclined Black students—by which Black pupils within desegregated classrooms are denied access to full educational opportunity.

Compounding the issue is the decreasing number of Black teachers who can talk honestly with Black students and their parents in terms they understand about the personal value, the collective power, and the political consequences of choosing academic achievement. Assessing the benefits as well as the costs of deseg-regation, another teacher discussed this theme. One consequence of desegregation, she concluded, is that it is now more difficult for African-American teachers to adopt the multifaceted and protean roles of admonisher, urger, and meddler:

> I think that integration, when I'm talking I could talk about it two ways. It's like integration is great and we need to know each other, but they miss the big picture. I know that one way integration is worthwhile because you're going into the work force. But, on the other hand, it's been so detrimental to kids. I mean maybe it's been great for White people. Because I don't think the kids even know where they're supposed to be themselves. The kids say, "Well I've got a C, so hey, that's wonderful." But, see nobody Black would let him get away with that. They would say, "You know you're supposed to do better than that," in the olden days. What integration as a whole has done to the Black teacher? In the olden days you would just stand there in front of your class and just tell 'em, you can't do that. I mean, I can't do that when I got Black and White, you know what I mean? I mean you could do it in your own little way, but you can't just stand there and say,"You're being hurt by this, wake up and smell the coffee," kind of thing. They really don't understand what's happening to them. That's the sad part.

Contrasting his experience in segregated and desegregated schools, a teacher from North Carolina with 41 years in a rural North Carolina community expanded on this theme:

> The big difference was that I can see we were able to do more with the Black students. In other words, if I wanted to come in this morning, have my kids put their books under the desk or on top of the desk and I'd get up on top of my desk and sit down and just talk to them. Why are you here? Are you here just to make out another day? Or are you here because the law says you must go to school? Are you here to try to better yourself? This kind of thing I could talk to them about. Well, now I'm here to better myself. Well what must you do? What are the require-ments? Do you know where your competition is? And I could talk to them about things like that. Your competition is not your little cousin that's sittin' over there. Your competition is that White per-son over there in that other school. He's your competition. He's the one you've got to compete with for a job. And the only way

that you're going to be able to get that job is that you can't be as good as he is, you got to be better. And I could drill that into their heads. But once you integrated, I mean you didn't feel, I didn't I don't feel comfortable really in a mixed setting to really get into the things that the Whites did to us as Black people. I don't really feel too comfortable doing that in a mixed group because I think I know how I felt when they talked about me. And surely they have feelings even though sometimes I didn't think they had any, but that kind of thing we, I mean I, couldn't do. I didn't want to pull them aside because then they would feel that they had been moved out of the mainstream because then you were just talking to just Blacks, but this is the big difference that I saw that you couldn't do. Well, I guess another thing I got disillusioned with integration because of that type thing, because I could not get to my people and tell them all the things that they needed to know. I could not beat into their minds that they had to be better; that to compete with that White kid on an equal basis was not enough. I couldn't tell them that. I couldn't stop my class and tell him that so that he would understand. I think this is one of the things that they miss, Black kids, in general.

The result is an increasing passivity among Black students who have come to view academic excellence in strictly utilitarian purposes. Continuing, Everett Dawkins described students' reactions once schools were desegregated:

Black kids are not hungry now. There are some few of them that want to be on top, but they're not really hungry. They want to be there because they heard somebody say that it's nice to be on top, but they do not hunger and thirst after righteousness, if I can use that expression from the Bible. They don't hunger and thirst for it and the reason they don't hunger and thirst for these things is because nobody tells them that they need to hunger and thirst for these things. . . . There's nothing that's pushing them when they went into an integrated situation, they looked back they look at Martin Luther King's address and he said, "I have seen the promised land." They say, "I have reached the promised land. Now that I'm here I don't need to be concerned anymore."

African-American Values and Pedagogy

To confront these issues with their students, these teachers have consciously fashioned philosophies and pedagogies that draw on lessons from their own childhoods. They also incorporate classroom activities that are based on African-American community norms. When asked specifically about what sources they drew on to inform their teaching, several elementary teachers noted that their participation in church events and pageants where "every one had a part—even if it was as a lamb" influenced the way they currently structure their classrooms. Several pointed to the use of plays, choral reading, and poetry recitations as deliberate attempts to incorporate forms from the African-American church into their classrooms.

A community college teacher, with no teacher-training experience, articulated that one of her models for good teaching came from listening to the sermons of Black preachers. She noted they are ideal models because they teach, entertain, and keep people's attention. Moreover, they are able to take complicated theological material and make it understandable to the average person. Fieldwork undertaken in this teacher's classroom revealed that she incorporated the preaching style characteristic of African-American preachers as well as the expressive talk that characterizes African-American speech events to link the abstract concepts in the text to everyday life. These interactions differed from normal classroom discourse because they were gesturally as well as stylistically embellished. Prosodic features such as vowel elongation; changes in meter, tempo, and rhythm; cross-speaker anaphora; single speak repetition; manipulation of grammatical structures; and use of figurative language were salient features of this African-American speaking style. This strategy was but one of many this teacher used to involve all of her students in class discussion.[23]

Even when teachers did not mention that African-American norms undergirded their approach to teaching, I found evidence that an African-American ethos informed their teaching pedagogy. An urban high-school English teacher mentioned during an interview that discussions and debate formed an integral part of his pedagogy. Intended to engage his students in critical discussions of literature, these debates were not free-wheeling, non-purposeful rap sessions, but, rather, were exchanges designed to promote group understanding:

> When class begins you will see them (students) quiet up and when you leave you will see them—I'm trying to push them out the door to get to their other class, because I know how I demand getting to class on time. And they're still talking about what is going on

234

and they nag me because I don't give them the answer when they get in a heated debate about something, you see. A discussion. They get annoyed with me because I don't give them the answer. Part of my motivation is to get everyone involved, you see, so everyone is involved. As you will notice if you walk into my classroom, or you'll notice that soon after, if not right away, everyone is involved. I don't believe in standing in front of a class and expounding on something forever. I like for everyone to be involved. I don't believe in rappin', I mean not the rap song, but to me you have to discuss something meaningfully. You have to have some kind of a goal, or what have you, that you're trying to reach. But just to get in and, "I'm going to express my opinion," and rap about this, and argue and that sort of thing, back and forth. If you're not focusing on something specific, well, then, I don't go along with that. That's for the lunch room, or when you have your free time together. That's fine, but in the classroom, let's focus in on something that we're all striving for.

Explaining the responsibility of each individual for the group's learning, he continued:

I tell the students I'm just another member of the class. If this class goes wrong, you're just as responsible as I am because each individual is responsible for making this class work. Don't expect me to be the only one responsible for motivating this class. And I say, "The only way that you can contribute is by motivating this class. If it fails, you're responsible. You have to contribute, we all contribute and everybody listens when someone else is talking," or what have you. And it takes a while to get that sort of chemistry working, but it works.

The teachers' beliefs evident in their descriptions of classroom activities reflect some of the values that are at the heart of African-American communities.[24] In all of these descriptions, for instance, the relationships were marked by social equality, egalitarianism, and a mutuality stemming from a group, rather than an individual, ethos.

Most of what typically occurs in classrooms in the United States encourages competitive behavior and individual achievement. In contrast to this, much of the activity in the classrooms of these African-American teachers focused on the group not the individual. The activities emphasized cooperation instead of competition. In the minds of these teachers, learning is a social event, not primarily a competitive or individual endeavor. Unlike most classrooms, where the typical learning strategy matches one learner with a text, learning in these classrooms was structured as a social activity. Texts were interpreted by the group and it was only by talking collectively about the texts that they came to have meaning.

While these teachers accepted the institutional goal of developing cognitive growth, their collective personal definition of the teacher's role was not confined to the development of academic skills, but also included the social and emotional growth of students. All of the teachers interviewed conceived of their role as educators as broader than that assigned by the narrow, utilitarian purpose of schooling. From these teachers' perspectives, not only are cognitive and affective growth interdependent, but neither is achievable nor desirable without the other. A high-school teacher from a large West Coast city spoke to this point. This California Teacher of the Year supported the trend toward professionalization—including higher salaries for teachers as well as the corresponding accountability that would be demanded of them. However, she also worried about the seemingly singular emphasis on higher test scores that has become the focus of some who support professionalization. She worried especially about what the consequences of this movement would be for African-American students. Her concerns did not stem from disagreement with holding teachers accountable for student progress. She was troubled instead because, based on her 18 years of experience successfully teaching African-American students, she predicted that holding teachers accountable only for cognitive growth without concomitantly stressing affective development lessened the prospect that higher educational standards for Black students would be realized:

> T: I didn't believe that before the Commission's work, but I think that's gonna be the wave of the future, because if teachers make any demands, especially monetary demands, the way things are going now, you're gonna have to be accountable, that's why I think that, I keep saying I'm hopin' I'm outta the profession by then, but I think that everything is going to be judged by content. It's gonna just be like making Toyotas, that's what I meant by that Toyota statement.
> I: Toyotas!
> T: It's gonna be on production. How many kids score so and so on this test, or so and so. Like my one friend said, what she

said is "What they should do is pay teachers by the head. Then everybody would learn things." That's really what it's gonna boil down to.

I: Um hum.

T: And so that's the one course Shanker and those guys think is all right. I don't go for that because I'm more into the affective domain.

Recognizing that an appropriate pedagogy for Black students could not be limited only to academics but had to encompass all the other aspects of the students' lives, this teacher continued:

> I always point out those examples of other things that they can do and things that they can be, so I think that's probably what I give them—high and different expectations. I tell them that I really want them to learn to think by themselves and I want them to learn how to find things out. I think it's more important for me to let them know how to find out things than to give them everything because learning is a lifelong thing. I want them to be able to use it (education) as a lifelong thing and to have a quality of life based on knowing something about their history and literature. To live pretty much on their own terms and be anti-materialistic. Don't get caught up in what you own. You need certain things, but don't define yourself according to those things. I'm interested in self worth and inner beauty and all those idealistic kinds of things.

It could be argued that balancing the cognitive and affective domains is indispensable to more humanistic and caring relationships for all—not just Black pupils. However, among these teachers there was a shared perspective concerning the education of African-American students that was marked by a philosophical orientation that extended beyond the humanistic education others have proposed. There was evidence in these interviews of a "hidden curriculum" undergirding these teachers' practice. The teachers were concerned that their students master more than the content of specific subjects. And though the details of this hidden curriculum might be refashioned to suit context, individual teacher style, and level of students, its intention was to convey to African-American students, in terms they understood, the personal value, the collective power, and the political consequences of choosing or rejecting academic achievement. Without this dialogue, these teachers reasoned, African-American students were unlikely to be engaged in or committed to their own learning. This point was emphasized over and over in the narratives of other teachers with similar experiences.

Everett Dawkins, the high-school teacher who was quoted earlier, demonstrated how one aspect of this hidden curriculum manifested itself in his formerly all-Black classroom when he related his efforts to instill "hunger and thirst" for learning in his African-American students. Another illustration was provided by Jean Vander, a first-grade teacher who has taught in Boston's public schools since 1952 and is currently working in a low income school. Here Ms. Vander discusses how she approached first graders.

> T: Now ours (socioeconomic status) is very low. Very low, but this is what you got to zero in. Because these kids are not dumb and we are going to pay a price. These children are not dumb. They are very capable . . . if they were handled correctly— emotionally—if their needs were serviced all around, I think you'd have some real bright kids coming out.
> I: So what do you do?
> T: I really try to reinforce their self image all of the time and I praise all the good work. I try to involve some peer pressure. I talk to them a great deal. If they're reading I say, "You're doing very well, keep on doing this."

The above excerpt illustrates how, when seeking to connect them to the classroom, Ms. Vander tailored the hidden curriculum to the age and sophistication of her students. In the concluding section I will discuss further how such practices reflect teachers' uses and understanding of community norms.

Conclusion: Education or Schooling?

Some observers contend that irrespective of the particular culture schools exist in, families and community members have consistently undertaken the task of transmitting particular understandings, values, and behaviors to their young. The existence of schools, Herskovitz argued a number of years ago, tends to shift the responsibility for education away from the family to an outside institution.[25] Though there is a tendency to associate what goes on in schools with education, anthropologists and others working within an anthropological tradition offer insights into the different purposes of schooling and education.

Those who address the different functions of schooling tend to emphasize schools as instruments for maintaining the social order[26] or as institutions which are primarily responsible for cognitive development.[27] Though this differentiation is analytically useful, these functions of schooling are related and usually covary according to students' gender, social class, ethnicity, and race.

Two competing theories have been advanced that attempt to explain the widespread alienation of African-Americans from schools. Both bear significantly on the analysis that follows. The first one, the cultural mismatch hypothesis, contends that differences in communicative and interactional norms between home and school cultures are responsible for the failure of ethnic minority students.[28] The second hypothesis is that educational failure results more from social, political, and economic inequalities than from discontinuities in communicative patterns.[29] Uncritical adherence to either of these competing theories can cloud our ability to understand what teachers believe about education, how they respond to students, and, finally, to see what may actually be taking place in their classrooms. Taken alone, neither of these theories is adequate for explaining what the teachers described in this chapter know and do to achieve success with their students.

It is widely acknowledged that some teachers achieve much greater success with individual students as well as with particular groups of students than their colleagues in the same school do. All of the teachers interviewed for my study represent cases in point. Some researchers dismiss teachers such as these as anomalous cases—individuals whose successes are idiosyncratic and result mainly from some elusive and unique qualities or a special charisma rather than from well-reasoned understandings. Perhaps this is the reason why few efforts have been made to systematize the understandings, beliefs, and practice of such teachers. An unfortunate consequence is that though there is a large body of literature on teacher thinking, planning, and practical knowledge, it does not focus specifically on successful teachers who work with students who are currently defined as and pejoratively labeled "at risk." As a result, we know little about the thinking, pedagogical processes, understandings, or considerations of such teachers, nor do we understand how many of these teachers define their teaching situations, decide which roles and responsibilities to assume, and apply this knowledge to their practice.

Research has clearly shown that it is not merely shared ethnicity but shared cultural and social norms that affect the educational success of ethnic minority students. Gay's study found no difference between the way Black and White teachers interacted with Black students.[30] It is precisely this point that Labov argued when he called for community teachers.[31] He argued that persons who had not been socialized into mainstream teaching norms would make better teachers for African-American children than their college-trained counterparts. Labov incorrectly assumed, however, that successfully participating in mainstream institutions uniformly stripped individuals of their proficiency in community norms. Indeed, my own research into the communicative and performance competence of middle-class African-American women teachers challenged such an unqualified assertion.[32] It is also true, however, that schools and teachers who blame the victim—attributing student failure to family attitudes and supposed cultural deficits rather than to institutional racism and structural inequities—or the larger society for their own failure to reach African-American students, are unlikely to teach them successfully.[33]

Where they are closely linked, school and community interests can play complementary roles in promoting particular values, understandings, and behaviors—even if these contradict those of the social order. Such is the case with Amish schools, Black Muslim schools, the community-organized free schools that emerged during the 1960s and 1970s, and increasingly with contemporary African-American independent schools.[34] Researchers who have considered the success of such schools argue that just as the high rate of school failure among African-American children can be explained by the politics enacted between pariah children and host-group teachers, alternative schools are often places where cultural solidarity between teachers and students accounts for their success.[35]

How successful teachers of African-American students define their task and what they understand to be the goals of successful teaching remains largely unexamined. It is my contention that the teachers who participated in my study are successful because they are proficient in community norms—i.e., they are able to communicate with students in a familiar cultural idiom. Moreover, their success is also due to their understanding of the current as well as the historic social, economic, and political relationships of their community to the larger society. These teachers are not merely educating the mind—they are educating for character, personal fulfillment, and success in the larger society as well as for competence in the local community.

Notes and References

1. I acknowledge funding for this work from the University of Pennsylvania Research Foundation and the Spencer Small Grant Program. A Spencer Postdoctoral Fellowship from the National Academy of Education, a Carolina Minority Postdoctoral Fellowship, and a Smithsonian Faculty Fellowship enabled me to work full-time on this study. I am grateful to Jeanne Newman for her careful transcription of the interviews.

2. This chapter was written while the author was on leave (1989-1991) at the University of North Carolina at Chapel Hill.

3. I. Reed, "Reading, Writing and Racism," *San Francisco Examiner Image Magazine* August 1990: 27-28; B. Blauner, *Black Lives, White Lives: Three Decades of Race Relations in America* (Berkeley: University of California Press, 1989); S. Monroe and P. Goldman, *Brothers: Black and Poor, A True Story of Courage and Survival* (New York: Ballantine Books, 1988); H. Baker, "What Charles Knew," in *An Apple for My Teacher: 12 Authors Tell About Teachers Who Made the Difference*, ed. L. D. Rubin, Jr. (Chapel Hill: Algonquin Books, 1987); M. Fields and K. Fields, *Lemon Swamp: A Carolina Memoir* (New York: The Free Press, 1985); R. Kluger, *Simple Justice* (New York: Vintage, 1975); A. Murray, *Black Experience and American Culture* (New York: Vintage, 1970); S. Clark, *Echo in My Soul* (New York: E. P. Dutton, 1962).

4. H. Kohl, *36 Children* (New York: Signet, 1965); J. Herndon, *The Way It Spozed To Be* (New York: Simon and Schuster, 1968); S. Decker, *An Empty Spoon* (New York: Harper and Row, 1969); J. Kozol, *Death at an Early Age: The Destruction of the Hearts and Minds of Negro Children in the Boston Public Schools* (Boston: Houghton-Mifflin, 1967).

5. S. Lightfoot, *Worlds Apart: Relationships Between Families and Schools* (New York: Basic Books, 1978); P. Sterling, *The Real Teachers: 30 Inner-City Schoolteachers Talk Honestly About Who They Are, How They Teach and Why* (New York: Random House, 1972); G. Lerner, *Black Women in White America: A Documentary History* (New York: Vintage, 1972).

6. P. Conroy, *The Water is Wide* (Boston: Houghton-Mifflin, 1972).

7 R. Rist, "Student Social Class and Teacher Expectations: The Self-Fulfilling Prophecy in Ghetto Education," *Harvard Educational Review* 40 (1970): 411-451; R. Rist, *The Urban School: A Factory for Failure* (Cambridge: MIT Press, 1973).

8. M. Foster, "Constancy, Change, and Constraints in the Lives of Black Women Teachers: Some Things Change, Most Stay the Same," *NWSA Journal* 3 (1991): 233-261; M. Foster, "The Politics of Race: Through African Teachers' Eyes," *Journal of Education* 172 (1991): 123-141.

9. V. P. Franklin, *The Education of Black Philadelphia: The Social and*

Educational History of a Minority Community 1900-1950 (Philadelphia: University of Pennsylvania Press, 1979).

10. J. King, "Black Student Alienation and Black Teachers' Emancipatory Pedagogy," in *Readings on Equal Education, Volume 11: Qualitative Investigations into Schools and Schooling*, ed. M. Foster (New York: AMS Press, 1991); G. Ladson-Billings, "Returning to the Source: Implications for Educating Teachers of Black Students," in *Readings on Equal Education, Volume 11: Qualitative Investigations into Schools and Schooling*, ed. M. Foster (New York: AMS Press, 1991); P. Murrell, "Cultural Politics in Teacher Education: What's Missing in the Preparation of Minority Teachers," in *Readings on Equal Education, Volume 11: Qualitative Investigations into Schools and Schooling*, ed. M. Foster (New York: AMS Press, 1991); M. Foster, *It's Cookin' Now: An Ethnographic Study of a Successful Black Teacher in an Urban Community College*, unpublished doctoral dissertation, Harvard University, 1987; M. Foster, "It's Cookin' Now: A Performance Analysis of the Speech Events of a Black Teacher in an Urban Community College," *Language in Society* 18 (1989): 1-29; Foster, "Constancy, Change, and Constraints"; A. Henry, "Black Women, Black Pedagogies: An African-Canadian Context," paper presented at the American Educational Research Association Conference, Boston, MA, 1990; K. Lomotey, "African-American Principals: Bureaucrats/Administrators and Ethno/Humanists," in *Too Much Schooling, Too Little Education: A Paradox of Black Life in White Societies*, ed. M. Shujaa (Trenton, NJ: Africa World Press, 1994). All of this group, except Lomotey, describe teachers. Lomotey describes the philosophy and practice of principals.

11. D. A. Spencer, *Contemporary Women Teachers: Balancing School and Home* (New York: Longman, 1986).

12. All of the teachers' names are pseudonyms. The place names remain unchanged.

13. Foster, *It's Cookin' Now*; Foster, "It's Cookin' Now."

14. D. Jones, "Toward a Native Anthropology," *Human Organization* 29 (1970): 251-259.

15. J. Gwaltney, "Common Sense and Science: Urban Core Black Observations," in *Anthropologists at Home in North America: Methods and Issues in the Study of One's Own Society*, ed. D. Messerschmidt (New York: Random House, 1980), 46-61.

16. J. Lytle, "Minority Student Access to and Preparation for Higher Education," paper presented at the Annual Meeting of the American Educational Research Association Conference, Boston, MA, 1990.

17. The teachers were placed into regions using the 1989 *Statistical Abstract of the United States*, 109th edition, which divides the States into nine regions.

18. Foster, "It's Cookin' Now"; M. Foster, "The Power to Know One Thing

is Never the Power to Know All Things: Methodological Notes on Two Studies of African-American Teachers," paper presented at the Annual Meeting of the American Educational Research Association Conference, Boston, MA, 1990; Foster, "Constancy, Change, and Constraints"; Foster, "The Politics of Race"; M. Foster, "Just Got to Find a Way: Case Studies of the Lives and Practice of Exemplary Black High School Teachers," in *Readings on Equal Education, Volume 11: Qualitative Investigations into Schools and Schooling*, ed. M. Foster (New York: AMS Press, 1991), 273-309.

19. Foster, "Constancy, Change, and Constraints."

20. Foster, "It's Cookin' Now"; Foster, "Constancy, Change, and Constraints"; Foster, "The Politics of Race"; Foster, "Just Got to Find a Way."

21. For a discussion of the term "recreation explosion" with respect to the development of coastal South Carolina, see: J. Russell and R. G. Silvernail, "The Impact of Recreation on Coastal South Carolina," *Business and Economic Review* 13 (1966): 3-8.

22. "Black Enterprise Survey Results," *Black Enterprise* August 1990: 85-94.

23. Foster, *It's Cookin' Now*; Foster, "It's Cookin' Now."

24. Foster, *It's Cookin' Now*; Foster, "It's Cookin' Now"; R. Abrahams and J. Szwed, "Introduction," in *After Africa: Extracts from British Travel Accounts and Journals of the Eighteenth and Nineteenth Centuries Concerning the Slaves, their Manners, and Customs in the British West Indies*, eds. R. Abrahams and J. Szwed (New Haven: Yale University Press, 1983), 1-48; S. B. Heath, *Ways with Words: Language, Life and Work in Communities and Classrooms* (Cambridge: Cambridge University Press, 1983); J. Szwed and R. Abrahams, "After the Myth: Studying Afro-American Cultural Patterns in the Plantation Literature," in *African Folklore in the New World*, ed. D. Crowley (Austin: University of Texas, 1979), 65-68.

25. M. Herskovitz, *Man and His Works* (New York: Alfred A. Knopf, 1947); M. Herskovitz, *Cultural Anthropology* (New York: Alfred A. Knopf, 1964).

26. Y. Cohen, "The Shaping of Men's Minds; Adaptations to the Imperatives of Culture," in *Anthropological Perspectives on Education*, eds. M. Wax et al. (New York: Basic Books, 1971), 19-50.

27. J. Bruner, R. Oliver, P. Greenfield, et al., *Studies of Cognitive Growth* (New York: John Wiley and Sons, 1966).

28. F. Erickson, "Transformation and School Success: The Politics and Culture of Educational Achievement," *Anthropology and Education Quarterly* 18 (1987): 335-355.

29. J. Ogbu, "Variability in Minority School Performance: A Problem in Search of an Explanation," *Anthropology and Education Quarterly* 18 (1987): 312-334.

30. G. Gay, "Ethnic Minorities and Educational Equality," in *Multicultural Education; Issues and Perspectives*, eds. J. Banks and C. A. McGee Banks (Boston: Allyn and Bacon, 1989), 167-188.
31. W. Labov, *Language in the City: Studies in the Black English Vernacular* (Philadelphia: University of Pennsylvania Press, 1972).
32. Foster, "It's Cookin' Now."
33. J. King and G. Ladson-Billings, "Dysconscious Racism and Multicultural Illiteracy: The Distorting of the American Mind," paper presented at the Annual Meeting of the American Educational Research Association, Boston, MA, 1990; Lytle, "Access and Preparation."
34. For a brief discussion of contemporary African-American independent schools, see: "Taking Knowledge into Our Own Hands: Black Private Schools," *Emerge Magazine* October 1990: 28-29.
35. C. Cazden, "How Knowledge about Language Helps the Classroom Teacher—Or Does It: A Personal Account," *Urban Review* 9 (1976): 74-90.

Chapter Ten

Literacy, Education, and Identity Among African-Americans: The Communal Nature of Learning*

Vivian L. Gadsden
University of Pennsylvania

Literacy and education are valuable possessions which African-American families have respected, revered, and sought as a means to personal freedom and communal hope from the time of enslavement to the present. Approaches to interpreting literacy and education in the African-American communities are deeply entrenched in the differential meanings ascribed to schooling and education and to their community-determined purposes, functions, and uses. Literacy, as Harris found, has been attached historically to the uplift of Black people—uplift steeped in understanding the traditions and beliefs of literacy and education as communal knowledge, hence group strength.[1]

This chapter focuses on literacy and education as a dualism that is perceived as an individual possession and communally embedded

* A version of this chapter was first published in *Urban Education* 27 (1993): 352-369.

commodity within many segments of the African-American community. Using information from a study of 25 African-American adults, the discussion focuses on multiple interpretations of literacy that link it to education, and how literacy and education shape identity within the community. Moreover, the discussion addresses identity formation by examining the ways these translations of literacy and learning have been conveyed to subsequent generations. The discussion is based on the premise that literacy should be seen as a continuous, ever-changing activity, transformed by critical life events, translated as a result of life-span transitions, and defined and shaped by cultural and community beliefs about the nature of education and the expected rewards of learning.

Background

Until the past decade, research on the ethnic and cultural aspects of literacy and education, specifically research on African-American learners, focused almost exclusively on the ways in which culture serves as an impediment to literacy and educational achievement.[2] What is especially striking about these accounts is the variability in the explanations of the nature and impact of schooling and education within the African-American community put forth by researchers and educational critics.[3] For example, the well-intentioned and often informative reports that emerged during the 1960s[4] and others in the 1970s attempted to describe Black children's educational achievement and in doing so, often associated the obstacles to Black children's literacy and school achievement with their culture, family life, and community.[5]

Generally limited to descriptions of Black urban life and education, many of the studies reinforced images of a community that devalued education and hard work to achieve it. Etzkowitz and Schaflander wrote that "love, warmth, hygiene, education, and family stability [we]re absent from most Negroes" and that there were "practically no pluses in Negro ghetto culture . . . [only] bitterness and despair, nihilism, hopelessness, rootlessness, and all the symptoms of social integration in the poor speech, poor hygiene, poor education."[6]

The pictures of African-American life included several overlapping characteristics. First, the images were minimally accurate, at best, and constrained by a distinctively Western, middle-class interpretation of education and success in non-dominant communities.[7] In many of these studies, some of which used qualitative methods, the researchers interpreted interview and observational data with the severe disadvantage of knowing little or nothing about the socio-political or human histories of the communities they studied. Second, by invoking the "medical model" in which African-American children and families were seen as afflicted and needing to be nursed back to health, the studies, in fact, resulted in greater support for programs to remedy the educational and social problems experienced by African-Americans in urban areas. At best, the studies emphasized "a slice" of Black life embedded in well-defined urban enclaves, generally in Northern cities. Excluded from these discussions, however, was any mention of African-Americans in other contexts (e.g., the South and rural areas) or of the historical precedents (e.g., racism, educational inequality, and social inequity) that contributed to the problems.

At about the same time or shortly after these reports appeared, less widely cited works were also published, e.g., Billingsley's writing on Black families in America;[8] Barnes' work on the Black community as the source of positive self-concept for Black children;[9] and Hall, Cross, and Freedle's definition of stages in the development of Black awareness.[10] These reports provided a different (and many would argue broader) perspective on Black family and life experiences. While they acknowledged the existence of problems within the Black community that militate against school success for many Black children, their interpretations of the problems and projections of solutions affirmed the view that the Black child and family valued education and were both capable and willing to make sacrifices to ensure the education of the child.

The mismatch in the analyses of Black life by African-American researchers and interpretations by non-African-American researchers has been a source of ongoing debate, nested in, but not limited to, intellectual banter and battering. Historical accounts by researchers such as Anderson,[11] Holt,[12] and Harris[13] frame a view in which education and literacy are perceived by African-Americans to be not only important but also eminent in their position within the Black family, church, and community. Research by Foster,[14] Siddle-Walker,[15] and Irvine[16] examines some of the same issues within a time-comparative context. They investigate current portrayals of Blacks as noncaring and bound to the underclass by tracing, over time, educational activities and perceptions of educational access within African-American communities. While these and many of the other studies discussed earlier have obtained similar findings, the interpretation and meaning of the findings, the attributions that have been attached to what was heard, and the conclusions that have been drawn have varied widely.

The basis for this mismatch, as Foster notes, may be that researchers who are not African-Americans are "less biased and able to discern patterns in the Black community and differences among Blacks more clearly than Blacks themselves."[17] A second explanation is that the interpretive discussion of the information gathered is greatly affected by untested assumptions and subtle prejudices with which many researchers who are not Black enter the study of African-American life.[18] A third explanation is that insiders to a culture are less influenced by racial stereotypes about their group and less likely to shy away from exploring more rigorously "the intracultural variability and complexity among members of their own community."[19]

Initially, this mismatch appears to be split along racial and cultural lines, with White researchers providing a view of African-American life that is decidedly different from that provided by African-American researchers, other researchers of color, or White researchers who have immersed themselves in the community in order to understand it.[20] On the surface, it appears that one faction attributes the problem to the victim—in this case, African-Americans—while the other attributes the problem to institutional factors, such as racism. Despite where the issues are stacked, however, the problem appears to lie, at least in part, in the degree to which cultural differences affect how researchers interpret what they see when they look into African-American communities and schools, and what they hear when the voices of African-American parents and children speak about literacy, education, and their capacity to find, achieve, and retain access to education.

The discussion of education and schooling in the African-American community, as may be true in any community, is tied to the development of literate competence. Where culturally diverse communities may differ, however, is in the importance they assign to the purposes of literacy and education, and the linkages among language, literacy, and representations of culture—most comprehensively discussed in reading and linguistic research over the past 25 years.

From the 1960s to the present, research on reading and the African-American learner has revolved around notions of language and linguistic competence and development, i.e., the presence or absence of a linguistic culture for Black children and the viability of Black linguistic codes, meanings, and structure to the reading process itself and school success. The result of these discussions sometimes approached combat about Black English. Several views were set forth during this period. The first one, the "deficit" theory, described reading failure in terms of the linguistic deprivation of Black children. Bereiter and Engelmann[21] and Deutsch[22] suggested in their work that Black children's spoken language was unstructured, undeveloped, and deficient. Thus, these children, the writers argued, did not have an adequate foundation on which to build language skills in standard English, and, as a result, had cognitive deficiencies which obstructed any attempt to succeed in abstract tasks typically required in schools and by a standard English curriculum.

The second one, the "different" theory, suggested that the language of Black children was highly structured, systematic, and logical.[23] Researchers such as Baratz,[24] Labov,[25] Smitherman,[26] and others argued that Black children spoke a "different" language which did not render them any less linguistically capable than children who spoke standard English. Reading researchers such as Ruddell[27] and Goodman[28] suggested that while the differences between Black English and standard English might cause reading problems for some children, Black children showed a high degree of language competence when they translated standard English messages they heard into their own expression.

Although the latter descriptions of Black children's reading strengths and abilities provided a more balanced context for discussing literacy development among African-American children, they only began to present a view of reading ability or, more broadly, literacy as requiring explanations for the nature, importance, and quality of these children's cultural experiences, their social relationships, and their community in the development of literate competence. Research findings reported in the 1980s have not changed this situation entirely but have expanded the emphasis in the field to include the impact of culture on literacy learning. Researchers have begun to rely on actual field experiences as sources of information. Moreover, practitioners are assuming roles as researchers and are beginning to examine their own practice in order to be responsive to all children and to explore alternative approaches to teaching reading. Researchers have also denoted literacy as more than experiences related specifically to books;[29] instead, it is viewed as a life-span experience and as encompassing a wide range of everyday practices about how people come to acquire literacy and develop definitions and beliefs about literacy.

Literacy and Education:
Life Perspectives in a Southern Community

The variety of studies, including those by Delpit,[30]Heath,[31] Delgado-Gaitan,[32] and Taylor & Dorsey-Gaines,[33] that examine the use of knowledge and cultural practices in developing literacy within diverse communities, has provided theoretical bases for investigating issues in literacy. The case study described here is borne out of this tradition, but has been equally encouraged by studies and writings on the Black experience by researchers such as DuBois,[34] Billingsley,[35]Blassingame,[36] and Strickland.[37] It explores the issues of access to and transformations of literacy by examining the historical and contextual factors that contributed to the informants' views about literacy.

Since the signing of the Civil Rights Act of 1964, changes in the way African-Americans are perceived in contexts related to literacy and the utility of schooling for improving life have resulted in a loss of hope and increased cynicism for many African-American families.[38] Many of these changes have been attributed to the discontinuity of inner-city life and weakening of the support systems that the extended family provided in the South.[39] The case study described in this chapter is one small phase of a multi-level study designed to explore the impact of these factors—gender, race and racism, family structure, parent-child interactions, kinship, and distance—on literacy meaning within African-American families. The larger study attempts to examine the definitions and translations of literacy meaning and traditions across four generations of adults and children within 25 families. It is an effort to examine the ways in which the interpretations of literacy and success have evolved or eroded across four generations, to understand views of schooling and literacy, and to identify incentives to active engagement in literacy and schooling.

Context of the Study

The families are originally from a small community in rural South Carolina. Beginning with the second generation of informants, adults in the study began to migrate to the Northeast. However, at least one-half of the families have stayed in this Southern community. The case study is based on information provided by the first generation, people presently in their seventies and early eighties. The families represent a cross-section of participants in the first generation. They differ in such characteristics as level of education, gender, income, number of children, and marital status. Of the informants in the first generation, seven are men and 18 are women; two have been in marriages for 50 or more years. In addition, one woman who has been a dominant force in the community but has no children was also interviewed. Schooling ranged from third grade to post-baccalaureate studies; two people have earned master's degrees. The average number of children is six.

Over 200 hours of interviews were conducted over a 2-year period. All 25 adults were interviewed using open-ended life history methods. I asked the informants about their childhood, family and community life, schooling experiences, views of literacy, experiences with literacy, personal aspirations and goals for their children, and sources of inspiration. The experience was a unique challenge because here is a community where respect for heritage is foremost, education is valued for the sake of learning, and literacy is equated with "learning something."

The Community

This Southern community is a village, an enclave of people, traditions, and sometimes unbridled boldness. It is a community dominated by five or six major families. For years, the best thing that an outsider could do was to marry into one of the major families to give himself or herself an identity. Outsiders were (and are) scrutinized carefully and not given immunity until they demonstrate that they, in fact, bring something to the community or family—property, intellectual ability, good looks, money, social status—and still they may be marginally accepted.

It is a community in which many of the early freed men and women were far more literate than their White counterparts. More than one-half of the informants are the children of parents born into slavery, and are, thus, the first generation in their families to have been born free.

The expectations of children to be successful are great, although not all children are enormously successful or realize their parents' dreams. Many have gone to college, but many left the area after high school to move North. Once in the North, however, they were expected to maintain a close relationship with the home community, even within later generations. For years, this practice was successful, and people felt that the North held opportunities. However, as is true of other communities across the United States, many of the bonds that were once embedded in these communities have been wrought with tensions resulting from crime, drugs, and other problems. Until recently, most of what is known about these problems was only hearsay from the North and from the news media. There is growing, but still relatively little, crime in the area. The crime that does exist is described as "serious," and doors cannot be left unlocked, as was generally done until recent years. Many of the older community members attribute the problems to the people from the North, often returning home with many of the trappings and problems of life in large urban areas.

The White community is barely visible and has not been able to sustain the mainline effect of the African-American community; there is no comparable educational or personal success by Whites within the village and town. With the exception of a few Whites in leadership roles (e.g., the mayor), many other positions are held by local African-Americans. This is in sharp contrast to 25 years ago when a rash of incidents occurred to protest widespread integration attempts. The local professionals are generally White, although the village can boast of many successful African-American professionals who left the community in search of educational opportunity or employment. The older African- Americans in the community, however, have held on to their hope that they will one day have "one of their own" to come back and serve the community in a professional position, such as a local physician or dentist.[40]

Unpacking the Meaning of Literacy and Education

When we were growing up, a few people could read and write, and I guess that if people ever really thought about the term literacy, they would probably define it as reading and writing. But, when I think of the people we respected in this community, some could read, and some could not. But, they could think and somehow get their work done, provide for their families, make decisions, and . . . whatever. These weren't people who just went to school to learn to read. We saw people as smart or able, and sometimes that meant that the people were learned, and sometimes it meant that they had gone to college. What was always important was that the person had enough sense to treat people—elders and other folks in the community—with respect. That was the real sign of an educated person—to understand his community, his people, and then still be able to go right on and move ahead in life. We valued education and success for our children. So, if you want to know how I would define literacy as a Black person, let's say it's reading; let's say it's writing or knowing how to survive in this world—and most of all knowing how to combine all of these things so that you appreciate who you are as a Black person and so you never forget your history. You understand?[41] (Mz. Lennie, 82-year-old)

Mz. Lennie's voice was important to this study. While discussing issues of literacy is, more or less, a matter of course in the day-to-day existence of literacy researchers, I heard in her comments a quiet, though riveting and resonant, message from my childhood: to reconcile scientific inquiry and school-based knowledge with the integrity of my own history, a different twist from the way I have been trained to see research and to conduct it.

My questions to the informants focused on their perceptions of what it means to be literate or educated and on the effect of events and transitions on that meaning. This question initially evoked little response until it was reworded to focus on life events. Literacy was always described in terms of school attendance while education was described as the successful meshing of school and real life in the community. Each person had attended a three-month school in a small, one-room schoolhouse. The experience in the schoolhouse was preparation for accomplishing tasks at home and in the community. The most obvious enactment of literacy occurred in church with the reading of Sunday School lessons and the Bible. These activities encouraged people to seek personal meaning and spiritual uplift. This tradition continues and is evident in the fact that despite the complexity of interpreting the Bible, as literary critics have noted, the people (parishoners) attend Sunday School classes around the community and, as one informant noted, "from 1 to 101, come prepared to understand the Bible lesson!"

In many of the area churches, the structure of Sunday School discussion groups—called classes and resembling traditional school classrooms—typifies the educational premises for participating in community activities. Literate activities have a life-experience orientation, sometimes fundamentalist in its message but mostly motivational and political. Discussion group membership is usually based on age, that is, people of similar ages are often in the same discussion group. However, every class, except infant classes, includes people from across age ranges. This is especially true in adult classes where discussion group members may be as young as 30 and as old as 88. The decision about which group to join is based, as Mz.

Shettie, an 83-year-old, stated, on "whether the teacher [group leader] is a good one, . . . whether [he or she] is able to get everyone involved, . . . and whether [the class members] leave the class feeling [more knowledgeable] and better than when they entered." These high expectations were mentioned consistently in conversations with informants, such as Mz. Laura who commented on her eight years of schooling:

> Going to school three months was like going to school now for three years! When we went to school, we never knew how long we would be there. The most important thing was learning to read and write. We needed to be able to do the transactions at the store, for the cotton. Some people had hopes of going on to get more grades or even going to college. But not too many people knew much about college, and there were not many people who could tell us a lot.
>
> It just seemed as though if we could learn to read like that teacher and learn to do it fast, it would make all the difference. Everyone was excited too—our parents and the old folks. We wanted to make the teacher proud, too. But people had to make choices, and the times were hard. So, we got as much book learning as we could and read on our own. I read all the time to this day, and I made my children read to me.

Mr. Adams spoke of having left school as the end of learning to read:

> You know, people say that the schools back then didn't teach a lot, but learning to read meant everything to me. You got an education! Of course, some children were better readers than others, and you had no time to waste. I didn't really know how far knowing how to read would take me, but I always thought it would take me far. The teacher was someone we knew and respected. My teacher, she was tough, now. She made you get your lessons, and if you didn't, she talked to your parents, and . . . well, you got your skin tore up . . . not just because you didn't do your lesson but because you disrespected the teachers by not doing it. Lots different these days, huh?
>
> Well, you know, I wasn't able to get the learning that I wanted. But, when I didn't get it for myself, I got it for my children. All have a high school diploma, and 4 of the 6 finished college. I depend on them, even when I know I can handle things. I want them to know that I respect what they know. Literacy, I guess,

meant just knowing how to read at that time, and the people who learned to read and could stay in school, . . . well they became some of our top people in this here community—the professors [local educators].

Education was often parsed by the need for people to go to work and help provide for the family. Most of the people who felt confident about their reading stated that even after they left formal schools, they participated in various literate activities which they defined as reading notices, keeping minutes of church meetings, reading the hymnal and prayer books, outlining hymns, and "making up programs." They seemed to operate under the assumption that, as Mz. Lennie stated, "those who can, do, and those who can't do as well, help. Not all people are respected but most often because they won't do or won't help." Some informants stated that people in the community purchased books for their children, when they could, and read these books themselves, or helped their children "sound out" the words; in short, they helped their children using approaches from their school and classroom experiences, but only the most confident appeared to do so.

Once people went to work, their definitions changed as a function of the new transition. Men worked hard on the farms and/or got jobs at the local mill or factories in adjoining towns. Since most people owned their land, they put effort into developing the land. At about the same time that people took on the responsibility of employment, they also assumed the responsibility for families. Literacy became a functional activity, and while people continued to value book reading and learning, they were confronted with the reality of ensuring a livelihood:

> I used to think about reading sometimes, but literacy at this point became survival—how to get the most out of the land, how to make it from day to day. To tell you the truth, I used to work from sunup to sundown, and when I came home, I was naturally too tired to read or care much about reading. My children were born during the Depression and nobody had anything. So we spent all of our time figuring out how to make ends meet. I guess that was the education. (Mr. Duncan)

Still another important event occurred when children were born into a family. Parents demonstrated the value they placed on literacy by ensuring that their children attended school regularly to receive book learning. Thus, the school was perceived as an institutional structure to prepare children to survive and excel in the larger world, and education became a blending of "book learning, understanding their people, and [negotiating] the realities of a 'segregated, unjust' society" (Mz. Lennie). This was an important experience because with the exception of the "Jeanes teacher," a person who came in to teach basic literacy and self-care, the classes were taught by local people. Mrs. Tyler commented:

> I thought it was something that my children were going to school, and I figured that these White folks would someday give just enough of a break maybe for some of the Black children to someday be something, you know, not have to leave home. When my children went to school, I watched all that reading start over again. I used to see them read, and I bought them books—religious stories. Knowing how to talk to the teacher about my child was an important thing to me. I knew my children would succeed where I couldn't. But, you know things were so bad in the South, a lot of people understood that their children might move away for the opportunities. But, some of them could have stayed right here because the North was not much better, just different. Anyway, I had to know how to speak well and ask the teacher and principal the right questions.

But Mr. Young stated:

> When I sent my children to school, I stopped thinking about learning for myself and thought about getting it for the children. I was still trying to figure out how to keep them in school without sacrificing my crops. I didn't want to pull them out, but sometimes, I kept them out at the beginning of the year. We were figuring out how to survive.

In general, literacy constituted a set of functional tasks, even once children entered school. For Mrs. Tyler, literacy became speaking and representing oneself well. She commented on the importance of posture, speaking, and behaving, especially when she is around her children's "professional friends." Mr. Young kept a more basic view of literacy. Despite his stated valuing of literacy and demonstrations of pride in the successes of Blacks in the community, neither Mr. Young nor his children has experienced much academic or economic success. His hope lies in his grand-daughter, the first in his family to attend college.

Several of the informants are living alone now, and literacy has come to mean thinking, reading, writing, and speaking to complete tasks that they once thought outside their purview of need or ability. With adult children in the North or elsewhere, many have been forced to deal with the powers that exist—medicare and doctors— on their own. Reading and understanding constitute literacy for most. One woman stated that "with all her doctors' bills and the fast talking of doctors' receptionists and the insurance representatives," she has to read everything and make sure she has a "handle on things." People rely on friends and, as Fingeret suggested, on networks for support, for helping them with difficult literacy tasks, thus continuing to enact the notions of literacy and education as communal learning and community success.[42]

Interpreting the Issues

Our review of the interviews and observations coupled with subsequent discussions with the community people about the information obtained suggests that they view education as having community-empowering potential. The community members—in and outside of school in this community—have developed views of literacy and schooling that are rooted in the belief that African-American children, like all children, have a right to literacy. Access to *literacy* is achieved through schools, but access to *education* may be accomplished only through mutual understanding, respect for the community, and a sense of cultural identity. This message of school as community-centered was discussed by educational progressivists and critics in the 1930s. Counts identified schools as one of many important institutions, along with family, culture, and religion.[43] Teachers, in turn, were challenged to engage in the struggle to ensure a fair and just life in society. In the 1980s critical theorists reiterated this discussion.[44]

This generation's views of schooling and education were formed often as a result of their exposure to the successes of other African-Americans, their interpretations of what it took for these people to be successful, and their dedication to finding "a way out" for their children, even if they did not understand fully where success would lead their children. Most wanted their children to be successful in school, many wanted their children to go to college and return to their communities to serve, but all seemed to accept the fact that the racial issues in the community constrained opportunities for education and for educated African-American youth.

What can we conclude from this phase of the study? The immediate response is that we can conclude little. The information provided by the informants contributes to an understanding of the beliefs and life events of a small group of people in a Southern community, and through discussions with the informants, some trends or commonalities in thinking emerge.

First, literacy meanings and definitions are tied to the opportunities available for access to literacy. These opportunities may exist in structural contexts (e.g., within school buildings or society) or within the individual. Second, for these African-Americans literacy has historically had cultural and community-specific meanings. Their view of literacy was individually devised in many cases because there were relatively few African-Americans in this community who held college degrees during the informants' youth, although, as they pointed out, "there were highly learned people." Third, school was the basis for some definitions, but people translated literacy for functional tasks and, therefore, interpreted literacy for daily living. Only a few people stopped thinking of themselves as literate because they could no longer go to school. Fourth, despite doubt about literacy for themselves, literacy was seen as "something that no one could take away." It was the medium to success. Fifth, literacy was (and is) seen as ongoing and never-ending, with new changes and twists. As one informant commented, "What you need to know now is much more than what you used to need to know to get by; learning is a powerful thing!" Finally, the enactment of the Civil Rights Act of 1964 was seen as the most significant event to ensure access to literacy. It is not clear whether these views persist in the same measure within this generation or will persist in subsequent generations. Yet, many informants state that if they were young now, they would learn everything and read all the books they could.

The acquisition of literacy and uses of knowledge are tied to the transitions that people make and to understanding life and work in communities, as Heath suggested.[45] These interviews have the potential for adding to our knowledge of beliefs and definitions. The importance of these factors to these adults and their children is undeniable, but the issues must be seen within the context of the community and community members' beliefs about respect. They are intertwined with the community members' sense of self, history, and hopes for educational achievement.

We never really thought about literacy as people now call it. . . .
So, if you want to know how I would define literacy as a Black
person, let's say it's reading; let's say it's writing or knowing how
to survive in this world—and most of all knowing how to combine
all of these things so that you appreciate who you are as a Black
person and so you never forget your history. (Mz. Lennie)[46]

Notes and References

1. V. J. Harris, "African-American Children's Literature: The First One
    Hundred Years," *Journal of Negro Education* 59 (1990): 540-555.
2. T. Holt, "Knowledge is Power: The Black Struggle for Literacy," in *The
    Right to Literacy*, eds. A. A. Lunsford, H. Moglan, and J. Slevin (New
    York: Modern Language Association, 1990).
3. J. D. Anderson, *The Education of Blacks in the South, 1860-1935*
    (Chapel Hill: University of North Carolina Press, 1988); E. V. Siddle-
    Walker, "Effects of Brown vs. Board of Education on an Exemplary
    Black School in Caswell County, North Carolina," paper presented at
    the Annual Meeting of the National Academy of Education, Stanford,
    CA, 1991.
4. J. S. Coleman, *Equality of Educational Opportunity* (Washington,
    DC: Government Printing Office, 1966); D. P. Moynihan, *The Negro
    Family: A Case for National Action* (Washington, DC: Government
    Printing Office, 1965).
5. Although I use "African-Americans" throughout the chapter, I use the
    term interchangeably with the term "Black" because the informants
    identify themselves as Black, not African-American, and because much
    of the work written during the 1960s and 1970s referred to African-
    Americans as Black.
6. H. Etzkowitz and G. M. Schaflander, *Ghetto Crisis: Riots or
    Reconciliation?* (Boston, MA: Little, Brown and Company, 1969).
7. A. Billingsley, "Family Functioning in the Low-Income Black
    Community," *Social Caseworker* December 1969: 563-572.
8. A. Billingsley, *Black Families in America* (Englewood Cliffs, NJ:
    Prentice-Hall, 1968).
9. K. Barnes, "The Black Community as a Source of Positive Self-Concept
    for Black Children: A Theoretical Perspective," in *Black Psychology*,
    ed. R. L. Jones (New York: Harper and Row, 1972).
10. W. S. Hall, W. E. Cross, and K. Freedle, "Stages in the Development of
    Black Awareness: An Exploratory Investigation," in *Black Psychology*,
    ed. R. Jones (New York: Harper and Row, 1972).
11. Anderson, *Education of Blacks*.
12. Holt, "Knowledge is Power."
13. Harris, "African-American Children's Literature."
14. M. Foster, "Educating for Competence in Community and Culture:

Exploring the Views of Exemplary African-American Teachers," in *Too Much Schooling, Too Little Education: A Paradox of Black Life in White Societies*, ed. M. Shujaa (Trenton, NJ: Africa World Press, 1994).

15. Siddle-Walker, *Effects of Brown vs. Board of Education*.

26. J. J. Irvine, *Black Students and School Failure* (New York: Praeger, 1990).

17. M. Foster, "Constancy, Connectedness, and Constraints in the Lives of African-American Teachers," *National Women's Studies Journal* 3 (1991): 236.

18. Billingsley, "Family Functioning."

19. Foster, "Constancy, Connectedness, and Constraints," 236.

20. Many White researchers have examined major issues in the African-American Community and have done so uncompromisingly.

21. C. Bereiter and S. Engelmann, *Teaching Disadvantaged Children in the Preschool* (Englewood Cliffs, NJ: Prentice Hall, 1966).

22. M. Deutsch, *The Disadvantaged Child* (New York: Basic Books, 1967).

23. J. C. Baratz, "Teaching Reading in an Urban Negro School System," in *Teaching African-American Children to Read*, eds. J. C. Baratz and R. C. Shuy (Washington, DC: Center for Applied Linguistics, 1966); W. A. Labov, "Linguistic Research on Nonstandard English of Negro Children," paper presented to the New York Society for the Experimental Study of Education, New York, 1965.

24. Baratz, "Teaching Reading."

25. W. A. Labov, *Language in the Inner City: Studies in the Black English Vernacular* (Philadelphia, PA: University of Pennsylvania Press, 1972).

26. G. Smitherman, *Talkin' and Testifyin': The Language of Black America* (Boston, MA: Houghton-Mifflin, 1977).

27. R. B. Ruddell, "The Effect of Oral and Written Patterns of Language Structure on Reading Comprehension," *The Reading Teacher* 18 (1965): 270-275.

28. K. Goodman, "Dialect Barriers in Reading Comprehension," *Elementary English* 42 (1965): 853-860.

29. D. Bloome and J. Green, "The Social Contexts of Reading: A Multidisciplinary Perspective," in *Advances in Reading/Language Research* Vol. 1, ed. B. Hutson (Greenwich, CT: JAI, 1982); S. B. Heath, *Ways with Words* (Cambridge, England: Cambridge University Press, 1983); D. S. Strickland, "Literacy and the Black Learner," keynote address, paper presented at the Conference on Literacy among Black Youth, University of Pennsylvania, 1989; D. Taylor and C. Dorsey-Gaines, *Growing Up Literate: Learning from Inner City Families* (Portsmouth, NH: Heinemann, 1989).

30. L. Delpit, "The Silenced Dialogue: Power and Pedagogy in Educating

Other People's Children," *Harvard Educational Review* 56 (1988): 280-298.

31. Heath, *Ways with Words*.
32. C. Delgado-Gaitan, "Mexican Adult Literacy: New Directions for Immigrants," in *Becoming Literate in English as a Second Language,* eds. S. R. Goldman and K. Trueba (Norwood, NJ: Ablex, 1987).
33. Taylor and Dorsey-Gaines, *Growing Up Literate.*
34. W. E. B. DuBois, *The Souls of Black Folk* (Greenwich, CT: Fawcett Publishers, 1903).
35. Billingsley, *Black Families in America.*
36. J. Blassingame, *The Slave Community* (New York: Oxford Press, 1972).
37. Strickland, *Literacy and the Black Learner.*
38. J. U. Ogbu, "The Consequences of the American Caste System," in *The School Achievement of Minority Children: New Perspectives,* ed. U. Neisser (Hillsdale, NJ: Lawrence Erlbaum, 1986).
39. S. B. Heath, "Oral and Literate Traditions among Black Americans Living in Poverty," *American Psychologist* 44 (1989): 357-373.
40. The community is in much need of local professionals and has sought to attract them to the area. Educators are respected as professionals because they are willing and tireless resources for the community. Work by Siddle-Walker (in preparation) examines the role of such an outstanding educator in rural North Carolina.
41. I have avoided writing the responses in the native dialect of the informants because they asked me not to do so.
42. A. Fingeret, "Social Network: A New Perspective on Independence and Literate Adults," *Adult Education Quarterly* 33 (1982): 133-146.
43. G. S. Counts, *Dare the Schools Build a New Social Order?* (New York: John Day, 1932).
44. M. W. Apple, *Education and Power* (Boston: Routledge and Kegan Paul, 1982); M. Fine, "Silencing in Public Schools," *Language Arts* 64 (1987): 157-174; H. A. Giroux, "Introduction: Literacy and the Pedagogy of Political Empowerment," in *Literacy: Reading the Word and the World*, eds. P. Freire and D. Macedo (South Hadley, MA: Bergen and Garvey, 1987).
45. Heath, *Ways with Words*.
46. This work was supported by funding from the Spencer Foundation/National Academy of Education and National Center on Adult literacy (NCAL) at the University of Pennsylvania, which is part of the Educational Research and Development Center Program (Grant #R117Q00003) as administered by the Office of Educational Research and Improvement (OERI), U.S. Department of Education (USDE), in cooperation with the Departments of Labor and Health and Human Services. The opinions expressed here do not necessarily reflect the position or policies of the NACL, the OERI, or the USDE.

Too Much Schooling

Part Four

African-Centered
Pedagogy:
An Absolute Necessity
for African-Centered
Education

Introduction to Part Four

When discussing African-centered education I believe that more emphasis should be placed on pedagogy than on curriculum. My reasoning for this is that pedagogy conveys the importance of the teacher to the education process while curriculum is too often reduced to documentation. Working with and in independent African-centered schools for nearly 20 years I have seen good teachers grounded in African-centered thinking use European-centered, racist materials to teach brilliant African-centered lessons. I have seen European-American as well as some African-American public school teachers grounded in European-centered thinking use curriculum materials written by our best African-centered thinkers in ways that trivialize and misrepresent the content. These experiences have convinced me that it is the African-centeredness of the teacher's thinking that determines the African-centeredness of the teaching.

Becoming African-centered in one's thinking is an ongoing process of personal transformation. I was born in the heartland of the United States and steeped in Bible-belt patriotic propaganda. Personal transformation for me has meant perpetually deconstructing the assumptions I learned growing up in that environment in order to center my own thinking in the cultural history of African people. This process has touched my thinking about virtually every aspect of reality. Even though I lived in a supportive African community in a small town, I was surrounded by European American images and versions of reality on television, on radio, in the newspaper, in school, and in the economic and political life of the town. The impact was such that it was difficult during my formative years to locate myself in the cultural history of African people. I learned that George Washington never told a lie and that he crossed the Delaware standing up in boat. I did not learn that he was a slave holder. Also, I did not learn until I was well into adulthood that George Washington Carver, as a boy, had lived less than an hour from my childhood home. Nor did I learn who Booker T. Washington was although, I remember sitting in church on Sundays staring at his portrait on the back of a paper fan. I thought it interesting that his picture should appear on the church fans when the only other picture so placed was that of a white Jesus wearing a white robe in the middle of a flock of white sheep. Recalling and analyzing these experiences and others similar to them has been an important part of my personal transformation.

Becoming African-centered in one's thinking necessarily involves a critical analysis of the social order and a historical understanding of one's position in it. This is a process of realization that entails deconstructing socially constructed versions of reality. We come to understand reality objectively through our interaction with the external environment which includes other people engaged in their own interactions and reality forming processes. We subjectively organize these experiences in our minds and draw upon them to make sense of subsequent interactions and to identify ourselves in relationship to others. While I have presented an overly simplified version of a complex process within human development, my purpose in delving into this area is to make the point that the social context into which we are born imposes a material reality that provides a context for much of what we understand to be real. The United States is a society in which the politically dominant cultural orientation is rooted in Western European cultural history. Thus, even though we as people of African descent can lay claim to inclusion within the continuum of African cultural history, we typically know more about the myths and legends of Europe than about the movements of African people through time and space. Consequently, European views of the world, including versions of European/American relationships with Africa, are often more accessible and influential in our thinking than are African interpretations.

Deconstruction of assumptions about social reality that validate European-centered hegemony is a necessary, but not sufficient condition for African-centered personal transformation. There must also be a process of reconstructing social reality—both objectively and subjectively—based on one's understanding of African cultural history and perception of one's location in it. This is the process of centering oneself. It involves purposeful learning about African cultural history and critically reinterpreting what one has been taught. It requires seeking out perspectives other than those legitimated by the European American elite who have shown time and time again that they will do virtually anything to maintain dominance in their social order. As one continues to grow and develop in his/her understanding of African cultural history s/he also locates himself/herself differently within in it. Consequently, we will reconstruct assumptions about reality many times throughout our life spans. The important thing to understand about this process is that one's movement through time is not the same as climbing a mountain; there is no peak whose attainment marks the end of the climb.

African-centered thinking is a process of personal transformation that brings with it the responsibility for changing oppressive social conditions. This is a collective exigency for the betterment of humanity. African-centered pedagogy, because it proceeds from African-centered thinking, is also evolutionary in its development. Part Four of this book consists of three chapters that explore the philosophy and practice of African-centered pedagogy. In Chapter Eleven, "BEing the Soul Freeing Substance: A Legacy of Hope in Afro Humanity", Joyce Elaine King and Thomasyne Lightfoote Wilson present a philosophical foundation for the pursuit of African liberation pedagogy. They extend discussion beyond non-critical approaches to "multi-cultural education" in order to embrace the freeing of thought from oppressive pedagogies that oppose social change. Chapter Twelve, "African-centered Pedagogy: Complexities and Possibilities", by Carol D. Lee focuses on the need for an African-centered pedagogy and the aims that such a pedagogy must address if it is to be instrumental for African-American liberation. She provides examples of the implementation of such a pedagogy drawn from the New Concept Development Center, an African-centered independent school she helped to found in Chicago. Agyei Akoto's "Notes on an African-centered Pedagogy" is Chapter Thirteen. This seminal chapter offers a detailed analysis of the critical role African cultural history plays in establishing a context for African-centered pedagogy. It is argued that such pedagogy must not only be liberatory in its intent, but, that, in order to be truly African-centered, it must have nation-building as its goal.

These authors give us frameworks that go well beyond superficial interpretations of African-centered education and pedagogy. Their collective focus is on helping us to recognize and challenge cultural domination while constructing a new world order that is given meaning by African understandings of humanity and humanness.

Chapter Eleven

*BE*ing the Soul-Freeing Substance: A Legacy of Hope in AfroHumanity*

Joyce Elaine King
Santa Clara University
Thomasyne Lightfoote Wilson
San Jose State University

Speak the truth to the people . . .
Free them with reason
Free them with honesty
Free the people with Love and Courage . . .
And Care for their being
—Mari Evans[1]

. . . We lose about ten thousand children every year to poverty. That's more kids over a five year period than we lost in the Vietnam war. But where is the outrage?
—Marian Wright Edelman[2]

* A shorter version of this chapter was previously published in *Journal of Education* 172 (1990): 9–27.

A Prescient Hope in the Substance of Afro Humanity

True human freedom means BEing equitable in one's soul, especially learning to nourish well-being and differentness in self and other persons. BEing free is based on knowing one's own humanity from within. This chapter concentrates on the prescient hope for humankind that is rooted in the foundation of all people's Afro/human beginnings in the Olduvai Gorge of East Africa.[3] We recognize that the substance of this Afro humanity, with its legacy of hope, is a fundamentally African quality of existence that involves being attuned to the human spirit within while attending to humankind and the earth. Embracing humankind's Afro humanity offers hopeful potential for expanding and assuring an equitable human landscape that could foster non-oppressive and non-defensive uses (not misuses) of the diversity of all peoples. Recognizing and living the existence of Afro humanity is soul-freeing. This living means participating in the creative possibilities that come from BEing equitable with each other. In the universal truth of humankind's beginnings there is also the hope of being free from the Western cultural bias against Africa and against being one's *self*.

The cultural bias against Africa and the racial slavery it justified are products of a "way of being" that instituted all manner of slave-master exploitation, degradation, and human suffering associated with the mission of civilizing Africa and the "New World." This mission set in motion devastating consequences for people and the earth; overturned meanings of "being civilized" continue to undermine the possibilities for equitable existence by distorting the energy of relating freely and humanely throughout the world. For example, it has been widely assumed that the "Negro race" was "inferior" and "incapable of making any substantial contribution to civilization."[4] Derogatory assumptions about Africa (the "Negro Other" and "Blackness") cast aspersions on humankind's Afro/human beginnings from which our souls and the world need to be freed.

More is at stake in all this than the vindication of Africa. The possibilities for true freedom—beyond legal liberty—to respect "different" persons and to care for diverse peoples, rather than to shun, fear, and oppress them, are part of the hopeful legacy of Afro humanity; these are facets of what we explore in this chapter. We consider two aspects of un-free existence. Both obstruct the equitable possibilities Afro humanity offers. Metaphorically speaking, these possibilities for BEing equitable reside in each person's "seed" of human existence. What we want to emphasize is that each person can BE the soul-freeing substance of Afro humanity. The potential—to exist fully in alignment with one's human spirit—is already present in each of us. Unfortunately, the "dominant" values of United States' society do not nourish the seed of Afro/human existence and schooling does not value Afro humanity in its store of knowledge.

Bias against Africa and Blackness is manifested in school knowledge, definitions of intelligence, and processes of knowing. This bias is the first obstacle to equitable existence we will discuss. Second, we will consider how Euro-American cultural imagery and identity, grounded in these "dominant" biases, derogate Africanity—and humankind's African referent—thereby obstructing one's deeper view and appreciation of the Afro/human existence of all people. The dominance of so-called "civilized" culture distracts people of African ancestry from the worth of their own existence and undermines, for all people, the worthiness of personally experiencing the truths of one's inviolate soul. Maya Angelou suggests the latter as a value from which we must not be moved.[5]

Finally, this chapter concludes with a brief discussion of the implications of cultural domination and resistance for liberating pedagogy. In other words, we concentrate on possibilities for learning to BE free from inhumane energies implicit in cultural domination. We explore the need for knowing humankind's Afro humanity and being human.

Afro Humanity's Hopeful Legacy

What is the soul-freeing substance of Afro humanity? What does it mean to have access to the vitalness of one's Afro/human soul?

> *Human vitalness* refers to aliveness of the human spirit expressed with honest vigor; responding and relating with attentive presence; being awake; looking; seeing, tasting, and engaging in non-oppressive uses of the power of one's autonomous soul; participating in self's human rights and responsively demonstrating the Afro humanity of caring, closeness, creating, and calling for truth.

Human vitalness, then, frees the soul to BE equitable. It is the substance of Afro humanity in which there exists the potential and yearning for human complementarity and equitableness. This soul-freeing legacy reflects the beneficent capacity to nourish and care for one's self, others, and the earth. It is the fundamental nature of the Afro/human soul which all people can BE (can regenerate in themselves). The desire to act in tune with the messages of one's soul (to BE the substance of Afro humanity) resonates as a universal truth. This can happen without dismissing specific frames of cultural identity that structure human behaviors.[6] Yet, disbelief in, as well as misuses of, human vitalness have become common in miscreant purposes and performances, both of individuals and society. This is shown in the socialized knowledge and values of the "dominant" culture that are reflected in normative schooling, all of which seem aimed at de-legitimizing humankind's African referent. Such schooling distorts, denies, and overturns the potential of Afro humanity, and consequently we do not have access to the spirituality and universality Afro/humanity offers. That is, the society of the classroom, like the "dominant" culture, becomes void of human vitalness and attentive presence.

> *Attentive presence* means fully existing emotionally with self's human spirit (recognizing that it is akin to the human energy of the moment manifested in self and others); staying attuned especially amid conflicts, contradictions, and ambiguities that accompany the randomness of relating; listening with the heart during human exchanges; exhibiting compassion with self and others while relating; facilitating human diversity and human dignity.

Despite the potential of Afro/human nature, as a reservoir of hope for humankind, its beneficent qualities are devalued and desecrated.[7] Chances diminish daily to BE our Afro humanity and to use its inherent qualities beneficially. Examples of daily disregard for chances to BE our Afro humanity can be seen in work and the work place, especially in the way work debases human existence and turns people into artificial, desiccated objects.[8] Paradoxically, society's "throw away" people—with no work—who are trying to "get a life," as Black folks say, are further dehumanized in the scramble for status, power, and money by any means.

In lieu of these polluted, overturned, and oppressive "uses" of humankind, we are offering alternative vistas for humanely equitable existence. Like W. E. B. DuBois we dream . . .

> of a world of infinite and invaluable variety . . . of true freedom: in thought and dream, fantasy, and imagination, in gift, aptitude, and genius—all possible manner of difference, topped with freedom of individuality . . . to stop this freedom of being is a blow

at democracy. . . . There can be no perfect democracy curtailed by color, race, or poverty.[9]

Our dream of human equitableness and true freedom is a vision of *can be* possibilities for human existence. In this hopeful vision of regenerated Afro humanity, in which the "mode" of being human transcends hierarchy as the normative social model, human beings would BE more than political or human "capital" and more than consumers and makers of products—even though these might be worthy endeavors.[10] In an abbreviated form the freeing legacy of hope that Afro humanity offers includes: (1) willingness to approach one's own and others' human vitalness without being trapped into proving one's legitimacy and credibility;[11] (2) the urgency to relate with attentive presence; (3) choosing not to be "at war" in human contacts and instead, choosing to engage with others non-oppressively; and (4) fostering human exchanges that are not warped by the inhumane energy of buying and selling, especially at prices "dictated by others."[12] In a social context of beneficent and nonviolent human exchanges all persons involved aim to satisfy needs and wants through human connections *with* others. This connectedness refuses to place psycho-social price tags on people; such "prices" are outcomes of stratifications that rank humans vertically and pander to the implicit inhumanity of trying to be "better than" (or feeling "less than") another in style, stardom, class, and "power over."[13] Finally, Afro humanity offers (5) the socio-emotional intimacy of sharing in truth-seeking and truth-speaking amid gender equitableness.[14]

We realize that an epistemology of equitableness and societal "systems" for regenerating this vision of Afro humanity have not come into being, not even in current goals and assessments of "valuable" and "proper" education.[15] We believe, however, that people are capable of being aligned with and nurturing soul-freeing human vitalness, that it is possible to exist daily in full contact with the substance of one's Afro humanity—to be present *in* and *with* the vitality of one's soul. This is a task for education—to help us learn hopeful principles of human existence. Hence, we are proposing principles of human equitableness for regenerating the Afro/human seeds of humankind. We offer these principles as Seven Bases to facilitate an equitable context for nourishing the biosocial needs and wants of humankind. These Seven Bases represent the beneficent qualities of humankind's Afro/human nature. (Table 1)

Table 1. Contextual Paradigm for Human Equitableness

Contextual Paradigm for Human Equitableness	Base #1 Socio-emotional Initiation--is for awaking human vitalness; not shunning otherness; persons are willing to approach and not avoid differentness;	Base #2 Facilitating Human Intersections-- stresses making human contacts; showing attentive presence to differentness despite ambiguities, absurdities, conflicts, and confusion in a willingness to touch and to care;	Base #3 Electing Access to Self--calls for looking at and seeing one's predispositions and prejudices;
Base #4 Initiating the Regeneration of Knowledge-- involves owning" one's biased and stereotypic knowledge, bigoted views and behaviors and offering one's personal testimony (preferably without guilt and defensiveness);	Base #5 Seeking Truths and Wisdom-- requires attentive presence NOW in truth-seeking and truth-speaking as a pilgrim on the journey of germinating and using one's seed of human existence;	Base #6 Participating in Human Complementarity- -entails being conscious of the dynamics of human connections, valuing and connecting one's humanity with "different" persons and peoples; learning with diverse traditions as a member of earth's human family; caring about healing oppression, addictions, abuses, and violence;	Base #7 Experiencing an Equitable Philosophy-- indicates one's commitment to BEing equitable in spirit and behaviors, not violating or abusing self and others; not participating in "authority over" roles and interactions, not needing to be imperialistic, nor desiring to oppress or to be a victim, instead facilitating "win-win" energy with others' offerings.[16]

*We admit the need for a language and vocabulary that is itself free and consistent with Afro humanity's potential for equitable existence. The Seven Bases (see Table 1) mirror qualities of human vitalness for freeing ourselves to learn a language and vocabulary of freedom that *can be* based on human equitableness. An interim application of the Seven Bases can evolve as elements of soul-freeing education are learned and used. Stated differently: these Bases offer principles for human equitableness which have cosmic dimensions beyond liberation, per se. We offer them as a foundation for learning what freedom really means in the social context of BEing spiritually and vitally ourselves as human beings who practice Afro humanity.

Black Abduction and Education Beyond Liberation

We want to re-state that the soul-freeing legacy of Afro humanity is an ancient "gene" available for all people.[17] We also recognize that "New World" Black folk are direct heirs to the essentials of collective identity and equitable consciousness that are inherent in this legacy. Despite the realities of racial slavery in the Black Diaspora, the derogation of Africa and Blackness does not negate this legacy; instead it increases the necessity of surviving by keeping human vitalness alive. Indeed, the elusive concept of African-American "soul" expresses human vitalness and keeps alive the yearning for complementarity and attentive presence in human contacts. We sense a universal truth when African-Americans affirm that "We are family."[18] These are fundamental qualities of BEing that reflect an African ethos *and* the universality of Afro humanity. Of significant concern is that the universal substance of Afro humanity hoped for is often excluded, debased, and sometimes disavowed in what schools and "dominant" scholarship transmit as valued and authoritative knowledge, particularly about Africa and people of African descent. In other words, to clarify an earlier point, racist schooling distorts realities and abducts Diaspora Africans from their Afro/human cultural moorings; this schooled severance is world-wide and includes the African continent. Teachers participate in this abduction, often unknowingly, as a result of their own mis-education.[19] Several aspects of schooling are involved; they include: (1) biased school knowledge; (2) illusions of societal "normalcy," normality, and culture espoused by the educational establishment; (3) the mis-education of teachers as bearers of a "dominant" yet decaying vision of social equality; and (4) barriers in ways of knowing and perceiving presumed realities and truths—including those in the "worlds" of diverse peoples. Biases and inequalities that become standard realities of the "dominant" culture are continually transmitted through the "hidden" curricula and teaching strategies of the educational establishment.[20] These biases (as valued standards) help to maintain hierarchies of human value and worth; they are elements of a racist epistemic authority that construes difference, in general, as illegitimate. Furthermore, as standard (normative) societal realities, the biases in schooling subscribe to concepts of Africa and Blackness as non-good "Otherness."

For instance, the "Whitening" of Egypt in school textbooks continues with the omission of scholarly evidence, including primary sources, which documents that indigenous people in Egypt were "basically Negro."[21] The African origins of Greek culture and civilization are similarly omitted.[22] Furthermore, textbook discussions of "our human ancestors" frequently give the impression that "culture" and "civilization" reached their earliest and "highest" developments outside Africa, in the Middle East, and Europe (for example, cave paintings in France and Spain and the domestication of certain grains in the Middle East are given greater historical significance than earlier African techno-cultural developments). While some recent texts acknowledge that African-American history does not begin with slavery, others maintain that enslaved Africans "lost" their culture. Yet Africans, as heirs of Afro humanity, did not come to the "New World" "culturally empty handed."[23] In general, however, normative schooling does not incorporate the African ethos and related knowledge, scholarship, and aesthetics in the socio-cultural foundations for teaching and learning.

Inevitably, the derogation of the African heritage, values, and contributions to the world slanders and deprecates humankind's African referent; all people are victimized by this enslavement of human knowledge and consciousness. Although schooling that enslaves the mind (and dictates behaviors) in this way reaps a bitter harvest of psychic trauma and distorted consciousness among all people involved, it is particularly destructive to the vanishing self-value and socio-cultural fabric of Diaspora Black folk.[24] Black children and their parents recognize the social taboos of looking Black and being African. Blacks feel the impact of the school and society's wish to deny us opportunities to know and be conscious of ourselves, especially as full participants in the wealth and beneficent complementarity of Afro humanity.

Visible scars of racism, violence, disaffection, abuses, and misuses of self and others attest to the non-freedom of Afro/human vitalness. These scars can be viewed as results (and metaphors) of the abduction and the unhealthy educational enslavement of African-Americans. They are conditions of slave-master environments that steal the soul. Hence, it is impossible to "fully understand racism [and racist schooling] in present-day America unless we understand it in part as a reflection of a Western bias against African culture."[25] It is also impossible to BE equitable unless we acknowledge the damage which the derogation of Africa and Blackness has wrought on the souls of all people. Thus, Blacks are not alone in feeling isolated from our Afro humanity. Beyond this spiritual aridity which affects us all we can choose a journey toward BEing freely equitable and caring human beings.

Pledging Allegiance to BEing Free

Our quest is for educative environments with energies that nourish human consciousness and heal the vitality of the human spirit. With this chapter we are eavesdropping on the voices of our souls as we explore truths for creating an African liberation pedagogy, or more precisely, truths needed in an African pedagogy for freeing the Afro humanity of all people. We add this exploration of alternatives to a tradition of scholarship which disclaims allegiance to schooling that enslaves. In this endeavor we join other scholar/teachers working within a "Black perspective"[26] who have advocated the freeing of education for socio-political, cultural, spiritual, and economic liberation; these scholar/teachers include Grace Lee Boggs, Hazel Carby, Septima Clark, W. E. B. DuBois, Janice Hale-Benson, Vincent Harding, June Jordan, Julius Nyerere, Carter G. Woodson, and Sylvia Wynter, to name a few.[27] As scholars and human beings we, the authors, realize as did Mary Leakey when approaching seventy, that human bonding required her to align her existence with the truth that she and her work belonged to everyone "since it concerns the human origins that are common to the whole human race."[28]

We want to emphasize a vision of human existence beyond liberation from socio-economic oppression because true freedom entails "the emancipation of human knowledge" from anti-human normative "regimes of truth" which also enslave.[29] Thus, we are seeking education that nurtures "cognitive autonomy" and transcends dysconscious, unfree habits of mind.[30] Since the academic "achievement gap" and "failure" of African-American students in school are outcomes that reflect the biases and inequities of the "dominant" culture, we are calling for "political-pedagogical" energies that aid in the regeneration and use of the freeing legacy of Afro humanity;[31] these energies of equitableness will not permit human vitalness to be abducted, overturned, abused, and misused when confronting racism and oppression.

The Illegitimacy of Difference:
A De-Africanization Paradigm

From the perspective of Afro humanity, equitableness connotes horizontal human exchanges of diverse abilities and disabilities; it does not mean "tolerating" or superficially "celebrating diversity." For this reason we regard the "willingness" of the educational establishment to "accept" multiculturalism with skepticism.[32] The view of multiculturalism that appears to be gaining dominance (and which is reflected in the rhetoric of liberals and neo-conservatives alike), seems to be a retreat from the world of infinite and "invaluable variety" encompassed in "true freedom" (not curtailed by poverty, skin color, or gender) which was the dream of DuBois.[33] Although current multicultural teaching strategies and content claim to affirm cultural diversity, and notwithstanding the views of multicultural teaching contributed by James Banks, Christine I. Bennett, Donna M. Gollnick and Phillip C. Chin, Christine Sleeter and Carl Grant, and others, today's visions of multicultural education remain barely ameliorative.[34] In the final analysis, "we are not saved"[35] from the inequities implicit in concepts of societal "normalcy" and the school's de-valuation of human worth implicit in the Euro-American ontology of the human.[36]

Ameliorative ideologies of multiculturalism parallel a paradigm of "pluralism" that omits differentness in its ontology. In fact, there is almost an illegitimacy of difference in this paradigm and—like integration and desegregation reforms—this pluralism can foster an "illusory inclusiveness" (Cornel West's term). Such an illusion of socio-cultural inclusion de-legitimizes Africa and Blackness as "difference" worth valuing fundamentally.[37] This is evident when textbooks and other educational materials include selected aspects of the African/Diaspora heritage that seem to reinforce White values while African-centered scholarship and interpretations are excluded. A survey of high-school seniors in San Francisco, California[38] supports what Black educators have known all along, that Black students are keenly aware of and negatively affected by the misrepresentation of their heritage in schooling.[39]

A truth is that many advocates of multiculturalism are loyal to and want to preserve the existing social order, which is romanticized as a mosaic that represents "our national identity." Yet autonomous cultural identity is not socially acceptable in this paradigm; it is disparaged as racist, divisive "multicultural particularism" that undermines "democracy" and disrupts societal harmony.[40] The reactive furor of self-described "pluralists" regarding New York's proposal for a "curriculum of inclusion" is a case in point.[41] The New York proposal calls for authentic inclusion of diverse cultural histories and rejects the kind of cultural amalgamation which is often involved when "racial and ethnic minorities are woven into the central story"[42]—in the guise of "democracy," or *e pluribus unum*.

Otherness Revisited in the Paradigm of Pluralism

There is, of course, a more truthful representation of the "American Experience" of immigration and the processes which formed the American "national identity." Despite the Euro-American viewpoint of the U.S. national character in most school textbooks, the United States is not the triumphant accomplishment of a "Nation of Immigrants." This White-male-Euro-American version of history (or his/story) cynically justifies an intellectual hegemony and values which fuel vertical human ranking, oppression, and planetary destruction. (Even if "teacher editions" suggest otherwise in their declarations of "fairness" of representation, the justification of Euro-American-White-male hegemony in student texts often remains the unchallenged "authority," especially with regard to the experiences of African, Native-American, and society's "throw away" people.)

Europeans (and European-Americans) justified the domination and exploitation of African people on the basis of negative conceptions of "Otherness"; this allowed a Euro-White world to perceive Africans as wild and "primitive souls" to be saved by Western Civilization. Africans were seen as non-human chattel to be bought, sold, and enslaved for a profit (and for their own good, it was thought). They were considered immoral savages to be rescued from the backwardness of the "Dark Continent." Thus, Africanity and Blackness were the antithesis of the idealized White "civilized" cultural norm, the socially acceptable "mode" of being human. Or as Sylvia Wynter points out: "At this level of Otherness the 'negro' was not even considered, since he was not imagined to have languages worth studying, nor to partake in culture, so total was his mode of Nigger Chaos."[43] In this world-wide paradigm there was no culturally legitimate place in either Euro ontology or epistemology for African knowledge, languages, values, customs, and mores: African existence was excluded from the proscription of "civilization."[44]

A passage from *Uncle Tom's Cabin*, the anti-slavery novel first published serially in 1851–52, illustrates the culmination of the White Self juxtaposed with the African Other in American cultural mythology. The myth reflects the derogation of Africanity and Blackness that symbolized the invisibility of the Afro/human substance within African existence. In the novel there stood the non-existence of the non-civilized Black child, Topsy, in her "place" beside the White child, Miss Eva; Topsy becomes a metaphor for the passive, non-vitalness that is assumed in Black Topsy. Both Topsy and Miss Eva are in their customary ranks; as such, they are not attentively present—one is made absent by a presumed lack of human beingness. So the novel reads:

> There stood the two children, representatives of the extremes of society. The fair, high-bred child, with her golden head, her deep eyes, her spiritual, noble brow, and prince-like movements; and the black, keen, subtle, cringing, yet acute neighbor. They stood the representatives of their races. The Saxon, born of ages of civilization, command, education, physical and moral eminence; the Afric, born of ages of oppression, submission, ignorance, toil and vice![45]

As a European settler society, this nation-state was not founded on "multicultural" principles (as the mythology of "pluralism" maintains); it was founded on a romanticized notion of a "civilized" White Nation.[46] The society evolved from its European parentage through historical precedents which have brought the USA to its current crisis of national identity and character.[47] Social institutions, including religion and schooling, developed to implement these assumptions to support the "civilized" myths of a White nation; these assumptions and institutions (especially schools) were bound to give credence to the distorted image of the African Other as a negro creature hardly on the scale of being human.[48] Assumptions of African savagery became institutionalized cultural imagery—standardized symbols for a racist duality of human and non-human beings.[49] When placed in "school knowledge" the false ontologies this duality established excluded the truths of humanity in all its diversity, cultural specificity, and truthful universality. Out of this ontological duality Whites imagined Self and Other in opposition and in hierarchical relation: Whites were superior in every way that mattered.[50] Consequently, Blackness came to signify "the Ontological Lack or absence from 'true' being" that was used to justify slavery and colonization in the Diaspora and in Africa.[51] Versions of this ontology in the USA justify the denial of society's promised blessings of liberty, equality, and justice for all. This is the historical evolution of the changing Euro-American "template of identity."[52] We repeat, these early American "ethnic

notions" of African Otherness and White national identity were institutionalized in the epistemological order of racist schooling and subsequent socialization that virtually de-Africanized school knowledge,
stripping it of the beneficent uses of human vitalness and denying the
humanity of African people.

Although racial enslavement in the United States supposedly
ended with "emancipation," the cultural ideology of White "civilization" was perpetuated through schooling that was intended to
educate "African-Americans . . . to serve others and not themselves."[53] Nearly one hundred years later *Brown vs. the Board of
Education* pushed the society to confront the contradictions of
"separate but equal" Jim Crow schools. Even so, segregation and
institutionalized inequality persist in ostensibly desegregated schools.
Thus, the legal liberty of "emancipation" inexorably falls short of true
freedom.

The Terror in Things Not Seen

Despite recurrent cycles of Black electoral victories and incremental access to middle-class lifestyles, African-Americans continue
to live with the mundane terror of society's oppressive and overtly
hostile bias against Africa and Blackness.[54] Care for and nourishment
of Blackness are not social givens. For example, the crack cocaine
epidemic is terrorizing Black communities, threatening and devastating our Afro humanity. This terror is palpable in the testimony of
activist educator Aisha Kareem who calls it "the war we must win";
she understands it is a result of "the brutal bite of poverty":

> Our children are found with their backs to the wall. . . . The street
> gangs who traffic in drugs present a serious threat to the welfare
> and future of our children who are stalked and surrounded by the
> gangs and forced through violent intimidation, actual physical
> beatings, and outright murders to succumb to drug use and drug
> trafficking.[55]

Of course, drugs and violence are not endemic to the Black
community, and the complicity of those who perpetrate this erro-
neous view is deplorable.[56] We regard this violence as a consequence, at least in part, of the "cultural and economic domination"
of Black folk.[57] We want to elaborate on this cultural domination
and the possibilities for cultural resistance to it that we observe,
particularly among Black youth, which has implications, as we will

show, for liberating pedagogy.

From our perspective the violence and terror which plague Black communities reflect human vitalness that has been overturned by White "civilized" cultural imagery. In this imagery Whiteness is privileged as a more valued symbolic cultural identity while Blackness is derogated. Given that Whiteness is symbolically worthy and Blackness is de-valued and distorted as worthless, Black youth are denied access to an autonomous inspiration for self-valuing and self-understanding. Jeffrey Prager's insight regarding the Black experience illuminates this dialectic:

> It is not the mere fact that blacks hold a dual identity in this coun-
> try which has constrained achievement; to one degree or another,
> every ethnic group and racial group has faced a similar challenge.
> The black experience in America is distinguished by the fact that
> the qualities attributed to blackness are in opposition to the qual-
> ities rewarded in society. The specific features of blackness as cul-
> tural imagery are, almost by definition, those which the dominant
> society has attempted to deny in itself, and it is this difference
> between blackness and whiteness that defines, in many respects,
> American cultural self-understanding. For blacks, then, the effort
> to reconcile into one personality images which are diametrically
> opposed poses an extraordinarily difficult challenge.[58]

Without true knowledge of themselves and of the dominant society, Black youth have experienced the terror of a distorted self—made in the image of the White "American self-understanding" that is transmitted in school. Though less visible than the overt violence of poverty, this terror thwarts socio-emotional initiation needed to approach one's terrorized self (seeTable 1, Base 1), thereby block-ing the urge to "correct" one's overturned human vitalness; hence there is disinterest in freeing self to BE a beneficial participant in the vitality of complementarity (Bases 2-7). This freeing, which makes the fullness of one's Afro/human existence possible is blocked by White "civilized" values that uphold the socialized taboo on Blackness. In contrast, Black youth could discover the beneficial qualities of their collective identity in their Afro humanity. In sum-mary, we believe that the lure of riches from drugs, for too many Black youth, emanates partly within the bankrupt American Dream of money, prestige, stardom, status, and power.[59] Since Black youth presumably "lack" the White "qualities" of being which the domi-nant society values, their youthful desire is to have the rewards any way, by any means, as quickly as possible—rather than to choose the wealth of the beneficent qualities of Afro humanity. Neither schooling nor "street" values prepare them to make such a choice.

Precedents of Freedom: Beyond Terrors Not Seen

In the 1960s James Baldwin, in "a talk to teachers," offered a powerful assessment of what Black [or Negro] children should be taught in school. Baldwin said:

> Now if I were a teacher . . . in any Negro school, and I was dealing with Negro children, who were in my care only a few hours of every day and would then return to their homes and to the streets, children who have an apprehension of their future which with every hour grows dimmer and darker, . . . I would try to teach them [and] make them know—that . . . those agonies by which they are surrounded are a criminal conspiracy to destroy [them]. . . .[60]

Baldwin's vision is relevant. He is referring to a conspiracy which involves the derogation of Blackness we discussed earlier. In the minds of educators this conspiracy, which is not always a conscious one, takes the form of "theories" of cultural deprivation, beliefs about cultural deficits, "absent" Black fathers, and perceptions of inadequate Black mothers.[61] Baldwin went on to say that he would teach a Black child "that he must decide at once that he is stronger than this conspiracy . . ." and that ". . . refusing to make peace with it [this conspiracy] and . . . destroying it depend on *what he decides he is worth.*"[62] Finding one's truthful Afro humanity in the context of this derogatory conspiracy is a mean challenge.

Baldwin's wisdom on this point is profound: He is telling teachers how to prepare Black children to approach the terror of White "civilized" values with a clarity of soul that is available in the powerful fundamentals of their Afro humanity. Indeed, for any oppressive system to persist, it must maintain within the oppressed the belief that something lacking in themselves makes them deserve their de-valued state. This "invisible" terror of cultural domination is not so easily seen. It resides in the politics of societal normalcy and is hidden in the ideological framework and symbolic imagery that give birth to the violence of poverty and inequitable power. All this appears legitimate and produces guilt, defensiveness, and blame rather than outrage, resistance, regeneration, and healing.

The African Ethos in the Context of Oppression

We have reviewed the cultural context from which Euro-American self-understanding and identity evolved in opposition to the imagined savage and dreaded "Nigger Other" qualities attributed to Blackness. We wanted to demonstrate how the cultural imagery—on which White identity, privilege, and power depend (for their legitimacy)—overturns the vitality in the human spirit of Black folk, and in equal measure, makes "good" White folk dysconscious, as the proscribed boundaries of "goodness" and "badness" dehumanize "Others." Hence, the Euro-American "mode" for a human context is "inhuman."[63] The point we want to stress here is that the human vitalness African-Americans autonomously express is a Black self-value; it involves conscious awareness that "I-BE-WE-EXIST," and "I and you ARE worthy human beings." This is the human spirit of worthiness and soul-sovereignty that Baldwin was talking about. It is a spirit of human vitalness that can demystify Whiteness and "nihilated" Blackness,[64] as well as correct the illusions of "success" *for a few*, achieved in the context of oppression.

African-Americans have maintained an autonomous sense of self-value, that is, a "viable human spirit in the context of oppression,"[65] through a fundamentally African mode of collective identity, spirituality, and moral detachment from societal normalcy.[66] The transcendental nature of this African quality of existence, found in what we refer to as human vitalness, is evident in a contemporary Black cultural form, namely, "rap" music. "Rap" is an expression of culturally autonomous extended self-affirmation (i.e., collective affirmation) that has historical roots in the African ethos.[67] This collective affirmation is demonstrated as "rappers" strut about, energetically relating while seeking truths and wisdom. While their messages are at times unintelligible to persons unfamiliar with either Black culture or the idioms of the "street"—and these need to be differentiated—they affirm the "I am, because we are" African ethos. The meaning is: We are complementary participants and members in "the family." In defiance of the terror against the souls of Black folk, rappers express this unity (and diversity) in boldly extended, self-assertive chants, power anthems, and societal indictments to the beat of ancient African rhythms. Andrei L. Strobert, a Brooklyn-based scholar/musician says, "A lot of the rhythms that they use are Ibo rhythms, from the Ibo tribe of Nigeria."[68] Do the rappers know this? Should they?

The truth-seeking testimony of politically conscious rappers is an example of the African oral tradition of griot-truth-speakers. Although some rap music stresses anti-human societal values, including violence, sexism, and crass materialism, the music mirrors realities of the society where many people "are coming from." Explicitly sexual lyrics may be offensive, even misogynist, but rap music, with its own ambiguities and contradictions, exposes societal hypocrisy concerning standards of human value. The June, 1990 arrest of the rappers "2 Live Crew," for violating Florida's "obscenity law," is an example of this hypocrisy. Are poverty, homelessness, and hunger obscene in the land of plenty—in the USA, the "envy" of the world? At its best rap music can be seen as an expressive form of cultural resistance which shows us what we need to approach and attend to in ourselves (See Table 1, Bases 1 & 2).

Amid the violence and terror of domination, poverty, and dehumanization, this rap art form suggests possibilities for educators to use the fragments of cultural memory and human consciousness reflected in the music to develop Diaspora literacy;[69] this can help to regenerate the Afro/human legacy. Film-maker Ben Caldwell sees in rap or hip-hop culture "the age-old warrior element of teenage energy that is both vigorous and positive."[70] If "black youth are unwittingly merging aspects of [African] culture as old as their ancestors," what cultural products for freeing Afro/human vitalness from the illusions of the society might these youthful, truth-seeking griots produce if schooling permitted them really to know and love themselves? The lyrics of rap music and its cultural forms can be the focus of critical discussion and analysis. This might also be a point of struggle for teachers who want to develop a "meaningfully relevant" curriculum.[71] Could educators who really love Black children, and who perceive their heritage as a legitimate source of knowledge and human experience, use this cultural form in a liberating pedagogy?[72] If so, would this not be support for the creative struggles of Black youth to value themselves and to survive the war that society is waging against them?

What If Educators Really Loved Black Children?

The Afro/human legacy as we envision it calls for a pedagogy that challenges the social justifications of poverty, sexism, human ranking, exploitation, racism, and unhealthy environments. It gives no power to the colonizing mission of schooling that denies the African heritage of human equitableness. This pedagogy for freedom hardly coincides with assumptions of the "dominant" culture about Black existence, societal normalcy, and normative criteria for school "success"; all of these are meant to prove the power of the nation-state—to give appearances of national "success." An incident at an educational research conference illustrates one of the many ways that prevailing norms of school success deny possibilities for human equitableness (and the legitimacy of Black existence):

> When the keynote speaker, Robert Slavin, was asked if his findings regarding the success "minority" students achieve through cooperative learning strategies also applied to "model minority" Asians, he explained that his research focus was on Black students. But he added quickly with a laugh: "Maybe we should give all the Black kids Japanese mothers." The raucous laughter that erupted nearly drowned out another researcher's rejoinder: "No, no! Let's give 'em Jewish mothers!"[73]

Dare we search for a liberated pedagogy? What can be the impact of African liberation pedagogy in this political climate, especially when Black children are being held "hostage" in systems not designed to free them? How can these Black children function as themselves when African knowledge and culture are disrespected and people of African ancestry everywhere are under siege? In Toronto, Canada a 16 year-old Black youth was shot by the police, with apparent impunity, the same day the Black community was rallying to protest a museum exhibit presenting Africa from the White missionary perspective.[74] Amnesty International reports that police officers and death squads in Brazil are involved in the torture and murder of increasing numbers of poor Black "street" children.[75] Meanwhile, the Institute of Religious Studies in Rio de Janeiro is addressing the "inferiority complex" of poor Black Brazilian children through a program called: "What Is a Black Child Worth?"[76]

Michele Foster observes what she calls the "hostage theory" of Black education. In desperation Black parents seem to be saying: "If we can just get our kids in there with the others—who are White, have computers, or something else of value to the society—then they'll have to teach them something."[77] For example, Black parents in a Southern city in the USA say they are satisfied that good education is taking place in a predominantly White desegregated school if it has computers.[78] In San Francisco schools there is a West Coast California variation of this scenario:

Black students are "integrating" and generating money for

Cantonese and Spanish bi-lingual classes as a result of court-ordered desegregation. During lessons taught in their home language, the other children are involved in more advanced language-based activities in Spanish or Cantonese. The three or four Black children in these classes are often re-segregated into low skill groups for drill, practice, and remedial work in one of these languages of instruction. Teachers call on Black students by their Chinese or Spanish names. In one class a group of Black boys was observed eagerly practicing math drills in Cantonese; in another room a Black boy adamantly refused to participate in a Cantonese language lesson.[79]

Is the Black community being duped again? What are the multiple metapathologies in the postmodern duping of Black folk everywhere? We recognize the need to challenge societal illusions of inclusion and individualistic progress as did our enslaved ancestors who, when confronted with a slave system that denied their humanity and threatened Black existence, affirmed their human worth and value. A seminal truth they expressed in sacred song is still relevant: "Ain't you got a right to the tree of life?"

Our goal in this chapter has been to offer a beneficent context for living a humanely equitable existence (See Table 1). Our commitment is to offer elemental principles that can free Black children and all humankind from violence and oppression. We understand that the course we are taking addresses a need for de-colonizing current schooling that formally continues human bondage through teaching and polluted learning environments. A related task for all of us as educators is to develop a theoretical and epistemological base of teaching, learning, and culture that embraces the fundamentals of Afro humanity that can regenerate human vitalness and restore the continuity of history and cultural memory of African people. We take these positions because ameliorative education reforms tend to misuse (and abuse) culture to abduct Black people into the existing social order.[80] Therefore, a major task for educators is to place Afro humanity in our ontologies thereby going beyond a superficial "anthropology of blackness."[81] We suggest that Afro humanity, as a foundation in teaching and learning, can lead to the initiation of a truthful pedagogy, i.e., can bring about educative humane interactions and complementarity for freeing Black students and all learners to BE themselves with caring responsiveness for this society and the world. We also realize that further systematic study of Afro humanity and of formal, non-formal, and community-based education by and for African (and other-than-Euro-Western) peoples is needed.

In conclusion, we hope this chapter will challenge educative thought and scholarship concerning the type of human beings we want in society and the nature of the humanity we can BE. In this chapter we explored detrimental aspects of schooling that are not supportive of Afro humanity and human beings. We examined ways cultural domination denies the legitimacy of our Afro/human legacy and obstructs humanely equitable existence. The humanity that cares about all its different peoples requires fundamental societal and educational change not politically rearranged "pretty pictures" of society.[82] As Henry Giroux and Roger Simon suggest, "to propose a pedagogy is to construct a political vision."[83] While the world seems to be entering an era of freedom seeking, as reflected in the release of Nelson Mandela in South Africa, we are also witnessing the terror of racist violence throughout the world. The sores of inhumanity still need healing. The "political-pedagogical" vision we are proposing aims to facilitate this healing. We invite you to join the journey toward the wealth of human wholeness that calls for nothing less than a humane mode of being human.

Notes and References

1. Mari Evans, "Speak the Truth to the People," in *I am a Black Woman* (New York: William Morrow, 1970), 91.
2. Marian Wright Edelman, in conversation with Brian Lanker, *I Dream a World: Portraits of Black Women Who Changed America* (New York: Stewart, Tabari & Chang, 1989), 121.
3. We use the term Afro/human to connote a more universal conceptualization of "human" than is encompassed in "Western" ontology with its dualistic legacy. Joining "Afro" & "human" denotes their equivalence. Afro humanity is the substance of *soul-sovereignty* that is available to all human beings. We use upper case letters in "BE" and "BEing" to emphasize the possibilities of existing in alignment with self's Afro humanity (i.e., self's soul). This conceptualization of Afro humanity evolved through several decades of T. L. Wilson's field work in Africa: T. L. Wilson, "Notes toward a Process of Afro-American Education," *Harvard Educational Review* 42 (1972): 374-389; T. L. Wilson, "Let's Join Hands for Human Understanding," *Journal of Childhood Education* 56 (1980): 130-39.
4. S. C. Drake, *Black Folk Here and There*, vol. 1 (Los Angeles, CA: UCLA Center for Afro-American Studies, 1987), 127.
5. Maya Angelou, *I Shall Not Be Moved* (New York: Random House, 1990).

6. B. M. Ferdman, "Literacy and Cultural Identity," *Harvard Educational Review* 60 (1990): 181-204.
7. S. Slocum, "Woman the Gatherer: Male Bias in Anthropology," in *Toward an Anthropology of Women*, ed. R. Reiter (New York: Monthly Review Press, 1975), 36-50. P. Berger, and T. Luckmann, *The Social Construction of Reality* (Garden City, NY: Doubleday Anchor, 1967).
8. Hannah Arendt, *The Human Condition* (Chicago: University of Chicago Press, 1958). R. Leakey, "The Making of Human Aggression," in *The Making of Mankind* (New York: E. P. Dutton, 1981), 219-237. A. Montagu, "Aggregation Versus Isolation," in *On Being Human* (New York: Hawthorn Books, Inc., 1966), 37-46.
9. W. E. B. DuBois, *The World and Africa* (New York: International Publishers, 1965), 261.
10. D. Apter, *The Politics of Modernization* (Chicago: The University of Chicago Press, 1965).
11. J. Baldwin, *The Evidence of Things Not Seen* (New York: Henry Holt and Company, 1985).
12. Baldwin, *Things Not Seen*, 93-95.
13. Leakey, "Human Aggression."
14. P. Draper, "!Kung Women: Contrasts in Sexual Egalitarianism in Foraging and Sedentary Contexts," in *Toward an Anthropology of Women*, ed. R. Reiter (New York: Monthly Review Press, 1975), 77-109. Reiter, *Anthropology of Women*.
15. A. Bloom, *The Closing of the American Mind* (New York: Simon and Schuster, 1987). E. D. Hirsch, *Cultural Literacy: What Every American Should Know* (Boston: Houghton Mifflin, 1987). Diane Ravitch, "Diversity and Democracy," *The American Educator* 14 (1990): 16-20, 46-48. Diane Ravitch, and C. Finn, *What Do Our 17-Year-Olds Know?* (New York: Harper and Row, 1987).
16. T. L. Wilson, "Let's Join Hands."
17. T. L. Wilson, "Notes."
18. M. White, "We Are Family!: Kinship and Solidarity in the Black Community," in *Expressively Black*, ed. G. Gay and W. L. Baber (New York: Praeger, 1987), 17-34.
19. Joyce Elaine King, "Dysconscious Racism: Ideology, Identity, and the Miseducation of Teachers," *Journal of Negro Education* 60 (1991): 133–146. Joyce Elaine King, and G. Ladson-Bilings, "The Teacher Education Challenge in Elite University Settings: Developing Critical Perspectives for Teaching in a Democratic and Multicultural Society," *The European Journal of Intercultural Studies* 1 (1990): 15-30.
20. B. Gordon, "Toward Emancipation in Citizenship Education: The Case for African-American Cultural Knowledge," *Theory and Research in Social Education* 12 (1985): 1-23. E. Leacock, "The Influence of Teacher Attitudes on Children's Performance: Case Studies," in *The*

Social Life of Children in a Changing Society, ed. K. Borman (Hillsdale, NJ: Erlbaum, 1982), 47-64.

21. Drake, *Black Folk*, 129. See also C. A. Diop, *The African Origin of Civilization: Myth or Reality* (New York: Lawrence Hill, 1974) and R. Porteres, and J. Barrau, "Origins, Development and Expansion of Agriculture," in *UNESCO General History of Africa*, vol. 1, ed. J. Kizerbo (Berkeley: University of California Press, 1981), 687-705. For textbook examples, see B. Armento et al., *A Message of Ancient Days* (Boston: Houghton Mifflin, 1991) and M. Greenblatt and P. Lemmo, *Human Heritage: A World History* (Columbus, OH: Merrill], 1989). None of the sources identified here are referenced in these texts.

22. M. Bernal, *Black Athena: The Afro-Asiatic Roots of Classical Civilization*, vol. 1 (London: Free Association Books, 1987).

23. J. H. Clarke, "Social Studies African-American Baseline Essay," in *African-American Baseline Essays*, ed. Portland Public Schools (Portland, OR, 1988), SS1-85. C. L. R. James, "The Atlantic Slave Trade and Slavery: Some Interpretations of their Significance in the Development of the United States and the Western World," in *Amistad* 1, ed. J. A. Williams and C. Harris (New York: Vintage Books, 1970), 119-164.

24. Joyce Elaine King, and G. Ladson-Billings, "Dysconscious Racism and Multicultural Illiteracy: The Closing of the American Mind," paper presented at the Annual Meeting of the American Educational Research Association, Boston, MA, 1990. C. G. Woodson, *The Mis-Education of the Negro* (Washington, DC: Associated Publishers, 1933).

25. J. Hodge, D. Struckmann, and L. Trost, *Cultural Bases of Racism and Group Oppression* (Berkeley, CA: Two Riders Press, 1975), 40.

26. Drake, *Black Folk*.

27. Grace Lee Boggs, "Education: The Great Obsession," in *Education and Black Struggle*, ed. Institute of the Black World (Harvard Educational Review Monograph, 2, 1974), 61-81. J. Boggs, G. Boggs et al., *Conversations in Maine* (Boston: South End Press, 1978). Hazel Carby, "Schooling in Babylon," in *The Empire Strikes Back: Race and Racism in 70s Britain*, ed. Centre for Contemporary Cultural Studies (London: Hutchinson, 1982), 183-211. Septima Clark, and C. Brown, *Ready from Within* (Navarro, CA: Wild Trees Press, 1986). W. E. B. DuBois, "Does the Negro Need Separate Schools?" *Journal of Negro Education* 4 (1935): 329-335. Janice Hale-Benson, *Black Children: Their Roots, Culture, and Learning Style*, rev. ed. (Baltimore: Johns Hopkins University Press, 1982). Vincent Harding, "The Vocation of the Black Scholar and the Struggles in the Black Community," in *Education and Black Struggle,* ed. Institute of the Black World (Harvard Educational Review Monograph, 2, 1974), 3-29. Vincent Harding, *Hope and History* (Maryknoll, NY: Orbis Books, 1990). June Jordan, "Nobody Mean More to Me than You and the Future Life of

Willie Jordan," *Harvard Educational Review* 58 (1988): 363-374. Julius Nyerere, *Freedom and Unity/Uhuru Na Umoja* (Dar Es Salaam: Oxford University Press, 1966). Julius Nyerere, "Education," in *Education and Black Struggle*, ed. Institute of the Black World (Harvard Educational Review, 2, 1974), 100-105. Carter G. Woodson, *Mis-Education*. Sylvia Wynter, "The Ceremony Must Be Found," *Boundary/2* 12/13 (1984): 19-61.

28. Mary Leakey, *Disclosing the Past: An Autobiography* (New York: Doubleday, 1984).

29. Sylvia Wynter, "Beyond the Word of Man: Glissant and the New Discourse of the Antilles," *World Literature Today* (Autumn 1990): 645-46.

30. Sylvia Wynter, "Beyond the Word of Man," 645, uses the term "cognitive autonomy" to suggest a way of thinking that is independent of normative conceptual categories; Joyce King defines "dysconsciousness" as "an uncritical habit of mind (perceptions, attitudes, assumptions, and beliefs) that justifies inequity and exploitation by accepting the order of things as given" (King and Ladson-Billings, "Dysconscious Racism," 5).

31. Paulo Freire, and A. Faundez, *Learning to Question: A Pedagogy of Liberation* (New York: Continuum, 1989).

32. Ravitch, "Diversity," 16-20, 46-48.

33. DuBois, *World and Africa*.

34. James Banks, *Teaching Strategies for Ethnic Studies*, 3rd. ed. (Boston: Allyn and Bacon, 1984). Christine I. Bennett, *Comprehensive Multicultural Education: Theory and Practice* (Boston: Allyn and Bacon, 1986). Donna M. Gollnick, and Phillip C. Chin, *Multicultural Education in a Pluralistic Society* (Columbus, OH: Merrill Publishing Co., 1990). Christine Sleeter, and Carl Grant, *Making Choices for Multicultural Education: Five Approaches to Race, Class, and Gender* (Columbus, OH: Merrill, 1988).

35. D. Bell, *And We Are Not Saved: The Elusive Quest for Racial Justice* (New York: Basic Books, 1987).

36. Wynter, "Beyond the Word of Man."

37. Wilson, "Notes."

38. P. Ramirez, "Students Feel Unprepared for Life in a Multicultural Society," *San Francisco Examiner*, 7 May 1990, Special Report.

39. M. K. Asante, "Build Lessons for Students' Heritage," *New Jersey Education Association Review* (February 1989): 21-22.

40. Ravitch, "Diversity."

41. L. Hancock, "Whose America Is This Anyway?" *Village Voice*, 24 April 1990, 37-39. J. Leo, "Teaching History the Way It Happened," *U.S. News & World Report*, 27 November 1989, 73.

42. Ravitch, "Diversity."

43. Wynter, "Ceremony," 2.

44. V. Y. Mudimbe, *The Invention of Africa: Gnosis, Philosophy, and the*

Order of Knowledge (Bloomington: University of Indiana Press, 1988).

45. Harriet Beecher Stowe, *Uncle's Tom Cabin* (1852; reprint, New York: New American Library, 1981), 266-67.

46. See Thomas Jefferson, *Notes on the State of Virginia*, ed. W. Peden (London: John Stockdale, 1787; reprint, New York: W. W. Norton, 1972), especially pp. 138-139, for one example where Jefferson writes about his beliefs that Africans are naturally inferior to Whites. Space does not permit discussion of justifications of the oppression of others, including Native-Americans and enslaved Irish, for example.

47. H. Cruse, *Plural But Equal: Blacks and Minorities in America's Plural Society* (New York: William Morrow, 1987). L. Hancock, "Whose America."

48. G. Nash, and R. Weiss, *The Great Fear* (New York: Holt, Rinehart, and Winston, 1970). Woodson, *Mis-Education*. Wynter, "Ceremony." Wynter, "Beyond the Word of Man."

49. Versions of the "Nigger Other" exist in various contexts of cultural pro-duction including religion: J. H. Cone, *A Black Theology of Liberation* (Maryknoll, NY: Orbis Books, 1989), C. Salley, and R. Behm, *What Color Is Your God? Black Consciousness and the Christian Faith* (Secaucus, NJ: Citadel Press, 1988); advertising: C. Moog, *Are They Selling Her Lips? Advertising and Identity* (New York: William Morrow, 1990) ; "Western" visual and performing arts and popular media: A. Pasteur, and I. Toldson, *Roots of Soul: The Psychology of Black Expressiveness* (Garden City, NY: Anchor/Doubleday, 1982).

50. Drake, *Black Folk*. J. Pieterse, "White on Black: Notes for the Exhibition of Images of Africa and Blacks in the Tropenmuseum, Amsterdam (NL)," *The Journal of Ethnic Studies* 18 (1990): 93-109. Black folk are also envied for their humor, "naturally" superior dancing and singing abilities and other qualities. This contradiction persists in the dialectic of Blackness and Whiteness. See Hodge et al., Cultural Bases; Pasteur & Toldson, *Roots of Soul*; S. Stuckey, "Through the Prism of Folklore," in *New Black Voices*, ed. A. Chapman (New York: New American Library, 1972), 439-457; S. Stuckey, *Slave Culture* (New York: Oxford University Press, 1987).

51. Wynter, "Beyond the Word of Man," 641.

52. Wynter, "Ceremony," 34.

53. Clarke, "Baseline Essay."

54. Joyce Elaine King, and C. Mitchell, *Black Mothers to Sons: Juxtaposing African-American Literature with Social Practice* (New York: Peter Lang Publishers, Inc., 1990). M. Marable, "Toward Black American Empowerment: Violence and Resistance in the African-American Community in the 1990s," *African Commentary*, (May 1990): 16-21.

55. Aisha Kareem, *The War We Must Win* (Stockton, CA: The Academy for Human Development, 1989), 2.

56. Drug-related violence and death in the slums of Medellin, the main drug center in Colombia, reveal the global proportions of this problem. It is worth noting the less well-known fact that some youth gangs "hate the Blacks" there (R. Collier, "Medellin Drug War's Grim Toll," *San Francisco Chronicle*, 13 June 1990, 5, Briefing.

57. D. Richards, "The Implications of African-American Spirituality," in *African Culture: The Rhythms of Unity*, ed. M. Asante and K. Asante (Westport, CT: Greenwood Press, 1985), 228.

58. Jeffrey Prager, "American Racial Ideology as Collective Representation," *Ethnic and Racial Studies* 5 (1982): 111.

59. S. Terkel, *The Great Divide: Second Thoughts on the American Dream* (New York: Avon Books, 1988).

60. James Baldwin, "A Talk to Teachers," in *The Graywolf Annual Five. Multicultural Literacy: The Opening of the American Mind*, ed. R. Simonson and S. Walker (St. Paul: Graywolf Press, 1988), 11.

61. A teacher in an "exemplary" school told a student teacher there were "two kinds of Black students" in the class: the "White-Blacks" would make satisfactory academic progress; the "Black-Blacks" were "behavior problems" and were "less capable intellectually than the White-Blacks . . . because they don't have White values" (King and Ladson-Billings, "Teacher Education Challenge").

62. Baldwin, "Talk to Teachers," 11, emphasis added.

63. Richards, "African-American Spirituality."

64. Wynter, in "Beyond the Word of Man" translates "nihilated" from the French word, *neantise* (in Caribbean writer Edouard Glissant's work); it refers to the destruction of the Antillean "sense of identity" and the resulting "psychic disorder and cultural malaise" (p. 639).

65. Stuckey, "Prism of Folklore," 452.

66. Richards, "African-American Spirituality." Stuckey, "Prism of Folklore." Stuckey, *Slave Culture*.

67. See discussions of "extended self-concept and identity" in W. Nobles et al., *The KM EBIT HUSIA: Authoritative Utterances of Exceptional Insight for the Black Family* (Oakland, CA: The Institute for the Advanced Study of Black Family Life and Culture, 1985), 10; L. Semaj, "Afrikanity, Cognition, and Extended Self-identity," in *Beginnings: Social and Affective Development of Black Children*, ed. M. Spencer et al. (Hillsdale, NJ: Lawrence Erlbaum, 1985), 173-83; and G. Ladson-Billings, and J. King, *Cultural Identity of African-Americans: Implications for Achievement* (Aurora, CO: Mid-Continental Regional Educational Laboratory, 1991).

68. H. Allen, "Hip-Hop Madness," *Essence* 19 (April 1989): 79-80, ff.

69. Abea Busia borrows the term "diaspora literacy" from Veve Clark and defines it as: "an ability to read a variety of cultural signs in the lives of Africa's children at home and in the New World." See "What is Your Nation?" in *Changing Our Own Words: Essays on Criticism, Theory,*

and Writing by Black Women, ed. C. A. Wall (New Brunswick: Rutgers University Press, 1989), 197. See also, V. Clark, "Performing the Memory of Difference in Afro-Caribbean Dance: Katherine Dunham's Choreography, 1938-1987," paper presented at the Dunham Symposium, Stanford University, May 1989.

70. D. Trout, "I-Fresh," *California Tomorrow* 3 (1988): 41.
71. Joyce Elaine King, "Black Student Alienation and Black Teachers' Emancipatory Pedagogy," *The Journal of Black Reading and Language Education* 3 (1987): 3-13.
72. E. Anderson, "What Would We Do If We Really Loved the Students?" in *Black Students: Psychosocial Issues and Academic Achievement*, ed. G. Berry and G. Asamen (Newbury Park, CA: Sage Publications, 1989), 218-242.
73. Joyce Elaine King, Fieldnotes, 1987, Sociology of Education Association Conference, CA.
74. M. Lalonde, "Change Stance in Shooting Row, Black Groups Tell Toronto Police," *Toronto Globe and Mail*, 18 May 1990, A8-9.
75. *Jet*, 16 July 1990, 37.
76. Joel Rufino dos Santos, *Literatura e Crianca: I Encontro Local do Programa Quanto Vale uma Crianca Negra* (Rio de Janeiro, ISER, 1989).
77. Conversation with Michele Foster, August 1989.
78. J. Irvine, "Black Parents' Perceptions of their Children's Desegregated School Experiences," paper presented at the Annual Meeting of the American Educational Research Association, Boston, MA, 1990.
79. Joyce Elaine King, Fieldnotes, May 1990.
80. N. Burtonwood, *The Concept of Culture in Educational Studies* (Philadelphia, PA: NFER-Nelson, 1986). Mudimbe, *Invention of Africa*.
81. W. Strickland credits Robert Hill with this phrase in "Identity and Black Struggle: Personal Reflections," in *Education and Black Struggle*, ed. Institute of the Black World (Harvard Educational Review Monograph, 2, 1974), 137-43.
82. Simone de Beauvoir, *Les Belles Images*, trans. Patrick O'Brian (Paris: Gallimard, 1966; Cambridge, MA: Schoenhos, Pub., 1968).
83. Henry Giroux, and Roger Simon, "Ideology, Popular Culture, and Pedagogy," *Curriculum and Teaching* 3 (1988): 3.

Chapter Twelve

African-Centered Pedagogy: Complexities and Possibilities

Carol D. Lee
School of Education and Social Policy
Northwestern University

What manner of education will provide African-Americans with the voice to sing the sacred liturgy of their own culture? What manner of education will mold the African personality to thrive in a culture that has demeaned its character, denied its existence, and coordinated its destruction? How shall we sing our sacred song in a strange land? This is the fundamental contradiction that stands before African-centered pedagogy in the United States.

In this chapter I explain first why I believe African-American people need an African-centered pedagogy. Next, I address the implications for educational practice that such a pedagogy offers by focusing on the ways in which it demarginalizes and brings African-American culture to the center of the learning process. I provide illustrations of African-centered pedagogy in process within independent African-American schools and discuss the possibilities that develop when such a pedagogy is considered in the context of public schooling in the United States. Finally, I conclude with a discussion of African-centered pedagogy and its role in meeting the educational imperatives facing African-American people and their cultural life.

The Need for an African-centered Pedagogy

Conceptions of humanness are not universal, but are culturally and historically specified—although there are generalizations that apply across cultures. A fundamental flaw in Western conceptual foundations of education is their narrow interpretation of what it means to be fully human—to be man, woman, and child. Education is defined in ways that ignore time, space, gender, and culture. For example, in 1657 John Amos Comenius wrote: "The education that I propose includes all that is proper for a man and it is one in which all men who are born into this world should share . . . [to be] educated fully to full humanity."[1]

Similarly, in *Treatise on Pedagogies*, Immanuel Kant defined education as "the process by which man becomes man."[2]

What links these conceptions of education is that they reveal assumptions about humanity in which there is no recognition of the differences among human beings. Moreover, they have contributed to an unremitting cycle in which theories of learning and development have justified research that reproduces and reinforces Eurocentric paradigms. In this self-perpetuating process, conclusions are drawn from observations of White, middle-class samples and postulated as universal norms for development and learning.[3]

An African-centered pedagogy is needed to support a line of resistance to the imposition of Eurocentric biases. It is needed to produce an education that contributes to achieving pride, equity, power, wealth, and cultural continuity for Africans in America and elsewhere. In addition, such a pedagogy is needed to foster an ethical character development grounded upon social practice within the African community.

The African cultural character I speak of is neither monolithic or static. It possesses, even in its historical and geographic formations, an ontological foundation that remains constant—whether Yoruba or Zulu, African-Brazilian or African-American.[4] This constant existed in the ancient Egyptian concept of Maat which, according to Karenga, includes the following propositions:

1. the divine image of humans;
2. the perfectibility of humans;
3. the teachability of humans;

4. the free will of humans; and
5. the essentiality of moral social practice in human development.[5]
    Karenga also underscores the importance of an African conceptual foundation to overcome the cultural crisis in the African community.

> The key crisis and challenge in African life [is] . . . one of culture, the challenge to rescue and reconstruct the best of ancient African culture and use it as a paradigm for a renewed modern African culture and community. . . . Only in this way . . . [can] they speak their own special truth to the world and make their own unique contribution to the forward flow of human history.[6]

For contemporary African-American culture, Maat represents a historical model of ethical character that is centered in the African experience. Cultivation of such a model is required not only for resistance to political and cultural oppression, but also to sustain independent development. Pedagogical practices must be developed that support the continued development of this historical paradigm.

African-centered Pedagogy as a Relevant Praxis

We who seek to articulate an African-centered theory of learning and teaching must address many delicate questions. Among them are such a theory's similarities and differences with other progressive pedagogical frameworks, such as liberation pedagogy[7] and critical pedagogy.[8] Some goals, of course, are common attributes of all conceptions of pedagogy. Certain pedagogical practices, however, require cultural specificity. An effective African-centered pedagogy:

1. legitimizes African stores of knowledge;
2. positively exploits and scaffolds productive community and cultural practices;
3. extends and builds upon the indigenous language;
4. reinforces community ties and idealizes service to one's family, community, nation, race, and world;
5. promotes positive social relationships;
6. imparts a world view that idealizes a positive, self-sufficient future for one's people without denying the self-worth and right to self-determination of others; and
7. supports cultural continuity while promoting critical consciousness.

The challenge to researchers and practitioners who undertake the development of an African-centered pedagogy that encompasses the attributes I have described is to enact them in ways that are culturally accurate, politically viable, developmentally appropriate, and subject-matter sensitive. This task requires an integration of research and practice as well as an environment that does not consciously inhibit culturally sensitive development and practice.

African-Americans are not the only group in the United States focusing on the articulation of pedagogical principles that are specific to their cultural group. Culture-sensitive pedagogical principles have been articulated for native Hawaiian children;[9] Navajo children;[10] Pueblo Indian children;[11] Athabascan Alaskan children;[12] and for Hispanic children.[13] These efforts are critical given the current limitations of educational research in the United States and other Western countries. Rogoff and Morelli point out that:

> Cross-cultural research provides a breadth that has been more difficult to achieve when researchers have looked at cultural variation in our own nation and have tended to assume that the majority's practices are normal and the minority's practices involve deficits.[14]

The February 1989 issue of *American Psychologist* addressed from diverse perspectives the issue of culture and education in the United States. In addition, Dalton Miller-Jones noted that research focusing on African-American cultural styles and their relationship to education had had positive effects for all children over the past 30 years.[15] In a similar fashion, I expect that the implementation of African-centered pedagogical principles and research related to this process will broaden our knowledge of human learning by broadening the base of cases that instantiate our premises. The following are some of the fundamental questions regarding human learning for which research and practice related to African-centered pedagogy hold important implications.

- In urban, poor, single-parent African-American households, what is the nature of play and what are the cognitive foundations and socialization strategies that undergird that play?
- What story schema do African-American children display during oral storytelling in naturalistic environments and what are the implications of those schema or story grammars for story comprehension in early literacy and for writing instruction in cre-

ative writing, exposition, and argument in later grades?[16]

- What are the experiences that promoted African-American writers' creation of what Gates calls the "speakerly text?"[17]
- How can educators use African-American English speakers' understanding of and production of metaphoric and ironic talk in the form of signifying, sounding, etc. to promote children's comprehension of metaphor and irony in literature?[18]
- How can educators use African-American English speakers' signifying and sounding to enhance student writing?[19]
- What informal experiences in play and work do poor African-American children in urban and rural environments have with spatial relationships, quantities, logical operations, classification schemes, money, weight, and volume?
- What characteristics of these informal mathematical experiences share sufficient attributes of formal school-based mathematics to provide productive scaffolding for school learning?
- What effect can the incorporation of African contributions to mathematics, science, and technology into school-based curricula have on student motivation?
- How does the African and African-American tradition of socializing children through the indirect talk of proverbs and storytelling affect cognitive processing?
- How are the inferences from such indirect talk constructed and what are the implications of such construction for teaching African-American children (or other children) who are socialized in this way?

These questions are but the tip of an iceberg of potential foci for research that will support the articulation and elaboration of an African-centered pedagogy. Research in some of these areas has begun, but clearly more research will need to follow. This theoretical research must be coupled with strategic curricular implementation in environments that can maximize the effectiveness of instruction.

Placing Value on the Learner's Culture

Most conceptions of African-centered pedagogy focus almost solely on its motivational aspects and simply emphasize historical content. However, I propose that an African-centered curriculum positively exploit and scaffold productive community and cultural practices. In addition, it should extend as well as build upon the indigenous language. This pedagogy must consider the current socially routinized community practices. In so doing, it may have viable and powerful cognitive consequences for students. Indeed, African-centered pedagogy offers possibilities that go beyond self-esteem, historical accuracy, values clarification, and community empowerment—all of which are important consequences of education.

Recent research in cross-cultural psychology and schema theory supports the claim that cultural practices influence cognition.[20] These studies looked closely at how thinking is shaped by cultural contexts, but none looked sufficiently at the interaction of cultural contexts for learning outside the school and the learning that occurs inside classrooms. Moreover, none of the studies in these fields investigated a population of African-American subjects. Because of these limitations, continued research in African-centered pedagogy that builds on both community social practices and the indigenous language is needed to broaden our understanding of the interaction of culture and cognition and its implications for the transfer of learning. Schema theory would suggest that concept formation is based on a network of richly embedded associations.[21] The denser these associations, the more expert one's conceptual knowledge. This density may be defined in terms of content knowledge as well as associations of similarities and differences across ideas or processes. It has been argued that experts have routinized so many bits of information that they perceive overarching patterns with ease. Thus, if schools are able to identify critical and powerful ideas or practices in the cultural life of a community that map onto powerful skills that schools teach, two important results may follow. First, for individual children it may be possible to enrich and diversify the network of associations they are able to construct around specific concepts or skills. Second, the interweaving of home/community knowledge and school knowledge should broaden the scope of what we teach in schools as well as enrich the life of communities. The implications that derive from developing a deeper understanding of these cognitive associations are far reaching for any culturally sensitive pedagogy.

Molefi K. Asante argued that "the Afrocentric scholar finds the source of a people's truth close to the language."[22] The idea that language and thought are intimately linked has been speculated upon for many years.[23] Thus, it seems quite appropriate to search the language practices of an ethnically distinct community as a source for the caliber of social practices that Stigler and Baranes claimed can bridge school learning.[24] In a review of cross-cultural research that investigated the transferability of knowledge emanating from social practices to school mathematics, Stigler and Baranes included studies of Brazilian bookies and Liberian tailors in which unschooled and schooled cohorts were contrasted. They noted the following:

> Like the schooled bookies, the schooled tailors were successful in solving the nonpractical problems not because experience with formal schooling allowed them to solve decontextualized problems nor because schooling provided them with general problem solving skills, but because the nonpractical problems were similar to school problems, and, after years of schooling, they had become skillful school-problem solvers. The point here is that the problems themselves must be carefully examined, as well as the practical experiences of the subjects . . . all practical experiences are not necessarily equivalent, and some experiences may allow for better performance on school tasks than others.[25]

Despite such reported links between language and thought, the vast majority of research on language practices in the Black community has made direct claims of deficits.[26] In contrast to deficit theories, some researchers have recently suggested that schools do not recognize the linguistic strengths of African-American pupils. However, not even these researchers have offered any specific suggestions as to how the scaffolding of indigenous linguistic skills might occur in schools.[27]

Shirley Brice-Heath has made important contributions to our understanding of how cultural experiences are ignored in schools. She stated,

> The school has seemed unable to recognize and take up the potentially positive interactive and adaptive verbal and interpretive habits learned by Black American children (as well as other non-mainstream groups), rural and urban, within their families and on the streets. These uses of language—spoken and written—are wide ranging, and many represent skills that would benefit all youngsters: keen listening and observational skills, quick recognition and nuanced roles, rapid-fire dialogue, hard-driving argumentation, succinct recapitulation of an event, striking metaphors, and comparative analyses based on unexpected analogies.[28]

Heath admonished that "relatively few Black anthropologists or linguists have chosen to focus their research on language and culture patterns of Black Americans."[29] In the next section, I briefly discuss my research on signifying. It provides an example of a cultural practice based on language strengths that bridges home and school learning.

African-Centered Pedagogy in Process: The Case of Signifying

Signifying is a form of oral discourse within the African-American community that is characterized by innuendo, double meanings, and rhetorical play upon the meaning and sounds of words. As a discourse form, signifying has been the focus of much investigation.[30]

Signifying has been described as an attitude toward language and as a means of cultural self-definition.[31] It is a traditional form of African-American discourse which has been maintained across generations and across both rural and urban environments, and can easily be traced back to the period of the African-American Holocaust, known to many as slavery. There are many forms of signifying. In many communities, an African-American adolescent who cannot signify has no status and no style. Examples of sounding and the dozens, two popular forms of signifying are offered for illustration:

> You so poor the roaches and rats eat lunch out! [sounding]
> Your momma so ugly she went to the zoo and the gorilla paid to see her. [the dozens][32]

Because it involves the ability to process quickly words that do not mean what they seem on the surface, the cognitive requirements of signifying are similar to the tasks of constructing inferred meanings from written texts, a task that is both common and challenging in school classrooms.

Zora Neale Hurston called signifiers "big picture talkers" who "use a side of the world for a canvas" and "make crayon enlargements of life."[33] Hurston, an African-American writer who explicitly reveled in the beauty of African-American discourse, recognized that signifying is replete with metaphoric, figurative, and ironic talk. Studies by DeLain et al.[34] and Ortony et al.[35] pointed to the possibilities that signifying offers as a means of scaffolding the language strengths of African-American students in school contexts. DeLain et al. measured how skill in sounding, a form of signifying, correlated with the ability to interpret figurative language. They found that, for White students, general language ability predicted skill in interpreting figurative language. For Black students they found that skill in Black English predicted skill in sounding and that skill in sounding predicted skill in interpreting figurative language. Ortony et al.[36] used a research design similar to that of DeLain et al.[37] They found that skill in sounding was used as an effective scaffold for getting students to use concrete details and images to produce effective creative writing samples. Both these studies indicated positive academic outcomes when the language strengths of African-American students were recognized and utilized in school contexts.

In my own research[38] I have drawn analogies between the processing of signifying discourse and the processing of irony in literature.[39] In the tradition of Zora Neale Hurston, many African-American writers have produced "speakerly texts"[40] in which Black English abounds in the voices of characters and/or the narrator. One characteristic of African-American English which these texts draw upon is a high usage of figurative language to convey significant yet implied themes, symbols, and motifs. For example, in Hurston's *Their Eyes Were Watching God* I identified one hundred and sixty sentences/passages which are rhetorically metaphoric, proverbial, or oxymoronic. Each of these passages conveys an important theme, symbol, motif, or irony in the work.

Skill in the rhetoric of signifying should assist students in constructing meaningful interpretations of such passages. This process involves recognition by students of what Hillocks and Ludlow have identified as simple implied relationships and complex implied relationships.[41] Neither type of relationship is directly stated in the literary text. Each must be constructed by students as they piece together details that may be either localized within a small section of the text (i.e., simple implied relationships) or dispersed across the text (complex implied relationships). The skill needed to construct such interpretations is considered to be very difficult to learn and is one that U.S. schools have proven not very effective in teaching.[42]

These findings demonstrate some of the cognitive consequences that a culturally sensitive, African-centered pedagogy may have. The implementation of African-centered pedagogical principles is occurring within some Black independent schools and other educational institutions outside the public sector, including churches, social and fraternal collectives, and community organizations.[43] In the next section I will describe the application of African-centered pedagogy in the science curriculum of the New Concept Development Center, an independent African-centered school in Chicago.

African-Centered Pedagogy in an African-Centered Independent School

African-centered pedagogy is not a new phenomenon in the education of African-American youth. The African-American free schools during Reconstruction[44] and the Freedom Schools of the civil rights movement[45] represent two bench marks along this historical continuum. Since the early 1970s, hundreds of community-based schools across the country have developed and implemented a challenging curriculum which incorporates African and African-American history and culture. These schools have provided the most contemporary stage for the practice of African-centered pedagogy. Moreover, students in these community-based institutions have demonstrated a high level of mastery of academic skills as evaluated by standardized achievement tests.[46]

One important environment for the articulation and implementation of African-centered pedagogical principles has been the independent Black school as embodied through the Council of Independent Black Institutions (CIBI). The brief overview that follows describes some of the curricular activities that are common in CIBI schools and that reflect some of the goals we have identified as crucial to an African-centered pedagogy. These activities do not engage all the aims identified for this pedagogy. However they do legitimize African stores of knowledge, idealize community service, impart a worldview in which Africans master technology, and support cultural continuity while promoting critical consciousness.

The activities described here are typical of the type conducted in preparation for the National Science EXPO sponsored annually by CIBI since 1977. I choose to highlight activities in science and technology because much of the current emphasis on African-centered curriculum focuses primarily on the arts and secondarily on the humanities, but rarely on the sciences. When activities that may be construed as science-related are put forward, they are generally nothing more than storytelling—biographies of great African men and women.

These science units were done with students in grades one through five. Attention is called to the grade levels of the students because I want to emphasize that the work was challenging for such young students. It was undertaken because, in the spirit of such educators as Septima Clark and Mary McLeod Bethune, African-American educators in these independent institutions take for granted that *all* children are capable of learning. Moreover, the teacher's role is understood to be an extension of the parental role. Thus, whatever time, energy, or strategies are required to achieve success for these children will be marshalled. This conception of teaching is one in which the teacher sees his or her own personal future in the lives of the children s/he teaches. To be successful, an African-centered pedagogy requires this type of teacher attitude.

The exemplary units include one on the principles of aeronautics, one on architecture, and one on computer science. In the unit on aeronautics, students built a model wind tunnel and tested the effects of the position of the tail, rudder, and ailerons on the direction of an airplane in simulated flight. This set of activities was preceded by units on air pressure and air lift as exemplified by Bernoulli's principle. In conjunction with this unit, students researched and wrote about the role of Africans in American aviation, including the story of the famous Tuskegee Airmen. They also developed scenarios speculating on the source of the wooden glider in the Cairo Museum, presumed to be preliminary evidence of early attempts by ancient Egyptians to investigate the principles of flight.[47]

In the unit on architecture, students tested the strength of certain shapes in construction, particularly the truss in bridge and building construction. They then identified the triangle as the building block of the truss and traced the Egyptian's understanding of this function to the construction of the pyramids.[48] For the actual CIBI Science EXPO, students built model buildings and bridges out of straws and popsicle sticks. An African-American architect came in not only to evaluate the projects, but also to talk with the students about how he used his skills and his architectural firm to promote development in the African-American community.

In the computer science unit, several student volunteers in the computer science program at a local public high school came in to work after school with a group of elementary students on simple programming. The elementary students accumulated information from studies in Black history and developed a Black History quiz. With the assistance of the high school volunteers, the students then translated the quiz into a simple computer program. Other students worked on the base two binary system and developed an elementary circuit board illustrating how the computer counts and operates using binary-based on/off switches. At the Science EXPO an African-American businessman, who not only builds computers but also owns a computer company, came in to talk with the children about computers and to show them the inner workings of a computer. For the children, the computer specialist represented a living model of what they could become as well as an example of an adult who was giving his skills back to the community from which he had come.

Other projects included a hands-on demonstration of the Yoruba counting system. This activity was important in legitimizing a new source of knowledge for the students and also expanded their examples of how people count. In conjunction with units on Kemetic (Egyptian) history, students demonstrated the Egyptians' use of fractions in the marketplace and their use of simple machines in the building of the obelisk of Queen Hatshepsut. Several students from a CIBI school, while visiting the Washington Monument, observed that the monument was an obelisk. They noticed that it differed from the Egyptian model in that Hatshepsut's obelisk was carved out of solid granite, while the Washington Monument appeared to the naked eye to be built from blocks.

The independent African-centered school affirms the strengths that African-American children bring to school. These schools typically develop explicit goals that speak directly to African-centered ethical character development. Some clear examples are taken from the *New Concept Development Center Parent Handbook* in which the institution's expectations are clearly stated. The school intends that children learn to:

1. think critically and question everything;
2. understand history;
3. set good examples and accept just criticism;
4. practice a life-style which recognizes the importance of African and African-American heritage and traditions, and is geared to the values which will facilitate the present and future development of African people; and
5. be critical of self first and recognize that African values are only as just and correct as those who practice them.[49]

The unswerving belief in the ability of all children to be academically successful that is demonstrated within independent African-centered schools, coupled with the kind of curricular activities I have just described, promote a qualitative development that extends beyond simple literacy and acquisition of the skills needed to get a job working for someone else. These activities reflect African-centered pedagogical principles aimed at empowering students to create and to reflect on their creations and the impact such creations can have on their communities and families. Such activities inspire visions of a past and future in which Africans exert self-determination in the conduct of the communities in which they live.

Realities and Possibilities for Change in Public Schools

Consider the shortcomings in the implementation of the African-American component of the Portland (OR) school system's multicultural model[50] and the political turmoil surrounding the report "Curriculum of Inclusion" issued by the Task Force on Minorities: Equity and Excellence from the New York State Board of Education.[51] It is naive to believe that an African-centered curriculum based on an African-centered pedagogy will occur under such conditions. How, then, can an African-centered pedagogy fit into the framework of public schooling in the United States?

The implementation of African-centered pedagogy presents major challenges to public schooling. Among these challenges is the preparation of teachers. The implementation of an African-centered pedagogy demands teachers who advocate and are well grounded in the following principles and stores of knowledge:

1. The social ethics of African culture as exemplified in the social philosophy of Maat.[52]
2. The history of the African continent and Diaspora.
3. Political and community organizing within the African-American community.
4. The positive pedagogical implications of the indigenous language, African-American English.[53]
5. Child development principles that are relevant to the positive and productive growth of African-American children.[54]
6. African contributions in science, mathematics, literature, the arts, and societal organization.
7. Teaching techniques that are socially interactive and positively affective.[55]
8. The need for continuous personal study.
9. The African principle that "Children are the reward of life."
10. The African principle of reciprocity;[56] that is, a teacher sees his or her own future symbiotically linked to the development of students.

These attributes are extremely demanding, but are fundamental to the liberating aims of this pedagogy. Given such prerequisites it is difficult to believe that public schooling in a democratic and ethnically diverse country such as the United States can assume the responsibility to liberate any particular group of people. I do believe that it is possible to do the following within public schools:

1. Foster the development of the skills in literacy, numeracy, the humanities, and technologies that are necessary to negotiate economic self-sufficiency in the society;

2. Instill citizenship skills based on a realistic and thorough understanding of the political system, and support such citizenship skills by promoting questioning and critical thinking skills, and teaching democratic values;[57]

3. Provide historical overviews of the nation, the continent, and the world which accurately represent the contributions of all ethnic groups to the storehouse of human knowledge.

Even if public schools were to accomplish these things, the conditions necessary for African-Americans to achieve ethnic pride, self-sufficiency, equity, wealth, and power would not be met. For Africans in America to achieve such goals, a collective, although not monolithic, cultural and political worldview is required. Public schooling does not impart such a worldview.

These limitations of public schooling, as presently constructed, support the argument for the articulation and implementation of an African-centered pedagogy. In order to develop within public schools a more cohesive educational philosophy that will be sensitive to both current and future conditions, I believe researchers and practitioners must collaborate in lab school settings. These lab schools must have the philosophical and material resources as well as the historical practices to provide adequate support for collaborative activities. African-American independent schools and African-centered educational researchers potentially represent an ideal alliance for collaborative work toward the transformation of public schooling. Conclusions and practices developed through such collaboration would offer relevant and tested sources of curriculum content and pedagogical principles for the African-American component of multicultural curricula in public schools.

Conclusion

In the context of a multi-ethnic, democratic society, attention to African-centered pedagogy amidst calls for multicultural education creates serious tensions.[58] We must address the question of how an African-centered pedagogy reinforces intra-ethnic solidarity and pride without promoting inter-ethnic antagonisms. An African-centered pedagogy must include a conceptualization of American society as a culturally diverse entity within which ethnic solidarity is required in order to negotiate, acquire, and maintain power. This pedagogy should promote intra-ethnic solidarity among African-Americans while at the same time providing strategies for coalitions with other groups with similar needs and interests. American society is not a melting pot, but rather a mosaic of diversity. We must honestly address the question of what the implementation of an African-centered pedagogy means in different settings—such as a classroom in which many ethnic groups are represented or a public school whose population is entirely African-American.

In addition to complex issues within the United States, there are also complex international considerations. The issues related to the formulation of an African-centered pedagogy are relevant to Africans world wide. However, the functions and cultural specificity of such a pedagogy will be qualitatively different as social contexts vary among countries as diverse as the United States, Brazil, Australia, Nigeria, and Azania (South Africa). For example, certain socio-political and historical factors are important in accounting for differences in the levels of educational achievement among Caribbean Blacks in the United States and in Great Britain. A similar comparison may be made between the differences in educational achievement between Koreans in Japan and Koreans in the United States.[59]

An African-centered pedagogy must direct African-American children and African-American people out of the "peculiar sensation" observed by W. E. B. DuBois, of "this double-consciousness, this sense of always looking at one's self through the eyes of others."[60] Rather, African-centered pedagogy must take up the mantle of the griots as Ghanaian novelist Ayi Kwei Armah reveals in the prophetic novel *Two Thousand Seasons*.[61] African-centered pedagogy must help students see beyond "the howling cacophony" that may engulf them. Its activities must link them to "those gone, ourselves here [and] those coming." African-centered pedagogy can help students "listen far toward origins," and can offer them some tools with which they can figure out their "way." Their voices and self-analysis must be strengthened in order to "make this knowledge [of themselves] inevitable [and] impossible to lose."

There is a lesson to learn from scholar/practitioners as diverse as George Washington Carver, W. E. B. DuBois, Ida B. Wells, Cheikh Anta Diop, Mary McLeod Bethune, and Carter G. Woodson. They have all demonstrated that with a strong cultural sense of self, with a commitment to and connection with one's people, we may emerge out of low circumstances, take in the knowledge of the world, and give special gifts to all of humanity.

Notes and References

1. J. A. Comenius, *The Great Didactic of John Amos Comenius*, trans. and ed. M. W. Keatinge (1657; reprint, New York: Russell and Russell, 1967).

2. J. Dewey, *Democracy and Education: An Introduction to the Philosophy of Education* (New York: The MacMillan Company, 1916), 95.

3. M. Apple, *Ideology and Curriculum* (London: Routledge and Kegan Paul, 1979); J. Banks, "Ethnicity, Class, Cognitive and Motivational Styles: Research and Teaching Implications," *Journal of Negro Education* 57 (1988): 452-466; D. Miller-Jones, "The Study of African-American Children's Development: Contributions to Reformulating Developmental Paradigms," in *Black Children and Poverty: A Developmental Perspective*, ed. D. Slaughter (San Francisco: Jossey-Bass, 1988), 75-92; J. Ogbu, "Cultural Diversity and Human Development," in *Black Children and Poverty: A Developmental Perspective*, ed. D. Slaughter (San Francisco: Jossey-Bass, 1988), 11-28; National Alliance of Black School Educators, Inc., Task Force on Black Academic and Cultural Excellence, *Saving the African-American Child* (Washington, DC, 1984); D. Slaughter and G. McWorter, "Social Origins and Early Features of the Scientific Study of Black American Families and Children," in *Beginnings: The Social and Affective Development of Black Children*, eds. M. Spencer, G. Brookins, and W. Allen (Hillsdale, NJ: Lawrence Erlbaum Associates, 1985), 5-18; J. Stigler and R. Baranes, "Culture and Mathematical Learning," *Review of Research in Education* 15 (1989): 253-306.

4. M. K. Asante, *Afrocentricity* (Trenton, NJ: Africa World Press, 1988); C. A. Diop, *The Cultural Unity of Black Africa* (Chicago: Third World Press, 1978); *The Book of Coming Forth by Day: The Ethics of the Declarations of Innocence*, trans. and commentary M. Karenga (Los Angeles: University of Sankore Press, 1990); J. Mbiti, *African Religion and Philosophy* (New York: Anchor Books, 1970); W. Nobles, "African Philosophy: Foundations for Black Psychology," in *Black Psychology*, ed. R. Jones (New York: Harper and Row, 1980), 23-36; J. A. Sofola, *African Culture and the African Personality* (Ibadan, Nigeria: African Resources, 1973); S. Stuckey, *Slave Culture* (New

York: Oxford University Press, 1987); N. Warfield-Coppock, *Afrocentric Theory and Applications, Vol. 1: Adolescent Rites of Passage* (Washington, DC: Baobab Associates, 1990).

5. Karenga, *Book of Coming Forth*, 26.
6. Karenga, *Book of Coming Forth*, xi.
7. P. Freire, *Pedagogy of the Oppressed* (New York: Seabury Press, 1970).
8. H. Giroux and P. McLaren, eds., *Critical Pedagogy, the State, and Cultural Struggle* (Albany, NY: State University of New York Press, 1989).
9. R. Gallimore, R. G. Tharp, K. Sloat, T. Klein, and M. E. Troy, *Analysis of Reading Achievement Test Results for the Kamehameha Early Education Project: 1972-1979* Tech. Rep. No. 102 (Honolulu: Kamehameha Schools/Bishop Estate, 1982); R. Tharp, "The Effective Instruction of Comprehension: Results and Descriptions of the Kamehameha Early Education Program," *Reading Research Quarterly* 17 (1982): 503-327; R. G. Tharp, C. Jordan, G. Speidel, K. H. Au, T. W. Klein, K. C. M. Sloat, R. P. Calkins, and R. Gallimore, "Product and Process in Applied Developmental Research: Education and the Children of a Minority," in *Advances in Developmental Psychology* Vol. 3, ed. M. E. Lamb, A. L. Brown, and B. Rogoff (Hillsdale, NJ: Lawrence Erlbaum Associates, 1984), 91-144.
10. C. Jordan, R. G. Tharp, and L. Vogt, *Compatibility of Classroom and Culture: General Principles with Navajo and Hawaiian Instances* (Working Paper No. 18) (Honolulu: Kamehameha Schools/Bishop Estate, 1985); S. White and R. G. Tharp, "Questioning and Wait-time: A Cross-Cultural Analysis," paper presented at the Annual Meeting of the American Educational Research Association, New Orleans, 1988).
11. V. P. John-Steiner and H. Osterreich, *Learning Styles among Pueblo Children: Final Report to the National Institute of Education* (Albuquerque: University of New Mexico, College of Education, 1975); W. A. Winterton, "The Effect of Extended Wait-time on Selected Verbal Response Characteristics of Some Pueblo Indian Children," *Dissertation Abstracts International* 38, 620-A (1977).
12. C. Barnhardt, "Tuning-in: Athabaskan Teachers and Athabaskan Students," in *Cross-Cultural Issues in Alaskan Education*, vol. 2, ed. R. Barnhardt (Fairbanks: University of Alaska, Center for Cross-Cultural Studies, 1982); R. Scollon, *Narrative, Literacy, and Face in Interethnic Communication* (Norwood, NJ: Ablex Pub. Corp., 1981).
13. L. Moll, "Literacy Research in Community and Classrooms: A Socio-Cultural Approach," paper presented at the Conference on Multi-Disciplinary Perspectives on Research Methodology in Language Arts, National Conference on Research in English, Chicago, 1990.
14. B. Rogoff and G. Morelli, "Culture and American Children: Section Introduction," *American Psychologist* 44 (1989): 341.

15. Miller-Jones, "African-American Children's Development."
16. I acknowledge the important contributions to this question made by Heath, Michaels, and Gee: S. B. Heath, *Ways with Words: Language, Life and Work in Communities and Classrooms* (Cambridge: Cambridge University Press, 1983); S. Michaels, "Sharing Time: Children's Narrative Styles and Differential Access to Literacy," *Language in Society* 10 (1981): 423-442; S. Michaels, "Narrative Presentations: An Oral Preparation for Literacy with First Graders," in *The Social Construction of Literacy*, ed. J. Cook-Gumperz (Cambridge: Cambridge University Press, 1986), 94-116; J. Gee, "The Narrativization of Experience in the Oral Style," *Journal of Education* 171 (1989): 75-96). I also applaud Shirley Brice Heath's admonition that "Relatively few Black anthropologists or linguists have chosen to focus their research on language and culture patterns of Black Americans" (S. B. Heath, "Language Socialization," in *Black Children and Poverty: A Developmental Perspective*, ed. D. Slaughter (San Francisco: Jossey-Bass, 1988), 32). Several significant projects in naturalistic environments by African-American researchers include Mitchell-Kernan, Potts, Stockman and Vaughn-Cooke, as well as on-going research by Mahiri (C. Mitchell-Kernan, *Language Behavior in a Black Urban Community* Monograph no. 2 (Berkeley: University of California, Language Behavior Laboratory, 1971); R. Potts, "West Side Stories: Children's Conversational Narratives in a Black Community," paper presented at the Biennial Meeting of the Society for Research in Child Development, 1989; I. Stockman and A. F. Vaughn-Cooke, "Reexamination of the Research on the Language of Black Children: The Need for a New Framework," *Journal of Education* 164 (1982): 157-172; I. Stockman and A. F. Vaughn-Cooke, "Addressing New Questions about Black Children's Language," in *Language Change and Variation* eds. R. W. Fasold and D. Schiffrin (Philadelphia: John Benjamin, 1989); J. Mahiri, *Language Use and Literary Features of Pre-Adolescent African-American Males in a Neighborhood-Based Organization* (Chicago: University of Illinois, 1990). It has become more commonly accepted in ethnographic research that indigenous participant-observers may have insights into the discourse that others do not (Heath, "Language Socialization"; M. Saville-Troike, *The Ethnography of Communication: An Introduction* (New York: Basil Blackwell, 1989). The investigations of stories of personal experience within diverse communities by Miller, Potts, and Fung reflects sensitivity to the potentially privileged role indigenous members of a speech community may have in ethnographic research (P. Miller, R. Potts, and H. Fung, "Minority Perspectives on Narrative Development," paper presented at the Annual Meeting of the American Educational Research Association, 1989.
17. H. L. Gates, *The Signifying Monkey: A Theory of Afro-American*

Literary Criticism (New York: Oxford University Press, 1988).

18. Taylor and Ortony, and DeLain, Pearson, and Anderson, have established a relationship between expertise in African-American English, sounding (a form of signifying), and comprehension of figurative language in metaphor and simile (M. Taylor and A. Ortony, "Rhetorical Devices in Black English: Some Psycholinguistic and Educational Observations," *Quarterly Newsletter of the Laboratory of Human Cognition* 2 (1980): 21-26; M. T. DeLain, P. D. Pearson, and R. C. Anderson, "Reading Comprehension and Creativity in Black Language Use: You Stand to Gain by Playing the Sounding Game," *American Educational Research Journal* 22 (1985): 155-173. However, these studies do not use naturalistic texts and so the question of any transferability of this relationship to literary understanding remains open. Lee addresses the issue of transfer and the conditions of instruction which might promote transfer (C. Lee, "Signifying in the Zone of Proximal Development," unpublished paper, University of Chicago, 1990).

19. Arnetha Ball has initiated an excellent study which identifies structural patterns of discourse that emerge in writing samples from African-American high-school students (A. Ball, "A Study of the Oral and Descriptive Patterns of Black Adolescents in Vernacular and Academic Discourse Communities," paper presented at the Annual Meeting of the American Educational Research Association, 1990). How to exploit these structural patterns in enhancing student writing, however, remains an open question.

20. M. Cole, "The Zone of Proximal Development: Where Culture and Cognition Create Each Other," in *Culture, Communication and Cognition*, ed. J. Wertsch (New York: Cambridge University Press, 1985), 146-161; H. Ginsburg, J. K. Posner, and R. L. Russel, "The Development of Mental Addition as a Function of Schooling and Culture," *Journal of Cross-Cultural Psychology* 12 (1981): 163-178; A. A. Kulah, *The Organization and Learning of Proverbs among the Kpelle of Liberia*, unpublished doctoral dissertation, University of California, Irvine, 1973; Laboratory of Human Cognition, "Contributions of Cross-Cultural Research to Educational Practice," *American Psychologist* 41 (1986): 1049-1058; J. Lave, "Cognitive Consequences of Traditional Apprenticeship Training in West Africa," *Anthropology and Education Quarterly* 7 (1977): 177-180; H. J. Reed and J. Lave, "Arithmetic as a Tool for Investigating Relations between Culture and Cognition," in *Language, Culture and Cognition: Anthropological Perspectives* (New York: MacMillan, 1981); A. Petitto, "Practical Arithmetic and Transfer: A Study among West African tribesmen," *Journal of Cross-Cultural Psychology* 13 (1982): 15-28; A. Petitto and H. Ginsburg, "Mental Arithmetic in Africa and America: Strategies, Principles, and Explanations," *Internal Journal of Psychology* 17 (1982): 81-102; G. B. Saxe, "Culture and the

Development of Numerical Cognition: Studies among the Okaspmin of Papua, New Guinea," in *Children's Logical and Mathematical Cognition*, ed. C. Brainerd (New York: Springer-Verlag, 1982), 157-176; S. Scribner and M. Cole, *The Psychology of Literacy* (Cambridge: Harvard University Press, 1981); Stigler and Baranes, "Culture and Mathematical Learning."

21. R. C. Anderson, "Some Reflections on the Acquisition of Knowledge," *Educational Researcher* 13 (1984): 5-10; F. C. Bartlett, *Remembering* (Cambridge: Cambridge University Press, 1932); D. E. Rumelhart, "Schemata: The Building Blocks of Cognition," in *Theoretical Issues in Reading Comprehension*, eds. R. J. Spiro, B. C. Bruce, and W. F. Brewer (Hillsdale, NJ: Lawrence Erlbaum Associates, 1980).

22. M. Asante, *Afrocentricity: The Quest for Method*, unpublished paper, Temple University, 1989, 11.

23. J. Bruner, *Actual Minds, Possible Worlds* (Cambridge, MA: Harvard University Press, 1986); J. Bruner, *Acts of Meaning* (Cambridge: Cambridge, MA: Harvard University Press, 1990); L. Vygotsky, *Thought and Language* (Cambridge, MA: The MIT Press, 1986); M. M. Bakhtin, *The Dialogic Imagination*, ed. M. Holquist, trans. C. Emerson and M. Holquist (Austin: University of Texas Press, 1981); J. Britton, *Language and Learning* (New York: Penguin Books, 1970).

24. Stigler and Baranes, "Culture and Mathematical Learning."

25. Stigler and Baranes, "Culture and Mathematical Learning," 282.

26. C. Bereiter, "Language Problem for Culturally Deprived Children," in *Language Programs for the Disadvantaged: Report to the NCTE Task Force on Teaching English to the Disadvantaged* (Champaign, IL: National Council of Teachers of English, 1965); C. Bereiter and S. Engleman, *Teaching Disadvantaged Children in the Pre-School* (Englewood Cliffs, NJ: Prentice-Hall, 1966); J. S. Coleman, E. Campbell, C. Hobson, J. McPartland, A. Mood, F. Weinfeld, and York, *Equality of Educational Opportunity* (Washington, DC: U.S. Government Printing Office, 1966); M. Deutsch, ed., *The Disadvantaged Child* (New York: Basic Books, 1967); T. J. Farrell, "I.Q. and Standard English," *College Composition and Communication* 34 (1983): 470-484; C. E. A. Jencks, *Inequality: A Reassessment of Family and Schooling in America* (New York: Basic Books, 1972); G. W. Karger, *The Performance of Lower-Class Black and Lower-Class White Children on the Wepman Auditory Discrimination Test: The Effects of Dialect and Training and the Relationship to Reading Achievement*, unpublished doctoral dissertation, Harvard University, Graduate School of Education, 1973; D. R. Olson, "From Utterance to Text: The Bias of Language in Speech and Writing," *Harvard Educational Review* 47 (1977): 257-281; E. W. Orr, *Twice as Less: Black English and the Performance of Black*

Students in Mathematics and Science (New York: W. W. Norton and Company, 1987).

27. Heath, "Language Socialization"; S. B. Heath, "Oral and Literate Traditions among Black Americans Living in Poverty," *American Psychologist* 44 (1989): 367-373; DeLain, Pearson, and Anderson, "Black Language Use;" Gee, "Narrativization of Experience;" Michaels, "Sharing Time;" Michaels, "Narrative Presentations."

28. Heath, "Oral and Literate Traditions," 370.

29. Heath, "Language Socialization," 32.

30. R. D. Abraham, *Deep Down in the Jungle: Negro Narrative Folklore from the Streets of Philadelphia* (Chicago: Aldine, 1970); M. Andrews and P. Owens, Black Language (Los Angeles, CA: Seymour-Smith, 1973); R. Brown, *Die Nigger Die!* (New York: Dial Press, 1969); M. Cooke, *Afro-American Literature in the Twentieth Century: The Achievement of Intimacy* (New Haven, CT: Yale University Press, 1984); H. L. Gates, "The Bness of Bness: A Critique of the Sign and the Signifying Monkey," in *Black Literature and Literacy Theory*, ed. H. L. Gates (New York: Methuen, 1984); Gates, *The Signifying Monkey*; Z. N. Hurston, *Mules and Men* (New York: Harper and Row, 1935); T. Kochman, ed., *Rappin' and Stylin' Out: Communication in Urban Black America* (Urbana, IL: University of Illinois Press, 1972); C. Major, *Dictionary of Afro-American Slang* (New York: International Publishers, 1970). Mitchell-Kernan, *Language Behavior*. G. Smitherman, *Talkin' and Testifyin': The Language of Black America* (Boston: Houghton Mifflin, 1977).

31. Gates, "The Bness of Bness"; Gates, *The Signifying Monkey*; Mitchell-Kernan, *Language Behavior*; Smitherman, *Talkin' and Testifyin'*.

32. Mitchell-Kernan, *Language Behavior*.

33. Hurston, *Mules and Men*.

34. DeLain, Pearson, and Anderson, "Black Language Use."

35. A. Ortony, T. Turner, and N. Larson-Shapiro, "Cultural and Instructional Influences on Figurative Language Comprehension by Inner-City Children," *Research in Teaching of English* 19 (1985): 25-35.

36. Ortony, Turner, and Larson-Shapiro, "Figurative Language Comprehension."

37. DeLain, Pearson, and Anderson, "Black Language Use."

38. C. Lee, "Signifying as a Scaffold to Literary Interpretation: The Pedagogical Implications of a Form of African-American Discourse," paper presented at the Annual Meeting of the American Educational Research Association, Chicago, 1991.

39. W. Booth, *A Rhetoric of Irony* (Chicago: University of Chicago Press, 1974); M. Smith, *Reading and Teaching Irony in Poetry: Giving Short People a Reason to Live*, unpublished doctoral dissertation, University of Chicago, 1987).

40. Gates, *The Signifying Monkey.*
41. G. Hillocks and L. Ludlow, "A Taxonomy of Skills in Reading and Interpreting Fiction," *American Educational Research Journal* 21 (1984): 7-24.
42. I. V. S. Mullis, E. H. Owens, and G. W. Phillips, *Accelerating Academic Achievement: A Summary of Findings from 20 Years of NAEPs* (Princeton, NJ: Educational Testing Service, 1990).
43. J. D. Ratteray and M. Shujaa, "Defining a Tradition: Parental Choice in Independent Neighborhood Schools," in *Visible Now: Blacks in Private Schools,* eds. D. Slaughter and D. J. Johnson (Westport, CT: Greenwood Press, 1988), 184-198.
44. J. Anderson, *The Education of Blacks in the South, 1860-1935* (Chapel Hill: University of North Carolina Press, 1988); L. Bennett, *Before the Mayflower: A History of the Negro in America, 1619-1962* (Chicago: Johnson Publishing Company, 1962); V. Harding, *There is a River: The Black Struggle for Freedom in America* (New York: Harcourt Brace Jovanovitch, 1981).
45. F. Howe, "Mississippi's Freedom Schools: The Politics of Education," *Harvard Educational Review* 35 (1965): 144-160.
46. J. D. Ratteray, *Access to Quality: Private Schools in Chicago's Inner City,* Heartland Policy Study No. 9 (Chicago: Heartland Institute, 1986); J. D. Ratteray, *What's in a Norm: How African-Americans Score on Achievement Tests* (Washington, DC: Institute for Independent Education, 1989).
47. I. Van Sertima, ed., *Blacks in Science* (New Brunswick, NJ: Transaction Books, 1983).
48. This curriculum reinforces the premise that classical Egyptian or Kemetic civilization was created primarily by Black people. For further references, see: J. Carruthers and M. Karenga, eds., *Kemet and the African World View: Selected Papers of the Proceedings of the First and Second Conferences of the Association for the Study of Classical African Civilization* (Los Angeles: University of Sankore Press, 1986); C. A. Diop, *The African Origin of Civilization: Myth or Reality,* trans. M. Cook (New York: L. Hill, 1974); Diop, *Cultural Unity;* C. A. Diop, "The Peopling of the Ancient Egyptians and the Deciphering of Meroitic Script," in *Proceedings of the Symposium Held in Cairo from January 28 to February 3, 1974* (Paris: UNESCO, 1978); C. A. Diop, "The Origins of the Ancient Egyptians," in *The General History of Africa: Ancient Civilizations of Africa,* vol. 2, ed. P. Mokhtar (Berkeley: University of California Press, 1981), 27-57; D. D. Houston, *Wonderful Ethiopians of the Ancient Cushite Empire* (Baltimore: Black Classic Press, 1985); J. Jackson, *Introduction to African Civilizations* (New York: University Books, 1970); G. James, *Stolen Legacy* (San Francisco: Julian Richardson Associates, 1954); C. Williams, *The Destruction of Black Civilization*

(Chicago: Third World Press, 1974). Kemetic civilization is highlighted because, according to Dr. Cheikh Anta Diop, "ancient Egypt was the key classical African civilization given its abundance of documents, its level of achievement in various areas of culture and human knowledge, and its resultant significance to other African cultures as well as to world culture," (Karenga, *The Book of Coming Forth by Day*, xii).

49. *New Concept Development Center Parent Handbook* (Chicago: Institute of Positive Education, 1977), 1-2.

50. The unit plans developed by the Portland Board of Education do not meet the quality expected as a result of the superb baseline essays developed by Afro-centric scholars to provide a historical and philosophical framework for the African-American component of the Portland multicultural curriculum (Hilliard, personal communication).

51. Critics of this report cited by Hancock (L. Hancock, "Whose America is this Anyway?" *Village Voice* April 24, 1990: 37-39) assume that history is apolitical and that education is not an ideological as well as an intellectual enterprise. These critics cite Asian-American students and the fact that Japanese students learn to master Western culture as evidence that the Eurocentrism in American textbooks does not hinder the scholastic achievement of these populations. This argument skirts the issue of the limitations of Eurocentric bias in American textbooks and curricula. More importantly, it does not address the strong cultural foundations, ethnic solidarity, as well as ethnic complexities which inspire the academic performance of many groups of Asian-American and Japanese students (D. Slaughter, K. Nakagawa, R. Takanishi, and D. Johnson, "Toward Cultural/Ecological Perspectives on Schooling and Achievement in African and Asian-American Children," *Child Development* 61 (1990): 363-383).

52. Karenga, *The Book of Coming Forth by Day*.

53. DeLain, Pearson, and Anderson, "Black Language Use;" Gee, "The Narrativization of Experience;" Heath, "Oral and Literate Traditions."

54. J. E. Hale, *Black Children: Their Roots, Culture and Learning Styles* (Provo, UT: Brigham Young University Press, 1982); Warfield-Coppock, *Afrocentric Theory*; A. Wilson, *The Developmental Psychology of the Black Child* (New York: Africana Research Publications, 1978).

55. Hale, *Black Children*; Warfield-Coppock, *Afrocentric Theory*; M. G. Willis, "Learning Styles of African-American Children: A Review of the Literature and Interventions," *Journal of Black Psychology* 16 (1989): 47-65.

56. A. K. Armah, *Two Thousand Seasons* (Chicago: Third World Press, 1979); Mbiti, *African Religion and Philosophy*; Nobles, "African Philosophy."

57. A. Gutmann, *Democratic Education* (Princeton: Princeton University Press, 1987); L. McNeil, *Contradictions of Control: School Structure*

and School Knowledge (New York: Routledge and Kegan Paul, 1988).

58. Hancock, "Whose America."

59. C. Cortes, "The Education of Language Minority Students: A Contextual Interaction Model," in *Beyond Language: Social and Cultural Factors in Schooling Language Minority Children*, California State Department of Education (Los Angeles: Evaluation, Dissemination, and Assessment Center, California State University, 1986), 73-142; J. Ogbu and M. E. Matute-Bianchi, "Understanding Sociocultural Factors: Knowledge, Identity, and School Adjustment," in *Beyond Language: Social and Cultural Factors in Schooling Language Minority Children*, California State Department of Education (Los Angeles: Evaluation, Dissemination, and Assessment Center, California State University, 1986), 73-142.

60. W. E. B. DuBois, *The Souls of Black Folk* (Chicago: A. C. McClurg, 1903).

61. Armah, *Two Thousand Seasons*.

Chapter Thirteen

Notes on an Afrikan*-Centered Pedagogy[1]

Agyei Akoto
NationHouse Positive Action Center

The elaboration of an Afrocentric pedagogy begins with a description of the historical and political economic contexts in which the discussion occurs. The contemporary era of pluralistic cultural-nationalist expression coincides, not incidentally, with a leveling of the international political economic landscape. The era of the super-power nations whose whims determined the course of world events has come to an unceremonious end with the failure and collapse of state structures founded on one European form of grand socio-economic theory—Marxism (socialism and communism)—and the fragmentation and reordering of states bound to the other—capitalism.[2] This leveling of the world order has occasioned the flowering of national cultures that had theretofore been systematically repressed and stifled by both the Marxist and the liberal democratic regimes of the West. Both are European-centered phenomena and both have reaped gross profits from the Eurocentric hegemony in the international cultural, political, and economic spheres.

Eurocentric hegemony has been accomplished in two ways. The first is through methods involving simple brute force such as mil-

* The author's use of the letter "k" in the spelling of "Afrika" derives from the Kiswahili language. Its use is a long-standing tradition among many schools in the Council of Independent Black Institutions.

itary invasion and occupation; enslavement; forced migration; genocide; illegalization of language and tradition; imposed structural
dependency; and political repression. Secondly, Eurocentric hegemony has been accomplished through methods of mental manipulation such as religious indoctrination and mystification;
miseducation; racist scholarship; institutionalized racism; cultural
repression and subordination; and mass propaganda. The consequences of both methods have been the psychic and spiritual negation of the dominated people. Both methods of repression have
been cloaked in self-serving accommodationist myths such as the
melting-pot theory, the common culture, the democratic or feder-
alist ideal, the universal cultural ideal etc.

Expressions of nationalist or ethnocentric sentiments by
repressed nationalities have been and still are greeted with such
charges as separatism, reverse racism, incitation to racial animos-
ity, misguided militancy, Balkanization, and narrow nationalism.[3]
Defenders of the "American idea [of] common citizenship [in a]
multi-ethnic society"[4] revel in the collapse of European socialism and
the "evil empire" and have closed their eyes to the West's legacy of
genocide, enslavement, and pillage against Afrikans and
Amerindians. They have camouflaged and denuded the psychic and
moral significance of these acts in the tapestry, lights, and sounds
of Hollywood and TV merrymaking. This propaganda machine has
dulled the thinking capacity of the general population. In doing so
it has contributed to mass depoliticization and civic cowardice.
Moreover, it has functioned in concert with the myth-perpetuation
and social-reproductive agendas of the schooling system to mask the
fundamental socio-economic, cultural, and moral contradictions in
Western (European/American) democracies. As a consequence, the
viability of America's democratic experiment has been seriously
compromised.

Afrocentrism, then, must be understood in this historical and
global perspective. Afrocentrism is a nationalist cultural expression
of Afrikan people that seeks the truthful reconstitution of Afrikan
history and culture and the transformation of the Afrikan man and
woman and their world. As a worldview it is not isolated from the
events and dynamics of the world. It is informed by the struggles of
fellow Afrikans and by similar struggles of other people. It aspires
ultimately to inform concretely and positively the human condition.

Afrikan-centered education is the codification or systematic
expression of Afrikan people's will to recover, recreate, and per-

petuate our cultural heritage. As a dynamic enterprise, it enriches our culture as it acts to illuminate it and it enculturates the people whose collective and historical experiences shape and are shaped by it. Afrikan-centered education speaks to the Pan-Afrikan world and addresses the several national expressions of that world.

Finally, Afrikan-centered pedagogy is ostensibly concerned with the methodology of teaching. However, we cannot realistically deal with teaching methodology without first examining the nature of the teacher's character and the goals of teaching. The three queries to be examined in this discussion are: why? (the goals of Afrikan-centered pedagogy); who? (the teacher as cultural representative); and how? (the methods and goals of African-centered instruction).

The Goals of African-centered Pedagogy

The pedagogy of Afrikan-centeredness, like Afrikan-centeredness itself, is not a simple negation of the hegemonic assumptions of Eurocentric pedagogical theory. An Afrikan-centered pedagogy is concerned with the acquisition of self-determination and self-sufficiency for Afrikan people. It is ultimately concerned with truth and the "Afrocentric mission to humanize the universe."[5] Afrikan-centeredness as a worldview and as a comprehensive cultural whole presages an Afrikan-centered education which, in turn, entails the elaboration of an Afrikan-centered pedagogy. The Afrikan-centered pedagogy of which I speak is a studied, vigorous, and creative elaboration of the fundamental precepts of Afrikan culture and ideology.

The ends or goals of any pedagogy parallel or echo the overall goals of the educational system of which they are a part. That educational system itself must serve to perpetuate the nation-state and the underlying cultural reality that spawned it. As a consequence, the assumptions and principles that are fundamental to that nation-state and its dominant culture will be found in the methodology its agents use in the enculturation of all the society's members, particularly youths, and in every available medium. Education stands in the same relationship to the national culture as childbearing stands to the human species; that is, it assures perpetuation or permanence and continuity. The character, composition, direction, and vitality of education, like those qualities in human progeny, issue directly from the parents' essence. In the case of education, these qualities flow from the historical continuum that lies at the base of the national culture.

The reasons for the drain of talent, graft, nepotism, incompetence, and waste that Afrikan continental and diasporan nations experience can be found in the educational structures, philosophies, theories, subject content, and pedagogies inherited from colonialism. European colonial powers controlled the schooling provided for teachers and administrators for the singular purpose of maintaining Eurocentric thinking and behaviors. This type of schooling continues to serve and protect European economic and political interests. Jamaica, Kenya, Zimbabwe, Nigeria, and other former British colonies still employ vestiges of the British system including British and American texts and curricula. National exams are still often sent to Britain for evaluation. When the national educational system is modeled after the oppressor's, carried out in the oppressor's language, and the standards of success are still determined directly and indirectly by the oppressor, dependency and subordination of the indigenous culture can be the only result. Indeed, such an outcome was designed by the colonial powers. Because of their reduced capacity to contain the political and economic demands of indigenous populations after World War II, European colonial powers sought to protect their interests in independent Afrikan states by transferring power to "acceptable Afrikan collaborators" or by muting the "radicalism of popular leaders through 'material temptations'" and through physical removal where necessary.[6]

A potent transoceanic and transnational bond among Afrikans reflects the depth of the original cultural homogeneity among pre-colonial Afrikans as well as the gross and undifferentiated inhumanities of the holocaust of enslavement, colonial domination, and neocolonialism. Consequently, Afrikan-centered education within Afrikan-American communities or in Ghana, Zimbabwe, or Azania operates on the same principles and has the same goals. The essential goals are to achieve genuine self-sufficiency and self-determination. In each national context Afrikan-centered education seeks to develop the knowledge and skills needed to purge the process of education itself and the nation as a whole of the perverse effects of current, recent, and remote domination. Language, values, behaviors, images, systems, institutions, and relationships must all be thoroughly and critically re-examined. Afrikan-centered education includes the rediscovery of the essential truths that characterized the educational systems that were its immediate forebears in traditional Afrikan societies. Ultimately, Afrikan-centered education seeks to rediscover and reclaim its spiritual and material linkages with the classical civilizations of Kemet, Nubia, Axum, and Meroe.

The processes of rediscovery and reclamation, however, are not directed toward simplistic and misguided replication of either traditional Afrikan or European educational models. The needs of the contemporary world cannot be adequately met by superimposing the mores of classical and traditional societies. Much of the historical environment that occasioned the development of certain philosophical and social constructs no longer exists. Thus, the aim of Afrikan-centered education is not to reenact ancient rituals, values, behaviors, and relationships that have no relevance in modernity, but to illuminate those features of traditional and classical societies that are timeless and dynamic. The concept of Maat and the entire ethical and moral philosophy that surrounds it are invaluable. The concept of God in man; the essential "cooperative democratic" nature of traditional societies;[7] and the preeminence of family are all timeless values. Moreover, the general holistic conception of the universe and the concept of duty before right are also essential values found in traditional Afrikan societies.

In addition to the values that continue to be fundamental to traditional Afrikan societies, the political and social structures also warrant serious and critical attention. With modifications for technological developments, the structures and operations of the Asante confederation, Akan Abusua system, Njama Ya Itwika of the Gikuyu, Induna of the Zulu, and other traditional models might be better suited to Afrikans than the obviously inefficient structures inherited from colonial powers.

A common and tragic concession to political and economic expediencies among Afrikans is the uncritical adoption or continuation of European-based systems and philosophies of education. This practice can only result in continued dependency and subordination. Well-intentioned Afrikan educators seeking to fix the problems they experience with Eurocentric models of education will often turn to so-called progressive or radical education theories and practices that are also Eurocentric. These "radical" philosophies of Eurocentric thinkers who often proclaim themselves to be guided by precepts of social transformation and democracy are uniformly flawed in their incomplete treatment of cultural difference. Additionally, these well-intentioned Eurocentric theorists continue to assume a universality of cultural response and cultural ideal.

Paulo Freire, for example, whose philosophy and accomplishments have inspired many, retains an essentially Marxist analysis of social history that suffers from the same limitations as Marxism related to issues of culture and race. The assumption of universality that permeates Freire's writings is derived from a Eurocentric philosophical treatment of the relationship between knowledge and the nature of "man-world" relationships. This universalist perspective is typical among "radical" Eurocentric political theorists who routinely understate the significance of national and racial cultural differences. Freire's delineation of problem-posing pedagogy, dialogue as methodology, and cultural action is profound. His conception of culture anticipates a "metalanguage" of "revolutionary pedagogical principles" which is consistent with the general universalist orientation of his work.[8] He describes culture as a "superstructure which can maintain 'remnants' of the past alive in the substructure undergoing revolutionary transformation."[9] However, in spite of his apparent grounding in the "unity between subjectivity and objectivity" and "conscientization,"[10] Freire is nonetheless limited by the Marxist structural paradigm where culture is incidental to social relations and historical dynamics. That he fails to acknowledge or factor into his theories the rich, varied, and vigorous cultural traditions of Afrikan-Brazilians, who represent more than 50% of the population, can only be attributed to the theoretical limitations of his essentially Eurocentric and structuralist perspective.

For Freire, the past is synonymous with oppression and psychic invasion by the oppressor culture. There is no provision for the dynamic ethnocentric features that shaped social interactions and relationships. These features further shaped the traditions, philosophy, morality, art, and spirituality that predated the era of capitalist domination. They are coterminous with that era and will likely usher in the succeeding era. Freire echoes Fanon on the regenerative impact of the liberation struggle on culture and the oppressed. Fanon, however, links the fight for national existence intimately with the "fruitfulness, . . . the continuous renewal and deepening" of the national culture.[11] Fanon's concept of culture embraces the concept of broken continuity. This concept is also elaborated by Amilcar Cabral who posits that the dynamic of traditional culture—though aborted by colonialism—nonetheless provides the wellspring for national resistance and reconstruction.[12] Cabral's call for a process of "re-Afrikanization" is a call to reestablish the Afrikan historical continuum that undergirds Afrikan culture. It is clear that the disruption of that historical continuum explains the current cultural distortions and weaknesses of Afrikan political organizations and the dependency of Afrikan national economies. Given the reemergence of nationalism among Europe's and Asia's ethnic groups amidst the collapse of the Soviet Union and the continuing tensions among the traditional nations of Afrika, the tendency toward understating the significance of cultural difference should be sufficiently contradicted by reality to be permanently laid to rest.

The Teacher as Cultural Representative

Afrikan-centered pedagogy must focus on the process of illuminating the amassed wisdom and cultural legacy of one generation and bequeathing it to the succeeding generation. To ensure the continued and expanded viability of the culture this process must occur within a context of mutual discovery, inspiration, creativity, and reciprocity. An Afrikan-centered pedagogy is a pedagogy derived from the Afrikan historical continuum and cultural dynamics. It endeavors to stimulate and nourish creative and critical consciousness and to inculcate through study and application a firm and conscious commitment to the reconstruction of true Afrikan nationhood, and the restoration of the Afrikan historical/cultural continuum. Moreover, it represents an effort to create a dynamic and liberated Afrikan personality. That personality is realized as mwalimu (teacher) and mwanafunzi (student) interact with each other in a fashion that reflects their fundamental Afrikanity and simultaneously transforms their environments into dynamic models of liberty and humanism.[13]

The individual who assumes the role of mwalimu (teacher) must not only be involved in the study of the culture, but must be involved in a concrete and ongoing way with advancing the cultural and/or political interests of Afrikan people. The mwalimu comes before her/his students (wanafunzi) as a representative of the whole culture. Walimu (teachers) are entrusted with the task of inculcating the essential values of the culture and thereby play an essential role in guaranteeing its continuation. The mwalimu represents, in one sense, the limitations of tradition and the existing order while, in another sense, the student (mwanafunzi) represents the new order or unlimited potentiality. The mwalimu as a representative of the current order brings with her/him the accumulated wisdom of tradition and must seek to impart that wisdom in a way that inspires and fuels the new energy and unlimited potential of the student. The mwanafunzi must be so motivated as to welcome that wisdom as fuel for the long run and not as a burden. If that wisdom, the cultural treasure and inheritance of the nation, is perceived as burdensome, then the mwalimu and the nation have failed and the national-cultural continuity is in jeopardy. The mwalimu is the essential conduit and nexus between tradition and the potential of the nation.

The mwalimu can only be effective in fulfilling that task if he/she is an active participant in the working collective that is devoted to the cultural, political, and economic development of the Afrikan community. The mwalimu must bring enthusiasm, conviction, ideological clarity, moral integrity, and courage, as well as knowledge to the teaching/learning environment. If he/she is deficient in any of these areas, the respect of the students and the efficacy of the teacher/learner encounter will be compromised. Given the critical role that the mwalimu must play in maintaining and enhancing the national culture, it is no wonder that in classical Afrikan civilizations and in still viable traditional societies, the higher or core knowledge was entrusted to its most esteemed elders and spiritual leaders.[14]

Methods and Goals of Afrikan-centered Instruction
The Teaching/Learning Environment

The effective Afrikan-centered teaching/learning environment extends beyond the immediate relationship of mwalimu and mwanafunzi—teacher and student—and includes the active involvement of the family, the school as a community focal point, and the community itself (see Figure 1). Each of the several active elements, mwalimu, mwanafunzi, family, school, and community must be culturally and ideologically aligned. They must augment and reinforce the cultural context of the educative process. Parental involvement should be mandatory and facilitated by the organization of the school and the "communitarian" management philosophy of the school administration.

Parents should be intimately involved in the mwanafunzi's intellectual development and should be provided with opportunities for intellectual growth themselves. Parents should be expected to maintain an enthusiastic commitment to and involvement in cultural activities and to interact in positive ways with other parents and families. It is imperative that parents perceive their role as essential and substantive. Parental involvement in school management is facilitated through opportunities for representation on appropriate committees, involvement in school support and development projects, and ready access to information. Parents or families should receive periodic narrative evaluations of their participation in school affairs. In addition, the school itself must be seen by those involved with it

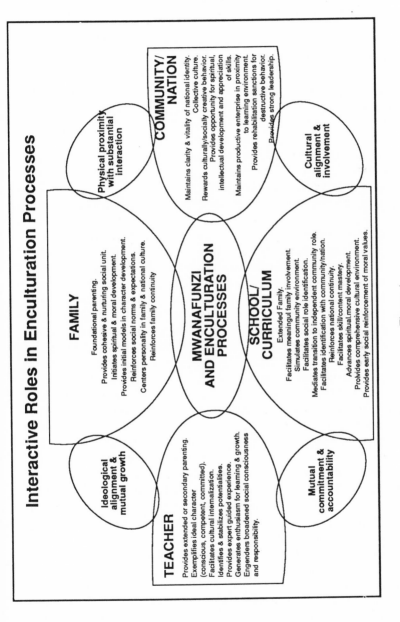

Figure 1

327

as the hub of a dynamic community that provides a variety of experiences for the cultural development and reinforcement of academic principles as well as opportunities for their application and reinforcement.

The Interactive Circle

The interactive circle (see Figure 2) is so potent and central to our cultural experience that it must be adapted to Afrocentric pedagogy. We have described the ideal relationship between the mwalimu and mwanafunzi as interactive, meaning that there is a vibrant exchange of information, mutual learning, and inspiration. This interactive and reciprocal communication between mwalimu and mwanafunzi is exemplified by the communal circle in traditional Afrikan societies. The circle, with its counterclockwise motion, facilitates spiritual communion in traditional Afrikan systems. When headed by the family elder or griot, the circle aids the intergenerational flow of history and culture.

The circle is particularly well suited to educe the active participation of all its members and it allows the mwalimu to easily adjust his/her posture from an egalitarian participant to one of mediator, facilitator, lecturer, adversary, or combinations and variations of all of these roles. The fluidity of the circle offers opportunities for the initiative and creativity of the mwanafunzi. The circle furthers the development of cooperative skills and a sense of reciprocity and mutual accountability. Moreover, it facilitates the development of both leadership and constituent skills.

The task of the mwalimu is to make the teaching/learning experience of the interactive circle sufficiently intense, stimulating, and comprehensive to both counteract Eurocentric cultural hegemony and facilitate self-determined, creative-critical synthesis, discovery, and commitment to a self-reflective cultural formation—an Afrikan-centered nationality. An explicitly collectivist and communitarian circle makes possible the kind of dynamic and reciprocal discourse that is essential to the development of the truly liberated Afrikan personality.

Dialogical Education

The dynamism of the discourse within the interactive circle is what Freire describes as dialogical education. The essence of dialogical education is . . .

INTERACTIVE CIRCLE

Social Placement of
Learning / Teaching Encounter

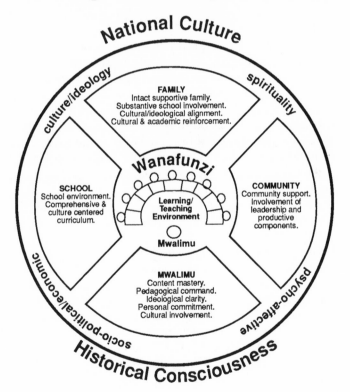

Figure 2

the encounter between men, mediated by the world, in order to name the world . . . [it is] the encounter in which the united reflection and action of the dialoguers are addressed to the world which is to be transformed and humanized.[15]

Such dialogue is perhaps more graphically demonstrated in the relationship between the traditional Afrikan master drummer and the master dancer.

The dancers move, and the musician finds the corresponding sounds. It is dialogue. Visible waves of body movement seek and are answered by audible waves of music. The dialogue continues. Sometimes it becomes a debate, a competition.[16]

The relationship of the mwanafunzi to the mwalimu is like that of the drummer to the dancer. The dancer follows the lead of the drummer. In following, and through dialogue, both are challenged and inspired to greater heights of artistry than anticipated. Ultimately, dancer, drummer, and the dance itself are transformed. Dialogue assumes a cultural and ideological context. Beyond the reality of physical, spiritual, and socio-political conditions there exist interests and perspectives on those conditions. Dialogue occurs as the mwalimu illuminates the historical and contemporary relationships and processes that constitute that reality and engages the mwanafunzi in critical-creative examination. This process occurs within a cultural and ideological context aimed at social/cultural transformation and reconstruction. The outcome is the transformation of both mwalimu and mwanafunzi.

Cultural Reconstruction and Reinvigoration

Reconstruction and reinvigoration of Afrikan culture and the rebuilding of the Afrikan nation/world must be the ultimate objectives of all pedagogy. Genuine dialogue, whether initiated within the interactive circle or directed by the mwalimu, must aggressively engage the mwanafunzi in intellectual exchange. This exchange arises out of work that is oriented toward general cultural-ideological goals. Each teaching/learning encounter must be informed by these objectives.

The independent schools within the Council of Independent Black Institutions' (CIBI)[17] structure have found it effective to incorporate valuing objectives as key components of instruction. Those valuing objectives employ the principles that form the Nguzo Saba as vehicles for imparting values that are consistent with and derived from the goals of Afrikan-centered pedagogy.[18] The principles that comprise the Nguzo Saba are Umoja for unity, Kujichagulia for self-determination, Ujima for collective work and responsibility, Ujamaa for cooperative economics, Nia for purpose, Kuumba for creativity, and Imani for faith.[19]

Consciousness of the ultimate cultural-ideological goals will be less obvious among younger wanafunzi. With younger children the mwalimu must engage them in dialogue that employs language and concepts appropriate to their cognitive development. The mwalimu must create a physical environment of displays, centers, and activities within the classroom that reflects not only the cognitive level of the mwanafunzi, but also the level of cultural-ideological consciousness that the mwalimu determines to be within the mwanafunzi's grasp. Beyond the actual physical displays, the dynamics of the classroom and the actual teaching/learning process should facilitate the development of the mwanafunzi's creative-critical thinking abilities. The development of these abilities requires that, in addition to the influence of the mwalimu's Afrocentric character described earlier, the actual content of the lessons reflect a balance of three considerations: (a) school-community prescribed curriculum content; (b) mwanafunzi interests; and (c) subject matter and activities that the mwalimu determines to be appropriate.

The progressive development of the wanafunzi's cultural consciousness will correspond with their relative cognitive abilities. With preschool, primary, and middle-school wanafunzi, the mwalimu provides the cultural-ideological focus. That focus is an implicit and essential component of the mwalimu's presence and must be a prominent feature in the mwalimu's character. The mwanafunzi must be aware of and visibly affected by the power of the mwalimu's cultural conviction, purposefulness, and ideological clarity. Equally important is the explicit elaboration of cultural-ideological goals in the contexts of formal instruction, mode of dress, classroom displays, language and vocabulary, expectations, and social interaction. Dialogue in this fashion is fundamentally generative. When undertaken as an essential component of a comprehensive educational program, its outcome goes beyond mere transformation to include an alteration of old perceptions. It gives birth instead to a new sense of the social order and to a new person—a liberated personality. That new perception of the social order and the liberated personality are thereafter sustained by the very dialogical methodology, the give and take, that brought them into existence.[20]

The necessity for the mwalimu to elaborate cultural-ideological goals is not to be confused with attempts to stifle creative critical thought. This is a simple recognition that all knowledge is culturally determined. Given the hegemonic nature of European culture coupled with the dominance and intractability of the popular media and the institutionally based perpetuation of that culture, the mwalimu, acting along with parents, school, and community, must consciously provide beacons that illuminate the truth of our history, our current condition, and our future as a people. The walimu of our Afrikan-centered schools would betray their mission if they engaged in actions that discouraged creative-critical thought or that divorced their discourse from the reality of the Afrikan struggle for cultural-historical truth and national reconstruction. Our children's, our wanafunzi's commitment to this struggle and to their culture and the ideology of national reconstruction can only be developed through the exercise of their individual thought processes. They must base their actions on the knowledge and discovery of historical truths through comparison, hypothesizing, and testing. Moreover, they must learn through debate, trial, and application; through analysis and synthesis; creative-critical thinking; problem resolution processes; and, finally, through final evaluation and decision making.

It is the absence of thoughtful and engaging dialogue based on creative and goal-oriented work that portends the presence of indoctrination and propaganda. Propaganda seeks to "invade the whole man, to lead him to adopt a mystical attitude and reach him through all possible psychological channels . . . and it does not tolerate discussion . . . it excludes contradiction and discussion."[21]

The Transformation of Student Resistance

The mwalimu's personal presence of authority and control must be balanced with compassion and sensitivity. Such a demeanor demands order and discipline yet it should encourage the pursuit of liberty. The mwalimu's presence should be further characterized by self-confidence, cultural awareness, and commitment as well as enthusiasm for learning and teaching. This presence will be apparent to the mwanafunzi who, always alert to "vibes" and the nuances of unspoken language, will respond in a way that ensures a productive and invigorated teaching/learning environment.

The initial response of wanafunzi in the classroom is usually one of clear resistance and challenge. Indeed, wanafunzi's demeanor is always characterized by some resistance, a certain measure of which is necessary and beneficial to the teaching/learning environment. That resistance is both a function of psycho-affective development and a manifestation of "oppositional behavior"[22] born of the repressive socio-political and cultural condition of Afrikan people. The resistance that the perceptive mwalimu will observe in the mwanafunzi goes beyond simple obstinacy, marginal self-motivation, negative attention-getting, or simple mischief-making, though it may be masked by these secondary behaviors. Given a functioning family/school/community environment and a capable and creative mwalimu, that resistance, like seedlings before the last spring frost, can be nurtured and shepherded into prominence.

It is the task of the mwalimu to facilitate the redirection of the mwanafunzi's energy away from reactionary individual challenge toward the social challenge of cultural/political analysis, study, and reconstruction of the Afrikan world. When that energy is nurtured, focused, and defined through Afrikan-centered dialogic methodology, student resistance has the potential to become the creative, irrepressible, and revolutionary spirit and force of a Harriet Tubman, Yaa Asantewa, Marcus Garvey, Malcolm X, Martin Luther King, or George Jackson.

Among male wanafunzi during the preadolescent and adolescent years, resistance and the accompanying urge to redefine perceived problematic situations is further intensified by the emergence of the "warrior spirit." It is the emergence of this virile and expansive warrior spirit that in traditional societies occasioned the prolonged isolation of the manchild. The purpose of that isolation was the inculcation of self-discipline, self-awareness, knowledge, and appreciation of tradition and the bounds and needs of social order. It was clear to our ancestors that the warrior spirit would be self-destructive and indeed would disrupt the very fiber of society in the absence of socially mandated training in discipline, order, and structured avenues for the application of that spirit. The current epidemic of self-destructive violence among our young males that now paralyzes our communities is a direct consequence of inadequate institutional capacity to direct that warrior spirit. There are three directions possible: (1) undisciplined and wanton mischief and self-destruction that serve to sustain our collective powerlessness and repression; (2) aggressive accommodationism that provides agency for Eurocentric hegemony to further entrench our subordinate social status; or (3) redirection to serve as a medium for national liberation.

It becomes the mission of the mwalimu, acting within the collective of family, school, and community to recognize that resistance, that spirit, and to heighten and focus it within a valuing context that is Afrikan-centered. The mwalimu's historical, cultural, and political knowledge should be comprehensive and include the mastery of some particular area of study. The mwalimu must be generally knowledgeable about the history of Afrika and the major events and themes that characterize it. He/she must additionally be knowledgeable about the involvement of Afrikans historically and currently in the discipline taught. That knowledge of history and the Afrikan cultural/ideological construct it engenders provide the context for the skills and processes that form the objectives of instruction.

Problem-solving and inquiry skills in math and science can be developed using social, historical, or technical situations that involve Afrikan people. The study of political parties, for example, could begin with a comparative study of single and seminal multi-party systems in Afrikan states. The crisis of drugs and homicides in our communities or the continuing legacy of instability among continental Afrikan states are socio-political problems that can be used to facilitate those thinking skills and processes. The problems of agricultural production, economic systems, and health issues on the continent and in the diaspora are areas particularly rich for math and science. The abundance of scientific data and technological options lends itself to research, synthesis, hypothesizing, and application skills. Creative-critical thinking, comprehension, and decision-making in the arts, literature, and the social sciences can be developed using information and examples from the Afrikan historical and cultural experience. In using experiences from the real world, the subject area is demystified and brought within the realm of the possible for the mwanafunzi and facilitates creative-critical analysis and the discovery of social relations. This real-life context enhances the interaction of the mwalimu and mwanafunzi, which must at all times be characterized by a reciprocity that occasions intellectual discovery and development by both.

We have seen occasions where well-intentioned walimu in independent schools and cultural enrichment programs have approached child and adult alike as psychic receptacles to be filled with historical truth. The truth thus implanted is then expected to neutralize the psychic and spiritual distortions and disorders born of miseducation and thereby bring forth a new person. There is no rebirth here, only dogma and the frail trappings of cultural consciousness. In fact, this approach in actuality demeans the intellectual capacity of the mwanafunzi and implicitly places the mwalimu in a dominant position similar to the hegemonic position of Eurocentric culture.

Both dogma and incomplete consciousness fail ignominiously when confronted by strong argument, material inducements, or the relentless propaganda of the popular media. Too many of the children and adults who have matriculated through our programs have abandoned the Afrikan-centered cultural framework because we were not successful in reaching them both psychically and spiritually. We erroneously assumed that the truth alone, once presented, would set them free. We naively underestimated the relentless and hypnotic effect of Eurocentric social propaganda.

Conclusion

It is true that many of our people are so culturally alienated through miseducation that engaging them in meaningful interaction is impossible. Beyond that, it is equally true that the battlefront for Afrikans in America is the consciousness of our people. Historically, Afrikans in America have vacillated between nationalist and assimilationist socio-political sentiments. Afrikan-centered education occasions the resurgence of a national consciousness and an urge for an independent national existence. Thus, this consciousness is neither new nor unique.

The Afrikan nationalist dynamics that underlie Afrocentrism have always been prominent in popular sentiment and in the social philosophy of the Afrikan population and its leadership.[23] Their immediate precedent was the Black consciousness movement of the sixties, and before that the period of the early twenties exemplified by the Universal Negro Improvement Association and its leader Marcus Garvey. The popular expression of this nationalist sentiment in the United States is very much like current nationalist struggles in Southern Afrika. Indeed, our two struggles have paralleled each other for very nearly a century and have been linked for that same period.[24] Moreover, Afrikan nationalist struggles parallel the resurgence of the repressed national cultures of Eastern Europe, the plethora of voices emanating from a disintegrating Soviet Union, and the resurgent militancy of Amerindians.

We must be vigilant. The powerful agents of the dominant culture will use every vehicle at their disposal to maintain their hegemonic grip on the minds of our people. It is the confident, capable, and committed mwalimu employing a broad repertoire of techniques within the interactive circle who stands as the first sentinel in our war to recapture our people's minds, engender the liberated Afrikan personality, and reconstruct the Afrikan nation/world.

Notes and References

1. A version of this chapter appears in the author's book *Nationbuilding: Theory and Practice in Afrikan-Centered Education* (Washington: Pan-Afrikan World Institute, 1992).
2. The reference here includes consideration of the divergent nationalist interests of Japan, a newly assertive and unified European Community, the U.S.A., and other capitalist powers. The World War II legacy of American dominance in international finance and productivity is being rapidly eroded, with fears of imminent decline prevalent within the mainstream American polity.
3. C. Krauthammer, "What's Left of the Left?" *U.S. News & World Report*, 21 December 1990.
4. J. Leo, "A Fringe History of the World," *Washington Post,* 12 November 1990.
5. M. Asante, *Afrocentricity* (Trenton, NJ: Africa World Press, 1988).
6. J. D. Hargreaves, "Toward the Transfer of Power in British West Africa," in *The Transfer of Power in Africa*, eds. Gifford and Louis (New Haven: Yale University Press, 1982).
7. Chancellor Williams, *The Rebirth of African Civilization* (Washington: Public Affairs Press, 1961).
8. P. Freire, *The Politics of Education* (New York: Bergin and Garvey Publishers, 1985).
9. P. Freire, *Pedagogy of the Oppressed* (New York: The Continuum Publishing Company, 1970).
10. Freire, *Politics of Education*.
11. F. Fanon, *The Wretched of the Earth* (New York: Grove Press, 1968).
12. A. Cabral, *Return to the Source: Selected Speeches of Amilcar Cabral*, ed. Africa Information Service (New York: Modern Reader, 1973).
13. Mwalimu and mwanafunzi and the plural forms, walimu and wanafunzi, are Kiswahili terms used respectively as titles of teachers and other adults, and of students within Afrikan-centered independent institutions.
14. See, for example: G. M. James, *Stolen Legacy* (San Francisco: Julian Richardson Associates, 1988); A. Hilliard, "Pedagogy in Ancient Kemet," in *Kemet and the African Worldview*, eds. Karenga and Carruthers (Los Angeles: University of Sankore Press, 1986).
15. Freire, *Pedagogy of the Oppressed*.
16. Y. Diallo and M. Hall, *The Healing Drum* (Rochester: Destiny Books, 1989).
17. The Council of Independent Black Institutions (CIBI) was formed in 1972 as a national organization of independent Afrikan-centered educa-

tional institutions. Activities of CIBI include teacher training, national student activities, curriculum development, clearing house for information on independent schools, and accreditation.

18. Council of Independent Black Institutions, *Positive Afrikan Images for Children* (Trenton, NJ: Red Sea Press, 1990).

19. M. Karenga, *Kwanzaa: Origins, Concepts, Practice* (San Diego: Kawaida Publications, 1978).

20. Fanon, *Wretched of the Earth*.

21. J. Ellul, *Propaganda* (New York: Vintage Books, 1965).

22. H. Giroux, *Teachers as Intellectuals* (New York: Bergin and Garvey, 1988).

23. Refer to the works of Lerone Bennett, Maulana Karenga, Sterling Stuckey, and Harold Cruse.

24. T. Martin, *Race First* (Dover: The Majority Press, 1976).

Part Five

Patterns of Resistance to European-Centered Schooling: Reclaiming Responsibility for Educating Our Own

Introduction to Part Five

The concluding part of this volume is a discussion about taking responsibility for our education. The three chapters included here are grounded in the real problem-solving activities of Diasporan African people in the United States and Great Britain. In each chapter the focus is on a particular concept for providing African-centered education that has been developed in accordance with community defined needs and available resources. The three contexts include full-time independent schools; part-time supplementary schools; and community-based rites of passage organizations.

It is important that we make an effort to visualize in these chapters the potential that exists to develop an infrastructure for African-centered education encompassing a variety of models. The three chapters included here can help us to construct a general picture of the options available to us for meeting our responsibilities to educate our people. We need to make our existing independent African-centered schools better, we must build such institutions where they are needed, and we have to create transitional models to serve our people until there are enough African-centered schools to meet our needs. The foundation already exists for a broad African-centered education infrastructure. It requires forging linkages among existing full-time African-centered schools; transitional models such as rites of passage programs; Saturday schools; after-school programs; Black supplementary schools; public school programs; study groups and so forth. One purpose of such linkages is to make it possible to hold forthright discussions about the educational needs within our communities. Another purpose is to access the capacities of the educational structures in place to meet those needs. A third purpose is to plan how unmet needs will be addressed

In Chapter Fourteen, "The Emergence of Black Supplementary Schools as Forms of Resistance to Racism in the United Kingdom," Nah Dove argues that the schooling of Africans in European-centered "educational" institutions is a method of subjugation. As culturally influenced institutions, European-centered schools play a major role in maintaining the interests of white-supremacy on a global and local scale. The rise of Black supplementary schools is analyzed as part of the resistance of Africans to this condition.

Chapter Fifteen, "Afrocentric Transformation and Parental Choice in African-American Independent Schools," is based on my analysis of parental rationales for enrolling their children in inde-

pendent schools. I focus on indicators of Afrocentric personal transformation evident in the explanations African-American parents
offer for enrolling their children in African-American independent
schools. This analysis facilitates a larger discussion about the nature
of Afrocentricity as a quality that is reflected in human consciousness. In the end I argue that it is inappropriate to treat the curriculum as the purveyor of Afrocentricity when it is actually the extent
to which Afrocentric consciousness exists among individual teachers and students that will determine how curriculum content is presented and perceived.

The concluding chapter, "The Rites of Passage: Extending
Education Into the African-American Community", by Nsenga
Warfield-Coppock analyzes the role of the adolescent rites of passage, in particular, can play in broadening the concept of education in African-American communities. Rites of passage are
described as immediate steps African-Americans can take toward
achieving personal and collective self-determination. In this chapter,
the historical roles of rites of passage in African communities and
current trends in African-American rites of passage are discussed.
In addition, recommendations are made concerning the development of rites of passage programs.

These chapters complete a volume that is unique because it is a
departure from the scholarship that addresses the education and
schooling of African people in diaspora as an issue of societal integration. The authors understand that the African historical-cultural
continuum, of which we are part, has an independent existence that
predates the United States, the United Kingdom and other European
nation-states whose cultures have had so much influence on people
of African descent. This understanding has led us to focus our concerns on how we, as Africans, take into account the centrality of our
cultural orientation to education. In doing so, we indicate new possibilities for theory and practice that emerge when it is no longer
assumed that education and schooling are overlapping processes for
Africans in societies in which multiple cultures exist and unequal
power relations sustain a racially hegemonic order among the members.

Chapter Fourteen

The Emergence of Black Supplementary Schools as Forms of Resistance to Racism in the United Kingdom*

Nah (Dorothy) E. Dove
State University of New York at Buffalo

Any serious attempt to examine the present critical situation of Black children in the context of Western schooling must address the dynamics of White supremacy and therefore racism as ideological and material realities in the lives of those children. In this chapter I look at the historical development of supplementary schooling in the United Kingdom. It is my belief that the establishment of these schools is a representation of African resistance to racism.

In recognizing the needs of the state and its influence on the schooling of populations, it is important to understand that racism is fundamental to White supremacy. During the historical construction of European institutions, Europeans of every national denomination, regardless of their class and sex, allowed their ruling elite to set the terms of their relationships with Africans and peoples of

*A version of this chapter was first published in Urban Education 27 (1992): 430-447.

color. In analyzing such conditions, I believe that the resulting racialized power relations took precedence over gendered and class relations. From this perspective one can more clearly see the collective role that European men, women and children have played in the oppression of African men, women and children. Importantly, the collective role that Africans must play to throw off the shackles of White supremacist oppression becomes imperative.

The ideology of White supremacy is one that all White people are able to participate in if they wish at any given time whenever it is desirable or advantageous. Racist belief systems have been necessary in the promotion of the ideological construction of White superiority and Black inferiority as an integral part of European centered culture and oppression.[1] Thus, regardless of who is teaching the children, anyone believing in and aspiring to the same European-centered cultural value system will undermine and devalue the potential for Africans to appreciate African self-worth and self-development as bases for self-determination. Those who control the state schooling systems in Britain and the United States are not about to alter the misinformation inculcated through their schools. Schooling of this kind is needed to reinforce the cultural values and beliefs that maintain the existing relations of power. These cultural values and beliefs have historically undermined the integrity and dignity of Africans while at the same time justifying African oppression.

Schooling in both the U.K. and the U.S. is a means of perpetuating racialized social relations of power. If we proceed from this understanding, we can comprehend why Black women and men are more likely to be incarcerated than White women and men; why Black men are more likely to be under- or unemployed; and why Black babies have a mortality rate twice that of White babies. The condition of African children as "underachievers" and "failures" in school can be described as symptomatic of the social, economic, political, legal, and psychological oppressions experienced by Africans living in the urban areas of the U.K. and the U.S.

The British Council of Churches Community asserts that "too many Black people are arrested without adequate grounds and receive longer sentences" than White people for similar offences.[2] According to the 1990 figures from the Prison Reform Trust Report, Black women and men are more likely to be stopped, arrested, charged, remanded, and then imprisoned than White women and men.[3] In the same report, figures show that African men and women are eight times more likely to be sent to prison than White men and women. Not coincidentally, Britain has the highest rate of African imprisonment in Europe in relation to the size of its African population. Black men represent 16% of the male prison population and Black women make 28% of the female prison population in a country where the African and Asian populations combined make up only 4.5% of the total. Moreover, the National Association of Probation Officers indicates that Black males and females comprised 20% of those remanded to prison in England and Wales during 1989.[4] These figures show a trend in the treatment of Africans which I contend is symptomatic of a long history of racist and classist oppression at the hands of White authority.

The situation in the United States for Africans is little different from that in the United Kingdom. For instance, statistics produced by the Urban League reveal African-Americans are underemployed at more than 2.2 times the rate experienced by Whites. Since 1987, figures on poverty compiled by the Center on Budget and Policy Priorities in Washington showed one in three African-Americans below the poverty level and numbers have increased since then. Although African-Americans comprise 12% of the nation's population, they account for 46% of the nation's prisoners. Nine out of ten African inmates are male and 54% are under 29 years old.[5] Marable asserts that the criminal justice system has become the modern instrument to perpetrate and maintain White hegemony. Sentences for Black men are far harsher than for Whites convicted for the same crimes and the death sentence is used far more readily.[6] Generally, in the U.S. and the U.K. African women and men live in the worst housing, hold the worst jobs, are disproportionately unemployed and underemployed, and are the poorest segment of either population.

Background of African Experiences in the U.K. and the U.S.

Britain benefited from the capital accumulation accrued from its slave colonies in the Caribbean and from its African colonies. Unlike the United States, however, it remained free from the presence of large numbers of Africans. This was essentially due to its size and the availability of White labor power. However, following World War II, Britain relied on U.S. aid to save its economy. This was a period of rapid economic growth. The migration of Black workers to Britain was defined by the need for insecure labor to supply the British manufacturing and service industries. Thus, the entry of African-Caribbeans to Britain in great numbers during the post-war period of the forties and fifties was related to the need for their labor power in the rebuilding of Britain. African workers were actively recruited by London Transport from Barbados, Trinidad, and Jamaica. The British Hotels and Restaurants Association also recruited from Barbados. African-Caribbeans came and filled the lowest paying jobs although many were actually skilled workers. Only 13% of the men and 5% of the women were unskilled workers.[7]

Experiences of racism in urban settings are similar in the histories of Africans living in the U.S. and the U.K. Ogbu compared the economic conditions of Africans in the U.K. and the U.S. and concluded that racial power relations in both societies exist within a caste system. He concluded from his research on racial stratification, and educational and employment opportunities for Black women, children, and men that there are limitations imposed upon achievement and success that exist outside the class dynamics already in operation. He further argued that the racial caste system is the basic determinant of social structure and that economic class is secondary. Within each caste exists economic classes and it is the caste relationship which determines the quality of life chances among the members of various classes that comprise the caste.

Ogbu considers the color caste system in Britain to be one that is not upheld by any formal law, as in the case of South Africa, but that shares features with South Africa's apartheid system nonetheless. White women, children, and men consider themselves to be superior to Africans within the same economic class and occupational or educational status as theirs. Intermarriage takes place infrequently and the progeny of mixed marriages cannot affiliate with Whites.[8]

For Africans, the racialized development of British social institutions takes precedence over both classist and sexist aspects. The consolidation of these institutions' racial, patriarchal, and classist hierarchies occurred prior to the European global conquest.[9] The development of capitalist institutions would not have occurred without the accumulation of wealth through the appropriation and exploitation of lands, minerals, labor power, and skills, and the annihilation of populations of peoples of color. As the European-centered, White supremacist aspects of this global conquest evolved, the racialized power relations that ensued were consolidated. Thus, existing social institutions were adapted to accommodate White empowerment—regardless of class, sex or ethnicity—above all others. This mode of organization was crucial to the establishment of African enslavement and the continued perpetuation of anti-Black racism. Although it can be argued that the institution of "slavery" no longer exists, the institutionalization of White empowerment over Black people is still in operation. In the next section I will discuss Black supplementary schools and the role they play in countering this process in Great Britain.

The Emergence of Black Supplementary Schools

In order to analyze what is happening to African children in British schools, we need to understand what is also happening to them outside school as well as what is happening to their parents and to Africans generally. We should not, therefore, isolate classroom activity from social organization. In Britain the needs of the state are reflected in the structure of the schooling system. There are three basic autonomous modes of schooling and educational information. There is a privileged type which is partly private and state funded for the families of the empowered. These schools are known as public schools. Next, there is privately funded schooling and finally, state-run schooling. Of the three, the state-funded schooling is most like public schooling in the U.S., i.e., it is paid for by taxes. This stratified schooling is suited to Britain's economic needs for a particular type of social class ordering. The racist and sexist dimensions of this social ordering need to be highlighted since their importance is often ignored.

In Britain, specifically London, the African response to the failure of state schooling to provide a "proper" education for Black children—those children who are predominantly African-Caribbean, African, or of mixed race—has been the establishment of Black supplementary schools. Classes are held in these schools mostly on Saturdays and some evenings in the week. The supplementary schools movement is indicative of both continued African resistance against racist treatment in schools and the recognition by Black parents of the influence and power of teachers and the school curriculum in both the "underdevelopment" and "development" of their children's academic potentials and skills. These steps by African parents to take responsibility for their children's education are indications of the importance they have assigned to Black self-development and Black self-worth as primary to achieving Black self-determination.

The rise of supplementary schools in urban areas can be traced to the early sixties when it was discovered that an inordinate number of Black children were being referred to schools for "educationally sub-normal" pupils. Some children in the London Borough of Harringay, were entering these schools directly upon arrival from the Caribbean to Britain.[10] In 1971, according to the report of the Parliamentary Select Committee, 5,500 immigrant pupils were put into special schools throughout England and Wales, mostly for the retarded. Caribbean children represented 70% of these children. In Greater London, 25% of all Caribbean children were in these schools. In the London Borough of Brent, 60% of primary school children and 70% of secondary school children in schools for educationally sub-normal pupils were Caribbean. In Harringay, although children made up only 10% of the school population, they accounted for 25% of those in schools for educationally sub-normal pupils.[11]

Also in 1971, Bernard Coard articulated and substantiated the Black communities' vociferous concern over this serious situation. Coard's book *How the West Indian Child is Made Educationally Sub-Normal* focused on deficiencies of the state education system and highlighted the internal dynamics of racism through a critique of culturally biased testing. More than a decade later, research carried out by Sally Thomlinson investigated the process of referral to schools for educationally sub-normal students and their assessment procedures, revealed that head-teachers involved in the referrals of 40 Black pupils believed behavioral/learning problems to be innate natural characteristics.[12] As a result of these and other similar findings, many African parents were convinced that the teaching of their children could not be left to the British state system and to White teachers who harboured such negative attitudes about African children.

It should be taken into account that the resistance by African parents to the state schooling system is not an isolated form of resistance. The undermining of African children in state schooling has created untenable conditions which have resulted in forms of resistance behavior among these pupils. Some of these behaviors have been defined by school personnel in psychological terms that relate to the students' cognitive development, behavior, and attitude. Consequently, behavior and attitude are frequently identified as the causes of low academic achievement leading to referrals for psychological assessments. The influence of educational psychologists has led to the legitimization of an institutional mode of behavioral analysis which informs specific methods of treatment. Thus, in the case of African children, their resistance to racism in the schools has been understood in pathological terms. Behavior patterns are regarded to be indicative of a certain type of child, i.e., Black, rather than symptomatic of institutionalized forms of treatment directed specifically at the African child.

In contrast, to date, there has been no attempt to define as pathological the backgrounds of teachers who have proposed the referral, assessment, banding, streaming, suspension, or expulsion of African pupils. Two educational psychologists, one from the London Borough of Camden and one from the London Borough of Hackney, told me that records would be kept in the near future by the School Psychological Services on the number of times individual teachers referred pupils. During my investigation in 1990, an educational psychologist confided that in one London borough, and perhaps in others, it is mainly White women teachers who refer Black boys. The psychological dimension of teaching practices and beliefs warrant further investigation especially in the light of the history of the over-representation of Black girls and boys in language units and schools for emotionally and behaviorally disturbed students.[13]

Given these racist conditions, many African parents have decided to place the education of their children under their own control and have turned to supplementary schools. These schools are not considered necessarily as schools that merely supplement mainstream schooling. Many parents and teachers believe that these schools provide a better education than that given by the state. In the next section I will discuss the findings from a study I conducted among the parents of children enrolled in some of London's supplementary schools.

Parental and Student Perceptions of Supplementary Schools

African parents in both the United States and the United Kingdom have been involved in alternative schooling for some time.[14] My investigation into Black supplementary schooling required gathering qualitative data through the use of survey questionnaires and interviewing. One of my objectives was to investigate whether Black-run supplementary schooling approaches education any differently than state-run schools. In other words, do teaching methods differ? Are teachers different? Does educational information differ? Another objective was to measure the success or failure of these schools. As a Black woman, parent, and supplementary school teacher myself, it seemed important to me to focus on parents' perceptions. I believe that parents of children in supplementary schools, perhaps more than any others, are able to make valid statements about the psychological dimensions of their children's progress and about the effects of supplementary schooling upon their children.

Many supplementary school teachers, in whose input I was also interested, were also mainstream school teachers, student teachers, community members, and parents. I believed that their interests in and commitment to the well-being of African children and, therefore, their judgements, were of value to my study. I also felt it necessary to highlight the pupils' perspectives out of recognition of how little credence is given to their experiences. Another point of relevance is that, as implied earlier, African-Caribbeans are the largest African population living in Britain so it is not surprising to find that the majority of the supplementary schools are directed by them. Also, underlying my investigation was the question of whether there is a case for full-time schooling based upon the supplementary school model, given the conditions of state schooling.

Fifty-five parents from nine supplementary schools answered the questionnaires, some more completely than others. They represented the interests of 100 children (51 girls and 49 boys) whose ages ranged from three years to 18 years. I also interviewed 20 parents and 30 children and their teachers from the schools. However, outside the context of the survey, I had been involved as an active parent governor in a secondary school and was very familiar with subject matter and circumstances. In fact, during the four-year period prior to conducting the study I had probably spoken with over 200 parents and met over 200 African teachers and several hundred African pupils.

Pupils' Perspectives

All the children spoken to preferred their supplementary school to their mainstream school. These are some of their responses.

*"I have learned so much that I am ahead in my maths class." (female, 14 years old)

*"I am ahead in all my subjects because I get taught here." (female, 9 years old)

*"As far as I am concerned I have never been taught anything at mainstream school. I was told from nursery onwards that I am expected to know the basics. What are those basics? I have never been taught them at school. I was given small hints in English, but because of one good teacher I learned about how to use commas this year. I've not been here long but I am learning." (female, 15 years old)

*"I didn't want to do O-levels at school, but since I came here I passed my O-levels in maths, English, and science. Since I have attended college, it is completely different, they believe in me. I am learning about electronics and doing my own research, now I find everything so much easier. This school really helped." (male, 18 years old)

*"I am ahead in maths and English, I have been here since I was 5 years old." (male, 11 years old)

*"I am doing well in maths, but I don't like mainstream school, I started this school at the age of 7 years." (female, 14 years old)

The pupils I spoke with felt very positive about attending their supplementary schools. They were convinced that their schools were helping them to develop academic skills. When the children discussed their mainstream school experiences with their supplementary school teachers, they often indicated that they were not encouraged. Moreover, being Black was perceived by their mainstream school teachers as being negative. One nine-year-old boy said:

> I think that being Black affects the way teachers behave towards me. We are told to speak out if we need help or if we disagree with something, but I get picked on because of this. I got sent out of the classroom because I was blamed for something I didn't do and I complained.

During these interviews, children often complained about what they perceived to be teachers' racism directed towards them because they were Black. In fact there was the general realization that they were attending supplementary schools to get away from the teachers' racism they experienced in mainstream schools. The children I spoke with felt positive about attending supplementary schools.

Parents felt that the teachers in supplementary schools had no preconceived ideas about their children's academic potential. Some parents had noticed that their children were treated differently in nursery school. They felt that their children were not encouraged to read or appreciate books during these formative years. They indicated that some teachers felt that Black children differed from Whites in the rates at which they developed academic skills and therefore should be encouraged to read at a later date. These perceptions by parents of teacher beliefs in the state-run schools are corroborated by the longitudinal study led by Barbara Tizzard that was undertaken by the Thomas Coram Research Unit in 1982. Researchers looking at the progress of a group of five-year-old Black and White boys and girls from nursery to infant school found that Black parents received less feedback about their children's progress and literacy than White parents.[15] According to supplementary school parents, teachers, and pupils, this results in a lack of motivation and a loss of confidence among students.

These perceptions are also consistent with findings reported in an ethnographic study conducted by Cecile Wright that focused on the experiences of fourth- and fifth-year African-Caribbean pupils from two schools situated in the North of England. After 900 hours of investigation and analysis that included looking at the processes used in these schools to assess the pupils' academic potential, Wright observed that:

> To the West Indian, the school seemed to be seen as a "battleground," a hostile environment insofar as it rejects their color and their identities.[16]

Wright found that the students believed that their academic performance was affected by their White teachers' attitudes, behaviors, and low expectations. In fact, children in both schools believed the system to be "rigged."[17] Students claimed that "bad" behavior was a response to "bad" treatment, rather than, as their teachers claimed, a result of "underachievement."[18]

Parent's Perspectives

In the light of these student responses, I was very much interested in finding out how parents felt about the relationship between supplementary school teachers and their children. Generally, parents were very satisfied with the teachers. Teacher characteristics were described by parents, who frequently praised their children's teacher in glowing terms: encouraging, positive role models, high expectations, helpful, respectful, motivational, relaxed, kind, gentle, understanding, caring, disciplined, and responsive. I do not mean to suggest that these characteristics are specific to Black teachers or supplementary school teachers. However, I am pointing out that, given their children's mainstream school experiences, parental demands for teachers who put the needs of Black children first take precedence over the needs of the state.

All the parents involved in the survey chose supplementary schools for their children because they were dissatisfied with state-run schooling. Parents also felt that racism in the state schooling system was responsible for the lack of a "proper" education. Some of the reasons supplementary school administrators said parents gave for choosing their schools included opportunities . . .
*to improve their children's academic performance;
*for more cultural learning;
*for more Black history;
*for exposure to positive images of Africans;
*to receive more support for children and parents;
*to keep children off the streets and involved in something positive;
*to build children's confidence.

Once their children were enrolled in supplementary schools parents were convinced that they were doing better. Moreover, they reported that their children's overall work had improved in state-run schools as a result of attending supplementary schools. When questioned further about the improvement in their children's academic work, some parents felt that the change was due to the attention and the general treatment provided by the teachers, the school environment, and the fostering of love of their "Blackness" and "Africanness" in the supplementary schools. This experience helped the children to better understand concepts in the three R's which they might not have understood so easily in the hostile environment of state-run schooling.

Parents were also asked to comment on changes they observed in their children that were perceived to have resulted from their supplementary school experiences. The following examples illustrate what they reported:
*A 5-year-old boy became positive and strong in his ideas.
*A 7-year-old girl looked forward to coming to supplementary school.
*An 8-year-old boy gained the ability to deal with abuse in his mainstream school.

*The concentration of 14- and 15-year-old sisters and their 10-year-old brother "vastly improved."

*A 7-year-old boy who was always bright did even better in his academic work and his attitude and behavior improved at home and in school.

*A 6-year-old boy and an 8-year-old boy wanted to attend school and do their homework.

*One 15-year-old boy improved in every aspect, however, his mother said "he does not use these qualities in his mainstream schooling."

*Another parent claimed, "my children had it in them to excel all the time . . . the sad result of this is that in spite of the hard dedicated work put in by the supplementary school teachers, the mainstream school will claim the credit for my children's progress."

These parents concluded, as did Cecile Wright, that the lack of academic success experienced in state schools was not a case of African children "underachieving." It was their belief that their children were unable to grasp certain concepts as a result of a hostile school environment. It was frequently perceived among the parents I interviewed that African children were being undermined in state-run schools through processes of assessment in banding, streaming etc. In similar fashion, Wright found that Caribbean children in her survey entered the secondary schools with a higher reading age than other children. However, determinations of pupil behavior, based upon teacher recommendations, were typically used to allocate children to bands. In this way Black students were downgraded so that a hierarchy occurred in the banding system based on ethnicity. Students of the African diaspora were usually placed at the bottom. Wright's figures showed that no Black children were placed in higher bands than their examination performances, yet there were cases of (Indian) Asian, and White pupils who were assigned to higher positions than their exam results warranted. In addition, Wright showed how student misallocation is related to teacher perceptions which, in turn, determine and affect the eligibility of Black students for examination groupings. The designation of children to inappropriate groupings influences their academic development and restricts their educational opportunities. As Wright asserts, school officials must recognize the schools' responsibility for the "achievement" and "underachievement" of their pupils.[19]

The Question of Full-time Alternatives to State Schooling

As I mentioned previously, in addition to improving my understanding of the impact of supplementary schools upon the children, I was concerned about whether the parents and students involved in supplementary schools would wish these schools to be full-time. Given their apparent satisfaction, this question took on even greater significance for me. Supplementary schools rely on minimal budgets which are often provided by a local government authority. Funding would have an obvious effect upon their ability to operate full-time. The operation of full-time Black independent schools is not an easy undertaking for Africans in either the U.K. or the U.S. However, this is especially the case in the U.K. because of the relatively small size of its Black middle class.

In the United Kingdom, unlike the U.S., there is not what could be considered a substantial Black middle class comprised of business people and professionals. The number of African women and men involved in the higher regions of the occupational hierarchy in Britain can be safely considered to be minimal. This state of affairs is due not only to the institutionalized racism involved in employment, housing, schooling, and the legal system which manifests itself in a de facto form of occupational segregation, but also to the more recent history of the African presence in Britain. Nonetheless, an overwhelming majority of the parents I interviewed in London indicated that they wished their supplementary schools to become full-time.

Grant-aided Black schools, outside the context of de facto segregation, have never been encouraged since they would be run by Black teachers and would cater to the specific needs of Black pupils. One such case is that of the John Loughborough school, a Seventh Day Adventist school, which at the time of my study, could boast of one of the highest levels of academic achievement in London. The school wished to avail itself to those who were unable to afford its relatively low fees. However, when the school attempted to become a state grant-aided school in 1990, its application was turned down by the Tory government.[20]

Winston Best asserts that the monetary provision for some London supplementary schools from the Inner London Education Authority (ILEA) has been negligible. These funds paid for the travelling expenses of some of the teachers and helpers and helped purchase some materials. The ILEA was disbanded in 1990 by the

Thatcher government because it was politically controlled by the opposition, i.e., the Labour party. Consequently, the acceptance of government funds was always a controversial issue among supplementary schools because of the desire among school leaders to maintain their autonomy from the interests of the state. For instance, one of the conditions for receiving funds required supplementary school leaders to meet regularly with the Multi-Ethnic Inspectorate.[21]

The parents and teachers of supplementary schools are particularly dedicated and committed to their work. They receive little remuneration and, in some cases, none for the time and effort put into running and maintaining these schools. Operating funds are raised by the parents at some of the schools. The interests of supplementary school teachers and parents are, therefore, not related to making a living. These schools are first and foremost concerned with serving the needs of their communities and gaining credibility on these grounds.

In summary, the findings of my study showed that the parents and the children who participated were satisfied with supplementary school teachers, their methods of teaching, and the schools' ethos. Overall parents believed that their children were doing well as a result of attending these schools. Many parents wanted their children to receive cultural information and Black history as part of the school curriculum. They believed that the schools had a positive effect upon their children. The level of their satisfaction is evidenced both by their responses during the interviews and to the items in the questionnaires, and by the fact that of the 82% who responded to the question about full-time supplementary schooling, every one of them wished their schools could be full-time. This represents a testimony of faith in Black schools that has developed as a consequence of the educational demands of some African parents, children, and teachers.

Conclusion

As I have stated previously, many of the parents and teachers I interviewed believe that supplementary schools provide a better education, albeit part-time, than that provided by the state. [The directors of those schools that offer an African-centered curriculum (8 out of the 9 schools that participated) believe, as do parents, that this type of curriculum has a positive effect on the children's educational and academic development.]

Since my arrival in the United States and my involvement with a full-time African-centered school, I have felt that there is good reason to be optimistic about the possibility of full-time independent Black schools. My wish is that the schools in London be developed along the lines of the model I am involved with. Some of the characteristics of supplementary schools, especially concerning the cultural affirmation of the Africanness of the children, are apparent in this school. I am aware from my own investigation into African-centered schools that cultural affirmation is central to the theme, philosophy, and ethos of these schools.

Studies conducted among parents of children who attend full-time African-American independent African-centered schools that have emerged in the U.S. during the last 20 or 30 years have obtained similar findings.[22] While there is a history of independent African schooling in the U.S. that dates from the time of the enslavement of African people,[23] the focus on cultural affirmation through an African-centered perspective as the context for gaining educational skills and knowledge is quite contemporary. I looked at the effects of supplementary schools on children according to their parents' perspectives, recognizing their independent Black status. At the same time, I explored the historical nature of the need for the development of these schools. My current involvement with an African-centered school has led me to believe that a future investigation into supplementary schooling should consider the importance of cultural affirmation to the parents and to the children. From my own study, which did not focus specifically on this area, I found that parents used supplementary schools in order for their children to receive a Black perspective, cultural understanding, Black historical information, a positive Black image, positive role models, a better learning environment, and the company of other Black children. These reasons may or may not show the importance of cultural affirmation for their children. Further questions in this area would have to be more specific.

The rise of supplementary schools in the United Kingdom may well parallel other forms of resistance to state-public schooling that have taken place in the United States, which is certainly an area for future study. I believe that an African-centered approach challenges the hegemonic scholarship that has pervaded European-centered educational systems from the conquest of Egypt by the Greeks. African-centered curricula and methods of pedagogy can help children learn to decipher lies and develop inquiring, scholarly minds.

The energies of children thus prepared may be channelled into the collective work of building institutions that rest on African values and beliefs as the bases for an alternative world vision.

Notes

1. D. Dove, *Racism and its Effect on the Quality of Education and the Educational Performance of the Black Child* (London, U.K.: University of London, The Institute of Education, 1990). D. Dove, *Racism and Resistance in the Schooling of Afrikans.* (Unpublished doctoral dissertation, State University of New York at Buffalo, Buffalo, NY, 1993.)
2. "Call to cut Black Imprisonment," *Caribbean Times* May 1, 1990. This is a London-based Black newspaper.
3. "Black Jail Figures Would Shame South Africa," *Independent* August 7, 1989. This is a leading White, national, British newspaper.
4. "Britain's Judiciary Hates Black Women," *Caribbean Times* January 16, 1990.
5. These statistics and many others concerning the quality of life and life expectancy of African-Americans can be found in *Newsday* January 2, 1990, a U.S. publication.
6. M. Marable, *How Capitalism Underdeveloped Black America* (Boston, MA: South End Press, 1983), 126-127.
7. P. Fryer, *Staying Power* (London, U.K.: Pluto Press, 1984), 373-374.
8. J. Ogbu, *Minority Education and Caste* (New York, San Francisco, London: Academic Press, 1978), 103, 245.
9. For more information on the development of European racialized hierarchies see: C. Robinson, *Black Marxism* (London, U.K.: Zed Press, 1983), 9-37. For information on the development of patriarchal relations of power, see: M. Mies, *Patriarchy and Accumulation on a World Scale* (London, U.K.: Zed Books Ltd., 1986).
10. F. Dhondy, *The Black Explosion in British Schools* (London, U.K.: Race Today Publications, 1982), 27.
11. Ogbu, *Minority Education*, 249-50.
12. S. Thomlinson, *Ethnic Minorities in British Schools* (London, U.K.: Heinemann Education Books, 1983), 29.
13. More recent figures on children in behavioral units in London shown in the 1988 ILEA report on "Characteristics of Pupils in Special Schools and Units" reveal the continuing trend of the over-representation of Black children in "special schools" from the Educationally Sub-Normal schools of the sixties to the Behavioral Units of the eighties.
14. I have labelled supplementary schools as forms of alternative schooling for African children in the U.K. As already noted, these schools rose in the 1960's as a result of the move by the state schooling to place Black children (in the main, African-Caribbean children) in "special schools," see the work of Best (1990) in *Against the Tide* (S. Olowe, ed.,

Against the Tide (London, U.K.: ILEA, 1990). Dhondy (*Black Explosion*) discusses the rise of these schools. The work of Ratteray and Shujaa *Dare to Choose* (Washington, DC: Institute for Independent Education, 1987) provides an historical perspective on African-American independent neighborhood schools.

15. A summary of the report findings can be found in the *Times Educational Supplement* No. 3692 (4/3/1987).
16. C. Wright, "Who Succeeds at School and Who Decides?" *Multicultural Teaching* 4(1) (1985): 12.
17. Wright, "Who Succeeds," 17-22.
18. C. Wright, "Learning Environment or Battleground?" *Multicultural Teaching* 4(1) (1985): 16.
19. Wright, "Who Succeeds," 22.
20. I lived in London in 1990 at the time of the Tory party's refusal to allow the school to become grant-aided.
21. Best in *Against the Tide*.
22. Ratteray and Shujaa, *Dare to Choose*.
23. See mention of the earliest independent Black school in Philadelphia, 1796 held in St Thomas' African Church by Absalom Jones, in H. M. Bond, *Education for Freedom* (Lincoln University, PA: Lincoln University Press, 1976), 65-80.

Chapter Fifteen

Afrocentric Transformation and Parental Choice in African-American Independent Schools*

Mwalimu J. Shujaa
State University of New York at Buffalo

African-American enrollments in private schools are increasing.[1] Although the majority of African-American students remain in public schools, it is clear that for a growing number of African-American families private schooling is viewed as a viable option.[2] This trend has deepened scholarly interest in the utilization of private school options by African-Americans.[3] In this chapter I use Molefi K. Asante's model of Afrocentric transformation as a framework for analyzing parents' perceptions of African-American independent schooling and their expectations of it. I am guided by an interest in knowing more about how African-American parents who have made this critical choice perceive its social and cultural significance.

*This chapter evolved from versions (a) published in *Journal of Negro Education* 61 (1992) 148-159 and (b) presented as a paper at the 1989 History of Education Society Annual Meeting in Chicago.

Background
Nomenclature
The nomenclature that describes African-American independent schools is still developing. The term "independent Black institutions" (IBIs) has been in use for at least 20 years. It was used in 1971 by the Congress of African People[4] and became the organizational identifier of the Council of Independent Black Institutions (CIBI) in 1972. Lomotey & Brookins differentiate between "traditional African-American private schools" and "independent Black institutions" (IBIs) by pointing out that IBIs focus on dealing with African-American culture as the basis for the curriculum.[5]

Ratteray and Shujaa introduced the term "independent neighborhood schools" to describe a broad range of schools located predominantly in urban African-American and Hispanic/Latino communities.[6] These schools represent "neighborhood-based, self-help responses to educational needs" in specific ethnic and cultural communities. Significant differences exist among independent neighborhood schools. Religious and secular schools are represented in roughly equal numbers. However, there is a cross-cutting distinction among the schools that reflects the extent to which emphasis is placed on building a cultural base and countering Eurocentric hegemony. In some independent neighborhood schools the cultural foundation is considered essential and in others it is essentially ignored.

Carter, who refers to "Black independent schools" (BISs), provides one more example.[7] In her study of parental choice, she contends that most BISs emphasize high academic standards but indicates that only some of them also emphasize an "Afrocentric educational model."

In this chapter, I consider the extent to which these observed differences in the degree of African-centered expression among African-American independent schools are also identifiable among the indicators of African-centered preferences expressed by parents whose children are enrolled in them. My intent is to facilitate a larger discussion about the influence of African-centered identity perspectives on parents' conceptualizations of education and its social context.

Conceptual Framework
African-American independent schools are products of the African-American social and cultural experience. They exist

because of perceived needs for social change and reflect analyses of schooling's role in achieving individual and group goals in the absence of needed change. We find, for example, that African-Americans in the northern states founded and operated schools for their own upliftment as far back as the 1790s.[8] We also find descriptions of how, following Reconstruction, African-Americans in the southern states combined their own resources to establish schools for themselves.[9]

Contemporary African-American parents' decisions to enroll children in African-American independent schools provide important channels to their perceptions of the social and cultural realities that influence their lives. These decisions involve careful consideration of other schooling options, most often public systems, that are well integrated into the societal infrastructure. They include assessments about the relationship of schooling to the social order and schooling's role in the attainment of individual achievement expectations. Most significantly, these decisions entail taking stock of one's own relationship to the social order and determining what type of schooling will provide one's children with the best preparation for life's challenges.

The Afrocentric transformation model was chosen for this analysis for several reasons. First, it is based on a theory that articulates social change as a process of individual/personal transformation. Second, it is specifically attuned to and emanates from African-American cultural and historical experiences. Third, it provides a means of reflecting on individuals' experiences with personal transformation. Each of these factors suggests that understanding an individual's decision to choose African-American independent schooling for his/her child will, in fact, also reveal something about that person's perceptions of him/herself and his/her social and cultural realities.

Asante's premise is that Afrocentric reconstruction of social reality is accomplished through an on going process of engagement in social interaction and individual reflection. Asante contends that an individual experiences four levels of transformation that can lead to and contribute to Afrocentricity as a level of critical consciousness. However, it should be kept in mind that individuals are not necessarily consciously engaged in becoming Afrocentric and not everyone becomes Afrocentric. Asante's levels of Afrocentric transformation are outlined below.

(1) "skin recognition"—Awareness of skin color and heritage as

characteristics that distinguish one as a person of African descent.

(2) "environmental recognition"—Awareness of discrimination and abuse within the environment attributed to one's skin color and heritage.

(3) "personality awareness"—Recognition of individual preferences related to one's heritage.

(4) "interest concern"—Demonstration of interest and concern related to the issues of people of African descent.

(5) "Afrocentricity"—Awareness of a collective and conscious will; constant struggle to interpret reality from an African-centered perspective.[10]

Asante's Afrocentric transformation model has antecedents in other theoretical constructs that describe the processes through which individual consciousness of one's own cultural and historical identity is liberated from Eurocentric hegemony. Frantz Fanon wrote of African intellectuals who, upon finding themselves "part of the body of European culture" and estranged from their own people, sought to reconnect with their national culture. These individuals exhibited what Fanon described as "phases of consciousness which is in the process of being liberated."[11] Amilcar Cabral referred to this personal transformation process among Africans as "returning to the sources." He described it as:

> a slow, discontinuous and uneven process, the development of which depends on each person's degree of acculturation, the material conditions of his life, his ideological training, and his own history as a social being.[12]

An additional example can be found in Paulo Freire's description of the development of critical consciousness. This process involves individual movement through several stages. The initial state of "semi-intransitivity" is one in which the decisions individuals make are essentially guided by biological necessity. As perception expands, individuals achieve transitive consciousness which has two levels. "Naive transitivity" represents an understanding that people are the makers of history, but is characterized by over-simplification of complex problems and reductionism. In contrast, critically transitive consciousness is denoted by depth of analysis, complex reasoning, and adaptive problem solving.[13]

When used as a conceptual framework, Asante's Afrocentric transformation model enables recognition of different levels of social reality reinterpretation approaching Afrocentricity. Analysis of parents' discourse about their schooling decisions contributes to our understanding of the extent to which Afrocentric reinterpretation influences their choice of African-American independent schools. Moreover, such information extends our understanding of how African-Americans interpret their educational needs in the general societal context.

Design of the Study

I conducted a secondary analysis of transcripts of interviews conducted by a colleague and myself as part of a national study of parental choice related to independent neighborhood schools.[14] The study was conducted under the auspices of the Institute for Independent Education. Informants included 35 parents whose children attended nine schools in eight cities. All of the parents had children enrolled in schools that were owned and operated by African-American individuals, families, organizations or churches and had enrollments made up entirely, or almost entirely of African-American students.

The respondents were selected by their respective school administrators according to membership within the following categories:

(a) leadership group—a person who holds an office in the school structure or parent-teacher organization, or regularly assists with administration or teaching;

(b) active non-leader—a person who regularly attends meetings, serves on committees;

(c) inactive—someone who attends few meetings and does not serve on committees;

(d) established—a person who has been a parent at the school for at least two full years;

(e) new—someone who has been a parent at the school for less than one full year.

The interviews were tape recorded and transcribed. Interview data were coded with the assistance of *The Ethnograph* (qualitative analysis software for personal computers). The coding process began with the content analysis of the interview transcripts. During this initial coding step, the transcribed data were reduced to units for analysis by identifying specific statements that contained parents' reasons for selecting a particular school.[15]

Once the data were reduced in this manner, categories were constructed for typological analysis using Asante's Afrocentric transformation model.[16] Typological analysis is flexible enough to serve both descriptive and generative purposes. In a descriptive sense, I located parents' responses within the context of the Afrocentric transformation model. However, the power of this form of analysis is derived from the ability it offers to generate new themes within the categories of a typology. Herein, I present the data in a way that gives meaning to the levels of Afrocentric transformation through analysis of the discourse provided by parents whose children attend African American independent schools.[17]

The information we have about Afrocentric qualities among independent African-American schools generally rely on descriptions based on investigator-created (etic) categories.[18] Because of this, we are left without a means of determining how consistent the researchers' interpretations are with the views of the people involved in these schools. This study provides descriptions in the participants' own language (emic categories). In this manner, the opportunity to evaluate my interpretations offers the reader a means of assessing the validity of the findings.

Findings
Skin Recognition

In the context of school choice, skin recognition can be viewed as the most basic level of African-centered awareness. Virtually all of the respondents made statements that demonstrated their awareness encompassed and transcended "skin recognition." This means, according to Asante's criteria, that the parents were aware of and accepting of their identities as African-Americans. Skin recognition consciousness may in fact represent just enough awareness to prevent a parent from avoiding an African-American independent school because it is African-American. We asked parents about their views regarding the cultural needs of African-American children. In some instances, the fact that a school was African-American did not seem to be an important factor in choosing it for their children. There were also instances when parents we interviewed would make it a point to emphasize that they were not specifically interested in an African-American independent school. As the example below shows, some even gave indications that it was merely coincidental that the particular school their children attended was all African-American.

> When we made the choice we really were not looking for a Black program. We chose this school because it had a good program and it happened to be Black. But, had we found a good program in a White setting we . . . I would not have a problem putting [our daughter] there. [6.001-467]

We found in other instances that skin recognition did play a role in some parents' decisions to choose an African-American independent school. One mother was hesitant to discuss her feelings in this area because she felt her views might be interpreted as prejudice. When she became more comfortable with us, she had much to say about the negative images of African-American people that seemed so pervasive to her. She wanted her daughter's school to teach her positive things about being Black.

> I would like for [my daughter] to know that being Black isn't bad, you know, like it's been taught when I was growing up, you know. White peoples' beauty, you know, the differences between White and Black, Black is bad, White is good, you know, everything depicts that. I want her to know that Black is not bad. Being Black and your hair not being straight, that's not bad. That's what I want her to know. I don't want her to be prejudiced, but I want her to know that her people are, you know, good, too. [6.003-368]

In one of the religious-based schools, skin recognition was evident in a parent's expressed satisfaction with the pictures in the school where the images of Jesus Christ were described as being ". . . not so White. He's got more of a color tone to him."

Skin recognition is the beginning. It is perhaps no more than the mere acceptance of what one sees in the mirror each morning. But, it is a beginning to the process of deconstructing Eurocentric cultural hegemony and it has produced sufficient awareness to contribute to some African-American parents' decisions to place their children in African-American independent schools. Subsequent levels of consciousness that can contribute to Afrocentric awareness may be built upon the consciousness embodied in skin recognition. Interpretation of the data show that even though most of the parents we interviewed had transcended this level of awareness, its tendencies could still be detected. However, if skin recognition is not transcended it is possible that parents could become satisfied with something as simple as images that are "not so White." Next, I will discuss indications of environmental recognition, the next level of awareness described by Asante.

Environmental Recognition

There were many instances in which parents expressed strong feelings of resentment about living in a social environment in which African-Americans have experienced forced segregation. They felt segregation was wrong. Acutely aware that their choice of schools could be interpreted as contradictory to such beliefs, parents were often careful to avoid giving the impression that they were voluntarily segregating their children by enrolling them in an African-American independent school. However, these parents did make it quite clear that they believed they were protecting their children from the harmful effects of a hostile social environment by enrolling them in an African-American independent school.

Environmental recognition was evident in parents' feelings that their children would be protected from the psychologically damaging effects of racism during their formative years. One father felt that

> . . . if kids go into a predominantly White environment those school systems will change them. You know you see a Black kid that's maybe not groomed properly. Whereas, here in a Black environment, he's going to get that tender loving care that he needs, in a White school that kid could very well be labeled as a kid with a problem—with learning disabilities because nobody wants to take the time to get close to him. [6.001-790]

His wife later described a scene she observed in their son's African-American independent school that confirmed her husband's feelings about the school.

> One day I was in here, a little boy came in. She [the teacher] say, "You didn't brush your hair, sweetheart." She came, she said, "come here" and she got a brush from somewhere and she lotioned him up and greased his little face and brushed his little hair and he looked like a little doll, you know. [6.001-810]

Insulation from society's racism was also sought by one mother who indicated that she wanted her son to attend a racially mixed school once he had obtained a solid grounding with his own people in the African-American independent school.

. . . by the time he reaches secondary education level and high school, I would want him to be in an integrated school only because I feel at this particular time I think that Black teachers are more sensitive to the problems of Black students. And in the primary years and maybe on up to the sixth or even eighth grade even, I think they need that foundation of their heritage with their people. [9.003-474]

Asante suggests that environmental recognition is consciousness borne from otherness. It is a sense of being made real as a result of discrimination and abuse in a racist society. The parents we interviewed are shown to have thought of African-American independent schools as places that afforded their children sanctuary. They utilized the schools to buy time for their children so that they could develop as free as possible from the limitations imposed by racism. For some, like the mother who hoped her son would be ready for what she termed "integrated schooling" by the time he reached high school age, environmental recognition seems to mark the extent of their Afrocentric transformation. For others, the transformation process includes both skin recognition and environmental recognition, but also transcends these levels to include personality awareness.

Personality Awareness

The next level of Asante's model of Afrocentric development is personality awareness. At this stage of development individuals demonstrate awareness of personal qualities and preferences that they relate to their cultural identity. It represents recognition of a cultural self that is unique. It is not a self derived of otherness. The attribution of personality characteristics to one's culture does not mean that the individual's thinking is Afrocentric. It does suggest, however, that the person is aware that some things in his/her environment have special appeal because he/she is African-American. The desire to foster this awareness in their children was a significant influence on some parents' preference for an African-American independent school.

I looked at six schools. It was interesting because in the Washington area you have a choice, apparently, between sending your child, at this particular age, to either a school where he or she is a minority. . . . Or, you have a choice of sending them to a school where it's all Black. . . . I know there's a need

for both kinds of exposures. My choice was based on the fact
that he's going to be in White environment soon enough as far
as I'm concerned and that I think I prize higher than education
or almost anything else, a positive self-concept. I don't think you
can start too early instilling that in kids and I assumed that [name
of school] would be the place that he would be able to get that.
[1.003-046]

This statement suggests that this Washington, DC parent felt it was
particularly important for her child's personal development to be in
an African-American independent school. Her comments indicate
that her level of Afrocentric development heightened her awareness
of the impact that the ethnic make-up of the school can have on a
child's self-concept. This awareness critically influenced her choice
of schools.

I found it particularly interesting that, for a number of parents,
it was simply the presence of African-American role models that
seemed to satisfy the expectations generated by this level of awareness. They wanted more than symbolic evidence of cultural identity
affirmation. These parents seemed to be concerned with the examples established by the adults in the schools and the totality of the
school environment. A Chicago mother discussed the advantages
she believed her child's school provided.

Well, the advantages are to be able to love yourself more as being
Black, I think, or getting real self appreciation. To know that
Black people can function and have these kinds of establishments
that run successfully. . . . I'm glad that these children are having
a chance to grow up in surroundings where they can see. [9.004-
621]

An Atlanta mother shared a similar view.

I want my son to have a very positive self-image about himself and
about Black people in general and about what they can do. And
I think to give him that positive self-image for him to be around
Black professionals, to be around Black students and see that
achievement is, indeed, possible. So, because I believe that, I live
in a Black community, I work with community organizations . . .
I shop in a Black community. I don't go across town because I
believe that by supporting our community we make it strong and
I want that positive self-image to also be fostered in my son. So,

> I chose a Black school. In fact, I have never considered going to a White school. [7.003-455]

Personality awareness represents an important threshold. What we are able to see is that these parents are not retreating from negative treatment in the general society, but are actively building and defining a sense of African-American community. They regard the African-American independent school as a part of that community and view the decision to enroll their children in such schools as consistent with the process of community-building.

Interest-Concern

The fourth step toward Afrocentricity Asante describes is "interest-concern." Asante states that "this level accepts the first three levels and demonstrates interest and concern in the problems of Blacks and tries to deal intelligently with the issues of the African people."[19] This level of awareness was exhibited in the many expressions by parents that described the importance of learning about African and African-American history and culture. Many parents indicated expectations that African-American independent schools would provide their children with a stronger knowledge base in African/African-American history and culture than they had received themselves. Indeed, the data from this study offer numerous examples of this. One mother from Washington, DC pointed out that growth in her own knowledge about Africa was facilitated by what her daughter brought home from school.

> There are a lot of things that [my daughter] has learned that she's come home and taught me. I mean, a lot of stuff about Africa that she has learned and about famous Black people that I've never even really heard about. [1.001-298]

A mother in Atlanta wanted schooling that would not make her child anti-White, but would foster love for his own culture.

> I don't mean for my child to be pro-Black and anti-White but I want him to know everything there is to know about his culture and about his background as . . . a Black child. [7.002-487]

Another illustration is provided by a mother whose child attends an independent African-American school in Baltimore:

I picked [this school] because he will be with some Black students. He gets along well . . . with both [Black and White children]. I haven't met a child yet that he cannot get along with, White or Black. But, I want him to know about his own heritage which I was really never taught. You know, I'm learning now myself. [3.002-854]

Statements like these help to illustrate how important it is to some African-American parents who choose African-American independent schools that their children learn more than they did in school about their cultural heritage. They typify the interest and concern about the problems of African-American people that Asante believes characterize this level of awareness. Moreover, they show that parents are utilizing African-American independent schools as a means of redressing the marginalization and devaluation of African-American culture in U.S. society.

Afrocentricity

Afrocentricity, Asante argues, "is above all the total use of method to effect psychological, political, social, cultural and economic change."[20] Moreover, it is a quality achieved "when the person becomes totally changed to a conscious level of involvement in the struggle for his or her own mind liberation."[21] Two key terms to consider in Asante's conception are "consciousness" and "struggle." Afrocentric consciousness implies a state of awareness in which one understands the need to evaluate symbolic reality as a social product that is never neutral. That is, symbolic reality always reflects a cultural point of view. The question that Afrocentricity demands that one address is whether that point of view reflects a reality grounded in the experiences of African people. Afrocentric consciousness enables individuals to recognize incongruities in their perceptions of reality and to reinterpret situations and phenomena in a manner that is consistent with the collective interests of African people.

The use of the term "struggle" implies that Afrocentric transformation is a continual process in which individuals constantly interpret new social situations. The individual involved in Afrocentric transformation in learning to define social reality with African cultural history at the center of his or her consciousness. For African-Americans this becomes an internal conflict in which Afrocentric consciousness is in constant conflict with Eurocentric hegemony.

These criteria are such that I am unable to determine solely from these interview data whether any of these respondents can actually be described as having attained Afrocentric awareness. Some of these parents may have attained Afrocentric awareness; my sense is that most have not. I have argued that when parents decide that it is important to send their children to an African-American independent school because they want them to learn about their culture, they are articulating interest and concern—a level in the process of awareness that more closely approaches Afrocentricity than does skin recognition. But, I cannot argue that evidence obtained through analysis of discourse alone is sufficient to draw conclusions about the totality of one's consciousness and practice. In fact, I have avoided making statements that would fix the consciousness of any of the informants at any particular level of Afrocentric transformation. What I have done is point out that there are clear indications that parental decisions to enroll their children in African-American independent schools are influenced by the parents' experiences within the U.S. social context while recognizing that these experiences relate very much to the social constraints imposed in a racist society. These experiences have enabled the parents we interviewed to demonstrate, through their discourse, evidence of increasing capacities to sort out the uniqueness of being an African in America and to begin the assumption of their share of the responsibility for shaping the future of African cultural history.

Conclusions

I have been able to show through examples two things. First, that the parents we interviewed do manifest characteristics that appear to reflect various levels of awareness that are consistent with Asante's steps toward Afrocentricity. Second, I have shown that the attributes of these levels of awareness influence these parents' decisions about schooling for their children.

These findings are significant for several reasons. First, when we consider that the number of parents choosing African-American independent schools is growing, the findings suggest that the number of African-American parents who are looking at schooling in its broader social context is also growing. By assigning dual priority to academic preparation and cultural awareness, these parents are demonstrating the capacity to differentiate schooling and education. These parents' decisions to enroll their children in African-American independent schools are efforts to obtain schooling that is more closely attuned to the values and beliefs they are developing within their own families. The school, therefore, is used by parents to extend the educational foundation begun at home. This pattern is clearly different from the trend toward the schools' assumption of educational responsibilities traditionally handled within families.

Second, these findings suggest a need to identify specific school characteristics that reflect levels of development toward Afrocentric education. Ratteray and Shujaa,[22] Carter,[23] and Lomotey and Brookins[24] have all noted that African-American independent schools can be differentiated according to the extent to which they stress Afrocentricity in their curricula. Further, at least one author cites evidence that African-American parents believe "it is important for their children to be exposed to an educational program which not only emphasizes high academic standards but also concentrates on an African-American educational perspective."[25]

It is essential that we not treat all of these schools as simply African-American "private" schools. Such a coarse classification prevents us from recognizing that these schools differ in such critical areas as mission, philosophy, and pedagogy. Ratteray and Shujaa found, for example, that these schools showed great range in the extent and manner in which Afrocentric symbolism was evident.[26] In some instances all images in the school reflected African and African-American influences. However, in others such symbolism was totally absent.

In Afrocentricity we have a concept but we lack concensus about the indicators that denote its existence in school settings. I believe that identification of such indicators can offer clues to the assumptions that underlie pedagogy and curriculum. Such indicators can help in making determinations about whether instruction is moving in the direction of Afrocentric constructions/reconstructions of social reality. However, we must keep in mind that Afrocentricity is a qualitative state. Its dynamism makes its enumeration through a particular set of characteristics infeasible. What constitutes Afrocentric interpretation in one temporal setting and situation is not necessarily so in another.

Third, my analysis is limited to parents' expressions at a particular moment in their lives. There is a need to do longitudinal research that would examine changes within individuals related to their movement toward Afrocentric awareness. Such longitudinal research would provide information about the influences of African-American independent schools on parents. Earlier research differentiated the reasons parents gave for keeping their children enrolled in an independent school from the reasons they gave for initially choosing the school.[27] The experiences that were made possible by becoming part of the school had clear effects on parents' perceptions of schooling and upon their subsequent expectations of schooling.

The data presented here offer strong indications that Afrocentric data both affects and is reflected in the way in which reality is perceived. By this I mean that "things" are not Afrocentric, but merely are able to be perceived in Afrocentric ways by individuals who have achieved this level of reality transformation. To me this seems fundamental. It is as simple as an observation that what is perceived as adinkra cloth by one person, is perceived only as African cloth by another, and as simply a piece of cloth with some designs on it by yet another. The "centeredness" is a quality of the perceiver, not the perceived.

I am concluding on this note because I am concerned about the uses to which Afrocentricity has been put in schools. Too often, it has come to be regarded as a quantity, rather than a quality, and, in some instances, even as a commodity that is bought and sold. In the context of education, Afrocentricity has often been linked with school curricula. I believe that the interviews with parents discussed in this chapter offer powerful evidence that Afrocentricity *is* a process of *individual* transformation, as Asante has initially argued. Viewed in this way, as I believe it should, it seems inappropriate to treat the *curriculum* as the purveyor of Afrocentricity when it is actually the extent to which there exists Afrocentric transformation among individual teachers that ultimately will determine how curriculum content is perceived and delivered through pedagogy.

Afrocentricity is one of those rare and fundamental concepts that is so powerful that the task of determining its meaning belongs to the people. Its interpretations will change as history is produced by the movements of African people through time and space and with the construction of new realities reflecting African life. Clearly, there is a need for additional research and discussion that focus on building a consensus of meaning around this important concept.

Notes and References

1. P. L. Benson, *Private Schools in the United States: A Statistical Profile, with Comparisons to Public Schools* (Washington, DC: U.S. Department of Education, 1991).
2. Institute for Independent Education, *African-American Enrollment in Independent Schools*, Research Notes on Education (Washington, DC:

Author, 1990).

3. D. T. Slaughter and D. J. Johnson, eds., *Visible Now: Blacks in Private Schools* (New York: Greenwood Press, 1988).
4. F. J. Satterwhite, *Planning an Independent Black Educational Institution* (New York: Afram Associates, 1971).
5. K. Lomotey and C. C. Brookins, "Independent Black Institutions: A Cultural Perspective," in *Visible Now: Blacks in Private Schools*, eds. D. T. Slaughter and D. J. Johnson (New York: Greenwood Press, 1988).
6. J. D. Ratteray and M. J. Shujaa, *Dare to Choose: Parental Choice at Independent Neighborhood Schools* (Washington, DC: U.S. Department of Education, 1987).
7. D. Carter, "Parental Schooling Choice: African-American Parents' Choice of Black Independent Schools," *Sankofa* 1 (1987): 11-13.
8. Ratteray and Shujaa, *Dare to Choose*.
9. H. M. Bond, *The Education of the Negro in the American Social Order* (New York: Prentice Hall, 1934); J. D. Anderson, *The Education of Blacks in the South, 1860-1935* (Chapel Hill, NC: University of North Carolina, 1988).
10. M. K. Asante, *Afrocentricity: The Theory of Social Change* (Buffalo, NY: Amulefi Publishing Company, 1980), 55-56.
11. F. Fanon, *The Wretched of the Earth* (New York: Grove Press, Inc., 1963), 220.
12. A. Cabral, *Guinea-Bissau: Toward Final Victory! Selected Speeches and Documents from PAIGC* (Richmond, BC, Canada: LSM Information Center, 1974), 42.
13. P. Freire, *Education for Critical Consciousness* (New York: Seabury Press, 1973), 18-20.
14. Ratteray and Shujaa, *Dare to Choose*.
15. K. Krippendorff, *Content Analysis* (Beverly Hills, CA: Sage, 1980), 29-31, 57-64.
16. Asante, *Afrocentricity*.
17. J. P. Goetz and M. D. LeCompte, "Ethnographic Research and the Problem of Data Reduction," *Anthropology and Education Quarterly* 12 (1981): 51-70.
18. Lomotey and Brookins, "Independent Black Institutions."
19. Asante, *Afrocentricity*, 56.
20. M. K. Asante, *The Afrocentric Idea* (Philadelphia: Temple University Press, 1987), 125.
21. Asante, *Afrocentricity*, 56.
22. Ratteray and Shujaa, *Dare to Choose*.
23. Carter, "Parental Schooling Choice."
24. Lomotey and Brookins, "Independent Black Institutions."
25. Carter, "Parental Schooling Choice," 13.
26. Ratteray and Shujaa, *Dare to Choose*.

Chapter Sixteen

The Rites of Passage: Extending Education into the African-American Community

Nsenga Warfield-Coppock
Baobab Associates

Historically, Africans brought to the shores of the Americas used the segregated church, the relationships among residents, and the make-shift or sanctioned schools to bring girls to womanhood and boys to manhood. Relatives of the same gender—aunts, uncles, grandparents, and older siblings—took on some of the nurturing and socialization processes. The African-American community is beginning, again, to take the responsibility for ensuring the proper induction and education of all of our offspring—including those who attend largely Eurocentric school systems and those who are in independent or private African-American educational situations. At every level of the African-American community coalitions are being formed to support rites of passage for the children.

Mbiti stated that initiation,

Marks the beginning of acquiring knowledge which is otherwise not accessible to those who have not been initiated . . . they learn to endure hardships, they learn to live with one another, they learn to obey, they learn the secrets and mysteries of the man-woman relationship, and in some areas, especially in West Africa, they join secret societies, each of which has its own secrets, activities, and language.[1]

While it is true that much of African-American children's technical knowledge is provided by the schooling system which trains them, many aspects of development and learning remain in the hands of each child's non-school community. African-Americans interact in interdependent ways. Accordingly, these non-school influences include parents, siblings, and other family members; mentors; peers; the church; community/recreational center staff members; as well as other people and organizations with whom they come in contact.

The establishment of rites of passage has become a grass roots movement that is swelling into a network of institutionalized practices. It is a model that can assist us in institutionalizing major traditional relationships and practices for African-American children, youth, and adults, including elders. This chapter will focus on the purpose, form, and potential impact of the rites of passage as an "institution" in African-American communities. I will briefly review the history of rites of passage, the current trends in African-American rites of passage, and finally, offer some recommendations and guidance for their use.

The Rites of Passage

A *rite* is simply a ceremony, ritual, or series of acts marking some significant occasion. *Passage* means the act or process of transition or movement from one place or condition to another. Thus, a working definition of *rites of passage* is simply a set of activities or celebrations marking the successful transition from one life stage to another. In nature, plants are born (seeded) and go through the stages of growth to blossoming, bearing fruit, regeneration, and death. Animals, typically, have similar cycles. All beings contain a spirit, which gives rise to the concept of "universality of being."

The rites-of-passage concept must be viewed within this larger ecological frame of reference and not simply as an activity to improve the behavior of children and youth. Therefore, we start with an overview of the African-American "spiritual life cycle" focusing on rites of passage. African people-centered thought views the person as a spiritual as well as a physical being without the dichotomy evident in either the European-centered or Asian-centered world views.[2] Hence, the use of the term spiritual/life cycle to reflect the developmental progress of one's spiritual as well as physical existence.[3] A person's development—as best we as finite beings can conceptualize such a process—can be viewed as progress through a spiritual as well as a physical plane and as a process occurring at different levels of existence. The being enters the physical plane from the spiritual plane and then progresses through stages within the physical plane before again transforming into a being within the spiritual plane.

Every African-American person passes through a series of stages in his/her life time that are appropriate for ritual and ceremony.[4] These stages are cyclical and are repeated/duplicated as is the case with all life. The African-American spiritual/life cycle occurs as a series of seven distinct periods of transformation or transition—birth (the transition from the spiritual plane), puberty, early adulthood, marriage, mature adulthood, eldership, and death (the transition to the spiritual plane). Because social relationships are key in an African society, these stages are defined by the customary relationships expected of the person in each stage. In general, there is a spiritual community within which are the Supreme Being who may be referred to as the Creator/God/Jaweh/Nyame/Allah or by whatever name one's traditions have established; ancestors (the recently deceased); deities; the dead (long deceased); and the yet-to-be-born.

Historical Overview

Traditional African rites of passage were processes by which communities taught and reinforced all cultural beliefs, values, and practices. The rites were so well integrated into the African social systems that there was no need to identify them as something unusual or extraordinary. The rituals maintained the people's relationship to the Creator/spiritual entities (ancestors and deities) as well as to the Creator's gifts—nature and people.

Rituals and celebrations created order and passed on the understanding of the human relationships to the Creator and nature. Rituals during planting or harvesting seasons were typical in agrarian societies. Asking and thanking the Creator and spiritual entities for their blessings in order to ensure the survival of the people were included in these practices. People, too, were highly valued from the perspective that the Creator is present in all beings or things. Rituals and celebrations related to the progression of human beings through the spiritual/life cycle were an important part of community life.

Birthing rituals and naming ceremonies, puberty rites, marriage, eldership, and death rituals all fall within the typical practices of a people who understand and revere their relationship with the Creator and other spiritual entities.

The novel, *The Healers*, by Ayi Kwei Armah contains a relevant discussion of rituals and ceremonies as ways of maintaining order. Festivals provided the whole community with the opportunity to take part in rituals of wholeness. The author shares how the people of the tribe or community became scattered which disturbed the oneness that the festivals or rituals were established to reinforce.

> True, in the beginning each division kept for a while its fragmented remembrance of a past oneness, and still made hesitant invocations to a future unity. . . . Yes, for a while each fraction continued in some form of ceremonies meant to remind a scattered people of our common origin. But in some places the ceremonies died with time. In all places the ceremonies changed. Their intended meaning had been wholeness. But the circumstances under which they had been played out had been circumstances of division, circumstances of fragmentation.[5]

We know that African people are now scattered around the globe. Everywhere in the world where African people now live, similar wails of loss can be heard. The impact of Western-European cultural imposition has touched nearly every corner of the earth. With the scattering of African people and the inculcation of Western-European influences, the wholeness and harmony have been changed or, in some instances, destroyed. We see evidences of this daily on the front pages of our newspapers, in our conversations, in our businesses, and on the streets. Our people are stealing, killing, and self-destructing. We awaken from the lull of material comforts to find chaos around us. The rituals and order that we as African people used to know are no longer.

Rites-of-Passage Trends

Rituals and ceremonies are being instituted to assist us in reinforcing the traditions that are needed to carry African-Americans beyond mere survival to growth and liberation. This section will review some of the types of programs that are currently in their developmental stages or have actually been established as of the early 1990s in the United States. I will focus on the programs for young people; however, there is an overlap with programs for young adults and women.

National Rites-of-Passage Organizations

The original rites-of-passage movement coincides with the "Black Power" era of the 1960s. Many community-based organizations disagreed with the strategies emphasizing racial integration that were advocated by the major civil rights organizations. "Separatists" or cultural nationalists as they were called upheld the position that African-American institutions need not be "integrated" for all people to receive their rights as citizens. To this end, groups continued to form and to maintain independent schools, after-school cultural programs, and some adolescent rites-of-passage programs. Kwanzaa, for example, founded in 1966, serves as a ritual of wholeness in many communities.

The oldest rites-of-passage organization for the development of young males is known as Simba, which means young lions, and dates back to the 1960s in several cities in California and in St. Louis, Missouri. Today, Simba has grown to become a nation-wide movement, holding annual meetings. It has also established a female counterpart, Simba na Malaika, which has also grown from a community-based to a national organization.

The Sojourner Truth Adolescent Rites Society, Inc. (STARS, Inc.) grew out of a family-based rites-of-passage program in New York City during the 1980s. STARS, Inc., like Simba, promotes rites of passage for females and males through its lectures, conferences, and a book—*Transformation: A Rites of Passage Manual for African-American Girls.*[6]

School Rites of Passage

Since the beginning of the African-centered independent school movement, "rites of passage" has been the model or term used for graduations. Many of the Pan-African and culturally-based independent schools incorporate the rites of passage as part of their learning model. Very often the major rites of passage coincide with the transitions young people experience around the age of puberty, e.g., completing or beginning junior high school or moving to high school. Puberty rites for instance, are typically performed between the ages of 12 and 14.

Currently the movement is witnessing the introduction of rites-of-passage programs into public school systems. As in independent schools, these rites of passage usually occur at the puberty or junior high school stage. Typically, eighth graders or graduating ninth graders are selected to participate in extra-curricular activities that are usually headed by teachers and/or counselors who are familiar with and interested in offering such programs. To date, these programs have been received with skepticism by individual school administrations and are run on minuscule budgets. They receive little or no support from school funds. Outside funding is sometimes sought, but most often the funds to operate the programs come out of teachers' pockets or from other sources that teachers may come upon through resourceful contacts.

Therapeutic Rites of Passage

This rites-of-passage model is being introduced by culturally-based therapeutic agencies and communities. Rites are being introduced on an outpatient basis to young people who live at home as well as to those who live in homes as a result of their adjudication or inability to abide by the rules of their families. The therapy or counseling situation offers a prime opportunity for addressing the traditionally conflicting values and behaviors of young people. Foster addressed the psychological misorientation affecting young people who are candidates for therapeutic rites.[7] Funding may be private or governmental.

Church Rites of Passage

Many Christian churches have had children's and youth's classes for the teaching of religious lessons. The adults of these churches, noting the secularization of their young people, have sought ways to interest them in the churches' activities. To this end, more extensive youth programs are being developed to attract young people to church. Rites-of-passage programs are taking the place of or being added to the current youth-oriented church programs. Since part of the rites-of-passage programs typically include an introduction to spiritual development, many religious organizations are incorporating their own religious lessons.

Organizational Rites-of-Passage Programs

This grouping covers a wide array of programs that I have placed together in order to address their similarities. Social, sororal, and fraternal organizations have placed youth on their agendas. They have provided assistance to community efforts to develop youth programs that include mentoring, tutoring, recreation, apprenticeships, and rites of passage. Sororities and other women's organizations have modified the traditional cotillion to address the cultural and career orientations of young females. Teen mothers' programs are using rites of passage not only to teach young females what they may have missed by moving to motherhood so early, but also to offer guidance for raising their children. Fraternities and other men's groups are taking seriously the threat of African-American male genocide and are developing programs that address the typical behaviors of young males. These include the adoption of teen fathers' programs and rites-of-passage models.

Community-Wide Rites of Passage

In many cities with largely European-American populations, there is often a core of African-Americans who lead the cultural efforts for the enmeshed community. Usually in these cities most African-Americans know or know of each other and there are churches, fraternal organizations, and agencies where the traditions of the community are carried on. In many instances the city's one African-American bookstore serves as a beacon in the town by bringing materials and up-dated cultural resources to the community. Such communities may bring together the major culturally-based organizations and representatives from the schools and churches to establish rites-of-passage programs. Individual agencies and organizations will sponsor the rites, but support comes from the entire community. This trend, though relatively recent, offers one of the best climates for success as long as the major institutions are maintained.

Family-Based Rites of Passage

These rites of passage, like community-based rites, most often come from a group of families seeking culturally expressive social-ization for their teenage children. The knowledge that many of the interfacing organizations, e.g., schools, churches, community centers, and community-based organizations, do not offer cultural teachings has prompted families to combine their efforts to offer appropriate lessons and rituals for groups of teens who usually know each other through regular family interactions.

Government Agency Initiatives

Programs that eventually receive federal, state, or city funding have often been developed from seeds planted within community-

or family-based programs.

High risk youth. Due to a federal government initiative to address the rising use and abuse of alcohol and drugs, a great deal of money has become available to communities that normally would not have had access to funding for programs to serve African-American youth. The purpose of most of these programs is to provide primary prevention and early intervention services. With such funds, African-American communities have developed programs to assist latch-key children; the children of housing communities in high drug areas; abused children; low achieving children in schools, etc. Rites-of-passage programs have been identified as a proactive approach to saving children who are affected by multiple risk factors. These programs have generally been attached to community centers that receive various kinds of funding and resources.

Substance-abusing youth and adults. A variety of culturally appropriate treatment strategies have been identified for African-American youth and adults. When drugs reach the African-American community, the only way to address the source of the problem is through the cultural experience of the abuser. In the case of African-Americans, healing cannot begin until the oppressive factors in the life of the person, the family, or community have been recognized. Prisons and therapeutic communities can typically exert strong influences on their populations if the members are separated into smaller groups of 15 to 30 people. As a condition of release or early consideration for release, males and females are taken, usually separately, through intensive programs to address cultural and self-development needs, family and community relationships, as well as changes in criminal attitudes and behaviors. A truly rehabilitated individual becomes altruistic and seeks ways to continue his/her own personal learning, to re-establish positive relationships, and to assist in the raising of his/her family as well as in the growth of his/her community. The number of programs using culturally appropriate strategies, including rites-of-passage models, is growing.

Pregnant and post-partum women and children. Due to the severe mental and physical impact of drugs and alcohol on a fetus, the Office of Substance Abuse Prevention has included pregnant women in the initiative to lower the use of drugs. Along with methods (such as acupuncture) that encourage females to abstain from the use of drugs and alcohol during pregnancy, educational materials and programs are being offered to young women and their children. In some cases, a rites-of-passage model is being implemented to address the source and not just the symptoms of substance abuse. Other community-based and church programs, some of which are funded with state or city monies, are using the rites-of-passage model to address the needs of pregnant women and young mothers.

Individual Rites of Passage

The concept of holding individual rites of passage is contrary to the proper focus of African-American rites of passage. This will become clear as this chapter proceeds. The concepts of interdependence and bonding are important parts of African-American rites of passage and are not well suited for introducing to young African-Americans as individuals. To date, I have only heard of individual rites of passage that have been completed for African-American male children by their mothers (which lack authenticity) or by fathers who were neither inclined to working with nor bonded with other adult African-American men. The African-American youth rites of passage should be a group activity. This is the way our young people will be able to understand that they are part of a group and that their survival is interdependent with that of all African-Americans.

Analysis of the Trends

The preceding discussion of the various types of rites-of-passage programs has partially documented historical trends within this social phenomenon. It has also offered a basis for the analysis of future directions in this movement. An article by Kotler provides some insight into the stages in the life cycle of a social cause. The author presents a four-staged characterization:

1. Crusading stage—characterized by a small number of zealots dedicated to a mission. Success is defined by their ability to get their message across and attract new members.
2. Popular movement—still led by the original charismatic leaders, number/membership grows to include people without the same degree of commitment. The cause changes with adoption of new roles, definitions, and needed resources.
3. Managerial—leaders with managerial skills become more important as more formalized planning and goal setting ensue. Growth slows with increasing availability of resources.
4. Bureaucratic—the original zeal is lost, leaders are functionaries and the "cause" is run like a business with the concerns of policies, procedures, and public relations.[8]

The rites-of-passage movement is quickly moving from the crusading stage to the popular movement stage as it experiences growth in many areas and on many fronts. The fact that it has taken hold among governmental agencies creates a dilemma for some African-Americans because funding is being made available for programs that come from the cultural experience of African-Americans. There is suspicion that rites-of-passage programs may lose some of their original energy, intent, and cultural integrity because money is often tied to regulations. Another concern is that government money will not last forever. If communities do not take ownership of the rites-of-passage programs and institutionalize them in their lifestyles, these programs will leave right along with the federal and state initiatives. Finally, a popular movement moving to managerial and bureaucratic stages will lose the colorful continuity of the culture. For this reason, it is probably best that rites of passage continue as a community or organization-based and governed processes. Every community has a personality. Every rites-of-passage program should reflect the colorful variations in the imagination and creativity of its creators and community. To overly standardize the programs will lead to bureaucratization and loss of independently created initiatives.

Rites of Passage Training and Program Development

Establishing rites-of-passage programs is a serious commitment. It is a commitment not only to young people and to one's community, but also to oneself to grow and learn. It is impossible to produce a rites-of-passage program without learning new materials, attitudes, and behaviors. One's own emotional, psycho-social, spiritual, and intellectual states as well as unresolved personal issues must be contemplated prior to embarking on the process of helping to raise youth to an adult level. This is because the process is not currently founded on a historical set of values, and most people come with their own belief systems. It is said that one cannot teach or bring another person to a level past that which he/she has reached him/herself. Men and women who have unresolved issues with their fathers and mothers (usually more intense with a parent of the same gender) or carry the baggage of emotional trauma from a cross-gender relationship need to resolve these issues for themselves.

There is an African proverb that states that "One must come out of one's house to begin learning." Every new person whom one meets or experience that one has must be viewed as an opportunity to learn. Rites of passage are no different. There is no place for the behaviors and attitudes which accompany self-hate, color or class discrimination, and chauvinism or abuse of any kind. We are in the process of molding a new future for our people and we must heal ourselves first, and then be open to the multiplicity of viewpoints, opinions, and feelings we will encounter as we forge this new beginning.

Adults should be fully trained before they start working with young people. Training should be supplied by competently trained persons with the expertise to understand the personal, cultural, and organizational nuances of the experience. Many people think that they can train just because they have read some books on a subject. Teaching is not the same as training. Some come as trainers but carry few tools. If all you have is a hammer then everything looks like a nail. By cutting corners during the training process, many people, agencies, and organizations never realize their full capacities, resources, and potentials.

The three areas of focus for knowledge and skill acquisition through rites of passage are education, physical development, and spiritual development.[9] Educational materials should focus on the infusion of the information provided by the adults responsible for the various components of the rites-of-passage programs. Physical development is required for achieving a healthy balance between the spiritual and physical aspects of the person. Spirituality should be built into the learning of all children; however, spirituality and religion are not necessarily the same and should not be confused.

Several essential areas should be considered in the training and development aspects of rites-of-passage programs. I will briefly consider each of these components.

African-centered Orientation

Training should begin with a basic understanding of the Afrocentric orientation. This orientation must be clearly understood by all persons who are to be involved in rites-of-passage programs and who will be responsible for passing it on to young people. Intellectual knowledge as well as behavioral practices often need adjusting during the training process. The basis for the African-American rites-of-passage expression is African philosophy. There is a proverb that states, "Because the water is spilled it does not mean that the calabash is broken." We are Africans raised on American shores; but because we have been raised somewhere other than our continent of origin it does not mean that we do not still carry many of the values and beliefs of our ancestors. This area is one in which adults should be well grounded. Books and materials by myself and other authors such as Asante, Nobles, Karenga, and Hilliard are available to assist in developing an intellectual understanding of the African-centered orientation.[10]

African-centered Principles and Values

Values should be explored and adopted by the community as the rites-of-passage program evolves. Some of the basic principles that must be infused at the programmatic and behavioral levels include:

- *Interdependence*—The "I am because We are" concept that every person is important to the whole and that we must depend upon and support one another. Another aspect of this concept is the very traditional idea of mutual aid or helping each other out in times of need. Behaviorally, this concept needs to be passed on to young people through discussions and activities that point to how we rely on one another in our communities and families.
- *Cooperation*—The principle of cooperation is best taught by example and experience. Children must see adults cooperate for a purpose and have the chance to work cooperatively with each other to learn the concept.
- *Respect*—Respect is another principle that is best learned through example and modeling. Children who do not receive respect do not learn it nor practice it. There are many levels of respect that must be modeled and taught. It begins with self-respect and is manifested in the way one carries and treats oneself as well as the levels of respect demonstrated with peers, siblings, parents, elders, other people in general, and the property of others.
- *Reciprocity*—This principle is related to cooperation, interdependence, and respect for other people. The notion of "what goes around comes around" is a belief that has it origins in the universal order.
- *Unconditional Love*—Our children feel secure and important when they understand that we love them—no matter what. We show them love by correcting them for inappropriate behaviors and separating the behavior from who they are as a person.

388

I will discuss values separately. There are two established systems that adapt very well to African-American rites-of-passage programs. One is the Nguzo Saba and the other is from the ancient Kemetic (Egyptian) tradition. Among the advantages of the Nguzo Saba (otherwise known as Seven Principles) is the fact that this value system has been around since the 1960s. These principles have taken hold in many African-American communities. Children learn the seven principles if they practice or have heard of Kwanzaa.

Several of the ways the Nguzo Saba are currently in use in rites-of-passage programs are described below:

* A long-term community program (seven years) has selected one of the seven principles to learn and practice for a whole year. Umoja (Unity) will be learned thoroughly through activities of all kinds throughout the year. At Kwanzaa time the rites-of-passage group will present the Umoja night celebration. Each year that follows will focus on one principle. Exciting things can be accomplished with that much time. With the principle Kujichagulia (Self-Determination) for example, a communications project such as a newsletter, video, movie, or series of news reports can be learned, developed, and maintained. The principle Ujamaa (Cooperative Economics) could be applied by starting and maintaining a small business. Ujima (Collective work and responsibility) could be practiced through community-wide self-help projects including repairs, carpentry, or building.

* The principle Kujichagulia is typically practiced when young people learn about and adopt an African name. The night of Kwanzaa on which Kujichagulia is the focus is often integrated to include the community-wide adoption of African names (naming ceremony night).

* Another program focuses on one principle per month and accomplishes a shorter version of the long term (seven-year program).

In other rites-of-passage programs, the Nguzo Saba are applied in very specific ways:

* Young people work together in small groups to practice one principle, then present what they have learned.

* The values are used in every day terminology to model what the practices of the Nguzo Saba are.

* The rules of the rites-of-passage program are structured to highlight the practice of the principles.

The second value system that is currently in use is derived from

Maat—the basis of ancient Kemetic (Egyptian) tradition. Programs that use Kemetic principles often begin with a basis of seven or ten Virtues. These can be learned like a creed or used as the basis for teaching lessons and program activities as with the Nguzo Saba. Virtue was an essential part of the Kemetic growth process. Some of the most ancient traditions included the development of the qualities that put the neophyte in harmony with people, nature, and God. The original educational system, then, goes back to Kemet (Egypt) where the mission of education was spiritual —the goal was to become God-like or one with the Creator. The basic concepts are order, justice, truth, righteousness, discipline, balance, propriety, control of thought and action, harmony, and devotion to purpose.

Cultural Competence

All young people should know and appreciate their cultural origins. Americans of African descent have a long way to go to learn and appreciate African accomplishments and traditions. Adults must model this competence with more than just a few "Black facts." A day should not pass without learning, teaching, and reinforcing important information on Africans and African-Americans. By the time the child is ready for puberty rites, the basics should be known and increasing amounts of analysis and synthesis of the information can be accomplished. This is one reason why many communities have developed "pre-rites" programs that rely heavily on cultural knowledge.

Spiritualization

In a materialistic, secularized society that separates church and state, there is little room in daily life for a harmonious relationship with the Creator, much less for the calm that comes from that knowledge. Few things are as important as re-establishing that balance. For without a healthy spiritual-physical balance, disease of some sort will always be present or available.

> Spirit cannot be understood, it can only be experienced. One can only be spirit. We are content to let others travel the path of the intellect. They have already accomplished much and will still accomplish more. But the "highest truth" will always remain hidden from the person who merely follows his intellect and never learns the bliss of pure *being* to which the path of renunciation leads.[11]

The ancient Kemetic spiritual traditions are a good place to begin.

Bonding

This is an absolutely essential part of the rite of passage. People living in materialistic societies are so alienated from each other that bonding among peers rarely takes place. The rites, initiates should be bonded not only to each other in a brotherly and sisterly way, but also to the adults who assist them through this important process. Trust, loyalty, and respect must be created and fostered at all levels. Bonding and the understanding of its importance will assist in the growth of young people raised in a society where children kill each other over boom boxes and sneakers. This is the only way to re-create the harmony and wholeness of our traditional communities.

In current rites-of-passage programs, bonding is created through the use of retreats or separation of the young people from their families. This is based on the ancient practice of removing initiates from their familiar surroundings to help them in becoming priests, or in assuming other adult roles. Some programs use an initial retreat, orientation, or induction ceremony to create the sense of who the group is. As time progresses and lessons come to an end, a final retreat or private induction may precede the formal public ceremony.

Community Integration

The proverb, "It takes a village to raise a child" speaks to the essence of the need for community interdependence when it comes to rites of passage. Multiple parenting and extended kin relationships are part of the history of our people. Communities are linked and strengthened by interlocking networks of relationships, concern for the group, and in this case, survival through our children and youth.

In developing rites-of-passage programs, the best procedure is to undertake the process with broad knowledge of the community. This will enable the programs to draw support and resources from the community. The community, in turn, provides a set of checks and balances that enable the developers to assess the extent to which the rites-of-passage program is regarded by the community as serving its interests. Public ceremonies solidify the process as well as the knowledge of the initiates and their families.

Intergenerational Balance

To incorporate the traditional principle of elder respect, a council of elders should be established for each community.[12] The number and the gender of the members should be dictated by the size of the program or community so that undue burden is not placed on a small number of elders who must be available for various functions and activities for large numbers of children.

Councils of elders are often used to:

1. advise in programmatic development;
2. give council to individual children or youth;
3. oversee rites processes and practices;
4. assess the readiness of initiates for completion; and
5. serve as providers of stability and integration

with other parts of the community.

Conclusion

The rites-of-passage process represents the first step toward achieving self-determination and reclaiming our future as families, as educators, and as a nation. It is a stabilizing and centering process that links and bonds African-American children, youth, and adults. The intent and purpose of the rites-of-passage process is not simply to modify, change, or eliminate current "problems" faced by African-Americans. Rather, it is intended to have revolutionary and long-term effects. It seeks to radically change how African-Americans view themselves, their history, their organizations, and their institutions in both present and future contexts by providing each person with the necessary tools, skills, vision, and perspectives for both individual and collective success on a world scale.

Rites of passage, when conducted correctly, help us to reintroduce traditional African emphases upon inner values and strengths as opposed to the destructive emphasis upon outer materialistic values. Thus, one can say that the aim of the rites-of-passage process is to enable African-Americans to transform the influences of Eurocentric schooling and society in a radical African-centered manner. This transformation represents a movement among African people toward freedom and liberation and away from oppression in all its various forms.

The future of African-Americans depends on the ability of those with the necessary information and means to successfully re-create past successes for our children, youth, families, and communities. Rites of passage represent one of the best liberation tools re-created to date. It is a time-honored yet progressive format for educating children within an African-centered cultural orientation.

Notes and References

1. J. S. Mbiti, *African Philosophy and Religion* (New York: Anchor Books, 1970), 159.
2. M. Asante, *The Afrocentric Idea* (Philadelphia: Temple University Press, 1987).
3. N. Warfield-Coppock, *Afrocentric Theory and Applications*, vol. 1 (Washington, DC: Baobab Associates, Inc., 1990).
4. Warfield-Coppock, *Afrocentric Theory and Applications*.
5. A. K. Armah, *The Healers* (London: Heinemann, 1978), 5.
6. M. Moore et al., *Transformation: A Rites of Passage Manual for African-American Girls* (New York: STARS Press, 1987).
7. P. Foster, *Therapeutic Rites of Passage: A Culturally Competent Model for Intervention with African-American Youth* (Washington, DC: Kintu, Inc., 1990).
8. P. Kotler, "The Elements of Social Change," in *Creating Social Change*, eds. G. Zaltman and I. Kaufman (New York: Holt, Rinehart and Winston, 1972).
9. N. Warfield-Coppock and A. Harvey, *Teenage Pregnancy Prevention: A Rites of Passage Resource Manual* (New York: Commission for Racial Justice, United Church of Christ, 1988).
10. Asante, *The Afrocentric Idea*. M. Asante, *Afrocentricity* (Trenton, NJ: Africa World Press, 1988). M. Asante, *Kemet, Afrocentricity and Knowledge* (Trenton, NJ: Africa World Press, 1990). A. Hilliard, "Pedagogy in Ancient Kemet," in *Kemet and the African Worldview: Research, Rescue, and Restoration,* eds. M. Karenga and J. H. Carruthers (Los Angeles: University of Sankore Press, 1986). M. Karenga, *The African-American Holiday of Kwanzaa: A Celebration of Family, Community, and Culture* (Los Angeles, CA: University of Sankore Press, 1988). W. Nobles, *Africanity and the Black Family: The Development of a Theoretical Model,* 2nd. ed. (Oakland: Black Family Press, Institute Publications, 1985). W. Nobles, *African Psychology: Toward its Reclamation, Reascension, and Revitalization* (Oakland: Black Family Press, 1986). Warfield-Coppock, *Teenage Pregnancy Prevention.* Warfield-Coppock, *Afrocentric Theory and Applications.* N. Warfield-Coppock, *Life Cycle Rites of Passage: African-American Development Strategies* (Washington, DC: Baobab Associates, Inc., in press).
11. E. Haich, *Initiation* (Palo Alto, CA: Seed Center, 1974), 130.
12. Warfield-Coppock, *Afrocentric Theory and Applications.*

The Afrocentric Project
in Education

Molefi Kete Asante
Temple University

The Afrocentric project aspires to be a reconstructive and loca-tive educational and social idea. This means that it must be able to provide the outlines for distinguishing itself from other projects of educational and social advancement. I have tried to make the gen-eral contours of these outlines clear in my own work. The present work, *Too Much Schooling, Too Little Education: A Paradox of Black Life in White Societies*, with its educational focus, fits into the Afrocentric school of thought with its aim to develop subject-centered analysis and solutions for African children. This is neces-sary not only for the sake of definition but for the sake of comparison with other projects. As we have seen in this collection brought together by Mwalimu J. Shujaa, the emphasis on school-ing and the de-emphasis on education have crippled the African-American community. What is necessary is an orientation to knowledge that puts noble obligations ahead of material values.

We need to know the fundamental ways of knowing in order to examine what it is that we do as Afrocentrists. The requirements of science therefore are for a clear definition, an appreciation of epis-temology, and some substantive ideas about how one gains location in an Afrocentric sense. All educational ideas are therefore ideas about culture. The process of education is a process of socializing students into a particular social structure. Science is the principal path to a clear understanding of what is necessary for African-American children. We cannot dismiss science in an effort to grasp educational efficacy. In fact, Afrocentrists elevate science and respect it more than any other way of knowing. It is from the bases of science that we have been able to demonstrate the anteriority of African civilizations, the presence of Africans in Scandinavia during the 9th and 10th centuries, the blackness of the ancient Egyptians, and the validity of the African presence in the Americas in the 14th century. So we cannot and must not disparage science.

But we also accept other ways of knowing. I am particularly struck by the fact that my grandfather in South Georgia often seemed to have achieved some ecstatic knowledge on his many visits to the root doctors. Then there are the insights of musicians and mystics, the visions of saints and prophets, the revelations of poets and schizophrenics. Almost none of this knowledge can be achieved through the domain of science. In other words, the scientific method does not lead us to conclusions that the other ways of knowledge would give us. This is not to suggest that one way is better than the other but to affirm the variety of ways of knowing.

However, as an Afrocentrist interested in certain kinds of knowledge that might be useful for the advancement of the education of African-American children, I believe in the place of knowledge from observation and experiences. Using this type of method I am able to determine what is and what is not on the basis of the evidence, and not from some form of intuition or mysticism that might or might not be possible for the next person to catch. While I am certainly not a Baconian scientist hoping that I can collect all of the facts before I make a speculation, I appreciate the way Cheikh Anta Diop has handled the scientific method in his own work. Diop is the great example. He amasses his facts, sifts them according to theory to distinguish between the significant and the insignificant, and then makes his interpretation. In this manner, Diop sits at the head of the class in the scientific method of inquiry. Neither Francis Bacon, Rene Descartes, nor David Hume could have taught Diop anything about knowledge coming from the relationships of logical propositions and knowledge coming from empirical facts. Indeed, Diop's entire ancestral history has been one of scholarship, extending back before the time of Bacon and Hume. One could speculate on the role of the Jolof kingdom in the formulation of a West African science, particularly in light of the fact that the scholars and leaders of the Jolof culture such as Lat Dior, Sheikh Anta, and Cheikh Mbacke were directly related to Cheikh Anta Diop.

The authors of this volume believe in the revolution that is happening in education. They know that African-American children can learn and are committed to the principles of teaching and educating that will affirm the existence of children who will reach the highest heights if they are met with concrete examples of care and concern. The barriers to Afrocentric understanding have been battered down by the ramrod of truth and historical fact. Furthermore, we have seen our children learn to a greater degree than many thought possible in schools that have adopted an Afrocentric curriculum and pedagogy.

Theories about the education of children must incorporate all that we know about learning. African-American children at the Wesley Elementary School in Houston were shown to be able to score higher on standardized tests than White children from the rich suburbs of Houston after they were instructed in a manner consistent with the learning styles of African-American children. The strategic significance of the principle of incorporating all that we know is that we do not confine children to the pattern of learning or ourselves to the pattern of teaching inherited in the school system. If African-American children are active, physical, engaged children, then education must be active, physical, and engaged.

The authors of the chapters of this book are educators with special skills for observing the behaviors of African-American children; they are scholars who have studied the patterns of American education and have exposed themselves to the essential theories of human learning, but they have not forgotten the lessons of their youth, the lessons of their ancestors, the lessons of the grandmothers and grandfathers. These are the fundamental elements that are passed from generation to generation. As the scholar Wade Nobles is fond of reminding us, "Our parents taught us to be mo' better." This "more betterness" is the objective of education. We do not seek education to reign over others or to amass great wealth; we seek education to become better people which means to work for harmony and peace in the world.

Since education remains a method of socializing children into a society, we are in dire need to socialize our children for effective living in the 21st century. That means that the children must see themselves as contributing to the entire human project. The sustaining of a social and cultural impetus for the education of our children must come from the theorists, the practitioners, and the parents. Teachers must teach children to be all they can be. Parents must encourage children from the standpoint of their culture and background to engage information in a positive way. If African-American children are to be prepared for the future then we must take advantage of the lessons of the past and the working of the present. This book is a clear example of what must continue to be done. We must applaud this work as a practical instrument for the liberation of our children's minds.

This book is an attempt to illustrate and demonstrate some of the ways we can use our cultural base to educate children. There is nothing unfamiliar to the reader about this process; it has been the fundamental process of education in all societies. You cannot leave the education of your children simply to those whose purposes are different from your own and expect the children to grow up and follow the path of your ancestors. This is precisely why some people go so far as to say that if you want a child to be trained in a certain way then people who espouse views that are anathema to that way cannot teach the child.

The authors of this volume suggest that a well thought-out strategy to educate our children is the best form of bringing about change. The work in this volume should inspire an entire generation of Afrocentric educators to grasp the opportunity presented to us to save our children.

CONTRIBUTORS

Agyei Akoto is Executive Director of NationHouse Positive Action Center. Bro. Akoto is principal of NHPAC Sankofa Institute; a co-founder and director of the Black Star Land Development Cooperative; founder of Heritage Village Encampment; founder of the Pan Afrikan World Institute; founder and Ankobiahene of Ankobia, Inc.; Editor-in-Chief of *Sankofa: Journal of African Culture and Ideology;* and Curriculum Development Officer for the Council of Independent Black Institutions (CIBI). He is also the author of the book *Nationbuilding: Theory and Practice in Afrikan Central Education* (1992).

Molefi Kete Asante is professor and chair of the Department of African-American studies at Temple University in Philadelphia, Pennsylvania. Dr. Asante is recognized as being one of the most distinguished scholars in both African and African American aesthetics and culture. In addition, Professor Asante is the author of more than 200 scholarly articles and 35 books, including *KEMET, Afrocentricity and Knowledge.* His works have been translated into Spanish, French and Chinese. Dr. Asante is the creator of the first doctoral program in African American studies in the world and is the founder of both the Afrocentric Philosophical Movement and National Afrocentric Institute.

Ronald E. Butchart, Professor and Program Director, Education Program, at the University of Washington-Tacoma, holds a Ph.D.

in U.S. Social History from the State University of New York at Binghamton. He is the author of *Northern Whites, Southern Blacks, and Reconstruction: Freedmen's Education, 1862-1875* (1980); *Local Schools: Exploring Their History* (1986); and numerous articles and papers on issues in education, particularly nineteenth century African American education. He is also Director of the Freedmen's Teachers Project. Dr. Butchart currently serves as president of the American Educational Studies Association.

Jacob H. Carruthers is professor of Inner City Studies at Northeastern Illinois University and the director of the Kemetic Institute; both are in Chicago. Dr. Carruthers has written hundreds of essays. Among his major works are the books *The Irritated Genie: An Essay on the Haitian Revolution* (1985); *Essays in Ancient Egyptian Studies* (1984); and *Science and Oppression* (1972). Dr. Carruthers is a founding member of the Association for the Study of Classical African Civilizations and served as its president for five years.

Nah (Dorothy E.) Dove is a member of the Board of Trustees of Nile Valley Shule, an African-centered school in Buffalo, New York. Dr. Dove has been active in the Black supplementary schools movement in London since 1980s and was a co-founder of the Winnie Mandela School. She presently holds a Rockefeller Fellowship at the State University of New York at Buffalo where she is doing post-doctoral research for her upcoming book *Afrikan Mothers: Bearers of Culture, Makers of Social Change* (SUNY Press). Her research interests focus on racism and resistance in the schooling of African children on an international scale.

Michelle Foster is associate professor of education and African-American studies at the University of California Davis. A recipient of the National Academy of Education Postdoctoral Fellowship, her research interests include sociolinguistics, anthropology of education and the social and cultural context of learning. Her work has appeared in *Language in Society; Equity and Excellence in Education;* and *Theory into Practice.*

Vivian L. Gadsden is an associate director in the National Center on Adult Literacy (NCAL) and an assistant professor of education at the University of Pennsylvania. Her current research focuses on intergenerational literacy, poverty, and family development within African-American and other families of color.

Beverly M. Gordon is an associate professor of curriculum in the Department of Educational Policy and Leadership at The Ohio State University. Her research and scholarship weaves together curriculum theory and history, knowledge production and dissemination in teacher education, and African-American epistemology. Professor Gordon has published in such journals as *The Journal of Education; Theory into Practice; Theory and Research in Social Education; Urban Review.* She also has authored several book chapters. She has served as President and as Program chair of American Educational Research Association's Research Focus on Black Education Special Interest Group, and as curriculum consultant and author for the National Afro-American Museum and Cultural Center in Wilberforce, Ohio.

Violet J. Harris is an associate professor in the Language and Literacy Division in the Department of Curriculum and Instruction at the University of Illinois at Urbana Champagne. Her research interests are the history of African American literacy and children's literature. She is editor of *Teaching Multicultural Literature in Grades K-8* (1992) and co-editor of a poetry anthology — *A Chorus of Cultures* (1993).

Joyce Elaine King is associate professor and director of teacher education at Santa Clara University. Her research and publications address critical and multicultural teaching, African American education, women and social change, global education, Afrocentric teaching methods, and parenting. She is a former W.K. Kellogg Foundation fellow and she also completed a fellowship with the American Council on Education. In addition to articles in various scholarly journals, she wrote (with C.A. Mitchell) the book *Black Mothers to Sons: Juxtaposing African American Literature with Social Practice* (1990). Her most recent book is *Formulating a Knowledge Base* (with E. R. Hollins and W. C. Hayman, co-editors, SUNY, 1994).

Carol D. Lee is on the faculty of the School of Education and Social Policy at Northwestern University in Evanston, Illinois. She received her Ph.D. in Curriculum and Instruction from the University of Chicago. In addition, Dr. Lee has many years of experience as a classroom teacher at the elementary, high school and community college levels. She is a founder and former director of a twenty-year-old independent school in Chicago that infuses African-American culture throughout its curriculum. Her research interests and publications focus on cultural contexts for literacy instruction. She is author of the book *Signifying as a Scaffold of Literary Interpretation: The Pedagogical Implications of an African American Discourse Genre* (1993).

Kofi Lomotey is Chair and Associate Professor in the Department of Administrative and Foundational Services in the College of Education at Louisiana State University. He has written several articles and book chapters on aspects of urban school leadership and African-American education. He is author of *African American Principals: School Leadership and Success* (1989) and editor of *Going to School: The African American Experience* (1990). He is also the editor of the journal Urban Education.

Haki R. Madhubuti is a professor of English at Chicago State University and was named "Author of the Year for the State of Illinois" by the Illinois Association of Teachers of English (1991). He is a leader in the independent Black education movement, an award winning writer, publisher and educator. He is the founder. publisher and editor of Third World Press in Chicago, one of the largest Black publishing companies in the world. He has been poet-in-residence at Cornell University, University of Illinois (Chicago), Howard University and Central State University. He is author of *Black Men: Obsolete, Single, Dangerous?* (1990) and many other books.

Vernon C. Polite is an assistant professor in the Department of Education at the Catholic University of America. He was an elementary and secondary school principal in both public and private schools in Michigan from 1985-1991. Dr. Polite has been a Federal Programs Monitor in the U.S. Virgin Islands and Desegregation Director for the Boston Public Schools. Among his recent projects is editing a special issue of *The Journal of Negro Education* (1994) which bears the theme "Pedagogical and Contextual Issues Affecting African American Males in School and Society."

Joan Davis Ratteray is founder and president of the Institute for

Independent Education, a non-profit organization that provides training, technical assistance, and policy leadership to independent neighborhood schools nationwide. The Institute recently published *On the Road to Success,* a landmark study of how independent neighborhood schools prepare students for college and employment. She is also the author of *Center Shift: An African-Centered Approach for the Multicultural Curriculum.* Dr. Ratteray has served on the staff of the White House Conference on Families, as a research associate at The Rand Corporation, and as a faculty member at Howard University and the University of Maryland.

Nsenga Warfield-Coppock is president of Baobab Associates. She works as an organizational psychologist in the Washington, D.C. area. Dr. Warfield-Coppock serves as Director of Organizational Services for the MAAT Institute for Human and Organizational Enhancement, Inc. Her scholarly writings have appeared in *Black Books Bulletin; The Journal of Black Psychology;* and *Reflections on Black Psychology.* Her books include *Life Cycle Rites of Passage: African American Development Strategies* (1993). Additionally, Dr. Warfield-Coppock serves as Historian on the Board of Directors for the Association of Black Psychologists, and as an organizational representative to the Black Congress on Health, Law and Economics.

Thomasyne Lightfoote Wilson is professor emeritus of education at San Jose State University and an affiliate of the University of Nairobi in Kenya. Her professional interests include multicultural education, international and comparative education, socio-humanistic foundations, and teacher preparation. As a Fulbright Scholar she established an Institute of Research at the University of Liberia, and she has done anthropological fieldwork of families, values, and social change in Liberian and Zimbabwe. She is author of *Toward Equitable Education: Handbook for Multicultural Consciousness* (1976) and numerous articles concerning equitable education and community participation in education.

Index

2 Live Crew 285

A
Afonso I 43
African Free School 133
African Methodist Episcopal
   Church 132
Afrocentricity
   (Afrocentrism/African-centered-
   ness) 9, 24, 32, 52-53, 61-63,
   106, 265, 278, 321, 334-335,
   372-373
   definition of 320
   personal transformation 361,
   363-365
   in rites of passage programs 387
African-centered education 265,
   323
   Africanization and 52-53
   African-centered worldview and
   53
   analysis of 9
   definition of 320
   Black intellectual crisis and 41,
   51
   cultural knowledge, transmission
   of 29, 32
   cultural studies 5
   curricula 16, 128-129, 131-
   133, 136-138, 265
   in Black supplementary schools
   (U.K.) 356

in independent African-American
   (Black) schools 4, 5, 16, 23-27,
   32, 123, 29, 306, 330-332
   pedagogy 295-310, 319-335
   values, transmission of 5, 52
Akbar, Na'im 21
Akin, Emma 162-166
Akoto, Agyei 267
Alger, Horatio 158
Allen, Richard 132, 161
American Educational Research
   Association 70
American Freedmen's Union
   Commission 131
American Teachers Association
   137
American Tract Society 131, 157
American Youth Commission, The
   49
ancient Aryan project 52
Anderson, James D. 4, 68, 81-
   82, 102, 143-144, 148, 170,
   247
Angelou, Maya 271
Anta, Sheikh 396
Armah, Ayi Kwei 309, 380
Armstrong, Samuel Chapman 47-
   48, 95, 160
Asante, Molefi K. 31, 62, 300,
   361, 363, 369, 371-372, 388
Asantewa, Yaa 323
assimilation 230

at seba 42
autonomy 89, 96, 104, 284, 347

B
Bacon, Francis 396
Bacote, Clarence 103
Baldwin, James 283
Baltimore, Maryland 24
Banks, James 283
Banneker, Benjamin 160
Baranes, R. 300-301
Baratz, J.C. 249
Barnes, K. 259
Benezet, Anthony 45
Bennett, L. 137
Bennett, Christine I. 278
Bereiter, C. 249
Best, Winston 355
Bethune, Mary McLeod 4, 132, 305, 310
Bethune, Thomas Greene 160
Beyer, Landon E.
    crititque of *A Nation at Risk* 23
Billingsley, Andrew 247, 250
Black Independent Schools (BISs) 362
Blassingame, J. 250
Blyden, Edward Wilmot 31, 38-39, 45, 53-54
Boggs, Grace Lee 277
Bond, Horace Mann 92-96, 99-101, 109
Bontemps, Arna 155
Bowles, S. 148
Boykin, A.Wade 69
Brawley, Benjamin 154
Brawley, James P. 116n
Brice-Heath, Shirley 258, 301-302
British Council of Churches
    Community 344
Brookins, Craig 129, 362, 374
Brown, Charlotte Hawkins 132
Brown v. Topeka Board of Education (see also integration)

49, 96, 104, 126, 231, 281
Buffalo (NY) Public Schools 205, 215
Bullock, Henry Allen 93, 95, 99-100
bureaucrat/administrator role identity 206
Burroughs, Nannie Helen 132
Butchart, Ronald E. 82

C
Cabral, Amilcar 324, 364
Caldwell, Ben 285
California textbook adoption controversy 61
Capitien, Jacobus E. J. 44-45
Carby, Hazel 67, 277
Carlyle, Thomas:
    "The Nigger Question" and neo-slave system 46
Carruthers, Jacob H. 11, 179
Carter, D. 362, 374
Carver, George Washington 265, 310
Center on Budget and Policy
    Priorities 345
Cesaire, Aime 69
Chicago, Illinois:
    racism in public schools 2-3
    1919 race riot 51
Chin, Phillip C. 278
church (African-American) 234, 247, 253
    in fight for racial equality 3
    African Methodist Episcopal
    132-133
    rites of passage 382
CIBI (Council of Independent Black
    Instituttions) 4, 137-138, 304, 330, 362
    National Science EXPO 304-306
Civil Rights Act of 1964 250, 258
Clark, Lacy 32-33
Clark, Septima 277, 305

Index

Clarke, John Henrik 20
  education versus schooling 81
Coard, Bernard 348
colonialism:
  British 41
Columbus, Christopher 44
Comenius, John Amos 296
Comer, James P. 41, 71
Congress of African People (CAP)
  362
Conroy, Pat 222-224
Cooper, Anna Julia 148-150
Coppin, Fannie Jackson 132
Council of Great City Schools 225
Cox, Susan 166
Cross, W.E. 247
Crummell, Alexander 39
Cruse, Harold 4, 38, 60-61
cultural identity 257
Curriculum Infusion Project 206,
  212

D
Davis, William R. 94
Davison, John W. 83n
Dawkins, Everett 233
DeLain, M.T. 302-303
Delany, Martin 38-39
Delgado-Gaitan, C. 250
Delpit, Lisa 250
democracy, and African-Americans
  28, 96-97, 279
Descartes, Rene 396
desegregation, of U.S. public
  schools 49-50, 92, 96-100,
  103- 104, 126, 231-232
Deutsch, M. 249
Dewey, John 28-30
Diop, Cheikh Anta 62, 69, 310,
  396
Dior, Lat 396
dis-education (defined) 45
Dorsey-Gaines, C. 250
Douglass, Frederick 135, 160
Dove, Nah 12, 341

DuBois, W. E. B. 4, 28-31, 47-48,
  70, 85, 87, 89-90, 92, 94, 96,
  99, 101, 109, 135-136, 147-
  148, 150-152, 170, 223, 231,
  250, 272-273, 277-278, 309-
  310
  Frankfurt school, in relation to
  70

E
e pluribus unum 279
Easton, Hosea 38-39
Edelman, Marian Wright 269
education 15, 28, 31, 41, 82, 85,
  104, 106
and Afrocentricity (see also independent Black schools) 16, 24,
  39, 41, 51-52, 131, 136-39
  definition of 15, 28, 296
  dialogical 328-330, 333
  historiography of 85-122, 144;
  liberal progressivism in 92
  home schooling 23
  and literacy 247, 257
  "multicultural" 309
  prohibitions against 126
  regional differences in U.S. 214
  role of the teacher 236, 325-
  326, 332
  versus schooling (see schooling
  versus education)
Egypt, ancient (Kemet) 296, 306,
  322-323, 389-389, 396
  education in 42-43
Eleazer, R. 154
Engelmann, S. 249
Ethnograph, The 365
ethno-humanist role identity 204,
  213, 216
Etzkowitz, H. 246
Evans, Mari 269

F
Fanon, Frantz 4, 324, 364
Fingeret, A. 257

Fisk University 51, 138
Floyd, Silas 147, 158-162
Fontaine, William T. 69
Foster, Michele 33, 70, 180, 247-248, 286
Frazier, E. Franklin 4, 20, 37-40, 49
   American Youth Commission 49
Freedle, K. 247
Freedmen's Bureau 93, 102, 126
Freire, Paulo 4, 30, 152, 323, 328, 364

G
Gadsden, Vivian 180
Gallagher, Buell 97
Garvey, Marcus 4, 106, 137, 333, 335
Gates, Henry Louis 299
Gay, Geneva 240
Gintis, H. 148
Giroux, Henry 288
Gollnick, Donna M. 278
Goodman, K. 249
Gordon, Beverly M. 11
Grant, Carl A. 278
Greensboro, North Carolina 49
Gwaltney, J. 225

H
Hale-Benson, Janice 277
Hall, Prince 128
Hamilton, Alexander 133
Hampton Institute (Hampton University) 47-48, 138
Harding, Vincent 277
Hare, Bruce R. 31
Hare, Nathan 70
Harlan, Louis 92-95, 99, 101
Harris, Violet J. 82, 245, 247
Hayes, Rutherford B. 46-47
hegemony 11, 31, 108, 153, 170, 179, 266, 279, 319, 332-333, 362, 364

Hennessey, John P.
Henry, Annette 70
Herskovitz, Melville 238
Hilliard, Asa G. III 62, 388
Hillocks, G. 303
Hirsch, E.D. 30-31
Hogan, I. 155
Hollins, Etta Ruth 70
Holt, T. 247
homophily 205
Houston, Drusilla Dunjee 31, 43
Howard, Alice 145-147, 160-161
Howard University 85, 138
Hume, David 396
Hurston, Zora Neale 302-303

I
independent neighborhood schools 362, 365
independent Black institutions (IBIs) 362
Inner London Education Authority (ILEA) 355
Institute for Independent Education 23, 365
integration, of U.S. public schools (see desegregation)
Irvine, J.J. 247

J
Jackson, George 333
Jackson, Jesse 73
Jackson, Luther P. 90
James, George G.M. 62
Jay, John 133
Jim Crow 21, 97, 179, 281
John Loughborough School 355
Johnson, Charles S. 51, 94
Jones, James M. 69
   TROIS 69
Jones, Thomas Jesse 88
Jones, D. 225
Jones, Dalton-Miller 298
Jones, Absalom 132
Jordan, June 277

Index

K
Kant, Immanuel 296
Kareem, Aisha 281
Karenga, Maulana 138, 296-297, 388
Kenyatta, Jomo 41-42
King, Joyce E. 70, 267
King, Martin Luther, Jr. 73, 333
Kliebard, H. 148
Knight, Edgar W. 91
Kotler, P. 385
Kozol, Jonathan 1
Kwanzaa 381, 389

L
Labov, W.A. 249
Ladner, Joyce 69
Ladson-Billings, Gloria 70
Lake Mohonk Conferences on the Negro Question 46
Laney, Lucy 132
Leakey, Mary 277
Leavell, Ullin Whitney 95
Lee, Carol D. 15, 267
Lee, Spike 71
Leo, John 62
liberatory education 65
    role of African American scholars in 65-66
    pedagogy for 73
Lightfoot, Sarah Lawrence 71
Lincoln University (Pennsylvania) 46
literacy 245-259
Logan, Rayford W. 103
Lomotey, Kofi 15, 33, 180, 362, 374
Ludlow, L. 303
Luke, A. 148

M
Maat 296-297, 307, 323, 389
Mabee, Carlton 103
Mandela, Nelson 288
Mani Congo Nzinga a Nkuwa 43

Marable, Manning 21-22, 345
Marxism 319, 323
Mazrui, Ali 62, 71

Mbiti, John 69, 377
Mbacke, Cheikh 396
Meier, August 95
mis-education 46, 81, 137
    (defined) 45
    decolonization and 41
Mohraz, Judy Jolley 104
Morelli, G. 298
Morrisson, Toni 71
Mosier, R.D. 156-157
Muhammad, Elijah 132-133
Multi-Ethnic Inspectorate 356
Myrdal, Gunnar 96

N
National Association of Independent Schools 24, 162
National Association of Probation Officers 345
National Association for the Advancement of Colored People (NAACP) 96
Naylor, Gloria 71
Negro History Bulletin 167, 169
New York Manumission Society 133
New Concept Development Center (Chicago, IL) 304-306
New York (state) "Curriculum of Inclusion" 278, 306- 307
Nguzo Saba 137-38, 331, 389-390
Nicholson, David 61
Nkrumah, Kwame 11n, 43-44

Noble, Stuart G. 91
Nobles, Wade 388
Nyerere, Julius K. 41, 277

O
Office of Substance Abuse Prevention 384

Ogbu, John 74, 346
Olduvai Gorge 270
Ortony, A. 302-303
Osei, G.K. 44-45
Outlaw, Lucius 71
Ovington, Mary White 156

P
Palcy, Euzhan 72
Parham, Thomas A. 21, 69
Parker, Dorothy B. 89
Parsons, Kansas
   Frederick Douglass School 32-
   33
Payne, Bishop 132
pedagogy 65, 69-70, 73-75, 135,
   223, 225, 233-239, 265, 267,
   277, 281, 285-288, 295-310,
   357, 374
philanthropy 102, 126-127
Plessy v. Ferguson 143
Polite, Vernon C. 180
Portland (Oregon) public schools
   multicultural model 307
Prager, Jeffrey 282
Prison Reform Trust Report 344
public schools (U.K.) 347
Public School Society 13-134

Q
Queen Hatshepsut 306

R
race relations 26, 88-90, 98, 184-
   185
racial equality:
   illusion of in U.S. society 22
racism 2, 10, 12, 20, 52, 63, 73-
   75, 90-92, 97, 101-102, 107,
   230, 248, 285, 346, 353
   effects on consciousness 276
   institutionalized 320
   in public schooling 2
   social domination and 20
   racial inferiority ideology 20, 52,

73
   resistance to 143
   "minority" perspective 20, 25
   "Whiteness" 20, 31
Range, Willard 94-95
rap music 284
Ratteray, Joan Davis 24, 82, 128-
   129, 137, 362, 374
Ravitch, Diane 61-62, 65
Reconstruction 93, 100, 104-110,
   144, 304, 364
Reed, Ishmael 71
Rist, Ray 223-224
rites of passage 341, 342, 377-
   392
   definition of 378
Robinson, Jackie 231
Rogers, M. Crosby 169
Rogoff, B. 298
Ruddell, R.B. 249

S
San Francisco (California) high
   school students 278
Schaflander, G.M. 246
schema theory 300
Schlesinger, Arthur Jr. 61
Schomburg, A.A. 136
schooling *versus* education 3-4,
   10, 14-15, 17, 27-28, 32-33,
   39, 81, 205, 222, 238-239,
   245-246, 395
Searle, Chris 70
schools/schooling 1-2, 15, 17, 31,
   98, 101, 104, 106-107
   access to 123-41, 144
   Amish 240
   antebellum (U.S.) 81, 87, 98
   Baptist 132
   Black Muslim (Nation of Islam)
   132-133, 240
   Black supplementary (U.K.) 343-
   358
   Catholic 24, 127-128, 130
   "classical" 133-134

defined 15, 17, 28
function 16, 28, 222, 239
independent religious 127-128, 130
literacy 248
postbellum (U.S.) 87, 90
private 124-25, 361
industrial 47, 94-95, 102, 129, 135-136, 151
public (U.S.) 15, 75, 125-127
public (U.K.) 347
Quaker 127, 130, 134
reforms, intent of 22-23
resistance to 196, 348
state-run (U.K.) 347, 353
segregation 46, 49, 95-97, 99, 103-104, 143, 227, 368
Shackelford, Jane Dabney 152, 166-169
Shannon, P. 148
Shor, Ira 70
Shujaa, Mwalimu J. 5, 6, 15, 24, 128-129, 137, 205-206, 362, 374, 395
Siddle-Walker, E.V. 247
Simbas 381
Simon, Roger 288
Sims, R. 170
Sleeter, Christine 278
Smith, Nila Banton 147
Smitherman, Geneva 249
Sojourner Truth Adolescent Rites Society, Inc., The (STARS) 381
Southern Education Board 95
Spencer, Dee Ann 223-224
Stanfield, John H. 50
Stigler, J. 300-301
Strickland, D.S. 250
Strobert, Andrei L. 284
supplementary schools (U.K.) 341, 343-358
Swint, Henry L. 91, 93, 102
Sykes, Charles J. 63-65

T

Taxel, J. 148
Taylor, D. 250
Temple University 138
Thomas Coram Research Unit 352
Thomlinson, Sally 348
Tizzard, Barbara 352
Toronto, Ontario, Canada police violence 286
Toure, Sekou 66-67
Tubman, Harriet 333
Turner, Nat 126
Tuskegee Institute 48

U
Uncle Tom's Cabin 279
Universal Negro Improvement Association (UNIA) 335
Urban League 345

V
values and/or value systems 5, 52-53, 89, 233, 278, 331, 333-334, 344, 388-390
Van Sertima, Ivan 62, 69
Vander, Jean 238
Vaughn, William P. 93

W
Walker, David 31
Walker, Alice 71
Ware, Edmund Asa 160
Warfield-Coppock, Nsenga 342
Warner, Sylvia Ashton 70
Washington, George 265
Washington, Booker T. 47-48, 68, 88, 94-95, 135, 148, 160, 162, 164, 265
Washington, Mary E. 149-150
Wells, Ida B. 310
West, Cornel:
on postmodernism 59-60, 72
on Foucauldian model, 72-73
illusory inclusiveness 278
white supremacy:

K. 343

. social order 10

istance to 73-75, 343

e, Joseph L. 21, 69

berforce University (Ohio) 46

ilkerson, Doxie 104, 107

Williams, Chancellor 4, 62

Williams, Raymond 147-148, 153-154

Wilson, Thomasyne L. 267

Wilson, Amos 21

Woodson, Carter G. 4, 20-21, 31-32, 40-41, 45, 48, 81, 87, 92, 136-137, 147-148, 152, 166, 168, 170, 277, 310

Wright, Cecile 352, 354

Wright, Richard R. 88

Wynter, Sylvia 277, 279

X Y Z

X, Malcolm 73

Xavier University 138